The Prime Ministers

55 Leaders, 55 Authors,
300 Years of History

EDITED BY IAIN DALE

HODDER &
STOUGHTON

First published in Great Britain in 2020 by Coronet
An Imprint of Hodder & Stoughton
An Hachette UK company

3

Copyright © Iain Dale 2020

Illustrations © Zoom Rockman

A CIP catalogue record for this title is available from the British Library

Hardback ISBN 9781529312140
Paperback ISBN 9781529312164
eBook ISBN 9781529312171

Typeset in Bembo MT Pro by
Palimpsest Book Production Ltd, Falkirk, Stirlingshire

Printed and bound in Great Britain by Clays Ltd, Elcograf S.p.A.

Hodder & Stoughton policy is to use papers that are natural, renewable
and recyclable products and made from wood grown in sustainable forests.
The logging and manufacturing processes are expected to conform to the
environmental regulations of the country of origin.

Hodder & Stoughton Ltd
Carmelite House
50 Victoria Embankment
London EC4Y 0DZ

www.hodder.co.uk

In memory of my grandmother,
Constance Henrietta Dale (1894–1979),
who inspired my love of politics,
parliament and prime ministers.

'I am called repeatedly and insidiously prime and sole minister.'

Sir Robert Walpole

'The office of the Prime Minister is what its holder chooses and is able to make of it.'

Herbert Asquith

'The main essentials of a successful prime minister are sleep and a sense of history.'

Harold Wilson

'The most important thing as prime minister is trying to make the right judgments. In order to make good judgments, you need good advice; you need good principles, and you need a clear head, and you need to have a sense of equilibrium.'

David Cameron

Contents

Length of Premiership

Sir Robert Walpole – 20 years, 315 days
William Pitt the Younger – 18 years, 345 days
Earl of Liverpool – 14 years, 306 days
Marquess of Salisbury – 13 years, 255 days
William Gladstone – 12 years, 130 days
Lord North – 12 years, 59 days
Margaret Thatcher – 11 years, 209 days
Henry Pelham – 10 years, 192 days
Tony Blair – 10 years, 57 days
Viscount Palmerston – 9 years, 141 days
Herbert Asquith – 8 years, 243 days
Winston Churchill – 8 years, 240 days
Harold Wilson – 7 years, 280 days
Duke of Newcastle – 7 years, 208 days
Stanley Baldwin – 7 years, 85 days
Benjamin Disraeli – 6 years, 341 days
Ramsay MacDonald – 6 years, 291 days
Harold Macmillan – 6 years, 282 days
Viscount Melbourne – 6 years, 257 days
John Major – 6 years, 156 days
Lord John Russell – 6 years, 113 days
Clement Attlee – 6 years, 93 days
David Cameron – 6 years, 64 days
David Lloyd George – 5 years, 318 days
Sir Robert Peel – 5 years, 59 days
Earl of Derby – 3 years, 354 days
Edward Heath – 3 years, 259 days
Earl Grey – 3 years, 230 days
Arthur Balfour – 3 years, 146 days
Duke of Portland – 3 years, 84 days
Henry Addington – 3 years, 55 days

James Callaghan – 3 years, 30 days

Theresa May – 3 years, 12 days

Neville Chamberlain – 2 years, 349 days

Duke of Wellington – 2 years, 322 days

Gordon Brown – 2 years, 319 days

Sir Henry Campbell-Bannerman – 2 years, 121 days

George Grenville – 2 years, 86 days

William Pitt the Elder – 2 years, 77 days

Earl of Aberdeen – 2 years, 43 days

Spencer Perceval – 2 years, 21 days

Sir Anthony Eden – 1 year, 279 days

Earl of Wilmington – 1 year, 137 days

Marquess of Rockingham – 1 year, 115 days

Earl of Rosebery – 1 year, 110 days

Duke of Grafton – 1 year, 107 days

Boris Johnson – 1 year, 56 days★

Lord Grenville – 1 year, 43 days

Sir Alec Douglas-Home – 364 days

Earl of Bute – 318 days

Earl of Shelburne – 266 days

Duke of Devonshire – 226 days

Andrew Bonar Law – 210 days

Viscount Goderich – 131 days

George Canning – 119 days

★Boris Johnson had served 1 year and 56 days at the time this book was completed on 18 September 2020.

Foreword

EARLY PRIME MINISTERS were shy about admitting that they actually were Prime Minister. 'The term,' says this book, 'had French connotations'. People apparently feared – or claimed to fear – that the emergence of this figure heralded a 'foreign' and 'tyrannical political system'. In 1741 Sir Robert Walpole 'unequivocally' denied that he was Prime Minister (despite having been so for 20 years).

It was all humbug of course. Everyone knew that Walpole was a new species of minister who presided over cabinet and wielded executive power on behalf of the sovereign. Instead of importing foreign tyranny, the modern office of Prime Minister became a successful British export.

Today the world has scores of Prime Ministers, yet the Downing Street prototype remains stubbornly unique. None of my overseas colleagues stands in a continuous line of succession as long as the one you will encounter in these pages. Their powers are often defined by written constitutions; our Prime Ministership has been shaped and organised by history.

You will find that history in this book, the whole story from the beginning 300 years ago to the present (though I do not necessarily endorse every word). Many of my predecessors were giants, some had feet of clay, all possessed human foibles.

This book reminds us that Disraeli was 'mired in debt', Gladstone a 'fanatical chopper-down of trees' (and an equally zealous planter of them), and Pitt the Younger delivered some of his finest parliamentary orations while intoxicated.

But did you know that Gladstone forced the first railway companies to offer cheap fares, thereby becoming father of the commuter belt? Or that Pitt invented income tax as a temporary measure in 1799? As for Disraeli, he said that the 'first consideration of a minister should be the health of the people', words I have recently had cause to echo.

For all the momentous change, these titans would still find much to recognise. I live at the same address, preside in the same cabinet room and answer to the same Parliament. I feel the same reverence for the nation and the same weight of responsibility. And after three centuries and 55 incumbents, I think it's fair to say that the coyness about owning up to being Prime Minister is finally beginning to fade.

Rt Hon Boris Johnson MP
Prime Minister 2019–

Introduction

I HAVE LIVED THROUGH the premierships of a dozen of our fifty-five prime ministers. I have met eight of them and had dinner with five. It's always been a matter of fascination how someone climbs what Disraeli called 'the greasy pole' of politics to become the leading politician in the country. I've come to the conclusion that two factors are timing and luck. Being in the right place at the right time has a lot to do with it.

When I realised that April 2021 would mark the tricentenary of the appointment of the man widely regarded as Britain's first prime minister, Sir Robert Walpole, I decided to mark it with this book of fifty-five essays.

Part of my motivation was the realisation that even a political geek like me knows comparatively little about most of our prime ministers, especially those from the eighteenth and early nineteenth centuries. At my school it was as if political history didn't exist before Gladstone and Disraeli. There are several prime ministers I had never heard of, let alone knew anything about. Editing the essays has been an absolute pleasure and significantly added to my knowledge of our country's political history.

The thread running through the book is that each and every prime minister is a character in his or her own right. Having said that, it is almost impossible to assert what makes a good or a bad prime minister. Different times and circumstances require different qualities.

Many prime ministers throughout history have been charismatic, but nowadays to be a successful prime minister it is almost *de rigueur* to possess lashings of charismatic ability. Boris Johnson has it. Tony Blair had it. Theresa May and Gordon Brown didn't. Harold Wilson had it but Ted Heath didn't. Macmillan and Churchill had it, while Attlee didn't. Attlee was a hugely successful prime minister, but would he stand a chance of winning power in today's multimedia age? I doubt it.

The British prime minister has always been seen as *primus inter pares* – first among equals, chairman of the Cabinet. There is an ongoing debate about cabinet government and the effectiveness of cabinets in recent years. There is little doubt that today's version of a prime minister is most certainly more than an equal. The modern-day prime minister carries the aura of a president, rather than a prime minister. He or she may not be the head of state, but in today's world that's effectively what they are, or are viewed as. Tony Blair is perhaps the best example of this phenomenon.

The contributors to this book are a mixture of political academics, historians, politicians, commentators and journalists. David Campbell Bannerman has written about his great uncle, Sir Henry. Lord Bellingham has written about the prime minister his kinsman, John Bellingham, assassinated. Charles Pitt has written about William Pitt the Elder, who, I'm sad to report, is no relation!

My interest in the history of Prime Ministers was encouraged by the wonderful *Facts About British Prime Ministers* by J B Seatrobe, published in 1995. Where possible and where needed I have checked any disputed facts with this book and gone with Seatrobe's meticulous research.

If you enjoy the book you might also enjoy the accompanying podcast series called 'The Prime Ministers' in which I interview each author about the prime minister they have written about here. It is available on all the usual podcast platforms.

This is not an academic book. It is aimed at the general reader, as well as those for whom politics is a part of their daily lives. The contributors were asked to tell a story, to write in an engaging way, and above all not to be afraid of giving an opinion. I am grateful to all of them for the way they have responded, and I am sure you are going to learn just as much as I have from their brilliant essays.

Iain Dale
Tunbridge Wells, September 2020

The Office of Prime Minister in History

Andrew Blick

OVER THE THREE centuries since the ascendancy of Robert Walpole, what has changed, and what has remained the same? A key difference between then and now is that the existence of a prime minister is generally accepted. The role is an established part of our constitutional arrangements. In the early eighteenth century, by contrast, the post had no official existence. Furthermore, to describe someone as a 'prime minister' was a way of attacking them. The term implied a subject of the monarch who had obtained too much power. According to received wisdom at the time, the different royal ministers were equal in their responsibility to the ruler. As a phrase, it also had French connotations, suggesting the undesirable incorporation of the methods of a foreign, rival power and tyrannical political system into our own. During his time as First Lord of the Treasury between 1721 and 1742, when accused of being a prime minister, Walpole disputed this claim. As he put it to the House of Commons in 1741: 'I unequivocally deny that I am sole and prime minister.'

But while he might have wished to avoid having such a label attached to him, Walpole knew that he was the most important person in the King's government of the day, as did everyone else. After his fall from power in 1742, other politicians adopted some of the techniques he had used and themselves became pre-eminent. There were times when it was not quite clear that a single figure merited the title 'prime minister'. But generally, somebody was seen as being the senior member of the administration. There were good practical reasons for the existence of such a role. As Lord North, writing during the American War of Independence in 1778, explained to his monarch, George III: 'in critical times, it is necessary that there should be one directing Minister'. Alongside this view from within the system, public perceptions also developed. By the first decade of the nineteenth century, *The Times* was referring to the prime minister as though the office were an accepted part of the institutional landscape; as were participants in parliamentary debates. As of the mid-nineteenth century, controversy about whether there should be or was a premier had dissipated.

But actual formal recognition of the post lagged behind. William Gladstone noted in 1878 that: 'upon the whole, nowhere in the wide world does so great a substance cast so small a shadow; nowhere is there a man who has so much power, with so little to show for it in the way of formal title or prerogative'.

Change was coming. In the year Gladstone wrote these words, his great rival, Benjamin Disraeli, signed the Treaty of Berlin as the 'Prime Minister'. By 1885, *Hansard* had begun referring to the existence of the post when listing members of the government of the day. We can find uses of the term in Whitehall files by the early twentieth century, and in 1904, the forerunner to the *Civil Service Yearbook* (the *Imperial Calendar*) described Arthur Balfour as 'Prime Minister and First Lord of the Treasury'. Finally, in 1905, the role received clear formal recognition. In December of that year the prime minister received a position in the official order of precedence. But the first reference in an Act of Parliament did not come until 1917 – and the law in question dealt purely with the granting of a country residence to holders of the office, rather than any wider issues. Moreover, the term 'prime minister' appeared only in the supplementary schedule of the statute, rather than the main body of the text. Firmer recognition came two decades later, with the Ministers of the Crown Act 1937, though primarily it only set the salary and pension of the prime minister, rather than making any stipulations regarding the nature of the post itself. Following the early faltering acknowledgements of its existence, a diverse range of Acts of Parliament came to refer to the office of prime minister. Some were relatively minor in significance, involving, for instance, the appointment of Trustees of the British Museum. Others dealt with matters that were of more constitutional importance and could be of an exceptionally sensitive nature. The Security Service Act

1989, for example, placed the entity commonly known as MI5 on a statutory basis, and charged the Director-General of this agency with reporting on an annual basis to the Prime Minister and Home Secretary. The Constitutional Reform Act 2005 dealt with matters including the role of the prime minister in the selection of the Lord Chancellor and appointments to the senior judiciary; while the Fixed-term Parliaments Act 2011 provided the prime minister with a role in fixing the precise date of a General Election.

This process of defining the office of prime minister in law remained incomplete. As Tony Blair explained in a written answer to the House of Commons in 2001, 'there are more than 50 specific powers conferred on the office by statute'. But key aspects of the role were still 'not . . . defined in legislation. These roles, including the exercise of powers under the royal prerogative, have evolved over many years, drawing on convention and usage, and it is not possible precisely to define them.'

Blair added that '[t]he Government have no plans to introduce legislation in this area'. The *Cabinet Manual*, a text published in 2011, contained perhaps the most detailed official publicly available account of the office of prime minister ever to have appeared. Yet it had no direct legal force, and left much unsaid. For instance, the document asserted that premiers 'will usually take the lead on significant matters of state', but gave no explanation of the application of this principle: what did 'usually' or taking the 'lead' mean; and what were 'significant matters of state'?

The office of prime minister has changed in as far as it has become accepted as part of the constitution, gained official status and gained a degree of formal definition. But such coverage never became comprehensive. Consequently, the role has always had a considerable degree of flexibility. Different prime ministers could approach it in different ways, according to their own disposition and the circumstances in which they operated. But what has the actual role been, and how far has it shifted or remained constant?

Leadership and power

By definition, prime ministers have always been important political figures. They have had a leadership function not only within government, but for the country as a whole. Because of this prominence, an ongoing debate about the premiership has involved discussion of just how powerful it is – and should be. From the outset, a recurring criticism has been that the office is exercising an inappropriate degree of dominance over government.

Sometimes the objection has been the opposite one: that firm leadership is needed, but lacking. In 1775, James Boswell noted in his diary a complaint by Samuel Johnson (who ironically had once been among the opponents of Walpole) 'that government had too little power . . . there was now no Prime Minister. Lord North was only the agent for Government in the House of Commons . . . we were governed by the Privy Council; but . . . there was no one head there, as in Sir Robert Walpole's time.' Lord Palmerston became premier in 1855 at a time of perceived poor performance in the Crimean War. A reason for his accession was that he might offer the decisive approach that was absent under Lord Aberdeen. Harold Wilson, as Labour leader of the opposition, sought to maximise his appeal by presenting himself as the more dynamic alternative to Sir Alec Douglas-Home, whom he succeeded following the General Election of 1964. When giving evidence to the House of Commons Liaison Committee in 2002, Blair noted that premiers were likely to generate criticism of whatever approach they took. He explained: 'If you go back in politics I think Prime Ministers fit into two categories: those that are supposed to have a strong centre are accused of being dictatorial; and those that do not are accused of being weak.'

Sometimes observers have discerned a general pattern of development that extends beyond one individual. In 1904, the political commentator Sidney Low asserted that over 'the greater part of the past half century . . . The office of premier has become more than ever like that of an elective President'. In 1951, Harold Laski claimed that 'if we compare 1850 with 1950, or even 1900 with 1950, the centralisation of power in the Prime Minister's hands has proceeded at a swift pace, and . . . its judicious use is mainly dependent upon his own self-restraint'. In 1963, the Labour politician and journalist Richard Crossman wrote that '[t]he postwar epoch has seen the final transformation of cabinet government into prime ministerial government'. The 1960s saw a fierce debate between different commentators about whether or not the premiership was becoming dominant within the political system. This argument has continued to the present.

A further historical perspective on prime-ministerial power suggests that, rather than increasing, it has been diminishing. In 1899, Lord Rosebery wrote that, to 'the ordinary apprehension', the title 'Prime Minister . . . implies a dictator'. But 'the reality is very different'. Earlier in the nineteenth century, Rosebery held, it might have been possible for a forceful premier to exercise 'a strict supervision over every department' and be 'master of the business of each and all of them'. But now 'when the burdens of empire and of office have so incalculably grown, for any Prime Minister to discharge the duties of his high post with the same thoroughness . . . would demand more time and strength than any man has at his command'. A little over a century later, in 2007, Michael Barber, a former aide to Blair, asked: 'suppose the real problem is not the extent of the power the Prime Minister wields, but the lack of it? Suppose the problem is not the strength of the prime ministerial role, but its weaknesses?'

When considering the three-hundred-year history of the premiership as a whole, certain observations regarding the leadership role and the power it bestows are possible. Prime ministers have never simply been able to dictate outcomes. They have had to contend with a range of limitations, some of which have changed in their nature over time, but which have always existed in some form. A constant constraint has been other ministers. Under the UK system, government has been the work of a group of senior politicians, each with their own functions and powers, bound together in an institution that developed in parallel to the premiership, the Cabinet, becoming a clear part of the constitution during the nineteenth century (though like the premiership, lacking firm, legal definition). There has never been a principle of having a single minister in direct control of the executive. It became the accepted practice that the most important members of the government, comprising the Cabinet, made major decisions as a group, debating in private and uniting publicly around the conclusions reached. From 1916, the Cabinet became further entrenched after Lloyd George established a secretariat to record and transmit its conclusions, developing into the Cabinet

Office that continues to operate from the centre of government today. Acting as chair of the Cabinet, premiers have had to work through this collection of individuals and the institution that has bound them together. Furthermore, they simply do not have the personal or institutional capacity to take on the running of every aspect of policy. As the academic George Jones put it in 1965:

> The Prime Minister is the leading figure in the Cabinet whose voice carries most weight. But he is not the all-powerful individual which many have claimed him to be. His office has great poten-
> tialities, but the use made of them depends on many variables, the personality, temperament, and ability of the Prime Minister, what he wants to achieve and the methods he uses. It depends also on his colleagues, their personalities and temperaments and abilities, what they want to do and their methods. A Prime Minister who can carry his colleagues with him can be in a very powerful posi-
> tion, but he is only as strong as they let him be.

Sometimes prime ministers have possessed great strength. William Pitt the Younger, Robert Peel, Gladstone, Lloyd George, Winston Churchill and others have at various points appeared dominant within their governments. Pre-eminence of this kind has developed partly because the particular premier was exceptionally interven-
tionist by nature (others, such as Clement Attlee, seemed to be less so). It also arises because circumstances – perhaps political success, or an emergency such as war – made the will of the premier diffi-
cult to resist. But though it is attainable, such ascendancy has always proved fleeting. The configurations of forces that facilitate it are not permanent. As they change, the prime minister can weaken. Churchill, for instance, lost power at the apparent height of his success at the General Election of 1945. Thatcher, who might have seemed invincible for much of the 1980s, was removed by her own party in 1990. Indeed, as this latter case demonstrates, the very strength that a prime minister possesses can contribute to their subsequent downfall. The neglect of collegiality by Thatcher created increasing resentment among colleagues, some of whom eventually turned on her. Compounding this problem, a policy to which Thatcher was personally committed – the Community Charge or

'Poll Tax' for financing local government – proved a political disaster. Greater commitment to consensual decision making might have avoided this error.

Changing structures

Prime ministers, then, have always had to work subject to the changeable political climate of the time, dealing with a set of other players whose various levels of cooperation are also variable. Their power is therefore contingent both on their own skill and inclination, and on factors beyond their immediate control. It has always been changeable. But have such fluctuations taken place within the context of longer-term shifts in the amount of power associated with the office of prime minister? The reality is more complicated. There have been alterations in the constitutional and political environment, but whether cumulatively they point in any one direction – towards more or less strength for the premiership – is difficult to state with certainty.

Handling the monarchy was once a great challenge. Rulers could be problematically assertive, pressing certain courses of action and resisting others. Walpole struggled to resist military engagements favoured by George II. Pitt the Younger resigned from office in 1801 because George III refused to countenance Catholic emancipation as a corollary of Union with Ireland. But rulers are now no longer politically active in the way they once were (though their presence is not completely eliminated). This transition, which occurred in particular during the nineteenth century, might be seen as representing a movement of authority away from the Palace and towards Downing Street. Yet at broadly the same time that this transfer was taking place, the Prime Minister was losing direct control over an institution that had been a crucial power base for most of the early prime ministers – the Treasury.

While the role of First Lord of the Treasury – a title held by all prime ministers today – is now considered honorific, it once signified actual responsibility for this great office of state and the policy portfolio that came with it. Before the role of prime minister became clearly accepted and established, most of those who in practice occupied this disavowed post, from Walpole onwards, held the office of First Lord. If they sat in the Commons, they combined this post with that of Chancellor of the Exchequer and presented the Budget themselves. Peel, on becoming premier for the second time, chose not to take on the latter post, conferring the details of Treasury work on a subordinate. He did so as a way of relieving himself of some of the burdens of office, allowing him to focus more on other matters. A decision driven by practical imperatives had long-term political consequences. The Chancellor of the Exchequer would become a major figure in the Cabinet in their own right, potentially a rival or future replacement for the prime minister, as was – for instance – Gordon Brown during the Blair period.

Another important transition has been the rise of the mass party, disciplined within Parliament, with public membership across the country. This phenomenon came about in response to successive enlargements of the franchise from 1832 onwards. Mass parties were in some senses a source of strength for premiers. They provided a solid base at Westminster and a campaigning organisation beyond. But they were not simply entities awaiting instructions from above. Communication and pressure could travel in both directions. Parties could be a problem for prime ministers as well as a benefit. Peel noticed this tendency early on. In 1846, shortly after the end of his second and last premiership, he remarked that '[t]here is too much truth in the saying "The head of a party must be directed by the tail." As heads see and tails are blind, I think heads are the best judges as to the course to be taken.' He found it unacceptable that a prime minister might be turned into 'the tool of a party', following 'the opinions of men who have not access to your knowledge, and could not profit by it if they had, who spend their time in eating and drinking, and hunting, shooting, gambling, horse-racing and so forth'. Peel concluded he would in future 'take care . . . not again to burn [my] fingers by organising a party'. In more recent times, the parliamentary parties of Major, Blair, May and Boris Johnson (prior to the 2019 General Election) created enormous difficulties for them. Members beyond Westminster might also exert pressure, as did Conservative activists over the European Union.

Some of those who have observed an increase over time in prime-ministerial power have connected it to the role of the civil service, arguing that it provided premiers with an important institutional support structure. It is certainly the case that the development of this institution, which made significant progress in the second half of the nineteenth and early twentieth centuries, had consequences for the way in which the office of prime minister functioned. But once again, the impact was not straightforward. Prime ministers have always had aides of various kinds. In this respect, though the occupant of the post is a single person, the premiership was from the outset a group effort. Walpole had a large team of assistants supporting him in areas such as policy advice, election management, parliamentary discipline, and promoting him to the public. He and his eighteenth-century successors employed staff by a variety of means, but they were not formally defined as prime-ministerial staff. In 1806, a single private secretary was finally attached to the First Lord of the Treasury; and (often slow) growth commenced in 1812 when a second official was added. They were always supplemented by other aides who were not formally part of the secretariat.

Different prime ministers utilised their teams according to their own preferences. Gladstone, for much of his four terms as premier, closely supervised his staff to ensure they were an extension of his obsessively systematic approach. His rival, Disraeli, by contrast, who had far less interest in detail, delegated much of the day-to-day work to a single trusted secretary, Montagu Corry. While no prime minister could operate without assistants, they were a potential source of difficulties. The distinguished historian and political thinker, Lord Acton, helped Gladstone in various ways during his premierships, but eventually seems to have become too convinced of his own importance. In 1892, shortly after assisting Gladstone during the election that returned him to power for the last time, senior Liberal figures, resenting the behaviour of Acton, combined to ensure that his role was downgraded.

The emergence of the civil service was significant because it eventually comprised a body of staff employed on a career-long basis, without attachment to any one politician or party. Before the 1920s, the team supporting prime ministers was largely made of people premiers had chosen to recruit, and who were likely to leave when they did. Civil servants brought with them the benefits of professionalism and attachment to a sophisticated bureaucratic machine, the workings of which they understood and could help facilitate. But they were not necessarily as attuned to the particular prime minister they supported, or as committed to achieving their particular objectives. They might well stay on when there was a change of incumbent. Career officials tended to have a degree of loyalty to the machine itself, and were in this sense not necessarily vehicles for the power of a given premier in the same way.

Prime ministers have responded to this arguable deficiency by recruiting their own aides. The use of special advisers on the prime-ministerial team (and elsewhere in Whitehall), commencing in 1964, is an example of such an initiative. Special advisers were recruited to bring qualities such as political commitment, communications skills or policy expertise that premiers felt they could not obtain from the permanent civil service. Sometimes they worked in specially created bodies attached to the prime minister. The prototype for this type of entity was the Prime Minister's Secretariat or 'Garden Suburb' that Lloyd George formed after becoming premier in 1916. Churchill followed this model when, like Lloyd George, he took on the office of prime minister during a world war, establishing the Prime Minister's Statistical Section in 1940. In peacetime, various other initiatives repeated this pattern: specialised bodies, made up at least partly of individuals recruited from beyond the career civil service, to support the premier in pursuing their particular objectives. They have included the Policy Unit (set up by Wilson in 1974); the Efficiency Unit (formed by Thatcher after becoming prime minister in 1979); and the Delivery Unit (established to support Blair in 2002). What none of these institutions has amounted to in itself is a fully blown 'Department of the Prime Minister', though some would hold that such an entity exists in practice if one takes into account the role of the Cabinet Office at the centre of government (and arguably, in the early days, the Treasury performed this function for its First Lord).

Continuity

There has, as the previous discussion shows, been substantial change in the office of prime minister over the past three centuries. But it is important to note certain aspects of the role that have remained relatively constant. They include:

- The basis in the support of Parliament, and in particular the House of Commons. Occupants of the post of prime minister hold that office because they are able to progress the business of Her or His Majesty's government through Westminster. Support from this institution is their source of strength, but it must be maintained. Once lost, so too is their power. If dissolving Parliament and electing a more compliant replacement is not a viable option, their position is untenable. This reality ended the career of Walpole in 1742, Theresa May in 2019, and others in between.
- Election management. While the size and diversity of the franchise has expanded enormously since 1721, securing sufficient levels of support distributed in a territorially advantageous way across the country has been essential throughout.
- Responsibility for ministerial and other public appointments, and patronage. Most obviously, the prime minister has been central to the construction of the government itself, as well as placing people in various other roles and generally cultivating goodwill as deemed necessary. These functions are a burden as well as a source of power. Matching eligible people to appropriate roles in government is not always easy. In a 1976 discussion of the task of reshuffling the Cabinet, Wilson explained that such exercises were 'anything but set-piece movements on a chess board . . . a re-disposition affecting a substantial number of ministers at all levels is like a nightmarish multidimensional jigsaw puzzle, with an almost unlimited number of possible permutations and combinations'. Furthermore, while those who benefit from prime-ministerial patronage might feel a degree of gratitude, resentment can generate among those who do not.
- Managing the machinery of government and the staff that operate it.
- Handling foreign policy and internal and external security.
- Leading government and acting as its public figurehead. This function, discussed above, is a vague but vital one, entailing the convening of ministers and departments, and ensuring that the administration as a whole has a general sense of coherence. The outward-facing aspect has been a challenge for all prime ministers. There have always been media of some kind, and they

have tended to look to the person who is premier at the time as in some way embodying the government of the day. Walpole recognised this tendency and deployed immense financial resources for propaganda purposes. But, however effective his public relations machine was, its scope was ultimately limited. He could not control public debate, or suppress the impressive body of literary talent – including Alexander Pope, John Gay, Jonathan Swift and Henry Fielding – that targeted him. Technological change has altered the way in which political messaging and commentary is disseminated: radio, television and the Internet have risen to prominence in succession to earlier media such as the spoken word; handwritten sheets; plays; songs; commemorative crockery; items of clothing; printed words; and visual images (though all of them continue to coexist). But as with so many aspects of the premiership, they provide opportunities not only to promote but also to undermine the objectives of the prime minister. It is not possible wholly to manage the media in the UK.

• The physical location. Walpole moved into a renovated Number 10 Downing Street – in fact at least two houses joined together – in 1735. George II designated it as the official residence of the First Lord of the Treasury. Thereafter, most prime ministers used it, at least as an office and often as a central London home. As well as being based at No. 10, prime-ministerial staff have also worked in nearby space, especially the complex now known as 70 Whitehall, to which No. 10 is connected by an adjoining door. But the continued use of relatively small main premises has helped sustain the character of the office of prime minister as a personalised team more than a large-scale administrative entity.

The sum of this historical analysis is that, where the office of prime minister is concerned, we should not confuse temporary fluctuations with substantial, lasting change. A prime minister may take office in circumstances of political turmoil, offering to resolve a particular problem. They might then secure a substantial majority at a General Election, securing compliance among a previously divided parliamentary party. The main opposition might prove unable to offer a coherent alternative to their government. The premier can appear to secure unchallenged dominance among ministers, allowing cabinet membership only to those willing to fit precisely into their plans. A prime minister in such a position might vest immense delegated power in their staff, and perhaps in particular in one senior special adviser. That individual might become so emboldened as to believe they can restore the control that premiers once possessed over the Treasury and the annual Budget process. The No. 10 team might also have devised various means of managing the messages that reach the public, through the bypassing and undermining of some established media outlets, and through the use of online communications techniques. In such circumstances, it might appear that a premier has managed to defy political gravity, and that more traditional principles of dispersed power and collective government will never revive. But historical evidence suggests they will return. It is not possible to suppress every divergent political force permanently. Mistakes will be made. Events will at some point undermine the power at the centre. Public criticism will find ways of emerging in some form. Rival points of authority will generate within the party, within Parliament, and within the Cabinet. The prime minister in question, like others before, will find their grip loosening, and will need to modify their approach, or face more severe consequences.

Andrew Blick is reader in politics and contemporary history at King's College London.

I

Sir Robert Walpole

3 April 1721 to 11 February 1742
Whig

By Mark Fox

Full name: Robert Walpole
Born: 26 August 1676, Houghton, Norfolk
Died: 18 March 1745, 5 Arlington Street, London. Buried at Houghton
Education: Eton; King's College, Cambridge
Married to Catherine Shorter (d. 1737), then to Maria Skerrett; 3 sons, 4 daughters
Quotation: 'The balance of power.' (13 February 1741)

BEFORE WALPOLE THERE were many powerful and pre-eminent ministers, but none were ever considered to be the prime minister. William Cecil and his son Robert would each have a reasonable claim to the title. Cardinal Wolsey or Archbishop Thomas à Beckett were as close in their time to the monarch they served and as politically powerful as it was possible for a subject to be, but they were never considered to be prime ministers. So what was it about Robert Walpole that has caused history to elevate him to the position of Britain's first prime minister? It was not a formal change decreed by the Sovereign or Act of Parliament. Neither was it a personal ambition of Walpole himself. Indeed, the charge of being the sole or prime minister was used as an attack against him by his opponents and one he felt obliged to defend himself from. It was rather his political skill, personal confidence and a fair share of good luck – a combination that has and will always play a critical role in a person's political career – that enabled him to dominate politics and national life for over twenty years as the principal minister in the government.

Walpole was born on 26 August 1676 into a prosperous and politically established Norfolk family. His father and grandfather both served as Norfolk Members of Parliament. They lived on an estate that had been in the family for more than four hundred years. Politics was in their blood.

Walpole was the fifth child of nineteen, and the third son, of Colonel Robert Walpole and Mary, an heiress. Colonel Robert rendered solid if unexceptional parliamentary and county service. He is chiefly remembered, other than for being Walpole's father, for holding the record for borrowing a library book. He borrowed a biography of the Archbishop of Bremmen in 1668 from the library of Sidney Sussex College, Cambridge, which was not returned for 288 years, in 1956, when his descendant accidentally found it in the library of the family's ancestral home, Houghton Hall. The colonel's death at the relatively young age of fifty on 18 November 1700 meant that his son could inherit both his seat in Parliament, where he would sit for the next forty years (for Castle Rising and then, with only a short interruption, for King's Lynn), and his share of the family fortune. Both would give Walpole a head start in politics, and he had not expected to inherit either.

Walpole was his parents' second surviving son. He planned to pursue the path common in second sons of the time and become a clergyman in the Church of England. Ecclesiastical preferment for someone of his social standing and connections would have been highly likely.

Leaving the work of helping his father to run the family estates to his elder brother, Edward, Walpole was sent to school at Eton, where he stood out for his academic success and became a King's Scholar, and then, after completing his time at school, he went up to King's College, Cambridge in April 1696. After two years, however, his university education was brought to a premature end and his career path changed for good with the death of his brother and his return home to take up the responsibilities and duties of eldest son and heir.

He married Catherine Shorter of Bybrook, Kent, on 30 July 1700. The marriage brought a dowry of £20,000 with it, a very considerable sum that helped to bolster the Walpole family finances. The marriage produced six children, although the paternity of their last child, Horace, who was born ten years after their fifth child, was the cause of speculation at the time.

Although the marriage lasted thirty-seven years and produced five children, it disintegrated into unhappiness and unfaithfulness, on both sides. Catherine died in Chelsea in August 1737 and is buried on the family estate at Houghton. Sexual incontinence being no bar, then as now, to being prime minister was something that did not unduly concern Walpole. He conducted a number of affairs, most notably with Maria Skerrett, whom he married shortly after Catherine's death. Maria brought with her a dowry of £30,000. She died in childbirth three months after their marriage and she too is buried at Houghton Hall. His relationship with Maria had been happy and he had shared his life with her openly even when Catherine was alive. They had a surviving illegitimate daughter, also called Maria, to whom King George II granted the rank of Earl's daughter when Walpole became Earl of Orford on leaving office in 1742, a signal mark of affection and respect for him from the King.

In addition to his owning and running a significant estate that encompassed land and property across Norfolk and Suffolk, and adding to his fortune with two significant dowries, Walpole was also an investor. He needed to be because, although the income from his estates brought in around £2,000 a year, his outgoings were substantial and his property carried significant mortgages. Early on, he bought shares in the South Sea Company. The collapse of that endeavour would lead to the infamous South Sea Bubble and a huge scandal, which would in time come to haunt Walpole. Nevertheless, at the time he bought early and sold his shares at the top of the market, making a fortune in the process. The resultant profit enabled him to lavish money on Houghton Hall.

Houghton Hall today is the seat of the Marquesses of Cholmondeley, but Walpole conceived this glory of Palladian architecture as not only a comfortable home for his family, heirs and successors, but as an outward symbol of his arrival into the highest rank of national life. Walpole relished his new home, built on his inherited family estate. He hosted lavish parties for the county and for his political colleagues. Each spring he would host his Cabinet over a three-week period at Houghton. This annual event became known as the Norfolk Congress. Walpole understood that entertainment and conviviality were not only expected as part of the responsibility of privilege and position, but also potent political weapons, and he was never shy about using both to full effect.

In addition to being very well educated and an established scholar, he invested heavily in one of the greatest private art collections the world has ever seen. He envisaged his new Houghton Hall as the principal and permanent home for this collection of art, Roman busts and wine coolers. The collection, known as the Walpole Collection, came to number hundreds of pieces and objects, and included works by Poussin, Rubens, Van Dyck and Rembrandt. His successors first added to and then sold off the bulk of the collection, with much of it ending up in the Hermitage Museum, and some in museums and galleries around the world. If a hinterland is an important asset to a successful politician, then Walpole was an early and outstanding example of it.

As soon as he arrived in Parliament, he became an active participant. 'It is obvious, that the people of England are at this moment animated against each other, with a spirit of hatred and rancour. It behoves you, in the first place, to find a remedy for these distempers which at present are predominant in the civil constitution.'

He was a man in a hurry. He had no significant aristocratic connection and he attached himself to the Whig interest following his father's political example. Within three years, in 1705, he gained his first political appointment – a member of the Council of the

Lord High Admiral. It brought with it a modest salary, which he needed because his expenditure outstripped his income, but more importantly it was the first visible outward symbol of political advancement. Furthermore, it was an appointment made by the Sovereign, Queen Anne, providing the first outward manifestation of the relationship with her, and subsequently her successor, that was to play such an important part in his rise to and maintenance of high office.

Further swift promotion followed as he became, successively, Secretary of War and Treasurer of the Navy. His ministerial career, however, came to an abrupt halt when the Tories came to power in 1710. They accused him of corruption in 1712 and Walpole found himself imprisoned in the Tower of London. By modern standards, a senior minister being convicted of a serious crime and being sent to prison would be a career-ending event. We live, however, in a more prurient and prudish era than did Walpole, so for him, who was to be continually accused of various forms of corruption throughout his long political career, it proved little more than a mild inconvenience to his progress. Nor did he ever much mind such accusations. Throughout this period he was active in Parliament and at his Norfolk estate, winning and maintaining friends and establishing his reputation through speeches and writing.

In 1714 Queen Anne died and was succeeded by her distant cousin the Elector of Hanover, to become King George I. His personal paranoia about his claim to the throne led him to intensely dislike the Tories, giving Walpole the opening he needed, and helping to enable the Whigs to remain in office for the next fifty years. In short order, Walpole would become a Privy Councillor, Paymaster of the Forces, First Lord of the Treasury, and, in 1716, Chancellor of the Exchequer. In just over eleven years, through personal talent and relentless energy, Walpole had overcome various political and personal setbacks to move ever closer to the top of British politics and the centre of power. He had built a formidable reputation as a parliamentary speaker and operator, and the Tories had tried to ruin him. They had failed, and in the many years that would lie ahead they would have plenty of time to rue their failure to stop his ascendancy.

There would be one further interruption, and a spell in opposition.

Here he honed his skills of debate and attack. The scandal of the South Sea Bubble would engulf the career of many of his contemporaries and rivals, but in April 1721 Robert Walpole was appointed once again First Lord of the Treasury and Chancellor of the Exchequer. In addition, he also took on the role of Leader of the House of Commons. These appointments marked the beginning of his long and extended period as the nation's undisputed leader and principal Minister of the Crown.

Walpole was adroit at using patronage to consolidate his power and advance his policy. He was effective at pandering to his royal master's obsessions and weaknesses, building a close team around him, pacifying parliamentary colleagues, and keeping himself and the country out of trouble at home and abroad. Abroad, he shied away from entanglements and confrontation. At home, he aimed to keep taxes low and to reduce the national debt. Peace, prosperity and living within one's means – generally effective and popular policies at any time. Indeed, so firm was Walpole's grip on power and high office to become that his administration would become known as the 'Robinocracy'.

His first great task was to tackle the scandal and fallout of the South Sea Company and its 'bubble'. He had been an early investor and many of his Whig colleagues were heavily involved in the enterprise in one form or another. Walpole, however, was able to use his formidable political and parliamentary skill to help impose a resolution and to shield his colleagues and their party. Through the considerable effort he put into this, Walpole was to earn much respect and loyalty from party colleagues.

The social discontent caused by the economic shock and scandal led to a stirring of the Jacobite cause. This caused King George I to be more than usually dependent on his favoured minister. Walpole was effective at quelling any insurrection and earnt the gratitude of the King for the rest of his reign. In the first two significant challenges of his ministry, Walpole had shown how to effectively balance the interests and concerns of people, Parliament and monarch in what we might think of today as a very good example of successful triangulation.

The accession of King George II in 1727 caused a hiatus in politics and Walpole's grip on power. Prevailed upon by his Queen,

Queen Caroline, to keep his father's First Minister in office, however, Walpole survived to thrive under a third Sovereign. His closeness to successive rulers was the principal means by which he retained and exercised power. By common consent, Walpole's mastery of debate and detail was better and more powerful than any of his peers and, historians tend to agree, better than that of any subsequent prime minister. His power, though, was not derived, as his successors' powers are, by controlling the House of Commons. Walpole's grip on power was gained through having the confidence of the Sovereign, who allowed him to use royal patronage for political ends. Thus Walpole was able to have an increasingly free hand to make appointments in the church, army and navy, the universities and other sinecures that were in the royal gift. In this manner, allied to his effective parliamentary oratory and skill, he was able to win the support and agreement of the House of Commons over an unprecedentedly long period of time – but he never controlled the House in the way a modern prime minister would expect and hope to do after a General Election victory. Walpole's use of patronage enabled his enemies to accuse him of corruption, a charge of which he took little heed.

In foreign policy Walpole resolutely pursued a policy of avoidance in foreign entanglements. This led his critics to charge that he was letting down Britain's allies, the Dutch and Germany, at the expense of keeping friendly with the French. In the end it was a trade dispute with Spain that was to force his hand and lead him to support a declaration of war – a move that was to start the beginning of the end of his long ministry. Throughout his time in office, however, despite the continuing upheavals and conflicts on the European continent that characterised the period, Walpole maintained Britain in a peaceful semi-disengagement. For a long while this policy abroad was bolstered by his domestic policy of keeping taxes low – something he was able to do because he did not need revenue to fund a war or military activity – and of paying down the national debt. It was an economic policy of a distinctly sensible and responsible nature from a person who was personally disposed to spend money and enjoy the finer things of life. His foreign and domestic policies proved for a long time both popular and effective.

Walpole's setbacks occurred as he sought to change the taxation system. He wanted to shift the burden of taxation away from the landed gentry to the new and increasingly prosperous merchants. He also wanted to tackle smuggling and excise-duty evasion. These changes brought a mixed response and damaged his popularity. When he tried to impose new taxes on wine and tobacco, and sought to move the place of taxation from the ports to the warehouses where they were stored, he was forced to withdraw the proposal; he subsequently removed from office all those on his own side who opposed him. Such tactics are not uncommon. Then as now the leader finds that all too soon there are more people on their own side who would like to see them displaced than there are those who are content for them to remain. Such is the eternal nature of parties and politics.

In 1732 King George II demonstrated his enduring affection for and confidence in Walpole by offering him the gift of a house across St James's Park from St James's Palace: 10 Downing Street. This was in reality a gift of three houses. Walpole resisted the proposal of a personal gift and instead accepted it on behalf of and attached to the position of First Lord of the Treasury. He had the three buildings remodelled and moulded into one house. The work took three years. Walpole would live there until he left office, after which, as he had wished, occupancy passed to his successor as First Lord, and so it has been ever since. The House has not always proved popular with First Lords of the Treasury. Walpole's five immediate successors did not choose to live there. More recently, after winning the 1974 General Election, Harold and Mary Wilson chose not to move back into No. 10 following their departure from it in 1970. They had had enough of the place and Wilson used it simply as an office until his resignation in 1976, returning to his home in Lord North Street each evening.

From 1737 onwards signs of persistent unpopularity began to dog Walpole and his administration. He had won the 1734 General Election well enough, but he lost seats. The number of opponents in his own party began to grow. Influential periodicals and publications became more persistent and strident in their criticism. Sheer longevity in office began to take its natural and inevitable toll. More seriously, the opposition of the Prince of Wales undermined Walpole's single most important hold on power, his relationship

8

with the Sovereign. The Prince of Wales was the de facto leader of the opposition to his father, the King, and therefore to Walpole and his ministry. The Prince attracted around him many of the new generation of rising stars, who increasingly saw Walpole as old and outdated. All this took its toll on him. In 1737 his first wife died, and in 1738 his new second wife also died, adding to personal as well as political strain.

He won yet another General Election in 1741, but as some of his successors have found to their own cost, winning a General Election is a necessary but not certain indicator of longevity or success in office. The Spanish war he had tried so hard to avoid, did not approve of and was vocal in his criticism of was nevertheless his prime responsibility to prosecute with vigour. He seemed – and worse, was perceived as being – unable to do so. Despite winning an election barely a year earlier, he was forced to resign, bringing to an end the most extraordinary and exceptional political career of his generation.

On 11 February 1742, Walpole resigned, and in anticipation of his departure King George II created him Earl of Orford, Viscount Walpole and Baron Walpole of Houghton. It would become common practice until fairly recently for departing prime ministers to accept an Earldom. Here, as in so much else he did, Walpole was setting a precedent for his successors as prime minister even as he was departing the scene.

Lady Mary Wortley Montagu recalled in 1748 that 'it was a maxim of Sir Robert Walpole's that whoever expected advancement should appear much in public. He used to say, whoever neglected the world, would be neglected by it.'

Walpole was a prime practitioner of his own maxim. Barely had his father died than he launched himself into public life. Through standing for election, conduct of a busy and hectic social life, the building of an outstanding and historic home, and his cultivation of a close personal relationship with the monarchy he exercised a personal political supremacy that far outreached the formal powers of the premiership.

He lived for barely another three years after leaving office. For many of his successors who have, like Walpole, held the highest office, exercised supreme power and become accustomed to being at the very epicentre of national events, political retirement can be a harrowing and diminishing time of life. Not so for Walpole. He enjoyed the continuing favour of King George II and was known to do so. His difficult relationship with the Prince of Wales was improved by his effective efforts to ward off questions and threats to the Hanoverian legitimacy. He spoke infrequently in the House of Lords, took satisfaction from helping push out his successor from office and installing a protégé of his own, and enjoyed spending time at his estate.

Robert Walpole died on 18 March 1745. He is buried at the family estate. His example of political moderation, prosperity at home, peace abroad and personal connection with Sovereign and public still provides today the outstanding model for sustained political success.

Mark Fox is a journalist, commentator and a former parliamentary candidate.

2

Earl of Wilmington

16 February 1742 to 2 July 1743
Whig

By Robin Eagles

Full name: Spencer Compton, Earl of Wilmington
Born: 1674 (exact date of birth unknown), Compton Wynyates
Died: 2 July 1743, St James's Square, London. Buried at
Compton Wynyates
Education: St Paul's School; Trinity College, Oxford
Unmarried: several illegitimate children
Quotation: 'No sir, you have a right to speak, but the House
have a right to judge whether they will hear you.'

SUNK WITHOUT TRACE is only a slight exaggeration when it
comes to describing the historical memory of Spencer Compton,
who, as Earl of Wilmington, succeeded Sir Robert Walpole as Britain's
second prime minister. Indeed, in some ways to describe him as

prime minister at all is slightly misleading. At least one contemporary observer reckoned that in 1742, Compton was being considered
as just one of a potential triumvirate of 'prime ministers'. Besides,
as the cartoons depicting the rush for office on Walpole's fall made
only too plain, Compton was far from the most prominent of those
jostling to replace the 'Great Man'. In one, a procession of grandees
lining up to receive awards from George II is headed by Lord
Carteret (effective head of the new ministry), with Compton
consigned to the end of the queue, out of focus, very nearly out
of sight.

Compton's near erasure from memory is not so very surprising
when one considers the nervousness with which he reacted to the
prospect of high office, but is the more so when one remembers
his early promise. By the close of his career he was dismissed as an
'old woman', but this was at odds with the independence of spirit
he showed when a young man by rebelling against his family's
traditional Toryism to embrace the Whig Party. He had enough
presence within the Commons to emerge as an effective Speaker
and was courtier enough to secure a series of significant offices,
largely the result of a close relationship with George II when Prince
of Wales.

Compton was a younger son of the 3rd Earl of Northampton,
and in establishing a political role for himself he was able to draw
on extensive family contacts, in spite of distancing himself from his
immediate family's traditional outlook. After a failed effort to secure
election at East Grinstead, a seat normally at the disposal of his
Sackville relatives, Compton was finally brought into Parliament by
Lord Cornwallis at Eye in 1698, which gives him the unique status
of being the only prime minister to have sat in the House of
Commons in the seventeenth century. A hiatus in parliamentary
service was then ended by a return to the Commons as one of the
MPs for East Grinstead, his Sackville sponsors this time proving
their worth, before progressing to one of the prestigious county
seats in Sussex.

Compton's early years in the Commons were fairly unspectacular,
but he soon became a close associate of Robert Walpole, both of
them being members of the Kit Kat Club, and he developed a
reputation for being a master of parliamentary procedure. He went

on to serve his political apprenticeship in the Commons, undertaking unflashy roles as a teller and a prominent committee-man. He played a key role in overseeing the passage of the Union legislation with Scotland, and continued to defend the arrangement when it came to be challenged a few years later. His first significant break came the same year when, in 1707, he was appointed to the household of Queen Anne's consort, Prince George of Denmark. Thereafter, his name was floated in relation to more high-profile roles, though nothing came of the rumours for as long as the Queen lived. Following the death of Anne, he finally achieved the distinction that had long been trailed for him with his election as Speaker. He brought a sense of aristocratic hauteur to the role, which he maintained for the next dozen years.

By then, Compton may have been thought of as rather ponderous, but he was not incapable of emotion. During the proceedings in 1710 against the incendiary clergyman, Henry Sacheverell, he was said to have 'trembled every joint and almost foamed at the mouth' when speaking in the debate. Fifteen years later, he again allowed himself a free rein when congratulating the managers of the impeachment of the disgraced Lord Chancellor Macclesfield, for wielding 'that sword of vengeance' so ably: 'You have stopped the cries of orphans, and dried up the tears of the widow, even those who must be insensible of the benefits they receive, ideots and lunaticks . . . will be partakers of the fruits of your labours . . .'

The crisis of his career proved to be the summer of 1727 when the country was surprised by the unexpected death of George I while he was visiting Hanover. Everyone expected that the Prime Minister, Sir Robert Walpole, whom the new King distrusted, would be put to one side and Compton nominated in his place. And this was what appeared to be transpiring as Walpole was ordered to refer himself to Compton. Walpole dutifully complied, declaring 'my time has been, yours is beginning'. At this point, though, Compton's courage failed him and, rather than take the initiative, he invited the outgoing premier to help him in composing the King's speech to be delivered to the Privy Council and in drawing up a new civil list. Walpole, bolstered by the not insignificant support of Queen Caroline, leapt at the chance and Compton slipped from being the man of the moment to yesterday's man in little more than a heartbeat. Lord Hervey was certainly in no doubt that 'if it had not been for the stupidity of Sir Spencer Compton, who did not know his own strength, or what use to make of it', Walpole would have been out and Compton installed as the new premier.

Perhaps what confirmed Compton's reputation as a third-rate individual, aside from Hervey's damning assessment of him as 'a plodding, heavy fellow, with great application, but no talents', was his apparent willingness to be sidelined. He allowed himself to be shifted from Paymaster General, an office from which he had managed to make a small fortune, to Lord Privy Seal and thence to Lord President of the Council. Lord Hervey provided a typically acid description of him presiding at a meeting of the council, 'with a great deal of dull dignity and becoming formality, his hands full of papers, his nose full of snuff, and his mouth full of nonsense'.

Along with the shifts in office, in 1728 he also agreed to be kicked upstairs to the Lords as Baron Wilmington (he was subsequently promoted again to an earldom). Promotion to the upper chamber in no way meant the end of his ambition: plenty of other hard-hitting ministers, many prime ministers among them, served as such from the Lords in the period; but in his case, the change of scene did appear to be a further step away from authority. That, at least, was probably Walpole's intention.

The relationship between the two men had deteriorated steadily through the 1720s. It is clear that Wilmington resented his rival's success and Walpole was keen to limit Compton's ability to act. On occasion Wilmington allowed his resentment to get the better of him, and flexed his muscles. He threatened to resign in protest at the proposed disciplining of a clutch of ministers who had rebelled over the Excise in 1733, but for the most part, he preferred to labour behind the scenes as an important member of one of the factions biding their time for Walpole to come unstuck.

Having missed his chance in 1727, Wilmington's ultimate achievement of the technical distinction of prime minister was decidedly inglorious. The loose coalition that engineered Walpole's downfall in early 1742 had initially looked for a significant broadening of the administration. This seems also to have been Wilmington's intention, but having failed to convince the King to take on board more than a handful of new men, he accepted office reluctantly as the figurehead of a caretaker administration led in effect by Lord Carteret. It is perhaps not insignificant, though, that one of those appointed to join him at the Treasury was his nephew, George Compton, who had been a resolute opponent of Walpole for several years.

Wilmington's short-lived administration was dominated by the early stages of the War of the Austrian Succession, though management of Britain's role was largely handled by others. In any case, within a year of assuming office Wilmington was said to be so ill that his death was believed to be imminent.

Some former Walpole supporters feared the consequences of him being carried off, but Carteret's response to his eventual demise in July 1743 was dismissive. He noted only 'that it was an event of great consequence and that he was sorry it happened at this time'. The speed with which Wilmington was forgotten may be attributable both to his comparative insignificance as a prime minister, and to his unfortunate bracketing between the colossus that was Walpole, and the long-lived ascendancy of the Pelham brothers who succeeded him. It was perhaps only by dying in office that Wilmington achieved real distinction.

Robin Eagles is editor of the House of Lords 1660–1832, History of Parliament *Trust.*

3

Henry Pelham

27 August 1743 to 6 March 1754
Whig

By Stuart Handley

Full name: Henry Pelham
Born: 25 September 1694, London
Died: 6 March 1754, Arlington Street, Piccadilly, London.
Buried at Laughton, Sussex
Education: Westminster School; Hart Hall, Oxford
Married to Lady Catherine Manners; 2 sons, 6 daughters
Quotation: Upon being informed of his death, George II was
heard to remark, 'Now I shall have no more peace.'

H ENRY PELHAM WAS arguably the most successful prime minister
in British history. As Enoch Powell once wrote, 'all political
lives, unless they are cut off in midstream at a happy juncture, end
in failure, because that is the nature of politics and of human affairs',

and when Pelham died in office at the age of fifty-nine, he was at the peak of his political powers, and had served over a decade in office as prime minister. His sudden death affected everybody in politics right to the very top.

Pelham had many advantages. He was the younger surviving son of a prominent Whig politician, Thomas Pelham, who had served as a Treasury lord in William III's reign, and whose favourable marriage in 1686 eventually led to the inheritance of much of the Holles estate by his elder brother of fourteen months, Thomas Pelham-Holles, Baron Pelham from 1712 and Duke of Newcastle. Pelham was involved in the London political scene from an early age, visiting prominent politicians as a matter of course, including the former Lord Treasurer, Robert Harley, Earl of Oxford, and William Wake, Archbishop of Canterbury.

Upon his return from foreign travel, Pelham was elected to Parliament for Seaford in a by-election in 1717. From 1722, he sat for the county of Sussex, a rare example of a politician on the rise sitting for a county (under place legislation, politicians had to resign their seats on accepting office, and this could be very expensive and risky in county seats, but, as it was, Pelham had no difficulty in winning re-election on three occasions after accepting office – such was his brother's hold over the county). An early indication of Pelham's future attitude was a vote in 1737 in favour of reducing the rate of interest on the national debt.

Pelham also had a good mentor, Sir Robert Walpole, for whom he often deputised in the House of Commons, and whom he described at one point as his 'oracle'. In return, Pelham was able to mediate successfully between his brother, Newcastle, and Walpole. Walpole, indeed, championed Pelham's credentials for high office, suggesting that he should be Chancellor of the Exchequer, and advising him not to let the opportunity slip, lest the chance never came again. Instead, Pelham became Leader of the House of Commons in July 1742, and by the time of the Earl of Wilmington's death on 2 July 1743, it had already been determined that he would take over at the Treasury. He became First Lord on 25 August 1743, and Chancellor of the Exchequer on 12 December 1743. He now held the same three offices that Walpole had done. However, Pelham was not the 'prime minister' in any meaningful sense until 1746.

The key to a successful eighteenth-century premiership was to have the support of a majority in the House of Commons and to culti-vate and retain the confidence of the monarch – in this case George II, who did at least prefer him to Pulteney. However, the King's confidence was bestowed upon Lord Carteret, the secretary of state, whose expertise in foreign policy and willingness to indulge the monarch's preference for protecting the interests of Hanover gave him a distinct advantage in the Closet. However, Pelham's position in the House of Commons gave him an advantage, and when Carteret's ambitious foreign policy, culminating in the Treaty of Worms in September 1743, and its supplementary conventions, which offered large subsidies to Austria and others, came under attack, Pelham was able to exploit the reversal in allied fortunes and engineer Carteret's dismissal on 24 November 1744.

Carteret's removal allowed Pelham to bring into office some Tories such as John Leveson Gower, Baron (later Earl) Gower and some of the followers of Lord Cobham (such as George Lyttelton and George Grenville) and the Duke of Bedford, to create a 'broad bottom' administration. Herein lay another reason for Pelham's longevity in office: his ability to disarm his opponents and weaken a formed opposition, by co-opting the most dangerous politicians into his government, leaving the discontented without effective speakers.

Pelham's problem now became the influence that Carteret was able to retain 'behind the curtain', owing to the confidence that George had kept in him. Nothing much could be done by Pelham during the national crisis of the Jacobite Rebellion of 1745–6, when governmental unity was essential. At the beginning of the Rebellion, Pelham was critical of the lack of urgency of some of his colleagues, especially the Scottish secretary, the Marquess of Tweeddale. As the situation deteriorated, Pelham exuded his characteristic calmness, and insisted on the recall of the Duke of Cumberland and some of the British troops employed abroad. He also played a key part in formulating policies to ensure the security of the regime in Scotland, and particularly the Highlands, such as the Heritable Jurisdictions Act of 1747.

With the Rebellion in retreat, Pelham forced the issue of Carteret's influence with the King. In a dramatic series of staged resignations,

Pelham, Newcastle and Lord Chancellor Hardwicke resigned on 11 February 1746. George II decided to try to form an administration without the Pelhams, based upon Carteret and Pulteney (now Earl of Bath). However, Pelham had covered his back well, and very few politicians were willing to join them. Instead, a succession of Whig grandees such as the Duke of Devonshire stood solidly behind Pelham and threatened to resign as well. Nearly two hundred MPs appeared at his 'levee' to demonstrate their support, and the City of London withdrew its offer of a loan of £3 million, the cry of 'No Pelham, No Money' being taken up. The City knew of Pelham's commitment to sound finance: Carteret may have dismissed him as a 'drudge', but he missed only four meetings out of over five hundred at the Treasury Board. Pelham and his fellow ministers immediately returned to office.

Pelham was now, in the words of J.H. Owen in *The Rise of the Pelhams*, 'Minister for the King in the House of Commons' and 'Minister for the House of Commons in the Closet'. After the exclusion of Carteret (now Earl Granville) from influence in 1746, he brought in William Pitt. He then neutralised the threat posed by the Prince of Wales by securing a dissolution of Parliament in 1747, a year earlier than scheduled under the Septennial Act, and fighting a General Election before the Prince could organise his extensive electoral interest in the Duchy of Cornwall. This resulted in an increase in the government's majority. The death of Prince Frederick in March 1751 presented Pelham with another tricky problem – how to prepare for a Regency should the King (who was sixty-seven) die before the new heir, Prince George (future George III, aged twelve), reached his majority. Pelham decided to back the claims of the Dowager Princess of Wales to be Regent (hemmed in with restrictions), rather than Prince George's uncle (the King's second son) the Duke of Cumberland, the victor of Culloden, and a military man suspected of autocratic tendencies.

The initial years of Pelham's premiership were concerned with war finance and the negotiations that led to an end of the Austrian Succession War in 1748. The conclusion of peace often caused problems for eighteenth-century governments; it was rare to deal successfully with post-war problems and expectations. The problem of dissatisfaction with the negotiated peace had been avoided by holding the General Election before the conclusion of the talks, and rather than lose power Pelham was able to consolidate his hold on the reins of government by concentrating on his role in charge of the nation's finances.

Pelham now dominated domestic politics, while his brother, Newcastle, conducted foreign affairs. Pelham's determination to reduce expenditure on foreign subsidies inevitably saw him attempt to circumscribe his brother's diplomatic manoeuvring. This often led to tensions between them, but the basic affection between the brothers ultimately prevented a complete breach. Credit for ameliorating the tension (occasionally exacerbated by disagreements over family finances and Newcastle's chronic indebtedness) rested with Lord Chancellor Hardwicke, who undertook the essential task of mediating between the two men.

Pelham was the archetypical finance minister, keen to minimise foreign commitments, especially subsidies to foreign powers for the use of troops; Lord Waldegrave, in his *Memoirs*, summed up his financial attitude as being 'averse to continual extravagance and useless subsidies'. The years after the peace of Aix-la-Chapelle saw him in his element as he managed to secure an unparalleled reduction in government debt in the early 1750s, consolidating the debt at a lower rate of interest (down from 4 per cent to 3 per cent), and even securing a reduction in the number of revenue officers. The debt reduction was achieved in the face of opposition from the Bank of England, the East India Company and the South Sea Company, a tribute to the skill with which Pelham built alliances with City financiers such as Sampson Gideon and the MP for London, Sir John Barnard. The latter had been encouraged to support Pelham's reforms by the minister's support in 1746 for the repeal of part of the City of London Elections Act of 1725, which allowed the claim of the Court of Aldermen to veto resolutions passed by the Common Council. With government expenditure subject to rigorous control, by 1754 the land tax (the benchmark of well-being for the landed classes) had been reduced from four to two shillings in the pound.

However, it was not only the administrative burden that Pelham sought to control. He was keen to keep public expenditure to a minimum on such things as propaganda, spending less on subsidising the press than Walpole. Peacetime did see him willing to forgo some revenue in the cause of social improvement; for example, he supported the Gin Act of 1751 (William Hogarth's prints of *Beer Street* and *Gin Alley* were issued the same year), which tightened the regulations concerning the consumption of alcohol in a bid to halt its perceived inducement to a life of idleness and crime. In this he joined with the bishops, an important part of his political coalition, and one that he knew it was important to conciliate while ensuring that they remained subservient in politics.

Governments in the mid-eighteenth century rarely imposed social legislation upon Parliament, but they were willing to allow privately sponsored public bills through the legislative process. If the statute subsequently threatened public harmony or the ministerial majorities in Parliament, or at a General Election, the legislation was swiftly reversed. One such measure was the Jewish Naturalisation Act of 1753, which allowed Jewish people to take the oaths of supremacy and allegiance without using the word 'Christian', which passed into law with little opposition, after having been trailed in previous sessions. The measure recognised the contribution to the British war effort of financiers like Sampson Gideon, and looked forward to rewarding the skills of other Jewish people. However, it was subject to a popular backlash, whipped up by opposition politicians. With a General Election imminent, Pelham decided that the threat to the government's majority was sufficient to allow the law to be repealed.

Pelham's government chose to allow through legislation to change from the Julian to the Gregorian calendar, which caused some disquiet among the populace, who demanded a return to their lost eleven days in September 1752. Another landmark Act, passed during his administration, was the Act establishing the British Museum in 1753, which provided for the purchase of several of the foundation collections.

Pelham had hitherto enjoyed excellent health, but in the summer of 1753 he became ill with a skin complaint, which he treated at Scarborough, a popular spa resort. The condition flared up again in December, and again in February 1754, and finally led to his death on 6 March. Pelham was in the process of revising his will when he died, so his will of 1748 (codicil 1751) came into operation.

As many contemporaries remarked, he died relatively poor, despite the lucrative offices he had held during his lifetime, including that of Paymaster General from 1730 to 1743. As heir to his brother, the family interest passed to his eldest daughter, whose husband, the Earl of Clinton, succeeded Newcastle as Duke of Newcastle-under-Lyme in 1768 (a title specially created for Newcastle in 1756).

For ten years Pelham had held together a diverse group of politicians, including men such as William Pitt and Henry Fox. His dominance of the political scene earnt him the soubriquet Henry IX. In truth though, the secret of Pelham's power lay less in acting like a monarch and more in a variety of his other personal qualities: he was unspectacular, quiet, calm and courteous; in more modern parlance, he was strong and stable.

Stuart Handley is Senior Research Fellow at the History of Parliament Trust.

4

Duke of Newcastle

16 March 1754 to 11 November 1756;
29 June 1757 to 26 March 1762
Whig

By Jeremy Black

Full name: Thomas Pelham-Holles
Born: 21 July 1693
Died: 17 November 1768, Newcastle House, Lincoln's Inn
Fields, London. Buried at Laughton, Sussex
Education: Westminster School; Clare College, Cambridge
Married to Lady Harriet Godolphin; no children
Quotation: 'We know that the brightest character may easily be
darkened by calumny.'

IN HIS NOVEL *Humphry Clinker* (1771), the Tory journalist Tobias
Smollett depicted Newcastle as a panicky fool at the start of the
Seven Years' War (1756–63). This was part of a tradition of trashing

the Duke in this way, one that, for the 1730s, left a memorable legacy in the shape of John, Lord Hervey's acerbic memoirs. So also with those of Horace Walpole. Indeed, when Newcastle came to the crunch, in 1756, in the controversy after the humiliating failure of Admiral Byng to relieve the besieged garrison on Minorca, he resigned as First Lord of the Treasury because he did not feel confident that he could ensure ministerial management of the House of Commons; and that despite a significant government majority there.

So why was it that Newcastle proved a key player in 'Old Corps' Whig ministries from 1724 until 1762, as well as being the most important politician in the House of Lords? The standard view was to attribute this to the oligarchical nature of the 'Old Corps' and to Newcastle's ability to control borough patronage, and thus select a number of MPs, as well as his willingness to spend lavishly to support the Whig electoral interests, which he did to the point of seriously endangering his finances. These factors were indeed important, and Newcastle was a particularly significant figure in the electoral politics of Yorkshire and West Sussex. He came from a background of great privilege. The eldest son of Thomas, 1st Lord Pelham, whom he succeeded in 1712, the young Thomas Pelham added the name Holles in 1711 when he succeeded to most of the estates of his maternal uncle, John, Duke of Newcastle. In turn, he was created Duke of Newcastle in 1715, and, in 1717 he joined another great Whig family, when he married Henrietta, the eldest daughter of Francis, 2nd Earl of Godolphin. These aristocratic connections helped ensure preferment at Court. In 1717, the young Duke became a Privy Councillor as well as Lord Chamberlain of the Household, a post he held until 1724, and, conspicuously favoured by George I, in 1718 he became a Knight of the Garter.

Nevertheless, the Duke brought more than patronage to ministries. First, for those led in large part from the Commons, as was the case with Sir Robert Walpole, Henry Pelham, and, to a degree, William Pitt the Elder, Newcastle essentially delivered the other House. This reflected his skill in managing government patronage, notably his attention to that of the Church of England, but also his busy attendance in the House. The Duke, furthermore, brought with him his brother Henry, who served as the ministry's business manager in the Commons while First Lord of the Treasury from 1743 to 1754 and who also helped to prevent relations between Newcastle and Walpole breaking down totally before their collapse in 1742.

Moreover, like all these men, Newcastle stood for policies: the patronage and management were to the point. In particular, Newcastle was convinced that chaos was the only alternative to Whig rule. Indeed, to him, politics was centrally entwined with the issue of the royal succession and the protection of both constitution and Protestantism. In 1715, as a Lord Lieutenant, Newcastle played a role in security during the Jacobite uprising, being particularly significant in the crucial county of Middlesex. Subsequently, as a secretary of state from 1724 to 1754, Newcastle saw protection against foreign support for Jacobitism as a major element in foreign policy.

The unexpected early death of Henry Pelham in 1754 led Newcastle to replace him as First Lord of the Treasury, and therefore prime minister. This reflected Newcastle's frenetic determination to retain control. In place of Pelham, Newcastle sought to entrust the management of the Commons to Henry Fox, but Fox refused to accept the task when he discovered that the Duke intended to retain full control of all government patronage and to manage the forthcoming General Election: that would have left Fox with responsibility, but without the power to give substance to his management. The politically weaker Thomas Robinson, who had been a diplomat, in contrast, proved more pliable. Newcastle told the Sardinian envoy that only Pitt was able to manage the Commons (by which he meant that he feared Pitt's opposition there), but that he had failed, despite very great efforts, to get the King to talk to Pitt, as George detested him.

As First Lord, and extremely busy on that account, Newcastle was compared to Walpole, but with the significant difference that he had to have others manage the Commons. In practice, comparison between Newcastle's periods of office as secretary of state and as First Lord is difficult, as the exigencies of approaching war and then war itself ensured that the situation from 1754 became more serious. As First Lord, Newcastle took a more direct role in foreign policy than Pelham had done, but he also had greater experience, as the most long-standing secretary of state ever. He intercepted diplomatic correspondence, frequently discussed foreign policy with foreign envoys, and also corresponded with British diplomats such as Andrew Mitchell in Berlin. Moreover, initially while First Lord, Newcastle had two secretaries of state (Holdernesse and Robinson) who lacked much political weight, skill or ambition, a situation that changed only when Robinson was replaced by Fox in November 1755.

Newcastle managed the 1754 General Election very well, but the opening stages of the Seven Years' War went badly, both in North America and in Europe. Combined with the difficulties of Commons management and with ministerial divisions, this led Newcastle to stand down on 27 October 1756. Newcastle's failure to create a strong ministerial combination to the King's liking eventually forced George's hand on the composition of the ministry, as a ministry under Pitt and William, 4th Duke of Devonshire, replaced that of Newcastle. However, Pitt discovered that he needed Newcastle's support to make the ministry stable, and on 29 June 1757 the Duke brought the political crisis to a close by forming a joint administration with him, an arrangement that Devonshire accepted. It was not initially clear that the ministry would be successful or lasting. Instead, to many commentators, it appeared likely that the differences between the two protagonists, and their drive to dominate, would soon split it. Pitt's position might have looked weak in terms of parliamentary management, as he did not command an interest or have any experience in managing the Commons. Nevertheless, thanks to his ability, magnetism, vigour and public resonance, Pitt's position was stronger than anyone else's, although not strong enough for him to direct a ministry by himself.

Pitt was especially weak at the Court, in the House of Lords, and with the leading financial interests. That made Newcastle necessary to him, while Pitt, in turn, served to blunt the critique from Tories and opposition Whigs, and, alongside the support of the 'Old Corps' produced by Newcastle, this situation ensured that 1758–61 proved politically stable, which was a valuable domestic basis for the delivery of repeated victories over France. The crucial importance of the financing of the war meant that Newcastle's post as First Lord of the Treasury was a key one. He was responsible for raising the vast loans the government required. Pitt also benefited greatly from Newcastle's hard-won influence with George II.

Newcastle's insecurity, however, made it very difficult for him to accept support without feeling fresh anxieties about its strength and/or duration. George, in contrast, could be explosive, but was generally steadier and more phlegmatic than the Duke. Indeed, Newcastle lacked both the personality and the position to sustain the political structure that his paranoia dictated: a concentration of decision making and power in his own person. He could not be a second Walpole, not least because he was not in the Commons. Newcastle wanted strong colleagues able to take the responsibility for decisions and, for that reason, operated best with Walpole, Pelham and Pitt. Yet he also wanted his colleagues subordinate and could not psychologically accept his own dependence on them: he was weak, but did not wish to acknowledge his weakness. George was not close to Newcastle, and this was a major source of the Duke's anxiety. Controlling neither Crown nor Commons, Newcastle sought to be a crucial intermediary between the two, but this was an unstable basis for political control.

Pitt helped Newcastle not only politically, but also psychologically, lessening the issues created by the Duke's indecisiveness and desire to share responsibility. The cooperative nature of ministries was the product of the absence both of party government based on a party organisation and of unchallenged royal direction that could be delegated to a favourite. Over three years of political infighting in 1754–7 had in some measure exhausted the participants, but it had also convinced them that a Newcastle–Pitt ministry was the best combination. There was little doubt that Newcastle's task would have been more difficult had Pitt remained in opposition, especially in terms of finding adequate leadership for the Commons, and that he believed that this was the case. As Newcastle found, war accentuated a central feature of the political system, namely that successful parliamentary management required competent leadership and acceptable policies, as well as patronage, and that, especially in periods of real and apparent crisis, such policies tended to take note of opinion 'out of doors', however manipulated and whatever was the arithmetic of parliamentary strength.

The situation was far less promising when George III succeeded to the throne in 1760. The young King saw the 'Old Corps' as corrupt and felt no expedient need to support them as his grandfather, George II, had done once he came to the throne. The initial crisis, that of 1761, focused on Pitt, and Newcastle, who also found him very difficult, understood why he had to go. Newcastle was to write to an ally, Devonshire, about Pitt in July 1762: 'I have long known his inveteracy to me . . . I have a great deal to complain of him, for his ingratitude for many years. In this reign, I own, I did, in concert with your Grace and my friends, prefer my Lord Bute to him.'

Indeed, Pitt was angered by Newcastle's refusal in 1761 to join with him in resisting the rise of George III's favourite John, 3rd Earl of Bute. However, that was not the issue by 1762. Newcastle found it difficult to accept the attitudes of George, notably his decision to end Britain's involvement in the German part of the Seven Years' War, and also the political views of Bute, and fell out with the latter over his determination to obtain peace, and his conduct of the government. Thus, having resigned that May, Newcastle ended up in the unexpected position of being in opposition. This was not a role that suited him, and he proved a poor and vacillating ally for Pitt against Bute in late 1762. Newcastle's last years were unsatisfactory. He returned briefly, in 1765–6, as Lord Privy Seal during the Rockingham ministry, but although Rockingham was a protégé, he was not now a major player. Newcastle lost office when George III turned to Pitt, now Earl of Chatham, in 1766. With Newcastle no longer at his side, there was nobody to take his place, and issues and circumstances were more divisive and less likely to produce countervailing pressures for unity than had been the case during the earlier ministry.

Ultimately, Newcastle's major contribution was to provide stability and continuity. It is easy to underrate this because the general attitude of politics is to look for change, notably reform. That, however, was not the major theme in this period. Indeed, in Britain as in continental Europe, the drive for reform repeatedly threatened stability. Newcastle was a key player in the process by which the Whigs lost their earlier radicalism. That could be seen as a failure, but, looked at differently, it helped ensure that the Whig position was stabilised and, thereby, able to survive the Jacobite challenge, which was serious.

Jeremy Black is Emeritus Professor of History at the University of Exeter.

5

Duke of Devonshire

16 November 1756 to 29 June 1757
Whig

By Elaine Chalus

Full name: William Cavendish, 4th Duke of Devonshire
Born: 8 May 1720, London
Died: 2 October 1764, Spa, Belgium. Buried at All Saints church, Derby
Education: Home schooled
Married to Lady Charlotte Boyle, Baroness Clifford of Londesborough; 3 sons, 1 daughter
Quotation: 'I have no motive but the King's Service.' (To George II's *maîtresse-en-titre*, Lady Yarmouth, November 1759)

WILLIAM CAVENDISH, 4TH Duke of Devonshire, was, according to Horace Walpole, appointed First Lord of the Treasury by George II at the beginning of November 1756, without having been asked. He had only returned from Ireland, where he had been a successful Lord Lieutenant, at the end of October.

He came back to a Westminster at war, and the war was not going well. Although the British had been fighting the French in North America since 1754, Britain had only formally declared war on France in May 1756. In June, Admiral Byng had lost the Battle of Minorca, thus depriving Britain of a vital Mediterranean base and setting off a seemingly interminable debate about Byng's personal culpability; similarly, in India, the East India Company had lost control of Calcutta to the Nawab of Bengal, sending horrifying tales of suffering in the 'Black Hole' of Calcutta back to England; and, throughout it all, the French had continued to threaten and encroach upon Britain's North American territories.

On the Continent, the Diplomatic Revolution was under way. Britain was now formally allied with Prussia to ensure protection of Hanover; Austria, followed later by Russia, had turned defensively away from Britain to forge alliances with France.

Nor were domestic politics reassuring. Newcastle, a peculiar combination of ambition and vacillating timidity, was unable to lead an effective ministry without powerful support in the Commons. Ideally, he needed both Henry Fox and William Pitt, but their rivalry, and particularly Pitt's intransigent desire for power, made crafting a stable administration almost impossible.

Court politics complicated matters yet further. George II disliked Pitt personally and distrusted his commitment to continental military involvement and the protection of Hanover: he therefore had been unwilling to give Pitt a senior office. Pitt in turn had used the loss of Minorca to attack Fox and Newcastle relentlessly in the summer of 1756. He had also performed a classic eighteenth-century political manoeuvre, effectively abandoning the King and Newcastle's 'Old Corps' Whigs in favour of the rival court of the young Prince of Wales and his mother at Leicester House.

George, Prince of Wales, had come of age in May 1756 and had immediately made his opposition to his grandfather's ministers clear. He had pointedly appointed his erstwhile tutor, Lord Bute, to head his Household as Groom of the Stole. Bute, an intelligent if rather haughty Scottish courtier, was not only a political outsider who lacked direct political experience, but he and the Prince also held idealistically 'Patriot' (anti-corruption, anti-party) sympathies. These threatened Whig hegemony and promised to bring the Tories, long in the political wilderness, back into power on George III's accession. Pitt, ever an opportunist, had recast himself in popular 'Patriot' mode, praising Lord Bute and roundly proclaiming his esteem for the Prince.

The combination of these factors, with the loss of Minorca uppermost, brought down the Fox/Newcastle administration. Fox, then Newcastle, resigned at the end of October 1756. The King turned first to Fox to form a ministry, but as he was unable to do so without Pitt, George II approached both Devonshire and Pitt, separately. Devonshire, although a lifelong friend of Fox and a long-time supporter of Newcastle, possessed that rare quality of being valued by the King and by politicians on all sides. Pitt himself commended Devonshire for office and agreed to serve under him. By the beginning of November, with matters still unsettled, the King ordered Devonshire to try to form a ministry. Devonshire agreed, but on the condition that he had the right to resign if he 'disliked the employment'.

By early November 1756, Devonshire was First Lord of the Treasury. As the head of arguably the most important great Whig family – George III's mother would famously, and aptly, refer to him as the 'crown prince of the Whigs' – he was an astute choice to lead what was understood to be an interim government. He combined the unquestioned authority and assurance of high aristocratic birth with outstanding wealth, extensive estates in both England and Ireland, and political influence and experience. He was beholden to no one and was free of the taint of the fractious politics of the preceding administration. Most importantly, he was known to be a worthy, honest and complaisant man. Even Horace Walpole, no friend of the Cavendishes, described the Duke and his father favourably, as 'the fashionable models of goodness, though their chief merit was a habit of caution'. This 'caution' was combined with diplomacy and a quiet ability to use his personal networks to outmanoeuvre difficult politicians and calm political situations, a skill Devonshire had demonstrated to effect while Lord Lieutenant in Ireland.

The Duke was not ambitious for power; his allegiance was to

the Crown. He appears to have accepted the post of First Lord out of duty and a sense of responsibility to King and country in a time of war. His primary political goal was to achieve domestic political stability and an enduring government. This meant finding a way to reconcile Newcastle and Pitt, something that would prove more difficult than prosecuting the war. Devonshire recognised that, despite his friendship with Fox, it was Pitt who had to be made secretary of state. Bringing the King around to give Pitt even half-hearted support was his first task. He achieved this through careful persuasion and, undoubtedly, as was his practice, through securing astute interventions by the King's mistress, Lady Yarmouth. Early in November, the Devonshire–Pitt ministry was formed.

The ministry proved to be short-lived and complicated. Political tensions between the Whigs and the Tories were exacerbated early in 1757 by the trial and eventual execution of Admiral John Byng. Pitt's poor mental and physical health added further difficulties. However, there were some notable achievements: in Europe, Newcastle's continental policy was continued, and British troops were sent to protect Hanover; elsewhere, the recruitment of Highlanders replaced Hanoverian and Hessian troops. The navy targeted and harassed the coast of France – and America took on increased strategic importance. More British troops were sent to America; contributions of men and money were demanded from the American colonies; and military action became more focused, first on Quebec and then on Louisbourg. Finally, at home, the passage of the Militia Act (1757) laid the groundwork for the creation of the modern militia.

Pitt's advocacy in the Commons for a pardon for Admiral Byng in early 1757 worsened his relations with the King and destabilised the ministry. Despite the best efforts of Pitt and his cousin Lord Temple, First Lord of the Admiralty, Byng was executed in March. The administration was fatally undermined, however, in April when the King's younger son, the Duke of Cumberland, refused to take command of the army in Germany unless there was a change of ministry. The King promptly took the opportunity to dismiss Pitt and Temple. The Devonshire–Pitt ministry was effectively at an end. Devonshire turned his attention in May to persuading the King to give Newcastle the authority to form a new government, and by the end of June, after playing a vital part in the negotiations that forged the Newcastle–Pitt ministry, Devonshire formally resigned. He was appointed Lord Chamberlain, but somewhat unusually continued to sit in the inner Cabinet. Here, he continued to play an important part as peacemaker and quiet tactician.

Devonshire's diplomacy was increasingly necessary after the accession of the young and politically naïve George III swept Lord Bute into power. With the supremacy of the Whigs under threat and relations between Pitt, Newcastle and Bute increasingly fraught, Devonshire did much in 1761–2 to ensure that sufficient harmony existed for the peace negotiations with France to go ahead. With Newcastle resigning after having been effectively pushed out of power by Bute in 1762, Devonshire withdrew from attending Cabinet and supporting government business. He then angered George III by refusing to attend a Cabinet council hosted by Bute on the final peace treaty. The dénouement proved farcical: having claimed that he lacked sufficient knowledge of the final treaty to attend, Devonshire travelled to London intending to take leave of the King before going north for Chatsworth. On the way to the capital, his carriage was passed by the King's coach. The King jumped to the conclusion that Devonshire was going to London to plot against him and then make a dramatic resignation; consequently, he not only refused to see Devonshire when he arrived at Court but also dismissed him as Lord Chamberlain. Furthermore, a few days later, he went so far as to physically erase his name as Privy Councillor.

Devonshire and Pitt worked together once more before Devonshire's untimely death at Spa, Belgium, in October 1764, aged only forty-four. In response to the passage of the highly unpopular Cider Tax in 1763, the Duke invited Pitt and other leading politicians to a dinner party in London, where they planned their opposition to the tax. This successfully contributed to Bute's own resignation in April 1763.

Elaine Chalus is Professor of British History and head of department at the University of Liverpool.

6

Earl of Bute

26 May 1762 to 8 April 1763
Tory

By David Torrance

Full name: John Stuart, 3rd Earl of Bute
Born: 25 May 1713, Parliament Close, Edinburgh
Died: 10 March 1792, South Audley Street, London. Buried at Rothesay, Isle of Bute
Education: Eton; University of Leiden
Married to Mary Wortley Montagu; 5 sons, 6 daughters
Quotation: 'A noble duke knows the difficulty to choose proper taxes.' (During a debate on the Cider Tax)

JOHN STUART, THE 3rd Earl of Bute, was the first Scot (and Tory) to become prime minister of Great Britain, a country little more than half a century old when he reached its most senior office. Memories of the 1745 Jacobite uprising (in the course of which

Bonnie Prince Charlie had reached Derby) were, in 1762, still fresh, and Bute attracted enmity on account of his nationality and perceived influence on King George III.

During his premiership, wrote Bute's sympathetic biographer J.A. Lovat-Fraser, 'he brought upon himself an amount of hatred and detestation rarely equalled in English history'. One contemporary pamphlet dubbed him the 'upstart Highlander', one of many (and often still recognisable) anti-Scottish tropes wielded against Bute during his term in office. Even in retirement, Bute was depicted as a malign manipulative figure, yet this bad PR – then as now – masks a respectable record among early British prime ministers.

Fittingly for a regal adviser, Bute was descended from pre-1603 Scottish royalty, with a family seat on the Isle of Bute (still inhabited by the family of the same name). He was born on 25 May 1713 close to the old Scots Parliament whose abolition in 1707 his paternal grandfather, Sir James Stuart (later the 1st Earl), had opposed. His son, the 2nd Earl and John's father, died at thirty-three, widowing his mother Anne Campbell, the 1st Duke of Argyll's daughter.

For his education, Bute went south to Eton and then to the Continent to study civil law at the University of Leiden. In 1736, aged twenty-three, he married Mary Montagu, the only daughter of Edward Wortley Montagu, who owned immense estates in Yorkshire. It proved a long and happy marriage, producing a remarkable six daughters and five sons, of whom the eldest, also called John, would become a notable politician and diplomat, as well as the first Marquess of Bute.

The 3rd Earl, meanwhile, became a Scottish 'representative' peer in 1737 (under the terms of the Anglo-Scottish Union, the Scottish peerage elected sixteen of their number to 'represent' Scotland in the Upper House), but was not re-elected in the 1741 Parliament, even though his maiden speech had impressed with its accomplishment. He retired for five years to the Isle of Bute, where he occupied himself with reading, improving his estates and his lifelong passion, botany.

In the mid-1740s Bute experienced financial problems and moved from Scotland to Twickenham, shortly after the outbreak of the Jacobite uprising. It proved fortuitous, for his introduction to Frederick, Prince of Wales – over a game of cards at the Egham

races – transformed his fortunes. In 1750 Bute was appointed Lord
of the Bedchamber to the Prince, although Frederick died the
following year. Bute continued his friendship with the widowed
Princess Augusta and thus had influence over her son George, now
heir to the throne.

By 1756, Bute was in charge of the young heir's household
(Leicester House) and made sure George was provided with an
education along Tory lines. Four years later he was with the Prince
when he received news of George II's fatal illness. Bute had a hand
in the new King's accession declaration and was subsequently made
a Privy Councillor, Secretary of State for the Northern Department
(having been re-elected a Scots representative peer in 1760) and a
ranger of Richmond Park, a rapid promotion that caused considerable resentment. It was said that an initial draft of George III's
first speech to Parliament spoke of glorying in the name of 'England',
but Bute induced him to change it to 'Briton', an acknowledgement
of the monarch's Scottish and Irish subjects that added to the
resentment.

Bute's good fortune manifested itself in other respects. When his
uncle, the Duke of Argyll, died, his power and influence passed to
Bute, while the death of his father-in-law left Lady Bute (who had
also been appointed a peer in her own right, as Baroness Mount
Stuart of Wortley) with a vast fortune. The great Jacobite families,
long absent from Court, now crowded Buckingham Palace, and in
1761 Bute was blamed for the resignation of William Pitt the Elder,
to whom he had once been close, over Pitt's support for a preemptive strike against Spain, then allied with France. When the
Duke of Newcastle resigned as premier on 26 May 1762, Bute –
already prime minister in all but name – took his place as head of
the Tory government.

As a result of his elevation to the premiership, Bute became even
more unpopular. Whigs resented him as an interloper; dissenting
ministers because they believed Bute had deprived them of a
generous government allowance; cartoonists because he was Scottish.
(Caricaturists, however, struggled to make him appear unattractive,
for Bute had fine aristocratic features and equally fine legs.) An
effigy of the new prime minister was suspended upon a gibbet at
one of Exeter's principal gates for two weeks before someone cut

it down. Satirists also claimed he had had an affair with the King's mother, which was almost certainly untrue given his religiosity and happy marriage. Everywhere he went, Bute experienced a rough reception, even threats of assassination.

Lyricists, reporters and pamphleteers were as cruel as the most vociferous tweeters of the twenty-first century. Bute was said to be attempting to restore the Stuart monarchy by the back door, bringing into English politics the despotic spirit of the Highland chief, evidence for which included his banishment of the name of the Duke of Cumberland, the 'butcher' of Scots lore, from the liturgy. One issue of the *North Briton* newspaper even consisted of an imaginary letter from the Old Pretender (the exiled 'James III') to the new prime minister. It made little difference that Bute had resigned the (Scottish) Order of the Thistle in order to be invested with the (English) Garter.

Bute, meanwhile, accelerated negotiations with France, which reached their conclusion in November 1762 and led to even more unpopularity. The new prime minister was blamed for ceding Guadalupe and St Lucia to France, although he was only following the logic of earlier talks conducted by the Duke of Newcastle. As a not inconsiderable *quid pro quo*, Great Britain gained Canada and stopped haemorrhaging cash as a result of the Seven Years' War, for which Bute received little thanks.

This 'Treaty of Paris' demonstrated his deep understanding of European politics, which added to Bute's self-confidence in office, something acknowledged at the time by subordinates. He also impressed foreign dignitaries in London, a useful dynamic as he drove the delicate Anglo-French peace process to a successful conclusion. Although Pitt, now Bute's leading nemesis, attacked the terms of peace as inadequate, it is hard from the perspective of the early twenty-first century not to view it as a major win for Great Britain and a considerable blow to French prestige.

Instead, the political focus was on Bute's alleged nepotism. There were complaints regarding the number of Scots in senior positions, which included the Lord Chief Justice of England and the Archbishop of York; Buckingham Palace was even nicknamed Holyrood. Yet Bute's relationship with Scotland appeared complicated. He does not appear to have ever taken King George III to his native land,

and while Bute inherited the stewardship of Scottish affairs from the 3rd Duke of Argyll, he delegated it to his brother, Stuart Mackenzie, as Lord Privy Seal of Scotland (an ancient office of state that only lapsed in 1922).

By the spring of 1763, Bute had carried a major Budget as well as peace with France, so his resignation on 8 April came as a genuine surprise, if a welcome one to his many enemies. Bute's explanation was ill-health and fear of making the Sovereign suffer on account of his own unpopularity, but in truth it seemed likely the opprobrium heaped upon him had made his premiership unendurable. Besides, his wife's inherited fortune meant he no longer required the financial perks of high office.

The antipathy towards Bute did not diminish with his resignation. His brother was turned out of office, as was the Earl of Northumberland, Bute's son-in-law. Bute himself retired from the House of Lords in 1780, seeing out his days at his Hampshire villa. In November 1790 he had an accident, falling over a cliff near his house. He never fully recovered, and on 10 May 1792 Bute died aged seventy-eight at his house on Grosvenor Square. He was buried back in Scotland on his eponymous island.

Although popular privately and obviously a devoted family man, this was rarely evident on the public stage. That mattered less in the eighteenth century than it would in the era of mass communications, but it still meant Bute's political achievements were under-appreciated, while his nationality enabled the opposition to mobilise public hostility – justified or otherwise – against him. As Lord Chesterfield once observed, the chief complaint against Bute, in and out of office, was his nationality, 'the only fault which he could not possibly correct'.

J.A. Lovat-Fraser, Bute's generally sympathetic biographer, argued that if prejudices against him as a Scot and a supposed intimate of Princess Augusta were put aside, then there was 'nothing in Bute's character that entitles either the historian or the politician to make him the object of his contempt or scorn'. Others have highlighted Bute's extensive patronage of the arts (he himself published a nine-volume work on botany) and his clear command of political strategy.

'I follow one uniform system,' Bute wrote of himself to Henry Fox shortly before his resignation, 'and that is founded on the strictest honour, faith and duty.' Most politicians, of course, want to believe such things of themselves, but in Bute's case he had arguably led an effective ministry in spite of considerable difficulty at home and abroad. Furthermore, Bute never allowed his considerable personal unpopularity to interfere with what he regarded as Great Britain's financial and imperial interests.

David Torrance is a political biographer, historian and a clerk in the House of Commons Library.

7

George Grenville

16 April 1763 to 10 July 1765
Whig

By Stephen Conway

Full name: George Grenville
Born: 14 October 1712, Westminster
Died: 13 November 1770, Bolton Street, Westminster. Buried at Wotton, Buckinghamshire
Education: Eton; Christ Church, Oxford
Married to Elizabeth Wyndham; 4 sons, 5 daughters

GEORGE GRENVILLE SERVED as prime minister from April 1763 to July 1765. He is most well known for his attempts to levy parliamentary taxes on the American colonies. Historians long have argued that Grenville's taxes provoked a crisis that marked the first phase of the American Revolution, which eventually led to the Declaration of Independence and the creation of the United States.

Grenville's background made a parliamentary career almost inevitable. His father was an MP, as was his maternal grandfather. George attended Eton and Christ Church, Oxford, before entering the Inner Temple and being called to the Bar. When he married in 1749, his wife was the daughter of an MP. By this stage, Grenville had already become an MP himself, elected for the borough of Buckingham in 1741. It was a seat with a tiny electorate – the thirteen members of the borough corporation – and was effectively in the control of Grenville's family. Unsurprisingly, he remained the borough's MP for the rest of his life.

In 1744, just three years after entering the Commons, Grenville began his ministerial career. At first, he served as a lord of the Admiralty, then, in 1747, he became a Lord of the Treasury. In 1754, he returned to naval administration when he was appointed to the office of treasurer of the navy. Senior ministerial responsibilities came in 1762, when he was made a secretary of state in the Earl of Bute's short-lived administration. In April 1763, when Bute resigned, Grenville replaced him as First Lord of the Treasury and effective prime minister.

Grenville inherited a difficult financial situation; the national debt had doubled in the course of the recently concluded Seven Years' War (1756–63) and wartime levels of taxation had to be continued just to cover the interest payments. He also had to grapple with the problems associated with a vast expansion of the size of the British Empire. New islands had been added to the British Crown's Dominions in the West Indies, making the French inhabitants subjects of George III. In West Africa, the source of most of the slave labour used in the American plantations, the British strengthened their position, while in South Asia, the British East India Company became a major territorial power in 1765, when the Mogul emperor in Delhi granted the company the right to collect revenues and administer justice in three of his Indian provinces. In North America, meanwhile, French Canada and Spanish Florida became British colonies, and the Crown's jurisdiction now stretched from Hudson's Bay in the north to the Gulf of Mexico in the south, and from the Atlantic seaboard in the east to the Mississippi in the west.

This vast new Empire had to be defended. Grenville's predecessor had already decided to base a regular army in North America after the war, to be used as a mobile force to be deployed against the French or Spanish in the event – assumed to be likely – of renewed conflict with the Bourbon powers. Grenville believed that this military force could be paid for only by parliamentary taxation (as a Whig supporter of the constitutional settlement of 1689, he was convinced that parliamentary control of the army was vital to preserve liberty). But Grenville also believed that the Americans should make a contribution to the costs of this army, sparing the hard-pressed British taxpayers, who had already resisted post-war attempts to levy new duties on English cider.

The first attempt to tax the colonies to pay for the army in North America came in 1764. The Revenue Act of that year imposed a range of duties on imports into the colonies – on foreign textiles, wine, and (most controversially) foreign molasses, or semi-refined sugar, used in North America to make rum. Grenville seems to have been inspired partly by a desire to preserve the colonies as a market for British manufactures (hence his duties on foreign textiles), but his main objective was clearly to raise money. The duty he imposed on foreign molasses was in fact lower than the duty imposed in 1733. But in 1733, the aim was to create a prohibitive tariff, which would prevent the import of foreign molasses into the colonies and encourage rum-producers in New England to buy (more expensive) British Caribbean molasses instead. In 1764, by contrast, the reduced duty was intended not to deter but to encourage foreign molasses to enter the British North American colonies, thereby boosting the revenue of the British government. The 1764 Act, furthermore, made clear that the proceeds would be devoted to helping to cover the costs of the British army garrison in North America.

The colonies began to mobilise in opposition to the 1764 Revenue Act, but what truly alarmed them was the prospect of further parliamentary taxation. Grenville, when he introduced his 1764 duties, suggested that more would have to follow and put the case for American stamp duties, which he thought would be cheap to administer and difficult to evade, as all contracts and official documents would have to be on stamped paper if they were to be legally binding. He discussed that matter with agents appointed by some of the colonies to lobby on their behalf, but most of the agents had no doubt that Grenville was personally committed to stamp duties and would not accept any alternatives. He was willing to be flexible on details (rates, exemptions), but not, it seems, on the principle. In early 1765, the Stamp Act made its way through Parliament with remarkable ease.

Grenville's hopes that the new tax would be accepted by the colonists proved over-optimistic. Resistance began with the elected assemblies of the different colonies, which saw themselves as the local equivalents of Westminster and argued that they possessed the sole right to levy taxes on their constituents. The resolutions of the assemblies reflected the very English political culture of the colonies; they invoked Magna Carta (1215) and the Bill of Rights (1689) as protections against arbitrary taxation by a body in which they were not represented. The same arguments appeared in the resolutions of the Stamp Act Congress, representing most of the mainland colonies, which showed the willingness of Americans to put aside local differences and unite to resist a threat that affected them all.

Grenville had already tried to answer colonial points about representation when he introduced his stamp duties. He accepted that taxation and representation were inextricably connected – this, after all, was a central principle of the British constitution – but he maintained that the colonists were in practice represented at Westminster. He acknowledged that there were no MPs sitting for colonial constituencies, but claimed that the Americans were 'virtually represented' by parliamentarians who took account of colonial views before they reached any decisions. His argument, while strange from a modern perspective, had some substance. Several MPs acted as paid agents for particular colonies; others were merchants who traded extensively with America; and still others had served in North America in the recent war, and knew colonial circumstances quite well. In this sense, the American voice was indeed heard.

Grenville's arguments about 'virtual representation' failed to convince Americans. Colonial writers pointed out that MPs had an interest in shifting the tax burden onto the shoulders of the Americans, who played no part in their election, to spare the money of their British constituents. But by this stage colonial opposition to the stamp duties had extended much further than polite exchanges in pamphlets or decorous statements of American objections in the resolutions of the assemblies and the Stamp Act Congress. Serious rioting occurred in northern towns. More importantly, merchants in colonial ports stopped importing British goods; their non-importation agreements were intended to last until the British Parliament relented and repealed the hated Stamp Act.

Repeal would have been very difficult to achieve if Grenville had remained in office. But in July 1765 the King finally tired of his First Minister. Grenville's fall had nothing directly to do with the crisis that his stamp duties had provoked. Rather, George III despaired of Grenville's insecurities. Grenville had become convinced that George was still consulting Bute (his boyhood tutor) and that the King's relationship with his former minister undermined his own authority. Grenville even tried to veto appointments that he thought owed much to Bute's influence. By July 1765, George III's patience was exhausted, and he replaced Grenville with a new First Minister, the Marquess of Rockingham.

Rockingham, who did not have the same emotional commitment to the Stamp Act as Grenville, piloted repeal through a sceptical Parliament, with Grenville resisting at every step of the way. At various times in the repeal process, Grenville's arguments seemed to be gaining traction. Many MPs were deeply concerned about the precedent that repeal would set. They worried that if the Americans established that Parliament had no right to tax them, then the colonists would go on to deny that Parliament had any right to legislate for them. What made them most anxious, it seems, was that the Americans would challenge the legitimacy of the seventeenth-century Navigation Acts, which regulated colonial overseas trade and were widely seen by MPs as the foundation of national prosperity and power.

At length, however, the Rockingham government's practical arguments won the day; non-importation, ministerial supporters argued, was inflicting enormous damage on the British economy, and repeal of this particular tax could be justified on those grounds, without endangering parliamentary sovereignty. The Stamp Act was repealed in March 1766, a little over a year after it was passed. To sugar the bitter pill, the Rockinghamites secured simultaneous approval for an American Declaratory Act, asserting Parliament's right to legislate for the colonies 'in all cases whatsoever'. Shortly afterwards, the same government passed its own Revenue Act, which lowered the duty on all molasses entering the mainland colonies, but applied it to the same purpose as Grenville had intended for his stamp duties. Neither the Declaratory Act nor the Rockingham government's own taxation of the colonies reconciled Grenville to the loss of the Stamp Act. He continued to remind MPs of the folly of repeal in speeches in the House of Commons right up to his last appearance a few months before his death.

Despite his obduracy, Grenville seems to have been widely respected in Parliament. In 1768, debate on a bill was suspended on the grounds that Grenville, who could not be present, had some objections to the wording of the preamble. Few MPs would have been accorded such a favour. Opponents as well as allies saw him as a committed 'Parliament man', determined to uphold the authority of the House of Commons. He approached the challenges of his premiership with the forensic debating skills of a lawyer and the obsession with savings and revenue-generation of an experienced financier. It was his misfortune that he misread the colonial mood and has gone down in history as an authoritarian figure; he would have seen himself as a true Whig and defender of the constitution.

Stephen Conway is Professor of History at University College, London.

8

Marquess of Rockingham

13 July 1765 to 30 July 1766; 27 March to 1 July 1782
Whig

By Jesse Norman

Full name: Charles Watson-Wentworth, 2nd Marquess of
Rockingham
Born: 13 May 1730, Wentworth House, Rotherham
Died: 1 July 1782, Wimbledon, London. Buried at York Minster
Education: Westminster School
Married to Mary Bright; no children
Quotation: 'The King can have no interests, no dignity, no
views whatever, distinct from those of his people.'

CHARLES WATSON-WENTWORTH, 2ND Marquess of Rockingham, was the eighth British prime minister to have held that
office since it took recognisably modern form in the hands of
Robert Walpole. But otherwise he was everything Walpole was not:

aristocratic, retiring in disposition if sporadically headstrong, a poor public speaker, personally incorruptible, but of limited energy and executive capability.

These are not in general the qualities of a successful politician, then or now. Rockingham spent little time in office, and his administration has been treated with icy condescension by historians ever since. For many, he is little more than a figure of fun, notable only for his love of the turf, for giving the St Leger its name, and for commissioning from George Stubbs a magnificent life-size painting of his horse Whistlejacket, which hangs today in the National Gallery in London.

His home, Wentworth Woodhouse, was the largest private house in Britain, with some 365 rooms (no one is sure exactly how many) and a magnificent East Front of 606 feet, the longest façade of its kind in Europe. But it was gravely damaged by Emanuel Shinwell and the post-war Labour government, which pushed open-cast coal mining right up to the house, apparently for reasons of class warfare, and it still stands in need of comprehensive restoration.

In fact, however, there are three linked achievements for which Rockingham must always command admiration. He formed and led for almost twenty years what is recognisably the first proto-political party; he was the friend and patron of Edmund Burke, the greatest philosopher-politician of the past three hundred years; and he supported Burke in and out of office while Burke laid down the intellectual basis of modern representative government.

Rockingham was born on 13 May 1730 in what was then called Wentworth House, near Rotherham, Yorkshire, the third child and only surviving son of Thomas, 1st Marquess, and Anne, daughter of the 2nd Earl of Nottingham and 7th Earl of Winchilsea. The family was fabulously wealthy: at a time when a gentleman could live on £300 a year, the young Marquess had an annual income of over £20,000, which doubled over his lifetime. He went to Westminster School in 1738, before completing his education via a Grand Tour in 1746–50; when his father then died, he acceded to the marquessate and got married. En route he had been gazetted a colonel, presented himself at the age of fifteen to the Duke of Cumberland as a volunteer against Bonnie Prince Charlie and the revolting Jacobites, and picked up what may have been a serious case of venereal disease. Possibly as a result, his marriage to Mary Bright – herself a considerable heiress – though loving and long-lasted, produced no children.

Rockingham spent the next decade learning to discharge the county responsibilities of a great aristocrat, improving his estates, gambling and horse-racing, and making periodic and occasionally successful forays into local politics. But he gradually became more active in Westminster. Family connections drew him close to the Duke of Newcastle, Walpole's Whig lieutenant and the great power-broker of the era, who followed his brother, Henry Pelham, as prime minister first in 1754 and then again, after a brief interruption, in 1756. In 1760 Rockingham was nominated for the Order of the Garter, and he assisted at the coronation of George III in 1761. But he had little taste for the new King's politics, for his willingness to intervene in politics, or for his favourite, the Earl of Bute, and resigned when Newcastle went out of office in May 1762.

The 1760s were a time of pressure-cooker politics in Britain, with six brief administrations – each unhappy in its own way – in a decade. The central question was how to deal with the financial and administrative aftermath of the Seven Years' War (1756–63), the first truly global conflict, in which Britain had defeated France across five continents and laid the foundations of an empire. With his wealth, modesty and personal charm, Rockingham had come to play a central role in organising the Whigs behind the scenes. When the other candidates all proved to be unpalatable to each other or to the King, he accepted the premiership in June 1765. He had never held ministerial office before, a characteristic he shares with Ramsay MacDonald, Tony Blair and David Cameron. It is an eclectic bunch.

In all, Rockingham was to hold office for only fifteen months, in two governments separated by sixteen years. The centrepiece of his first administration, which ended in July 1766, was the tumultuous repeal of the Stamp Act, a tax on legal documents and other goods levied to pay off war debt, and widely despised among the American colonies, which swiftly adopted the slogan of 'no taxation without representation'. In an effort to placate parliamentary hard-liners, the new government under Rockingham removed the duty

49

but passed a Declaratory Act, which insisted on Britain's right to tax in principle and only inflamed the colonists further.

Rockingham had hoped for a swift return to office, but in the event it took sixteen years. When he finally made it back in 1782, his focus was on ending the American War of Independence, and on relief of the poor. But viewed with hindsight, what matters is what happened – and what did not happen – in between.

Eighteenth-century political opinion tended to view parliamentary groupings outside government disparagingly under the heading of 'faction': unhelpful and adventitious alliances held together by patronage and self-interest, short in duration, and targeted on some specific political campaign or goal. But by the late 1760s, it was becoming clear that the Whig politicians around Rockingham – an estimated sixty MPs and thirty peers – did not conform to this description.

At their centre was the young Edmund Burke. Burke was a direct contemporary of Rockingham, but, as a university-educated Irishman of 'the middling sort', of radically different social and economic origin. By the age of thirty-five he had become the editor of an influential periodical and digest, the *Annual Register* and the third elected member of Dr Johnson's Club, and was increasingly recognised as a writer and speaker of genius. Dr Johnson himself was open in his admiration, once remarking that he did not begrudge Burke's being the first man in the House of Commons, for he would be the first man everywhere.

An astonishing sequence of events over a few months in 1765 saw Burke appointed as Rockingham's private secretary, Rockingham made prime minister, and Burke himself elected to Parliament. Although the administration quickly foundered, it did not – contrary to expectation and precedent – disintegrate after its loss of office. Instead, it retained its coherence and took shape as a distinct grouping in Parliament dedicated to the restraint of royal power, the protection of personal liberty and the constitutional settlement of 1688. In this, it was sustained by Burke's daring defence of the political party as a body of men 'united, for promoting by their joint endeavours the national interest, upon some political principle in which they are all agreed', and later by the famous description of the duty of a Member of Parliament in his *Speech to the Electors of Bristol*

(1774): 'Your representative owes you, not his industry only, but his judgement; and he betrays instead of serving you, if he sacrifices it to your opinion.'

Much of this was due to the personal charm and capacity to inspire loyalty of Rockingham himself, combined with lashings of patronage and financial support. Rockingham set the pattern, combining personal probity with a consistent adherence to a core of policy and insisting on his group's independence of both Crown and populace. At the start, Burke was a mere salaried secretary. But over time he assumed a crucial role, becoming at once the leading pamphleteer and an important business manager of the Rockingham Whigs in Parliament, moving them away from factional politics and helping to shape them organisationally and intellectually into the prototype of the modern political party.

As a result, when the political wheel at last turned again in March 1782 following the disastrous battle of Yorktown, the Rockinghams were ready to take office once more. They had not fragmented, as factions had fragmented before them. On the contrary, for sixteen years they had maintained a distinct political grouping, a core of shared policies, and a coherent political identity. They had, in other words, created the first outlines of the modern political party. Power had passed entirely peacefully to this party, large numbers of office-holders had been forced to leave, and the new government had arrived with well-understood legislative intent. It marked, perhaps for the first time, a genuine move of party from government into opposition and then back into government.

The Rockinghamites had returned to office, moreover, despite the resistance of the King, and in pursuit of a conception of cabinet responsibility that has since become the foundation stone of British government. In so doing, they had pushed Britain one more step towards a constitutional democracy, and away from a purely personal monarchy. It remains a remarkable and woefully under-recognised achievement; and Rockingham and Edmund Burke were – practically, intellectually and morally – at its centre.

The new government sued quickly for peace with the American colonists. Burke was appointed Paymaster General, the most senior post outside the Cabinet, and devoted himself to economic reform and the reduction of Crown patronage. But tragedy was to strike, with Rockingham's sudden death just fourteen weeks later from influenza.

Burke was distraught, and composed a valedictory inscription for the tomb of his patron, political leader and friend. Tying together person, party and politics, in part it ran:

> He far exceeded all other statesmen in the art of drawing together, without the seduction of self-interest, the concurrence and co-operation of various dispositions and abilities of men, whom he assimilated to his character, and associated in his labours: for it was his aim through his life to convert party connexion, and personal friendship, (which others had rendered subservient only to temporary views, and the purposes of ambition) into a lasting depository for his principles; that their energy should not depend upon his life, nor fluctuate with the intrigues of a court, or with capricious fashions among the people; but that by securing a succession in support of his maxims, the British constitution might be preserved, according to its true genius, on ancient foundations, and institutions of tried utility.

Framed as the vindication of an underestimated life, Burke's valediction to Rockingham is a fitting tribute to both men. But it also sets forth a reforming ideal of party politics that was compelling in its time, and remains inspiring to this day.

Jesse Norman is the biographer of Edmund Burke and Adam Smith, a former Paymaster General, and the Member of Parliament for Hereford and South Herefordshire.

9

William Pitt the Elder, Earl of Chatham

30 July 1766 to 14 October 1768
Whig

By Charles Pitt

Full name: William Pitt, 1st Earl of Chatham
Born: 15 November, Golden Square, Westminster
Died: 11 May 1778, Hayes Place, Bromley. Buried at
Westminster Abbey
Education: Eton; Trinity College, Oxford; and the University of
Utrecht
Married to Hester Grenville; 3 sons, 2 daughters
Quotation: 'The only way to have peace is to prepare for war.'
(1758)

WILLIAM PITT THE Elder was the British Empire's first war
leader, a hero of the people and the stand-out orator of his
age. He was also infuriating, complicated, prone to serious ill-health

53

and periods of mental breakdown. His leadership during the Seven Years' War secured his place in history, but his complex character provoked strong reactions in his lifetime and since. He has been judged as both a patriotic statesman and a self-seeking demagogue.

William's grandfather Thomas 'Diamond' Pitt had made a small fortune in India, which he used to encourage his sons into politics. Pitt's own father Robert and both his uncles were MPs and his two aunts married MPs. They were solidly gentry but not grand. He went to Eton (which he hated) and then to Trinity College, Oxford, leaving after a year for the University of Utrecht. As a young man he joined the King's Own Regiment of Horse, taking a commission in the gift of Viscount Cobham, who, having no children of his own, enjoyed mentoring young talent – 'Cobham's Cubs'.

Pitt entered Parliament in 1735 for the family seat of Old Sarum, and quickly made his name as an opponent of Walpole, who had, since 1721, dominated the political scene. Pitt's unrestrained speeches against the government gave him prominence as a 'Whig Patriot', the hawkish faction of the opposition. Walpole's policy of peace and prosperity had served him and his nation well for two decades, but it could not last forever and in 1742 his record-setting tenure ended.

As an advocate of war and an opponent of absolutist France, Pitt should have secured office when war broke out. But his opposition to Walpole had offended the King, and George II could not abide him. Pitt had ingratiated himself to the King's son and heir Frederick, Prince of Wales, the epicentre of opposition, as well as opposing military aid to the King's homeland territories in Hanover. When Henry Pelham and his brother the Duke of Newcastle formed a new administration in 1744, Pitt was overlooked despite his talent as a public speaker. He did not have his own following, making it safe for the Pelhams to exclude him. In response, he changed tack, moderating his language and shifting his allegiances, moves which were seen as unprincipled at the time. In 1746 he was finally appointed to government as Paymaster General, a role which did not require close contact with the King. Pitt's new-found flexibility and his potential to be a menace meant even the King now thought government was the safest place for him.

In office he worked hard and kept his head down, but by 1754 he was hungry for promotion. When he was again overlooked he let rip, 'like a torrent long obstructed burst forth, with more commanding impetuosity . . . haughty, defiant, and conscious of injuries and supreme abilities'. He was then removed from office completely. But the fortunes of war were turning to his eventual advantage.

The years leading up to the Pitt–Newcastle ministry, in power during the Seven Years' War (1756–63), show how slippery Pitt could be, and how careless with his contemporaries. His manoeuvrings were entwined in the *cause célèbre* of the ill-fated Admiral Byng. When war with France broke out in 1756, Byng's fleet failed to relieve the garrison on Minorca and he was tried by court martial. Pitt exploited this military failure, blaming the government, who in turn scapegoated Byng. When Byng was sentenced to death, it was assumed the King would show mercy, which he did not. When Pitt was in a position to plead for Byng's life, it was assumed he would do so, but he did not. By then, through a series of protracted negotiations and against the King's better judgement, Pitt was secretary of state, running the government with the Duke of Newcastle. The affair over Admiral Byng was, however, a stain on Pitt's character. When Byng was shot by firing-squad on a quarterdeck in Portsmouth, one contemporary remarked of Pitt, 'Sir, if this is the way you treat your friends, I hope you will always consider me as your enemy.'

The Seven Years' War was the first conflict on a global stage, from India to Europe, the Caribbean and North America. Pitt's strategy was to focus on defeating the French overseas while supporting Britain's continental ally Prussia, and it worked. The *Annus Mirabilis* of 1759 provoked Horace Walpole to say: 'Our bells are worn threadbare with ringing for victories.' At the war's end in 1763 Britain had displaced France from Canada and established an unassailable presence in India. To many this was down to Pitt, whose strategic brilliance was matched only by his lofty rhetoric. By focusing on the American theatre and knocking the French out of Canada and India, it can be argued that Pitt built the foundations of Britain's future greatness. Recent historians have challenged this view of Pitt, the strategic war leader. The war would have happened without him, they argue, and the victories were anyway won by commanders in the field, not by dispatches sent on twelve-week voyages from London.

But Pitt was central to overall victory, if not to every specific element. He made the coalition with Newcastle work, occupying the public stage while his partner fixed things behind the scenes. As someone who had irritated absolutely everybody in politics and who could exasperate even his close friends, he was able to stand above party faction and reach over the politicians to the people. He was pragmatic in office, building bridges with the King and accepting the logic of defending Hanover. And, vitally as a war leader, he gave spirit to the great national effort of fighting on many fronts and over many years. Writing in the nineteenth century, Macaulay, who was no fan of Pitt's, wrote: 'The national spirit rose to the emergency – that the national resources were contributed with unexampled cheerfulness – this was undoubtedly his work. The ardour of his spirit had set the whole Kingdom on fire.'

The accession of George III in 1760 put Pitt out of favour; the new King's favourite, the Earl of Bute, and Pitt did not get on. At the same time, France and Spain had formed a new alliance against Britain, encouraging calls for peace in London, something Pitt opposed. In 1761 he resigned.

Out of office, Pitt returned to form, attacking the government, alienating the King and his favourites, and infuriating former colleagues. When the Peace of Paris was signed in 1763, Pitt condemned it as a sell-out. He also took up the cause of the radical journalist and politician John Wilkes, further enhancing his self-image as a patriot and defender of liberty. This formed the myth of Pitt that would fuel the imagination of later generations, especially in America. The likelihood of another war with France never went away and Pitt exploited this, stirring up the public and encouraging nostalgia for his uncompromising wartime leadership.

In 1766 George III (with regret) invited Pitt to form a new ministry, hoping 'to extricate the country out of a faction'. Pitt accepted and took his seat in the House of Lords as the first Earl of Chatham. His decision to accept a peerage was motivated by his now near-constant ill-health – the House of Lords in the 1760s, as it is now, was a less stressful working environment than the Commons. But leaving the Commons proved an error and he was never as popular a politician when Earl of Chatham as he had been as Pitt, 'the Great Commoner'. He could no longer rely on his skill in managing the House of Commons, and his two years as the actual head of government from 1766–8 were uninspiring. For much of this period he was ill with stress, depression and the gout he had suffered from since his student days. In 1768 he begged the King to relieve him of office.

Out of office he returned to his natural home of opposition, reclaiming his image as a disinterested patriot and embodiment of national interest. His outspoken support for America fuelled further myths for future imperialists, who cast him as a prophet of the English-speaking peoples' shared destiny. He certainly wanted to avoid conflict with America. British soldiers fighting in the colonies horrified him: 'Will you sheathe your sword in the bowels of your brothers the Americans?' His speeches from this last phase remain popular with Americans to this day, giving him a place in the story of their nation's birth. But he never entertained American independence. Like Winston Churchill, who greatly admired him, Pitt imagined a relationship that acknowledged American rights without yielding any of Britain's pre-eminence.

On 7 April 1778 Pitt went to the chamber of the House of Lords for the last time to speak against withdrawing troops from America – whatever the colonies' rights, he could not countenance the loss of part of the Empire. As he rose to speak, he collapsed 'to all appearances in the agonies of death', and a month later on 11 May he died.

Pitt's state funeral reflected the contradictions of his life. Tens of thousands of people filed past his coffin; the House of Commons voted unanimously for a public funeral and monument in Westminster Abbey. But the Lords voted against going to the funeral at all and only one member of the government attended. Following the cortège was his nineteen-year-old son William Pitt. It is thanks to him that the Pitt of this essay is known not as Pitt, Chatham or even the 'Great Commoner', but as Pitt the Elder.

In his lifetime Pitt was described as shamelessly ambitious, hypocritical and vainglorious – and he *was* a massive blowhard. But he was also a 'Great Man', a war leader who gave the nation direction and purpose, who had a far-seeing appreciation of America and a vision for the British Empire. A generous and mostly positive verdict endured after his death and was entrenched by the Victorians. Most recent verdicts are more sceptical.

Beyond his wartime leadership, he was significant for his mastery of the House of Commons. His great successes there stand in contrast to his relative failure once in the House of Lords. Perhaps most importantly, he showed that, in an age of faction, reaching out above party to the people, especially commerce and the City, mattered. Pitt's predecessors had worked relationships at Court and used patronage to stay in power, Pitt appealed over their heads to the masses.

From this distance, one can see that emotional responses to Pitt are shaped by attitudes to Britain and her Empire. If the strains of 'Rule Britannia' and the defeat of absolutist France provoke feelings of pride, then Pitt is a hero. For some of his successors as prime minister he was a role model: cited, imitated and quoted by those whose self-belief whispers: 'I can save this country and no one else can.' Pitt will never appeal much to those embarrassed by Britain's great power status, achieved in the eighteenth century, arguably in 1759. But for those who see Pitt the patriot, he is a hero and role model still.

Charles Pitt is Corporate Affairs Director at Sovereign Housing Association and a former House of Commons researcher.

10

Duke of Grafton

14 October 1768 to 28 January 1770
Whig

By Andrew Thompson

Full name: Augustus Henry FitzRoy, 3rd Duke of Grafton
Born: 28 September 1735
Died: 14 March 1811, Euston Hall, Suffolk. Buried at Euston, Suffolk
Education: Hackney School; Peterhouse, Cambridge
Married to Anne Liddell, then Elizabeth Wrottesley; 7 sons, 9 daughters.
Quotation: 'Wisdom is at no time more conspicuous, nor more amiable, than in the acknowledgement of error.' (House of Lords, 30 May 1797)

AUGUSTUS HENRY FITZROY, 3rd Duke of Grafton, was the last in a series of short-lived, and increasingly reluctant, prime ministers in the 1760s. All of them faced a series of interrelated problems: a young and inexperienced King, keen to disrupt previous political norms, a country suffering in the aftermath of global conflict, and serious questions about political representation within Britain and across the Atlantic. They all struggled to address these issues adequately.

FitzRoy was born into privilege, but not necessarily the expectation of high office. His father was the younger son of the 2nd Duke of Grafton. The younger sons of aristocrats did not inherit land or titles themselves, thus keeping the membership of the House of Lords relatively constant for much of the eighteenth century, and so had to pursue other occupations, typically in the military or the church. FitzRoy's father, another Augustus, joined the navy and died at Jamaica during the early years of the War of Jenkins' Ear (1739–48). FitzRoy's uncle, Lord Euston, died in 1747, leaving FitzRoy as heir to the dukedom of Grafton and considerable estates in Suffolk and London (Euston station, constructed on Grafton land, takes its name from the family seat in Suffolk). The family had close connections with the royal Court – the first Duke was the illegitimate son of Charles II, and the 2nd Duke, FitzRoy's grandfather, enjoyed a long career as Lord Chamberlain, a member of George II's cabinet council and close friend of George II's daughter, Amelia. FitzRoy's education included a couple of years at Peterhouse, Cambridge, and concluded with a period spent on the Grand Tour in Europe, accompanied by a Swiss tutor.

FitzRoy was elected to the Commons at the first opportunity in November 1756, shortly after his twenty-first birthday. He had stood in two seats, Boroughbridge in Yorkshire and Bury St Edmunds in Suffolk, and was successful in both, opting to sit for Bury. His career in the Commons was short and uneventful. The death of his grandfather in May 1757 meant that he was elevated to the Lords as 3rd Duke of Grafton.

Grafton had married in January 1756. Although it was said to be a love-match, the typical motivations of eighteenth-century aristocratic marriage were also evident. Anne Liddell came from a wealthy gentry family, who made their money from coal mining in the north-east. Grafton acquired cash, through a substantial dowry, and Anne's family gained in social cachet. The important task of producing heirs was relatively successful, with four children, including the all-important son, born between 1757 and 1764. Nevertheless, tensions within the marriage quickly emerged. The Duke and his wife went on an extended continental tour in 1761, with the aim of restoring the Duchess's health and, possibly, their relationship.

Grafton's early political connections were distinctly Whiggish. He inherited connections with the Duke of Newcastle, but he also became close to Newcastle's coalition partner, William Pitt the Elder, and his brother-in-law, Earl Temple.

Pitt, Temple and Newcastle all opposed George III's desire to bring the Seven Years' War to a rapid conclusion, following the new King's accession in October 1760. George III was anxious to distance himself from the politicians associated with his predecessor, particularly Newcastle and the 'Old Corps' Whigs, and instead wanted to see his former tutor, John Stuart, Earl of Bute, promoted to a leading political position. When Grafton returned from the Continent in the autumn of 1762, he took a leading role in arguing against the proposed peace treaty in the Lords and attacked Bute. This soured his relationship with George III, who removed him from the Lord Lieutenancy of Suffolk as a result.

Bute was ultimately able to gain approval for the Peace of Paris, but at considerable personal cost. He resigned, despite the King's protestations, in April 1763. This left George III with a dilemma. Should he turn again to either Pitt the Elder or Newcastle, both of whom had opposed him over the peace, or should he seek another premier? Initially, the King opted for George Grenville, who had broken with Pitt and Temple, but nobody was convinced that Grenville would survive for long, so constant political manoeuvring persisted behind the scenes.

Grafton was careful during this period to maintain close contacts with many of the leading political figures and cultivated Newcastle's political heir, the Marquess of Rockingham, as well as the King's uncle, the Duke of Cumberland. Like Grafton, Cumberland was an enthusiastic follower of horse-racing, and Grafton's Suffolk estates were conveniently close to Newmarket. Race meetings offered an excellent opportunity for furthering social and political contacts.

By spring 1765, George III had grown tired of Grenville. His administration was mired in scandal over the failed attempt to censor the radical populist, John Wilkes, through General Warrants, and attempts to pose new taxes in America to defray the huge costs of the Seven Years' War were proving very unpopular. Moreover, Grenville's desire to control all official appointments was viewed as impertinent by the King. Consequently, George asked his uncle to open negotiations with the other leading politicians to form a new administration. Grafton was included because of his close connections with Rockingham and, particularly, Pitt.

It proved impossible to persuade Pitt to re-join the ministry at this stage. Nevertheless, Grafton was appointed Secretary of State for the Northern Department in the new administration. Grafton accepted office on the basis that active efforts would be made to conciliate Pitt, and it was hoped that his presence might entice Pitt to lower his demands, or at least not oppose Rockingham's administration actively. These hopes proved misguided and Grafton, angered that more had not been done to win Pitt over, resigned office in May 1766.

Grafton's political exile was short-lived. Rockingham's ministry fell in July 1766 and Pitt was finally persuaded to return, although he did not accept the traditional office of First Lord of the Treasury, but rather became Lord Privy Seal and accepted a peerage as Earl of Chatham. Grafton became First Lord of the Treasury, but had little influence on the wider construction of the ministry.

Grafton found himself in a difficult position. Chatham wanted to micro-manage the administration, but ill-health meant that he was increasingly absent from London. Grafton was left to manage day-to-day business, but was reluctant to set a firm direction himself, so long as Chatham remained around. The government's handling of America remained politically controversial and government majorities sank in the spring of 1767. With George's support, Grafton opened negotiations with the opposition and started to emancipate himself from Chatham. Although attempts to force Chatham's hand by asking him to either return to London or resign failed, by the summer of 1767 Grafton had effectively become prime minister in fact, as well as in name.

Grafton now attempted to strengthen his own position and the administration. The death of Charles Townshend allowed him to appoint Lord North Chancellor of the Exchequer. To win over some of the Bedford Whigs, Grafton agreed to split the secretary-ship of the Southern Department to create a new Secretary of State for the Colonies. The appointment of the hard-line Lord Hillsborough did little to conciliate the Americans. Grafton's administration contained various Whig groupings: some former followers of Chatham, some Bedford Whigs and some of his own friends. Grafton struggled to impose his own views on this diverse group, and collective responsibility proved illusory, not least because Grafton was inclined to do nothing when faced with difficult choices.

Grafton's administration faced two particular sorts of difficulties. Domestically, the re-emergence of John Wilkes was a cause of concern. Wilkes had been elected MP for Middlesex in 1768 during an election campaign marked by public disorder. Many, including the King, were anxious to make an example of Wilkes and the rioters. Grafton, mindful of Wilkes's popular appeal, was reluctant to act. Nevertheless, he was won round to supporting moves to exclude Wilkes from the Commons by Wilkes's claims that the government had deliberately killed some of his supporters at the Massacre of St George's Fields. Over America, Grafton, like other PMs in the 1760s, tried and failed to reach a compromise. Some in the Cabinet wanted compromise, while Hillsborough and others disagreed. Crucially (and fatefully), Hillsborough was able to win the argument that duties on tea should be maintained.

Grafton's political difficulties were matched by his private life becoming a matter of public concern. Grafton had begun a relationship with a courtesan, Nancy Parsons, while his wife was pregnant with their fourth child. Following the birth of the child, the couple had legally separated, with the Duchess being granted an allowance. When Parsons returned from the Continent in 1768, the Prime Minister was seen with her in public, causing considerable scandal. To make matters worse, Grafton's estranged wife was pregnant by her new lover, Lord Ossory, and Grafton now chose to prosecute her for adultery. Lady Anne agreed not to counter-claim, on condition that she be granted an annual allowance of £2,000, and so Grafton became the first divorced prime minister when the Act of Parliament finalising his separation passed in March 1769. Grafton married his second wife Elizabeth in June 1769 and the couple had twelve children.

Grafton's administration was subject to vicious attacks in the press during the summer of 1769 and Chatham chose this moment to reappear on the political scene in an attempt to destabilise the ministry. Government majorities during the autumn were worryingly small, and the resignation of Camden and Granby from the Cabinet in January 1770 sapped Grafton's resolve to continue. He remained in office until the King had persuaded Lord North to take over and then resigned on 30 January 1770.

Grafton returned to office, although not the Cabinet, as Lord Privy Seal, where he remained until falling out with North over America in November 1775. He was Lord Privy Seal again in 1782–83 under Rockingham and Shelburne. He was an opponent of the Fox–North coalition and generally supportive of Pitt the Younger, but did not return to major political office again.

Away from politics Grafton was a keen supporter of hunting and racing – both activities that were politically and socially valuable. He served as Chancellor of the University of Cambridge from 1770 and supported a number of liberal churchmen. Condemned by his critics as willing to place the pleasures of the flesh above all else, he was typical of a type of aristocratic politicians who saw political service as a necessary, if time-consuming, part of the public life, but who struggled to rule effectively in a period of rapid political change.

Andrew Thompson is a Senior College Lecturer in History at Queens' College, Cambridge.

II

Lord North

28 January 1770 to 20 March 1782
Tory

By Nicky Morgan

Full name: Frederick North, 2nd Earl of Guilford
Born: 13 April 1732, Albemarle Street, Piccadilly, London
Died: 5 August 1792, Grosvenor Square, London. Buried at All Saints church, Wroxton
Education: Eton College; Trinity College, Oxford
Married to Anne Speke; 3 sons, 3 daughters
Quotation: 'Your majesty is well apprized that, in this country, the Prince on the Throne, cannot, with prudence, oppose the deliberate resolution of the House of Commons.'

L ORD NORTH WAS the eldest of six children and the son of the politician, Francis North. His father was the 3rd Baron and later 1st Earl of Guilford, and his mother was Lady Lucy Montagu.

His mother died when he was just two, and in 1736 his father remarried the widow of Viscount Lewisham, who had been heir to the Earl of Dartmouth. As a result, his siblings included a step-brother, Lord Dartmouth, who was a lifelong friend and later became his Cabinet colleague for a decade.

His stepmother died in 1746 and his father remarried for the third and final time to the widow of the Earl of Rockingham.

Frederick attended Eton College from 1742 to 1748 and went on to study at Trinity College, Oxford. After leaving university, he travelled on the Grand Tour with Dartmouth. The two young men returned to England in 1754 in time for the General Election.

On 20 May 1756, North married Anne Speke, who was the daughter and heir of George Speke of White Lackington, Somerset, and his third wife, Anne. They had six children together.

Throughout North's life, two of the constants seemed to be a continual worry about money (or lack of it) and the letters to and from his father who he sounded out on a regular basis. He did not become wealthy until his father died in 1790 and he inherited estates in five counties worth more than £10,000 a year (around £1.5 million today).

North's father had been an elected MP for just two years before he inherited the family title as Baron Guilford and a seat in the Lords. His father was elected as a Whig, although in those days political parties and allegiances were much more fluid.

North therefore stood, unofficially, for the Whigs, but in reality he didn't get involved in Whig factions once elected. This stood him in good stead to garner broad support, including from the 100–150 'Country Gentlemen' MPs. They deliberately stood back from any direct party involvement. It also helped him to gain the backing of George III, who didn't like factions.

Many considered North to be a Tory. If he was, then he was a small 'c' Conservative who wanted the right outcome to the problem before him and not necessarily the popular outcome.

Undoubtedly, he became an MP because his father wanted it; he had a ready-made seat, which he held in eleven elections, but he was regarded (in fact he regarded himself) as unambitious.

In the General Election of 15 April 1754, he was elected, unopposed, as the Member of Parliament for Banbury. This was three miles from his family home at Wroxton.

It took him until 1 December 1757 to make his maiden speech. It seemed to be worth waiting for, though, and was praised as being full of promise, displaying two of his debating assets: self-possession and a powerful voice.

In his book, *North: The Prime Minister Who Lost America*, Peter Whiteley noted that North soon developed a reputation as a good administrator and parliamentarian, and was generally liked by his colleagues.

By 1759, his parliamentary prowess and first-rate connections (aided no doubt by the lobbying of his father) led to his appointment as a junior Lord of the Treasury during the Pitt–Newcastle ministry. North was quickly known for getting a good grasp of the nation's finances (unlike his own). Over time, four Chancellors trusted his abilities and judgement. He spent six years at the Treasury Board and clearly enjoyed the work.

During the Grenville ministry from 1763 to 1765, North's reputation as a good parliamentarian was cemented further as he made fifty speeches in the House and was chosen to speak for the government when another MP, John Wilkes, attacked both the Prime Minister and the King in his newspaper, *The North Briton*.

In 1765, North resigned from his position as a Lord of the Treasury when a government led by the Whig Lord Rockingham came to power. He probably thought the Rockingham administration would not survive for very long and that he would be better off out of government for a short period of time, in spite of the loss of a salary, which he would have felt very keenly.

He didn't have long to wait, and by the end of July 1766 he had been offered and accepted the role of joint Paymaster General in Pitt's ministry and became a Privy Councillor. With the role, also, came an official residence near Horse Guards.

In December 1766, Charles Townshend was dismissed as Chancellor of the Exchequer (an event that Pitt had returned to London for, after an absence of two months). North was Pitt's choice, but at first North refused the appointment. It is probable that the unhappiness of the ex-Chancellor was at least one factor in the refusal. The matter was resolved when, in early September 1767, Townshend unexpectedly died. Even then North hesitated because the offer coincided with his father being seriously ill. However, his father recovered and by mid-September North had finally accepted the promotion. In early 1768, North became Leader of the Commons as well. He continued to serve when Pitt was succeeded by Grafton in October.

Over the course of the next two years, North's position as Leader of the Commons made him the government's principal spokesman there, a position he was generally deemed to perform well in, even as the Grafton administration disintegrated.

It seems that George III started to make overtures to North about him becoming First Minister from mid-December 1769. Given North's nature and his prevarication over becoming Chancellor, it is likely that the King realised he might take some time to be persuaded to take on these additional responsibilities.

The year 1770 dawned with great unhappiness across the country at the state of politics and the economy. The government did win a key vote in the Commons (with the help of a speech given by North), but even in that debate it was attacked by two senior ministers and then undermined by a flood of resignations from the government bench. Grafton offered his resignation to the King in mid-January.

On 22 January the King summoned North again to meet him. North needed to be sure he could do the job. He was taking over a weakened administration and if he failed the political wilderness beckoned. But, at last, after defeating an opposition motion of censure, he accepted. By 31 January it was known that he had agreed, and after defeating another opposition motion with a majority of forty he was clearly on his way as First Minister. He retained the roles of Chancellor of the Exchequer and Leader of the House.

North became First Minister because of his abilities and his lack of factionalism, but he also had to be chosen by the King.

Even before North was summoned to become George III's First Minister, the two families had historical links. North's father had been appointed in 1730 as a Lord of the Bedchamber to the then Prince of Wales. In 1736 the Prince of Wales married, and in 1738 his wife, Princess Augusta of Saxe-Gotha, gave birth to their second child and first son, the future George III. The new Prince was six years younger than North.

There was some talk of the physical similarities between the new Prince and North. It seems unlikely from what is known of North's father and the lack of contemporary cartoons alluding to such a link that there was actually a blood relation between the two, but they were undoubtedly similar in character – which was probably a help to North as he managed the relationship with the monarch. North was also, later in his administration, in actual debt to the King, as George III settled some of North's debts. On the one hand it must have made sense to the King to have his First Minister focused on the role he needed him to perform rather than worrying about his personal finances, but it must have been an uncomfortable position for a minister to be in.

North's premiership started less than a century after the 'Glorious Revolution' and just over a hundred years after the English Civil War. The relationship between Parliament and the monarch and the exercise of royal power was still a very live question.

George III was responsible for trying to put together stable political administrations, which was not easy at a time of easily shifting political alliances. He did manage this with North's administration, which lasted from 1770 to 1782, and then with William Pitt (the Younger), whose administration lasted from 1783 to 1801. But apart from those periods, the fact that it was the King who summoned and dismissed ministers inevitably meant he was involved in the political life of the country in a way his successors would not recognise.

However, although George III, like most monarchs, had strong views on the issues of the day – particularly something as irrevocable as the loss of the American colonies – it seems that after making his views known to his First Minister (he often wrote to bolster North's spirits, or rather to encourage him to stick to the position they had agreed on) he would then accept his Cabinet's views on how to proceed, even if he didn't think their course of action would be successful.

North was seen as a great financier and used the annual lottery to raise money and induce government stockholders to accept repayment on terms favourable to the Treasury.

In 1775, he informed Parliament that the national debt had been reduced by £10 million, nearly all while he had been Chancellor of the Exchequer. His measures had also cut the annual interest burden by £500,000.

Unfortunately, however, these achievements were undone by the outbreak of the American War of Independence that same year, which led to government expenditure rising from £7 million to more than £20 million by 1780.

His first foreign crisis was dealt with successfully. When Spanish forces seized control of the British settlement on the Falklands in 1770, the government mobilised the British fleet, which prompted Spain's ally, France, to compel them to back down.

Apart from the restive American colonies, North also had to devote some attention, although perhaps not enough, to matters in Ireland and India. There is a report that he failed, on taking office, to read the papers presented to him about the situation in Ireland. But by 1778 a local defence force had been set up, as English troops had been sent to America. A reduction in trade, also due to the war with America, was causing economic hardship, and there were more calls for political reform. An Irish Trade bill did eventually pass through Parliament in 1780 after a two-year battle. North did not do much to address the underlying issues in the relationship with Ireland, but he did show flexibility over trade policy.

Meanwhile in India the issue had become how the Crown as well as The East India Company could benefit from Britain's increasing influence in the country. The set-up of The East India Company, which had become the pre-eminent European power on the Indian sub-continent, was giving cause for concern.

By 1771 both the financial state of the Company and the conduct of its affairs needed North's and Parliament's attention. The Company did attempt internal reform and a draft bill was put before Parliament, which then decided in 1772 that a Select Committee inquiry into the Company was necessary. North might have hoped the committee would provide the solution.

The Company's financial situation deteriorated further, and North realised the matter would have to be considered by the Commons again. There was, though, a huge gulf between the Company and the government. The Company wanted financial support but no regulation by the government. The government was clear that no financial support would be forthcoming until there was a radical overhaul of the Company.

In the end, three Acts were passed in 1773 – the Tea Act, the Loan Act and the Regulating Act. North did manage to introduce some degree of oversight of the Company. His natural instinct would have been for the government not to interfere in the affairs of a private company, but when that became untenable he, typically, opted for a pragmatic approach, which in time led to further reform.

If the Falklands crisis provided a model of success and the Irish and East India Company situations were partly contained thanks to North's pragmatic interventions, it was the ultimately broken relationship with the American colonies that came to define his premiership.

Much has been written about the American War of Independence. The emphasis here will be very much on North's role and conduct in the relevant years.

The seeds of the crisis with America were sown before North reached Downing Street. In 1764 Grenville had imposed stamp duties on documents in the colonies, matching the same duties already applied in Britain. The American colonies reacted very badly and ultimately the duties had to be repealed, although in doing so Parliament also passed a Declaratory Act stating that it was the right of Parliament to pass laws on all matters that would bind the colonies. It was this belief in the supremacy of the British Parliament over the colonies, fully subscribed to by North, that proved so intractable and fatally undermined any attempts at conciliation.

In 1767 Charles Townshend as Chancellor had introduced duties on American imports, including on tea. The intention was that the duties raised would be spent in America on the costs of the governance of the colonies.

The fact that the dispute stemmed from duties, particularly on tea, may have blinded British politicians, including North (and the monarch), both to the real grievance, which was that a Parliament thousands of miles away was deciding on the duties, and to the conclusion of the colonies that the way to correct this was full independence from Britain.

There were other factors that, if understood in London at the start of the 1770s, might have given ministers pause for thought. The American settlers had endured great hardship to build the colonies and they still retained their 'frontier spirit'; they were focused on their rights, which led to the rapid growth of representative government, as the colonies were taking increasing amounts of power into their own hands. London also underestimated the extent to which the colonies would work together.

The view in Britain was that the colonies were there for Britain's trading benefit and that, as long as they protected the trade routes with America, this gave them the right to be able to impose trade restrictions on the latter. It was a head versus heart debate. The British thought it was all about duties and trading rights. The American colonies had a much bigger ambition to be independent.

The 1773 Tea Act, designed to help the East India Company by getting rid of the export duty that applied to the Company, was deemed by Boston to be damaging to its interests, because they were still expected to pay the import duty. As history records, the tea was eventually dumped in Boston Harbour.

The response of the British Parliament was to pass the Boston Port Bill, and the Massachusetts Government and Justice Bills. They were essentially seen as punishment Acts. The view of the King was that the colonies should be mastered or treated as aliens. Public sentiment was on his side. North had led the government response, although in reality he wanted to find some accommodation, but there was no support for such a move. A General Election held in October 1774 left North's administration with around 321 supporters in the Commons it could rely on, out of 558 seats.

The election also meant the administration had a mandate for taking a very firm hand with the colonies. This did not stop North from trying to find some way of bridging the divide. In early 1775 the Cabinet authorised the exploration of a negotiated settlement and the devolution of tax policy. But by then the colonies had become a nation prepared to fight for their future, while Britain still thought this was a dispute about taxation powers.

In spite of North's private misgivings, he still took the lead in the introduction of a New England Trade and Fisheries Bill, which sent just the wrong signal to the colonies. North tried to adopt a 'middle way' position, which simply led to attacks from all sides and was out of step with public sentiment.

In any event it was too late. The first shots had been fired at Lexington on 19 April 1775. The war had begun and North now needed to be a wartime leader.

It is hard to know whether the criticism of North should be directed towards his conduct leading up to the war or his conduct during it. The eventual public view that North should bear responsibility for losing the American colonies stemmed not from the fact that there was a conflict, but because the British did not win. Once the war had started, there was a lack of clear strategic objectives and overall direction from London. The woefully slow communications meant that orders and reactions to events always came too late from the capital.

It is questionable what an eighteenth-century First Minister's role in a war was. North decided not to conduct the war himself, but to defer overall strategy to Lord George Germain, who was appointed American Secretary late in 1775, and the Earl of Sandwich. It could be said that North's role, through continuing as Chancellor of the Exchequer, was actually to organise the British army's supply lines and to arrange the loans to finance the war – both of which were successful, although the national debt ballooned as a consequence – and to keep the Cabinet united.

In late July news of the British defeat at Bunker Hill reached London. This triggered a Proclamation of Rebellion, issued by the government at George III's behest – effectively a declaration of war on the colonies. North did not particularly support the Proclamation, but nor did he use any political capital in stopping it. It was issued as the so-called Olive Branch petition arrived from the second Continental Congress. The petition was refused by the government, who refused to recognise the legitimacy of the Congress.

The war ground on – and political life in Britain carried on, although it was coloured by the ups and downs of the battles in America. North's predecessor, the Duke of Grafton, was sacked in November 1775, triggering an enforced reshuffle that led to the removal of North's stepbrother and ally, Dartmouth.

On 4 July 1776 the colonies made their Declaration of Independence. North's health waxed and waned as the war continued.

In early 1777 he was clearly ill and absent from front-line political decision making.

In October 1777 a corner was turned with the British surrender at Saratoga. Reports didn't reach London until early December. The government was still winning votes on the war in the Commons, but there was a growing realisation that the American colonists could defeat the professional British army. North believed the best outcome might now be an 'honourable stalemate'. However, George III remained confident of outright victory for the British.

Over the Christmas period there was one last serious attempt at a negotiated peace settlement. North hinted to the King that he should resign (he tried again in May 1778). Presumably he felt that a new First Minister might have more credibility in trying a new approach. The King refused to countenance it.

The peace plan, involving the appointment of three Commissioners, was unveiled and approved by the Commons in February 1778. The King was unconvinced by them and Parliament was deeply suspicious. North seemed to lose interest in them at this stage and the plan was ultimately unsuccessful, undermined by who was appointed, but also by the contradictory orders given separately to those involved in the military conflict. Perhaps if North had used his personal stature to back the Commissioners and briefed them properly, they might have had more success.

By autumn 1778 George III was losing patience with his ministers. France had entered the war to support the colonies in June 1778. Spain did the same in June 1779. It was now a truly international conflict. On 21 June 1779 George III took the highly unusual step of summoning a Cabinet meeting himself. North was in any event incapacitated following the death of his youngest son, aged only two, three days earlier.

The ministry was starting to slip. In April 1780 it lost the Dunning motion on the influence of the Crown over the administration. It was slow to react to the June 1780 anti-Catholic Gordon riots in London, which reached the outside of Downing Street. The King explored a possible coalition with the Whigs in Parliament in an attempt to broaden the government, but that went nowhere. A snap election in September 1780 only weakened the administration.

But even in early 1781 the administration continued to win votes on the war, and there continued to be a misplaced belief that there were more Americans who were ultimately still loyal to Britain. The final blow for the North administration was the British surrender at Yorktown on 17 October 1781 after a siege led by George Washington. Again, news only reached London on 25 November. North realised the war was over and independence inevitable. George III remained utterly opposed.

It was clear by February 1782 that the ministry would not survive. To his credit North realised that it would take a lost vote of confidence to persuade the King to change his ministers. The question was how to engineer such a thing without being the first First Minister to lose a motion of censure. On 20 March 1782, the King having accepted what must happen, North managed it (thus proving what a good parliamentarian he was) by speaking ahead of the proposers to make it clear that their motion was now unnecessary. Business in the House finished early, catching most members by surprise, but not North whose carriage was waiting. With some friends he went off to a family dinner party. His relief at laying down the burdens of high office was evident.

For most former prime ministers that would be the end of their political career. North remained highly influential, even as he enjoyed life outside the spotlight.

But the new Whig ministry was unstable. The leader of the opposition to North's administration, Charles James Fox, had a brief spell in government but quickly returned to the opposition benches. There was no love lost between Fox and George III.

The relationship between George III and North recovered, despite the King having been forced by North's actions to find new ministers, although it was soured by a dispute over a loan taken in North's name to finance the 1780 election. North maintained the money was borrowed at the King's prompting and the King was liable for repayment. The King disagreed.

By early 1783 it was clear that a more stable administration was needed in order to conclude the peace treaty with America. But too many potential ministers would not serve with each other.

In the end, North and Fox agreed to work together under the Duke of Portland. North justified this unexpected arrangement by saying that there were times when 'it highly becomes all honest men . . . to relinquish their personal feuds and temporary animosities, and unite their serious efforts, by one generous exertion, in the common interest'.

The alliance was opposed by most people, including North's father and George III. It is said that North regretted the alliance and yet, on his deathbed, he apparently told his family he had no regrets about the actions he had taken in his political life.

One of the major achievements of the coalition was the signing of the Treaty of Paris in September 1783, which formally ended the American War of Independence.

The King's opposition to the administration remained and, rather unconstitutionally, he ensured that the administration's East India Company Bill was defeated in the House of Lords. George III then asked both North and Fox to return their seals of office. The coalition was dismissed and North left office for the last time. He continued to represent Banbury without opposition until he succeeded his father as 2nd Earl of Guilford on 4 August 1790 and entered the House of Lords.

North's sight having significantly worsened from 1787, he started experiencing symptoms of dropsy five years later. He died on 5 August 1792 at his home in Grosvenor Square, London. He was buried at All Saints' church in Wroxton on 14 August. There is a fine monument in the church to the former prime minister.

Nicky Morgan is a former Conservative Cabinet minister and served as MP for Loughborough from 2010 to 2019. She was raised to the peerage as Baroness Morgan of Cotes in early 2020.

12

Earl of Shelburne

4 July 1782 to 26 March 1783
Whig

By Nigel Aston

Full name: William Petty, 2nd Earl of Shelburne
Born: 13 May 1737, Bride Street, Dublin
Died: 7 May 1805, Berkeley Square. Buried in All Saints
churchyard, High Wycombe
Education: Private tuition; Christ Church, Oxford
Married to Lady Sophia Carteret (d. 1771), then to Lady Louisa
Fitzpatrick (d. 1789); 3 sons
Quotation: 'It will appear from history that a partiality to continental states has always been destructive to the interest of this country.'

LORD SHELBURNE WAS never the most popular of politicians. In fact, he has few rivals as a premier either in his time or subsequently for inspiring distrust in colleagues – or potential colleagues. This unfortunate capacity for being awkward to deal with, one that he neither sufficiently registered nor adequately counter-acted, worked against the implementation of the ambitious range of reforming policy initiatives that he planned as prime minister, and was decisive in denying him the parliamentary support that he needed to continue beyond eight months in office. Yet, in that brief time, Shelburne managed to negotiate a peace settlement with the victorious American colonists at the end of the War of Independence and conclude peace preliminaries with their French and Spanish allies that looked to the creation of a peaceful European order based on free trade. For those reasons alone, his time as First Minister entitles him to a higher degree of recognition by posterity.

Shelburne was born in 1737 and grew up in Ireland as plain William Fitzmaurice, the eldest son of the Hon. John Fitzmaurice (1706–61), a scion of the Earls of Kerry, one of the oldest titles in the kingdom. John Fitzmaurice was lucky. When his immensely rich uncle, Henry Petty, Earl of Shelburne, died in 1751, he left his estates, his money and his name to his favourite nephew, and so John came to England, took up residence on uncle Henry's old estate at High Wycombe, and had the Irish earldom of Shelburne recreated for himself. Young William came with him, with Petty as his new surname and Viscount Fitzmaurice as his courtesy title. John got himself elected to the House of Commons in 1754 as MP for Chipping Wycombe, and courted Henry Fox (the father of Charles James Fox), the leading rival of Pitt the Elder in the Commons in the 1750s. His remaining ambition was a barony in the British peerage that would confirm his family's irrefutable standing in England, and it was gratified in 1760, just a year before his death.

William Petty was groomed by his father to make the kind of public impact in England that his own upbringing had not allowed him. William was tutored privately then sent to Christ Church, Oxford, to study alongside the sons of English Whig grandees, where, for all his advantages, he never quite fitted in, a condition that in a sense prevailed for the rest of his life. He resented his father's efforts at control. The closest thing to rebellion that young

Lord Fitzmaurice managed was to curtail his studies and join the British army in 1757. His service record in the Seven Years' War between 1757 and 1760 was one of distinction. In his lifetime, Shelburne had to put up with any amount of derogatory verbal abuse, but none of his political enemies thought to accuse him of cowardice.

He returned to England in 1760 at the beginning of George III's reign and immediately started on a political career for which he lacked neither ambition nor capacity. Unfortunately for Shelburne, he was quickly wrong-footed. First, his father, the 1st Earl, died in 1761 and he inherited large estates at Bowood in Wiltshire, Wycombe, and in Ireland. But it meant that he was catapulted into the Lords after less than a year as MP for Chipping Wycombe, and was therefore denied that experience of life in the Commons – a loss that invariably disadvantaged eighteenth-century peer premiers. Second, his original patron, Henry Fox, had relied on Shelburne to act as his spokesman in negotiations over the terms (a peerage for himself and retention of the lucrative Paymaster Generalship) on which he would leave Lord Bute's government once the Peace of Paris (ending the Seven Years' War) had passed the Commons. Shelburne fumbled his brief, and Fox would transmit to his indulged second son, Charles James, the enduring complaint that Shelburne was a disingenuous double-dealer who should never be trusted. But Shelburne had a tough skin and was too talented to be sidelined.

He entered government a month short of twenty-six as President of the Board of Trade in Grenville's administration in April 1763, only to resign the following September. Those six months had still given him time to engage with the problems of the expanding American frontier, and an enviable capacity for energy and information gathering as a minister.

At this point, Shelburne attached himself politically to Pitt the Elder and, until the latter's death in 1778, acted as his loyal lieutenant in Parliament at the head of the 'Chathamites'. Pitt famously regarded himself as above party politics – 'measures, not men' – and projected his appeal to the nation at large that had once fêted him; Shelburne's attitude was the same, but he had no compensatory national appeal and it left him with the besetting problem of never having enough political allies and an inadequate regard for those he did have.

Pitt, newly created Earl of Chatham, brought Shelburne (still only twenty-nine) back into office as a secretary of state in 1766, only to leave all his ministers to fend for themselves while he coddled himself at Bath. Shelburne soon found himself at odds with colleagues and the King over American policy and, tired of the squabbling, resigned his post in late 1768.

Shelburne spent the next fourteen years in opposition, mainly because he objected to the ever more coercive American policies of the Grafton and North administrations. Like his mentor, Chatham, he lost no opportunity in the Lords of urging the adoption of conciliation towards the colonists, of listening to their grievances about taxation, and securing them within a benevolent empire on the basis of partnership.

Shelburne was a formidable parliamentarian in these years. He was an eloquent if not always a clear speaker in his own right with a tiny but talented political following in the Commons, notably the partially blind former army officer Isaac Barré, and the brilliant barrister, John Dunning. Moreover, he was superbly well informed, drawing on a range of advisers led by Richard Price, radical dissenting minister and writer on political and financial questions; Joseph Priestley, Unitarian minister and chemist, his librarian at Shelburne House and Bowood; and Jeremy Bentham, startlingly original in his reflections on the links between jurisprudence and politics. But, in the divided Britain of the 1770s, pro-American policies were a minority option, and the Chathamite Whigs were a minority within a minority.

The main opposition in Parliament was led by the Rockingham Whigs, who made 'party' a principle, stood ready to grant American independence, and distrusted both Shelburne and Chatham.

The collapse of Lord North's administration in March 1782 brought Shelburne into office as Home Secretary (the first to hold the newly designated post) in uneasy harness alongside Charles James Fox as Foreign Secretary in a government led by Rockingham. The latter's death on 1 July flushed all the old suspicions about Shelburne into the open and ruptured this Whig alliance of convenience: Fox and the majority of the Rockinghamites refused to serve under

Shelburne as premier, but George III wanted him and the Earl formed a ministry dominated by – himself. Whereas Lord North had insisted that he was no more than first among equals, Shelburne acted during his months in office as the principal decision maker responsible primarily to the King rather than Cabinet colleagues. Ministers met regularly, but frustration at Shelburne's poor circulation of information to colleagues that could border on outright disregard caused several to quit their posts.

He was a difficult prime minister to serve. For all his capacities as a policy maker and far-sighted reformer who believed in efficient, enlightened government and a peaceful continent underpinned by free trade, Shelburne lacked the man-management skills that would have allowed him the chance to implement them. Though his intimates respected him and women liked him, he never cultivated enough friends in the world of Westminster and did little to counteract the insults ('the Jesuit of Berkeley Square' was a more polite tag) that his reputation for insincerity and what Lady Holland later called 'overstrained civility' attracted in that bearpit.

To his credit, Shelburne displayed and inspired confidence in his handling of peace negotiations with the Americans, the French and the Spanish in the winter of 1782–3 (his principal role in the diplomacy that ended the American War of Independence would be his greatest achievement), but his neglect of Parliament was his undoing. Always making a point of being above grubby 'party' considerations, he left it too late for his aides to secure a majority in the Commons, where he faced an unlikely alliance of the forces of North and Fox.

The peace preliminaries were narrowly defeated in late February 1783 and Shelburne quit the premiership in a pique, believing, unfairly, that the King had let him down rather than acknowledging his own failure to win the confidence of either his Cabinet or the Commons. For the next two decades Shelburne remained a powerful presence in the Lords, but he never returned to government. Significantly, he, who had recognised the talents of Pitt the Younger and made him Chancellor of the Exchequer in July 1782, was never asked by Pitt to join his own Cabinet.

It aptly indicates Shelburne's consistent failure to make those who recognised his talents actually want him as a colleague. He fascinated the young Disraeli, but too many of his contemporaries distrusted him and he was incapable of persuading them otherwise. Shelburne was destined to remain the odd man out, the great outsider.

Nigel Aston is an Honorary Fellow at the University of Leicester.

13

Duke of Portland

2 April 1783 to 18 December 1783

Whig

31 March 1807 to 4 October 1809

Tory/Pittite

By Richard A. Gaunt

Full name: William Henry Cavendish-Bentinck, 3rd Duke of Portland
Born: 14 April 1738, Bulstrode, Buckinghamshire
Died: 30 October 1809, Bulstrode. Buried at St Marylebone, London
Education: Westminster School; Christ Church, Oxford
Married to Lady Dorothy Cavendish; 4 sons, 2 daughters
Quotation: 'My fears are not that the attempt to perform this duty will shorten my life, but that I shall neither bodily nor mentally perform it as I should.' (On accepting the premiership in 1807).

Portland rose to high office through his impeccable Whig credentials: his great-grandfather, Hans Bentinck, was one of William III's principal supporters during the 'Glorious Revolution' of 1688, and his grandfather was given a dukedom for political services to George I. Portland was the eldest son of William Bentinck and Lady Margaret Cavendish Harley, heir to the 2nd Earl of Oxford. Styled Marquess of Titchfield, until he succeeded his father on 1 May 1762, from 1755 he assumed the surname Cavendish-Bentinck; this was formalised by royal licence in 1801.

As a fashionable young aristocrat, Portland completed a four-year Grand Tour of Poland, Germany and Italy. Thanks to the electoral interest of Lord Weymouth, his future brother-in-law, he was elected MP for Weobley in 1761. Portland's centrality to the Whig cousin-hood was reinforced by his marriage, on 8 November 1766, to Lady Dorothy Cavendish. The union – which lasted until Dorothy's death in 1794 – produced six children.

Although Portland succeeded to the dukedom in 1762, his mother (who lived another two decades) retained a life interest in large parts of the family estates. The dowager Duchess maintained her residence at Bulstrode, the family seat in Buckinghamshire, so Portland made Welbeck in Nottinghamshire the principal ducal seat.

Politically, Portland was a close colleague of the Marquess of Rockingham, in whose governments he served, first as Lord Chamberlain of the Royal Household (1765–6) and later as Lord Lieutenant of Ireland (1782). The Duke proved conciliatory towards Ireland, overseeing the repeal of the Declaratory Act (1720) and modifying Poynings' Law (1494), which tightly controlled the government of the country. When Lord Shelburne succeeded Rockingham as First Lord of the Treasury, Portland and leading Whig MPs, headed by the charismatic Charles James Fox, resigned and went into opposition.

Portland's modifying influence led to his appointment as First Lord of the Treasury, in succession to Shelburne, in 1783. He was not the King's first choice and his government has gone down in history as the 'Fox–North Coalition' – ensuring that posterity expunged any reference to his leadership. Portland was preferred because, while Fox and North were astute, practised politicians, neither of them could have independently sustained a government that commanded widespread support. The coalition signed the Peace of Paris (1783) with the United States of America, bringing the wars of independence to a conclusion. However, the government's proposal to grant the Prince of Wales a substantial income, and pay off his debts, when he turned twenty-one, upset George III. Relations were already fragile when the ministry's India Bill, which would have increased the power of Parliament in matters of patronage at the expense of the Crown, was introduced. The *coup de grâce* was delivered by the King himself, who let it be known, through Earl Temple in the House of Lords, that anyone supporting the measure would be considered his 'personal enemy'. The ministry was dismissed, without an audience, and the King sent out messengers to collect the seals of office. Portland was succeeded by the twenty-four-year-old William Pitt the Younger.

Portland remained the putative head of the Whig opposition after 1783. The aftermath of the French Revolution (1789) created extreme tensions for the Whig Party; those who supported the Revolution and its acts, like Fox and the Whig MP and dramatist, Richard Brinsley Sheridan, faced increasing assault from old friends and colleagues, notably the party's philosopher-statesman, Edmund Burke, and the bellicose William Windham. Portland struggled to sustain the party's fragile unity in the face of an internecine conflict that went to the heart of Whig ideology. The Earl of Malmesbury thought Portland 'benumbed and paralysed' by the situation – 'Nothing could be so painful.' Confronted with the increasing radicalisation of the French Revolution, the outbreak of war between Britain and France (1793), and the perceived threat of domestic radicalism in Britain, Portland was persuaded to lead the bulk of the Whigs into a governing coalition with Pitt in July 1794. In return for their parliamentary support, Portland secured a dispro-portionately high number of senior Cabinet roles, including his own appointment as Home Secretary (1794–1801).

Portland proved to be a keen defender of law and order, parrying threats from the London Corresponding Society, food rioters, and, during 1798, incipient rebellion in Ireland. He regarded all such assaults as 'a violent and unjustifiable attack on property pregnant with the most fatal consequences'. His knowledge of Irish politics, control of patronage, and access to secret service funds, helped induce the Irish parliament to vote through its own dissolution, and ensure the passage of the Act of Union with Ireland in 1800.

Pitt's resignation in 1801 fractured political allegiances into new combinations, but Portland proved a notable Cabinet survivor, serving (without contradiction) in the administration of his successor, Henry Addington (1801–4), as well as Pitt's second ministry (1804–6). Pitt's death, and the accession of the 'Ministry of all the Talents' under Lord Grenville (1806–7), placed Portland out of office for the first time since 1794.

Grenville's resignation, following the failure of his Catholic relief measures in 1807, meant that Portland emerged as best placed to head an administration committed to political stability and the support of the Crown. This was a testament to his own longevity and experience, but also to the fact that the emerging generation of Pittite ministers, Hawkesbury (afterwards Lord Liverpool), Perceval, Castlereagh and Canning, were driven, ambitious politicians, none of whom proved capable of unifying their colleagues. Though the head of a Pittite government, Portland maintained to the last that he remained a Whig.

Portland's second ministry was formed shortly before the Peninsular Wars began in Spain and Portugal. The government was bedevilled by political infighting among the two ministers charged with prosecuting the campaign, George Canning (Foreign Secretary) and Viscount Castlereagh (Secretary of State for War and the Colonies). Canning was incensed that troops which had been promised for Portugal were sent, on Castlereagh's order, to the Netherlands. On 24 March 1809, Canning wrote to Portland, accusing unnamed members of the Cabinet of inefficiencies in handling the campaign, and threatening resignation. It was clear that Canning wanted Castlereagh to be replaced by the ambitious Lord Wellesley. Portland, in declining health and worn out by political infighting, secretly agreed to make the change, but then failed to do so. The Cabinet fissure split wide open after Castlereagh discovered Canning's actions. Castlereagh demanded the 'satisfaction of a gentleman' and fought a duel with Canning at Putney Heath on 21 September 1809. Castlereagh, who was a crack shot, wounded Canning in the thigh; both of them subsequently resigned. Portland followed them soon afterwards. During August, he had suffered a seizure while travelling to Bulstrode; he resigned at the beginning of October 1809. Within a month, he was dead.

It was said of Portland that he 'possessed in an eminent degree the talent of dead silence'. There is no recorded speech or division involving him, during his brief spell as MP for Weobley (1761–2). The characteristic nervousness and embarrassment that he felt at making public speeches likewise limited his interventions in the House of Lords (1762–1809). Today, Portland is probably best known as the eponymous purchaser of the Barberini Vase – the Portland Vase – on display in the British Museum. It would be easy to dismiss him as an aristocratic non-entity whose position and prominence were quite out of keeping with his talents. Yet he engaged constructively and selflessly with the administrations of Rockingham, Pitt the Younger, and Addington, while valiantly striving to lead coalitions comprised of such combustible materials as Fox, North, Castlereagh and Canning. His period as Lord Lieutenant of Ireland demonstrated his ability to conciliate where necessary, and his time as Home Secretary showed his unyielding devotion to the defence of property against domestic radicalism and the threat of revolution. By taking the conservative Whigs into coalition with Pitt, in 1794, he unwittingly supplied the government with longevity and contributed to the emergence of the nineteenth-century Tory Party; as one of the midwives of the Act of Union with Ireland, Portland can be numbered among the first parliamentary Unionists. It was Portland's fate to be the head of two administrations in both of which he was overshadowed by senior colleagues. The fact that these governments were formed twenty-four years apart suggests that some of this misfortune is attributable to Portland's own character and temperament.

Richard A. Gaunt is Associate Professor in History at the University of Nottingham.

14

William Pitt the Younger

19 December 1783 to 14 March 1801;
10 May 1804 to 23 January 1806
Tory

By Mark Garnett

Full name: William Pitt
Born: 28 May 1759, Hayes, Kent
Died: 23 January 1806, Bowling Green House, Putney Heath,
London. Buried at Westminster Abbey
Education: Home schooled; Pembroke College, Cambridge
Unmarried
Quotation: 'England has saved herself by her exertions, and will,
as I trust, save Europe by her example.' (November 1805)

ALTHOUGH THE NAME of William Pitt the Younger is probably
well known today, most people will have difficulty saying much
about him beyond the fact that his father was another Prime Minister

called William Pitt, and that he took the job when he had barely become an adult.

Those with a bit more knowledge will be aware that Britain was at war with Revolutionary and Napoleonic France for much of his time as Prime Minister, so they will think of him primarily in terms of battles on land and at sea. More serious students of the past, primed by authors such as E.P. Thompson, will remember him as a tyrant on the domestic front – a willing tool of monarchical power, who embraced the cause of liberty only to betray it when it served his interests, using the pretext of the French Revolution to seek out and destroy any Briton who was foolish enough to express a sneaking admiration for democratic principles.

There is a scintilla of truth in all of the 'superficial' snapshots. Whatever his natural abilities – which were considerable – the Younger Pitt owed his freakishly early political elevation to the legacy of his father. He was indeed a notable war leader; he bore the main brunt of European conflict for more than a decade, although even his warmest admirers would have to admit that he made mistakes. While Pitt's 'reactionary' reputation is greatly exaggerated, he did show an alarming ability either to acquiesce, or actively to participate, in the prosecution of individuals who were actuated by principle – even some who had previously been his coadjutors in various causes.

Only on a closer examination of Pitt's career can one understand why he was venerated for so many years after his death. From this perspective, it can be appreciated that war was not the making of Pitt, but rather his undoing, and that he would have been the perfect leader to spearhead Britain's peacetime recovery from the loss of America were it not for the French Revolution.

Pitt was born just as his father's direction of British strategy in the Seven Years' War was yielding its greatest results. The year 1759 was remembered as one of almost continuous success for Britain – a veritable *Annus Mirabilis*. Although William was his father's second son, the euphoric circumstances of his first few months were bound to inspire parental hopes that he, rather than his elder brother John, would be a worthy successor. Fortunately for them, it seemed clear from a very early age that William had both the aptitude and inclination for a rigorous political training. Thus, he clearly enjoyed memorising and declaiming the speeches of classical orators, and although he was educated privately rather than undergoing the Etonian ordeal that had left his father deeply unimpressed, his juvenile feats were widely publicised.

Although he could show off his talents to people he knew well – and especially to adults – Pitt was sickly, and shy with his contemporaries. But at Cambridge University, where he matriculated at the age of thirteen, he made several lasting friendships. Through one of these connections he became MP for the 'rotten borough' of Appleby in January 1781. However, this came after an attempt to win one of the two seats for Cambridge University – hardly a 'democratic' constituency, but one with a very discriminating electorate by the standards of the time. Pitt came bottom of the poll in the General Election of September 1780, but secured the seat in 1784 and continued to represent the University until his death.

Pitt's father, now Earl of Chatham, died in May 1778 after delivering a final appeal for conciliation with America – a speech witnessed by William, who helped to carry the stricken statesman out of the House of Lords. If the Elder Pitt could not resist a hereditary title – presumably out of family pride – he had been staggeringly self-denying in financial terms. Despite all the lucre that he had secured for his country, he left his children little better off than he had been himself when he embarked on his remarkable career. The lack of an independent fortune meant that the Younger Pitt qualified himself as a barrister, and briefly worked in that capacity before the 1780 General Election called him to his true vocation.

In life, the relationship between father and son had been complicated; though Chatham was immensely proud of young William, it seems that he was unable to show his feelings, and in return William evinced respect rather than the deep affection he reserved for his mother (a representative of the powerful and gifted Grenville family). It is idle (though tempting) to wonder if William would have put his political career on hold if Chatham's health had held up for longer. As it was, he could enter Parliament as the legatee of a figure who had been more feared than loved during his lifetime; and after he delivered his maiden speech, it was easier to proclaim Pitt as a 'chip off the old block' (in the famous words of Edmund Burke) because the 'old block' had gone to the eternal scrap-heap.

Even so, the speech deserved the warm and almost universal praise it received. As a parliamentary performer, Pitt was very different from his great rival, Charles James Fox (1749–1806). Both were heavily influenced by the rhetorical masters of Greece and Rome; but while Pitt's oratory was confined within these 'classical' models, Fox could transcend them with brilliant passages that brought him closer to the 'romantic' aesthetic. The imperfect written record of their speeches makes it impossible to judge who was the better speaker (and the voting figures after their verbal jousts are even less reliable guides to their real merits). But at his best Pitt attracted rave reviews even when he was off-colour (due to nerves or intoxication), and almost invariably he commanded the Commons while he was speaking.

The prolonged political duel between Pitt and Fox was the second instalment of a rivalry that had begun with their respective fathers, who had been divided by temperament and circumstances more than by principle. In his maiden speech, William had supported a motion introduced by Fox, and the latter's supporters (including Burke) were understandably hopeful that the newcomer would join their ranks.

However, Pitt was a stickler for independence. Fox was more than a decade older than Pitt and never one to go to bed at midnight if the party was still in full swing; in any partnership between the two, the ebullient, gregarious Fox would have been the 'front-man', with Pitt as his ponderous, bashful heir apparent. Pitt's cool response to Fox's advances – his ability, as he put it himself, to ward off 'the magician's wand' – was thus an early instance of Pitt's gift for political calculation, as well as his tendency to inherit his father's feuds. In 'Pitt versus Fox II', the differences in temperament were equally acute. But more importantly, 'circumstances' proved decisive even against a temporary alliance. When the Prime Minister (and Fox's party leader) the Earl of Rockingham died in July 1782, George III replaced him with the Earl of Shelburne. Shelburne had been one of Chatham's most ardent supporters, but he had the unhappy knack of inspiring distrust among almost everyone he worked with. Fox, in particular, felt that he had been double-crossed by Shelburne in negotiations for peace with America, and refused to serve in a Shelburne ministry. Pitt felt no such reservations, and was duly appointed Chancellor of the Exchequer – within a few weeks of his twenty-third birthday. The position of Chancellor means a lot more now than it did in 1782, but nevertheless this could hardly be equalled, let alone surpassed, as an example of accelerated promotion.

Pitt's first stint in office didn't last long, but he did introduce several reforms that were designed to make government more cost-effective. Shelburne's government fell in February 1783, because the House of Commons refused to accept his peace deal with the American colonies. Desperate to avoid having to back down in his own (far more deadly) duel with Fox, King George appealed more than once to Pitt as an alternative prime minister. Again showing consummate judgement, Pitt played hard to get. George had to accept a government led by the infernal Fox, who compounded the royal humiliation by forming a coalition with Lord North, the King's long-suffering Prime Minister and fall-guy for the American disaster.

However, although he had lost a significant battle, George was a long way from the point of surrender. At his coronation, he had sworn an oath to defend the existing constitution, and (notwithstanding the anachronistic views of 'Whig' historians) he had good reason to deny that his job-description included compulsory acceptance of ministers who did not enjoy his confidence. A despot would have prevented the Fox–North coalition from taking office. As a 'constitutional' monarch, George acquiesced in the ministry until it gave him plausible grounds to dismiss it. George's *casus belli* – the coalition's India Bill – satisfied these conditions, since it seemed to wrest important patronage powers away from the monarchy. The King let it be known that any member of the House of Lords who voted in favour of the bill would no longer be considered his 'friend'. The idea that a misplaced vote might result in ostracism from regal favour wrought the desired effect; the Lords rejected the bill, leaving George with the pleasurable task of dismissing his ministers and forming a new and more agreeable government. This time, although the circumstances were hardly ideal, the Younger Pitt found it impossible to resist the royal summons.

Ever since 1783, Pitt's detractors have deplored his role in the King's strategy, arguing that he must have known about, and probably participated in, a fiendish plot to oust Fox and North. After all, the bearer of the fateful message to the House of Lords was a Grenville relative. Pitt, though, always treated the allegations with disdain. It seems likely that his air of irritated innocence was based on a creative interpretation of his own actions and motivations, suggesting that his brief career at the Bar had not been entirely wasted.

From a broader perspective, the episode shows that Fox (and, more surprisingly, North) over-rated the level of popular support for the (very imperfectly) elected House of Commons as against the residual power of the monarchy. Every serious political commentator knows that the last monarch to use a formal veto against legislation passed by Parliament was Queen Anne, in 1708. But this overlooks the various ways in which monarchs could block the passage of bills, so that they were never presented for signature. In contemporary parlance, George III enjoyed much more 'soft power' than Fox and North, and the twenty-four-year-old Pitt understood this much better than his seasoned adversaries.

Nevertheless, in accepting the King's commission, Pitt was like a promising football manager who, for his first job, agrees to take over a team in the relegation zone with no chance of winning any matches. His supporters in the Commons were heavily outnumbered, so that Fox and North could block any attempt to pass government-sponsored legislation – even, if they had been so minded, the Mutiny Act, which had to be renewed in order to keep the armed forces in being. To make matters worse, for understandable reasons Pitt had been unable to make any 'marquee signings' for his team, which consisted of untried newcomers and players who were past their prime. The only exception was the Lord Chancellor, Thurlow (1731–1806), who sported an unblemished record of being reactionary and wrong on every constitutional question, but had to be retained because he was essentially the King's spy in the Cabinet. The Earl of Shelburne, who had given Pitt his first government post, was not offered a position – a sign that the new Prime Minister was not minded to risk his authority by working alongside potential rivals, and that sentimentality was not prominent among his emotions.

The result, in parliamentary terms, was never in doubt. In every significant encounter – including on motions that invited the Commons to express or withhold 'confidence' in Pitt's regime – the government was beaten. Yet impartial observers could see that Pitt was being outscored rather than outplayed, and gradually the margin of defeat was reduced. By the beginning of March 1784, when it looked as though momentum had swung Pitt's way, the King dissolved Parliament. In the ensuing election, royal patronage was exerted on Pitt's behalf, but in itself this does not explain his land-slide victory, which gave him an overall majority estimated at around 120 seats. Among the survivors from this massacre of Fox–North forces was Fox himself, who squeezed home as the second elected member (behind a Tory) for the prestigious constituency of Westminster. This seat enjoyed a relatively wide franchise, and Fox had employed tactics that contemporary populists can only dream about; his glamorous supporter Georgiana, Duchess of Devonshire, openly traded kisses for votes. Pitt duly launched a futile and vindic-tive parliamentary campaign to unseat Fox for electoral malpractice. However, it should have been obvious to Pitt that, by the standards of his time, Fox's election for Westminster had been valid. In any case, Fox had already insured himself by being formally elected to a seat in the Commons in a non-contest elsewhere.

So why did Pitt do it? The obvious answer is that as MP for Westminster, Fox could speak with more credibility than would be available to him as the 'representative' for Tain Burghs in the Scottish Highlands (an honour that he won in 1784 by amassing three votes, compared to a paltry two for his Tory opponent). At least at some level, Pitt was probably expressing his revulsion against Fox's approach to public life, which featured wine, women and gambling at least as much as principle. Apart from the wine, Pitt had either shunned these pastimes or abandoned them after a few tentative trials. His personal finances were almost as disastrous as Fox's, but while his rival threw away his fortune at the gaming table, Pitt spent too much on beautifying the (fairly modest) properties he bought. While Pitt had immersed himself in classical literature, Fox merely flaunted his acquirements to bolster his image – a tactic not unknown in twenty-first-century Britain. Whatever he might have been, by 1784 Pitt was convinced that he had been called to serve his country rather than himself. Having adopted this austere public persona (accentuated by his physical features, including a beak-like nose that was a gift to caricaturists), Pitt was never likely to seek political salvation from a troupe of titled women distributing sexual favours.

Once he had established his authority, Pitt was able to construct a more congenial Cabinet. Again showing an astute assessment of contemporary politicians and officials, his appointments were generally shrewd. For virtually the whole of his tenure as premier, his chief lieutenants were his cousin William (later Lord) Grenville, and Henry Dundas, later Lord Melville. Having served as Speaker of the House of Commons, then briefly at the Home Office, Grenville was Pitt's Foreign Secretary for almost twenty years before becoming Prime Minister himself. Dundas held various offices, notably Secretary of State for War (1794–1801). Dundas was Pitt's senior by almost two decades, and the connection between them arose entirely from the good judgement of both, lubricated by a shared fondness for alcohol that allowed them to combine business with pleasure.

Pitt had no difficulty in choosing a Chancellor of the Exchequer, since he was determined to do that job himself. His essential task was to address the significant debts that Britain had accumulated in its fight to retain the American colonies. Tax increases were unavoidable, but Pitt ensured that they fell mainly on the consumption of luxury items. He also tried to reduce government spending by abolishing sinecures, which he found objectionable on moral as well as economic grounds. His stewardship of the nation's finances quickly earned him many admirers in financial circles, but his record was not unblemished. In 1786 he introduced a 'sinking fund', which he believed could eliminate the government's debts through the miraculous multiplying effect of compound interest. However, the scheme depended on a reliable surplus of revenue over expenditure, and the fund became an economic liability rather than a wonder-cure as Britain accrued new debts during the wars with France. Indeed, in 1799 Pitt was forced to introduce Britain's first income tax, making sure that this was 'progressive' rather than a flat-rate levy.

Back in 1786, war with France was the last thing on Pitt's mind. In that year his government reached a trade agreement with its traditional foe, on terms that were highly advantageous to British manufacturers. Pitt took a prominent role in the negotiations, rightly working on the assumption that, on this occasion at least, Britain was in a stronger position than a continental trading partner. But the agreement is commonly known as the 'Eden Treaty' after Britain's chief negotiator, William Eden (later Lord Auckland), who had been a supporter of Fox before Pitt appointed him as a special envoy. Pitt's intimacy with Eden's family was sufficiently close to arouse expectations in 1797 that he would marry his colleague's daughter Eleanor. For Pitt, however, Eleanor was only a pleasant but temporary distraction from public duties; he beat an embarrassed retreat from the field of courtship, giving rise to predictable speculation (at the time, and ever since, despite the absence of any evidence either way) about his real sexual inclinations.

In respect of domestic policy, Pitt's record during peacetime was not just defensible, but notably good. However, even in his early years he disappointed some of his admirers by failing to push through reform of Britain's irrational system of parliamentary representation. He did introduce, or support, several attempts to remove the most obvious 'anomalies'. However, the King regarded rotten boroughs as a bulwark of the constitution, and since so many members of the Commons and the Lords were beneficiaries of the system, Pitt was risking his authority even by showing favour to the cause of reform. On this score, his 'Whiggish' critics seem particularly wrong-headed, since the 1784 General Election suggested that a more 'democratic' franchise would actually have been helpful to Pitt.

The more serious charge against Pitt is that during the wars against Revolutionary France he turned from a moderate supporter of increased rights and liberties for Britons into a deeply *illiberal* figure. In 1794, for example, his government suspended habeas corpus, in response to allegations of treasonous cooperation between British radicals and the French government. On this score Pitt's defence seems particularly flimsy, since he promoted the prosecution of individuals whom he must have known to be idealistic rather than malignant. However, the 'Whig' charge against Pitt seems to be based on an assumption that the government was biased for ideological reasons, focusing its repression on 'radical' (i.e., pro-French) activities. In truth, it was at least equally concerned by violence perpetrated by 'Church and King' mobs, keen to terrorise any alleged sympathisers with the Revolutionary cause. If the only way to keep overall control of the situation was to throw a small helping of red meat to the reactionaries, Pitt was quite prepared to do so. He took similar tough action against the chief instigators of naval mutinies, on the Spithead and the Nore, in 1797.

Although Pitt lacked experience in foreign policy, he generally showed good judgement and was prepared to consult more seasoned practitioners. Throughout his time in office, his over-riding objective was to preserve the status quo in Europe, and thus to check the expansionist tendencies of other states. Although the Eden Treaty promised to open up an era of peaceful cooperation with France, Pitt continued to regard that country as the most likely source of trouble in Europe. In 1787 he responded quickly and successfully to the prospect of French intervention in civil disorder in the Netherlands. He gave a guarded welcome to the early stages of the French Revolution in 1789, taking the mistaken but understandable view that it would reduce the immediate threat from France and ultimately produce a less bellicose regime.

This is not the place for a detailed account of subsequent developments. In keeping with his pragmatic approach, Pitt held aloof from the initial attempt, led by Austria and Prussia, to restore monarchical power in France. Although the execution of Louis XVI in January 1793 was a key step towards British involvement, Pitt and his ministers were more alarmed by evidence that the French, fuelled by ideological fervour, were turning a struggle for existence into a war of conquest.

Pitt's efforts to check this impulse dominated the remainder of his life, and almost certainly shortened it. In part, his approach followed that of his father, using Britain's naval power to attack the enemy's territorial possessions outside Europe. But unlike Chatham, Pitt took little interest in the concept of empire; as a faithful student of Adam Smith, he saw no purpose in overseas annexations unless they contributed to the security of global trade; captured colonies were mainly useful as bargaining chips for the inevitable peace talks. Britain's army could achieve little on its own, so Pitt concentrated on building and subsidising alliances, whose shifting members (mainly combinations of Austria, Prussia and Russia) usually seemed willing to contemplate peace with a Revolution that they had once sworn to extinguish. Thus the most obstinate and effective opponent of the Revolution turned out to be the statesman who had the least violent objections to its stated principles.

Pitt found it difficult to contemplate a compromise peace with France because he believed that, in practice, Revolutionary principles would always lead to violence. The emergence of the five-member *Directoire* in 1795 opened a chink of light, since it was possible that these more 'worldly' rulers might be won over with bribes. But they were unlikely to compromise while France looked capable of taking on and beating all comers under the inspired Corsican-born general, Napoleon Bonaparte.

Pitt never met Napoleon – indeed, he only left British soil once, for a trip to France in 1783 – but he quickly decided (unlike Margaret Thatcher in respect of Mikhail Gorbachev) that this was not a man to do business with. While Pitt, and his rival Fox, were inspired by classical orators, Napoleon seemed more interested in emulating the military leaders of antiquity; and Pitt realised that, whatever his declared interests in peace, Napoleon had won his position through the sword and would have to keep proving his prowess to maintain his position. By 1801, the growing realisation that the military situation had reached a stalemate, and that Britain needed a pause in the fighting as much as France, probably helped Pitt to conclude that he should leave office, at least temporarily. The prospect of negotiations with Napoleon is unlikely to have appealed to him.

The main reason for the brief hiatus in Pitt's career, however, was the situation in Ireland. Pitt had proposed a trade agreement with Ireland soon after the Eden Treaty, but was thwarted by fears (exaggerated by the Foxites) that Britain's economic interests would suffer. During the wars against France, Ireland became an acute security problem thanks to its proximity and its largely disaffected population, whose Roman Catholic majority was denied crucial civil rights. Thus, when a rebellion broke out in Ireland in 1798, with (ineffectual) French support, Pitt's solution to the 'Irish Problem' was to push through a union of the island with the rest of Great Britain. While this measure was accomplished (by fair means or foul), and the United Kingdom of Great Britain and Ireland was formally inaugurated on 1 January 1801, Pitt rightly felt that the Union would be incomplete without the removal of the civil disabilities imposed on Irish Catholics.

Pitt had no difficulty in reaching this position, since he detested religious bigotry of any kind. However, King George saw things very differently. Although Pitt had kept him on his throne by outsmarting the designs of the dissolute Prince of Wales (abetted by Fox) during the Regency Crisis of 1789, George regarded the ascendancy of Protestantism as a non-negotiable element of his Coronation Oath. Pitt tried to persuade him, but seems to have recognised that the King was ready to dispense with his services, not least because he had begun to take crucial decisions without consulting George. In March 1801 Pitt relinquished office. His successor, Henry Addington, was in some ways a protégé of Pitt, but their connection arose from chance rather than choice, since Addington's father had been the Earl of Chatham's doctor.

Addington duly reached a peace agreement with Napoleon, and Pitt made supportive noises. But he was only biding his time for a comeback, and the Addington government only clung to office for so long as Pitt chose not to exercise his veto. Even Charles Fox tacitly accepted that Addington was inadequate compared to Pitt, and the two old foes joined forces to bring him down in April 1804.

Although he was clearly relieved to be back in harness – opposition never appealed to Pitt – he no longer enjoyed the health or the zest that had kept him going through his first ministry. The third coalition against Napoleon proved no more successful than previous instalments; news of the naval victory at Trafalgar (October 1805) was followed quickly by sharply contrasting tidings from the battlefields of Ulm and Austerlitz. Pitt continued, however, to believe that Napoleon would be defeated in the end.

The achievements of Pitt the Younger have been obscured by the passage of time, and in some respects his most remarkable feat – rising to the premiership at such an early age – has worked against his posthumous reputation, since it is easier to dump him in a class of his own rather than subjecting his record to a serious comparison with other prime ministers. Taking every factor into account, there is no reason to deny him a place in the first rank of British prime ministers, despite the fact that his record (in contrast to those of Churchill and his own father) was impaired rather than elevated by war.

Pitt also deserves recognition as the true inaugurator of a distinctive style of politics in Britain. If, in the 1980s, the Conservative Party was divided between 'Thatcherites' and 'One Nation Conservatives', Pitt the Younger, rather than Disraeli, was the model for the latter position. While dogmatic devotees of Adam Smith, like Edmund Burke, argued that the state should stand by while people starved, since the laws of the market were decreed by God, Pitt responded to famine as a human being should do, and used the power of the state for constructive purposes. His was a conservatism that was truly 'compassionate' as well as pragmatic; although perhaps he could have done more to press for the abolition of the slave trade, he kindled the spirit of reform in his friend William Wilberforce and did speak and vote repeatedly in its favour.

Pitt, in short, was like his near-contemporary, Mozart; and if their successors achieved more in politics or music, it was only because they were standing on the shoulders of real giants.

Mark Garnett is a political biographer and a senior lecturer at the Department of Politics, Philosophy and Religion at Lancaster University.

15

Henry Addington

17 March 1801 to 10 May 1804
Tory

By Stephen Parkinson

Full name: Henry Addington
Born: 30 May 1757, Holborn, Middlesex
Died: 15 February 1844, White Lodge, Richmond, Surrey
Buried at St Mary's church, Mortlake, Surrey
Education: Winchester; Brasenose College, Oxford
Married to Ursula Mary Hammond (d. 1811), then Marianne
Townsend; 4 sons, 4 daughters
Quotation: 'I have known the British constitution long: it has
often been in danger, but it has always scrambled through it.'

I F HENRY ADDINGTON is remembered at all, it is as a mediocre
prime minister better known for his time as Speaker and a reactionary Home Secretary. Apart from a laudatory three-volume life

by his son-in-law, he was the subject of no biography until 1965 – apart from the brief and bathetic *Addington, Author of Modern Income Tax*. Yet Addington does not deserve the obscurity and ignominy to which he has been consigned: both as Prime Minister and Home Secretary he faced down perilous challenges to the British constitutional settlement that he saw it as his lifelong duty to uphold.

Addington was the first middle-class prime minister. His father, a doctor specialising in mental illness, amassed a roster of fashionable clients including Pitt the Elder, 1st Earl of Chatham, during whose mental illness while premier Dr Addington provided 'judicious sagacity and kind care'. When Pitt the Younger was diagnosed with gout, it was Dr Addington who prescribed a daily bottle of port to cure it. An ambitious man, he encouraged the friendship between Pitt and his son Henry, two years his senior.

Henry attended Cheam School, then Winchester; he remains the only Wykehamist prime minister. A model pupil, he was heavily influenced by 'a fanatically narrow-minded and reactionary tutor', George Huntingford, to whom he stayed close, appointing him Bishop of Gloucester many years later. A lifelong and pious Anglican, William Wilberforce found Addington a man of 'pure and upright intentions, and of more religion than almost any politician'.

At Brasenose College, Oxford, Addington 'distinguished himself by no ordinary talent', and established a network of well-connected friends. He stayed on after graduating, then read for the Bar at Lincoln's Inn – alongside Pitt, rekindling a 'friendship which gave a distinctive colouring to his whole future life'. But the relationship was one-way, Pitt dropping Addington as he began to move in smarter circles.

Pitt was already prime minister by the time Addington was elected to Parliament – following his brother-in-law as one of the members for Devizes in 1784; he represented it unopposed for twenty-one years. He did not speak at all during his first two sessions, and only broke his silence when Pitt asked him to second the Loyal Address in 1786. He delivered a workmanlike effort, then barely spoke again, devoting himself to committees and reading. So it was a surprise in 1789 when Pitt nominated him for Speaker. Typically, Pitt was not solely motivated by friendship: he needed a docile supporter, and the unambitious Addington was a useful candidate to counter

Burke's criticism that the Chair was becoming 'a succession house, a hot bed for statesmen'.

The surprise choice turned out to be an excellent Speaker, 'esteemed and respected by all who knew him'. Addington's silent observation had given him a fine grasp of parliamentary procedure; patient and even-handed, he won the trust of members across the House, and was re-elected to serve for twelve years. He 'restored the dignity of the office', and was the first Speaker to be granted a salary and official residence in the Palace of Westminster. This was the apex of his relationship with Pitt: he dined with him often at Speaker's House, consoled him during his unhappy attempt at romance, stood watch over his duel on Putney Heath, and let him recuperate from illness at his home in Woodley, Berkshire in 1800.

The Speakership, however, held Addington back as a parliamentarian. It offered a false protection from interruption, invited pomposity and prolixity (something to which later Speakers have not proved immune), and discouraged partisanship, making Addington a poor defender of his own policies.

In 1801, Pitt had been prime minister for seventeen years and Britain at war with France for eight. Tens of thousands of troops had been lost. Poor harvests meant food shortages and misery at home. Britain stood alone and on the verge of defeat – living under constant fear of invasion and the burden of heavy taxes. Pitt was exhausted and ill. When George III vetoed his proposals for Catholic emancipation in the wake of Irish Union, Pitt misplayed his hand – or saw an opportunity for respite.

The King turned to Addington for help. He thought highly of the Speaker, who shared his view of Anglicanism as the foundation of the British constitution, and whose father had treated him when he was unwell during the Regency Crisis of 1788. He entreated him: 'Lay your hand upon your heart, and ask yourself where I am to turn for support if *you* do not stand by me.' Although Pitt had mooted him as a possible successor as early as 1797, Addington had no desire to supplant his friend. He sought a reconciliation between monarch and premier; only when it became clear that this was impossible – and with Pitt's encouragement – did he agree. The King embraced him: 'My dear Addington, you have saved your country.'

It was one of the most dramatic and unusual appointments to the premiership: a Speaker who had never served in government suddenly transferred to the highest office in the land – in the midst of a war that had sapped the nation's morale and ruined its finances, with a mentally ill monarch and an ambitious heir, and a new and tenuous Union with Ireland.

The crisis was compounded by another sudden illness of the King, and Pitt appeared to waver. Although he pledged Addington 'the most uniform and diligent support', Pitt's closest allies refused to serve. Addington turned to friends and family to fill the government – loyal but uninspiring choices who compounded his own deficiencies. But his Cabinet included two future prime ministers, Perceval and Hawkesbury (later Lord Liverpool), as well as Portland, who had already served as premier and would do so again. Addington's brother Hiley acted as an effective lieutenant and was 'highly successful in manipulating the press'.

Socially, as well as politically, Addington's administration was viewed as inferior. Dubbed 'The Doctor' after his father, many saw him as little more than a *locum tenens*. But Addington knew what medicine was needed: peace. He delivered it twelve months later with the Treaty of Amiens, securing the best he could with the hand he had inherited. Pitt gave the deal his support, and it passed with 'immense majorities' in both Houses. His next task was to repair the public finances. Delivering the first ever Budget speech in April 1802, Addington abolished income tax, an unpopular and inefficient invention of Pitt's, moving the burden to indirect duties on beer and malt. He was fêted by a war-weary, over-taxed nation, who gave him a huge majority in a General Election that July.

But the author of the peace did not expect it to last. He constructed coastal defences and raised a new militia – but more enlisted than could be trained, forcing an embarrassing change of policy. Addington made an unconvincing war leader: when the time came to declare war again in May 1803, he foolishly came to the Commons in the uniform of his local Woodley Cavalry. This absurd spectacle sealed his fate. A rejuvenated Pitt was waiting in the wings: it was a matter of when, not whether, he would replace him.

Soon after Addington had taken over from Pitt, the King drew them aside and said: 'If we three do but keep together all will do well.' Alas, it was not to be. Addington would never have assumed the premiership without Pitt's blessing; though he lost some of his awe for Pitt, he was always deferential to his old friend, making several efforts to entice him back to office, particularly when the resumption of hostilities looked inevitable. But Pitt was unwilling to serve under him – so Addington made the selfless suggestion that they share power under a figurehead such as Pitt's brother, Chatham. This, too, Pitt refused. Finally, Addington made 'an offer unique in the annals of British politics': to stand down in favour of Pitt and accept a subsidiary position – despite his standing with the King, the Cabinet, and Parliament. This, too, Pitt rejected, insisting on an entirely new administration, with Addington to depart for the invented role of Speaker of the House of Lords. The Cabinet protested. Pitt broke off negotiations, and his relationship with Addington deteriorated sharply. It was further soured by the poisonous campaign of Canning, an acolyte of Pitt's, who penned the wounding jibe:

> Pitt is to Addington
> As London is to Paddington.

It hurt because it rang true. Addington had three key deficiencies: 'He was not an aristocrat, he was not an orator and he was not William Pitt.' They rendered him unable to rouse the nation as Pitt had – vital in wartime. Although he stayed in office for a year after the resumption of hostilities, it was clear he was on borrowed time. His wartime Budget reintroduced income tax, albeit on a sounder footing with greater yield for less pain. But the government suffered from 'the general conviction, even among its own members, that any wartime administration that was not under Pitt was a patent absurdity'. Pitt, meanwhile, mobilised his supporters – even allying himself with Fox, his old foe, to whittle down Addington's majority in Parliament. When the King fell ill again, his loyal servant did not want to add to his burdens: on 29 April 1804 Addington told him that his position was 'hopeless'; on 10 May he handed back the seals of office and was replaced by the man he had replaced himself three years earlier.

Addington declined George III's offers to 'his truly beloved friend' – an earldom, a viscountcy, the Garter, a pension – but accepted the lifetime use of White Lodge, Richmond. It was only when the King succeeded in persuading Pitt to have him back in Cabinet in 1805 that Addington accepted the peerage that Pitt insisted on to avoid their sitting alongside each other in the Commons. This expedient was short-lived: when Pitt backslid on a promise to promote his allies, the new Viscount Sidmouth felt compelled to withdraw from the government.

Six months later, Pitt was dead. For all his betrayals, Sidmouth remained charitable towards his old friend. Hearing the sad news, he exclaimed: 'May everlasting happiness await him!' and spoke of 'the affection which has never been extinguished'.

Aged forty-six when he left Downing Street, Sidmouth lived for nearly four more decades. Though a plausible candidate to head new governments – not least after the deaths of Pitt and Perceval – he rebuffed all overtures, not coveting a return to the job that had sapped his spirits. But he served a further fourteen years in Cabinet under four of his successors – ten as Home Secretary under Lord Liverpool, 1812–22, maintaining order during years when Britain came closer to revolution than at any time in her history.

Sidmouth lived on into Queen Victoria's reign, a relic from another age. In the Lords, he continued to oppose Catholic emancipation and the so-called Great Reform Bill. He died, aged eighty-two, after a short bout of influenza on 15 February 1844, surrounded by his children – 'the happiness of my life'.

After Pitt's death, Sidmouth burned 'an immense mass' of letters between them, 'most scrupulously committing to the flames every letter, however interesting, that my conscience told me Pitt would have forbidden to be published had he then been living'. This makes it harder for the historian to make sense of their oscillating friendship, the anguish of which never left him. Whoever succeeded Pitt was always fated to be overshadowed by him; it is Addington's misfortune that he was followed by him too. But his premiership was more than a blip in the midst of Pitt's glory. At a critical juncture in Britain's twenty-two-year conflict with France, Addington negotiated a popular peace and restored the nation's finances – achieving what the great Pitt could not. An able administrator, his major failure was one of communication, as historian Philip Ziegler remarked: 'He was not a bad Prime Minister but he was bad at behaving like a Prime Minister . . . In the end, he could not even convince himself.' Yet he approached the premiership, like everything in his long and generally contented life, with selflessness and integrity. Replying to a letter of congratulation following his appointment in 1801, he wrote:

> I have done no more than my duty; and being actuated by that alone, and having no object but the good of my country, I have sought no political connections; but shall steadily pursue those measures which my own mind approves, and which I therefore venture to hope will be approved of and supported by parliament and the public.

It is not a bad way to approach that most difficult of jobs.

Stephen Parkinson is Director of the Conservative History Group and was raised to the peerage as Lord Parkinson of Whitley Bay in 2019, after serving as political secretary to Theresa May.

16

Lord Grenville

11 February 1806 to 25 March 1807
Whig

By Arthur Burns

Full name: William Wyndham Grenville
Born: 24 October 1759, Wotton House, Buckinghamshire
Died: 12 January 1834, Dropmore Lodge, Burnham,
Buckinghamshire. Buried at St Peter's church, Burnham
Education: East Hill School, Wandsworth; Eton College; Christ
Church, Oxford
Married to Hon. Anne Pitt; no children
Quotation: 'I can hardly keep wondering at my own folly in
thinking it worthwhile to leave my books and garden, even for
one day's attendance in the House of Commons.' (1803)

THERE ARE FEW prime ministers of whom the public know so
little as William Wyndham Grenville. Though premier for

barely over a year, Grenville made enduring contributions to British politics, policy and institutions over more than thirty years embracing both the loss of the American colonies and Waterloo. One might expect mere curiosity to be piqued by his being one of only two sons of prime ministers who then held the office themselves. His obscurity demands further elucidation.

The most obvious explanation is that Grenville was a colourless figure in an era oversupplied with big political beasts. Even his leading biographer concedes that Grenville was pious and haughty, with 'no apparent humour or vices'. He was an effective but un-inspiring orator. He was outshone even in dryness: indeed, by that other prime minister's son, William Pitt the Younger, with whose career Grenville's intertwined so closely.

Equally important, however, is that Grenville's career encapsulates the political flux of the late Hanoverian period, his enduring polit-ical connections being a function of family, not ideology. Grenville and associated 'Grenvillites' perforce navigated a complex political landscape produced by the fragmentation of the mid-eighteenth-century Whig Party, the incorporation of new forms of 'radical' and 'liberal' politics, the re-emergence of a recognisable 'Tory' grouping, the impact of wartime exigencies, and the fortunes of more charismatic political virtuosi. They did so in ways making it hard for later Liberal or Conservative political traditions to celebrate him as one of their own (it is telling that he was never accorded the standard Victorian tribute of a multi-volume 'Life and Letters').

Third, Grenville was an accidental prime minister. He had no ambition to lead a party, let alone the nation. His political ambitions were driven by a quest for financial security and status reflecting his position as a youngest son. They were already realised by his elevation to the Lords as Baron Grenville in 1790 and the acquisi-tion of lucrative sinecures, the potential loss of which, were he premier, constituted a significant disincentive to assuming that office (and expense). His most notable achievements came when he worked closely with others as a 'man of business' equipped with the skills and application increasingly essential as the demands of war and globalisation imposed unprecedented strains on state machinery. He was an exceptional right-hand man; in contrast, he lacked the social skills and flair for leadership, and knew it.

William Wyndham Grenville was born the fifth child of George Grenville and Elizabeth Wyndham on 24 October 1759, some three and half years before his father was appointed Prime Minister by George III. Both parents died in the same year as William was sent to Eton, 1770, but left clear marks on their son: from Elizabeth he inherited an uncomplicated Anglican piety; from his father a model of statesmanship that commanded respect rather than affection, founded on mastery of detail and pragmatic but stubborn commitment to policies. This complicated relations with the monarch they both served, and by whom they were at first resented and ultimately dismissed. Grenville's wider family situation ensured a future shaped by one of the most important Whig political connections, the 'cousinhood' embracing the Grenvilles, including his father and brothers, and the Pitts, Pitt the Elder having married Grenville's aunt Hester (in 1792 he himself would embark on a happy but childless marriage with Pitt's niece Anne).

Grenville shone at Christ Church, Oxford, both in mathematics and the classics, the latter furnishing a lifelong enthusiasm that would see him co-publish editions of the *Iliad* and *Odyssey* with Oxford University Press in 1800/1. After a short spell at Lincoln's Inn, his political career commenced in 1782 with his elder brother George (later Earl Temple and then Marquess of Buckingham) placing him as MP for the family borough of Buckingham, two years later William winning a county seat for Buckinghamshire that he would hold until his elevation to the Lords. When George accepted office as Lord Lieutenant of Ireland under Shelburne in 1782, William accompanied him as Chief Secretary, and it was here that his abilities were first demonstrated as he negotiated the Renunciation Act establishing Irish legislative independence. This impressed Pitt the Younger, with whom a friendship developed that sustained a long political collaboration. When Pitt emerged as premier following the fall of the Fox–North coalition (an event in which Grenville's brother's role forced his retreat from front-line politics), Grenville himself experienced the rewards of appearing as one of the King's friends in appointment first as Paymaster General and then to two key governmental bodies, the Board of Trade and the Board of Control for Indian Affairs, of which he became president in 1790.

Grenville became a key lieutenant to Pitt. Up until the outbreak of the Revolutionary Wars, they worked closely in applying insights gained from mutual reading of Adam Smith to trade policy with both Ireland and the Continent (Grenville was a key architect of the tariff-reduction treaty with France in 1786), reform of the East India Company, administrative reform and financial policy, where Grenville maintained that he had 'a larger share than I believe anyone knows' in the creation of the sinking fund intended to eliminate the burgeoning national debt. His managerial competence, meanwhile, was exemplified in a brief spell as Speaker of the House of Commons helping Pitt navigate the Regency Crisis associated with the King's mental illness in 1788–9, and then his elevation to the Lords to address a shortage of talent on the government benches. Higher office initially eluded him, partly because of his own preference for a second-order but comfortable career, and partly because his relations' perceived appetite for advancement and sinecures raised hackles in the highest places.

This changed when Grenville was appointed Secretary of State first for Home Affairs (1789) and then Foreign Affairs (1791), a post he would retain until he followed Pitt out of office in 1801 after clashing with the King over the Catholic Question, both men having come to regard increased toleration as a necessity for national security. Grenville helped shape British foreign policy through the challenges that followed the French Revolution in the context both of Cabinet divisions and rapidly fluctuating circumstances on the Continent. 'Bogey', as the effective leader of the Grenvillite connection was now nicknamed on account of his ungainly physical presence, began by focusing on combating domestic radicalism while trying to maintain neutrality between and distance from the continental powers; despite then working to form an allied coalition, he fell out with Pitt over the latter's willingness to subsidise Prussia's war efforts and commit to a Bourbon restoration. After 1795 Grenville was similarly unenthusiastic over Pitt's pursuit of peace negotiations on what he regarded as unsatisfactory terms, himself placing undue hopes on the potential of counter-revolutionary forces to work with other powers to deliver victory. After 1798 Grenville got more of his way, driving the formation of a second coalition to undertake continental operations rather than focusing on conquest further afield. Throughout, his best efforts met with at best partial success.

Despite contemplating retirement from politics aged forty-one after his resignation, Grenville instead found himself emerging as the effective head of a 'new opposition' critical of the peace settlement negotiated by Addington's ministry at Amiens. Grenville desired a broadly based ministry to confront Bonapartism once war recommenced in 1803; most observers would have envisaged this inevitably involving Pitt, but the tensions already evident now developed to the point where, in what has been described as 'one of the more extraordinary changes of course in modern history', Grenville failed to agree terms with his long-time associate and instead allied with Charles James Fox and his opposition Whigs, refusing Pitt's invitation to join his 1804 government since Fox was excluded. Yet he equally eschewed systematic opposition alongside Fox, a politician with whom he shared little positive beyond a commitment to Catholic emancipation. When Pitt died in 1806, adding to the political confusion, it was to the highly experienced Grenville that a reluctant King turned to form a new administration, even at the price of accepting Fox as Foreign Secretary.

In the circumstances, it is hardly surprising that much of the evident energy that Grenville devoted to his premiership went into the business of shoring up the novel political configurations that underpinned it, both through giving leading figures of all the four political factions his government embraced a genuine say in regular Cabinet meetings, and also seeking to expand this 'ministry of all the talents' to embrace a fifth: disgruntled Pittites. It was as part of this policy that he secured a General Election in the hope of demonstrating and reinforcing his support base in October 1806, which marginally increased his parliamentary numbers at the cost of stirring antagonisms, not least in a King who thought it unnecessary. His short tenure nonetheless also witnessed significant efforts to overhaul military recruitment and war finance on the domestic front, alongside unsuccessful multilateral negotiations with the French and fruitless military expeditions from Sicily to Buenos Aires designed to occupy Bonaparte until forces rallied to challenge him on the Continent. It was a third strategy to prepare for further conflict, a proposal to allow Catholics to serve in the army up to the rank of general and thus disarm discontent in Ireland, that saw Grenville provoke the King into demanding that his ministers pledge never to raise the Catholic Question again. Grenville declined to do so, and left office on 25 March 1807.

For the ten years that followed, despite having fewer followers in the Commons than Charles Grey possessed among Foxites, Grenville was effectively leader of the 'Whig' opposition to Pittite ministries that he came to regard as 'Tory' in their subservience to the Crown. His shortcomings as leader were exposed when the King's renewed illness offered an opportunity for a resumption of office in 1811 that Grenville bungled. In 1817 he handed over leadership to Grey and retired to private life save for penning occasional political pamphlets. Grenville survived a minor stroke in 1823 to rejoice in Catholic emancipation in 1829 and come to terms with the constitutional reform he had generally opposed in 1832, dying peacefully on 12 January 1834.

Grenville's single most important legislative achievement was the Slave Trade Abolition Act of 1807, where his parliamentary leadership enabled William Wilberforce's campaigning to realise an objective that Grenville had long supported. While one should not neglect the importance of the non-parliamentary forces that paved the way to abolition, or the limitations of the measure, this was a landmark decision. However, it is important also to recognise Grenville's contributions to the emergence of the nineteenth-century free-trade tradition in British politics and to new approaches to effective and efficient administration, at the same time as his dependence on sinecures and familial connection marked him out clearly as a product of the eighteenth century.

Arthur Burns is Professor of Modern British History and academic director of the Georgian Papers Programme at King's College London.

17

Spencer Perceval

4 October 1809 to 11 May 1812
Tory

By Henry Bellingham

Full name: Spencer Perceval
Born: 1 November 1762, Audley Square, London
Died: 11 May 1812, House of Commons. Buried at St Luke's, Charlton, Kent
Education: Harrow School; Trinity College, Cambridge
Married to Jane Spencer-Wilson; 6 sons, 6 daughters
Quotation: 'I have nothing to say to the nothing that has been said.' (During a Commons debate on corrupt electoral practices)

AFTER AN UNSEASONABLY cold and wet April, Monday 11 May brought bright sunshine, and it seemed that spring had finally arrived. The Prime Minister who stepped out onto Downing Street just before 5 p.m. certainly had a spring in his step. After a near disastrous start to his ministry, all the stars had aligned in his favour. The tide had turned in the Peninsular War; the illegal slave trade had been virtually stamped out; the Prince Regent was now his staunchest ally; and as an evangelical dyed-in-the-wool Conservative, he had fought off electoral reform.

He turned into Parliament Square, and into St Stephen's Entrance, and brushed past his old friend, Lord Francis Osborne MP. He stopped at the Hall Keepers Lodge, and he handed over his coat. It was at this point, for reasons that we will never know, that his private secretary and security officer peeled off.

He then rushed up the steps into the great Westminster Hall. In the pre-Great Fire House of Commons, the original Lobby doubled up as both Central and Members Lobby and it opened straight onto Westminster Hall. As he saw the Prime Minister approach, the Badge Messenger opened the large swing door into the Lobby. It was buzzing with activity, but suddenly there was a hush as people caught sight of the diminutive premier.

He was waiting just inside the second swing door leading to the chamber. The tall man with curly hair and a long saturnine face was stylishly dressed in a dark brown coat, a striped waistcoat, dusty yellow Nankeen trousers and Hessian boots. He had certainly dressed for the occasion as he now embarked on the final well-rehearsed act of his long-running search for justice. The expensive duelling pistols were well hidden in his specially designed coat pockets. John Bellingham then calmly stepped in front of the advancing PM, who apologised to him. At that point the assassin drew one of the pistols and shot the PM in the chest at point-black range. Spencer Perceval staggered forward and, as he collapsed, shouted, 'Murder, oh Murder'.

After being disarmed by the redoubtable former Coldstreamer, General Isaac Gascoyne MP, Bellingham was taken to the Bar, before being questioned and formally charged by two MP magistrates. One week later he was hanged.

Within hours, demonstrators had filled Parliament Square to celebrate the news. Even transporting the assassin from Parliament to Newgate proved a challenge. According to the diplomat George Jackson: 'By force only could they be prevented from mounting the coach. They were whipped off, beaten off amid vociferated applause and hurrahs for Bellingham.'

John Bellingham was a man of many contradictions: a bright accountant, who married well and doted on his three boys, and especially the youngest one Henry – but whose failed business dealings in Russia resulted in bankruptcy. A committed Christian who could be caring and considerate – he became so deluded and obsessed with his own grievances against the government that he decided to take the law into his own hands.

Was he really acting alone? Almost certainly yes. However, as Andro Linklater documents so well, there were plenty of people and organisations who had good reason to see the back of Spencer Perceval. Although John Bellingham had insisted throughout that he was on his own, only he really knew the exact answer to this question. He took it with him as the hangman completed his gruesome task.

The Percevals, who owned the 100,000–acre Egmont Estate around Kanturk, near Cork in Ireland, were actively involved in both the local community and politics. John Perceval was awarded a baronetcy in 1661. In 1733 his grandson, who was a long-serving MP, was created the Earl of Egmont. His son, the 2nd Earl, also went into politics, ending up First Lord of the Admiralty. When he was born in 1762, Spencer was the seventh son of his second marriage. The estate brought in £4,000 per annum (roughly £400,000 today), but as the seventh son, none of this was ever likely to filter down to young Spencer. He really would have to go and make his way in the world.

After Harrow and Cambridge, the Bar was the next logical step, and by 1786 he had been called to Lincoln's Inn. The following year he enjoyed a piece of outrageous good fortune: in a quite typical example of nepotism, his uncle, Spencer Compton, later 8th Earl of Northampton, arranged for him to be appointed Deputy Recorder on a salary of £1,000 per annum (£100,000 today).

By 1790 he had married Jane Wilson, the daughter of a wealthy former MP, and his legal practice really started to take off when he led for the Crown in the celebrated case against Thomas Paine and his subversive publication *The Rights of Man*. He also started to build a reputation as a formidable performer with illiberal and trenchant right-wing views on most subjects.

He soon enjoyed yet another stroke of nepotistic good fortune:

Northampton's MP was none other than his uncle Spencer Compton, whose father died in April 1796. He succeeded as the Earl of Northampton, and a by-election was duly called. With his uncle arranging a few well-timed local speeches, his adoption was a shoe-in. Elected unopposed in the by-election, Perceval then topped the poll in the subsequent General Election, and took his seat on 27 September as a fully joined-up Pittite. He made his maiden speech on 13 December in a debate on foreign policy. He began with a lengthy and thoroughly illiberal discourse on the constitution, and followed up with a vicious tirade against Charles James Fox. He concluded by saying that 'the country needed to be saved from the delusion of popular opinion, from the plausible fallacies of democratic theories and from the spirit of democracy!' It caused a sensation and the Pittites were thrilled with the young star.

He really hit his stride in a debate on the Assisted Taxes Bill. He spoke passionately about why taxes had to be raised to finance the war against Napoleon, and once again laid into Fox. It was a *tour de force*, and one of the greatest plaudits came from the Whig, Lord Granville Leveson-Gower, who described the speech as 'quite incomparable and one of the best he had ever heard'. Two themes keep emerging from these early speeches – total opposition to any kind of political reform; and equally strong opposition to Catholic emancipation.

Pitt was forced to resign in 1801 and was replaced by Henry Addington. In his first reshuffle, the latter made Spencer Perceval Solicitor General, and within eighteen months he had been promoted to Attorney General. To the great surprise of colleagues, he turned down the customary ex-officio knighthood. One can only speculate as to his motives, but as the son of an earl he was already The Hon. However, what caused consternation was the PM allowing him to continue his legal practice, and by this time his income had reached over £10,000 per annum (£1,000,000 today).

Spencer Perceval, the Attorney General, is best remembered for his vigorous prosecution of the Irish revolutionary, Colonel Edward Despard. It was during this time that he started to become an avid anti-slave trader. Guided less by his illiberal philosophy, but rather by his Christian beliefs, and encouraged by Wilberforce, he very deftly used his position to bring in an Order in Council to ban the slave trade in the new colony of Guiana. This sent a strong signal and ensured that the slavery agenda dominated the 1806 election that followed Pitt's death.

Unfortunately for Perceval, the Tories lost, and Lord Grenville formed the Whig-dominated coalition of 'All the Talents'. A hopeless leader, Grenville was then further weakened by the untimely death of Fox in September 1806. As the government fell into disarray, Perceval made a remarkable sixty-nine speeches in the 1806–7 session. In total exasperation, Lord Grenville even offered him a job in the coalition. However, he was enjoying opposition too much, and flatly refused.

By early 1807 the 'Talents' started to fall apart. On 19 March the King sent for the Duke of Portland. Although in poor health and fortified by regular doses of opiates, he seized his chance – presumably hoping that his ministry would last longer than the eight months of his first one in 1783.

Spencer Perceval had every reason to expect a top job, but when offered the Exchequer and Leader of the House, he initially declined, on the grounds that he genuinely knew little about finance. After a lot of pressure, he eventually succumbed, but very cannily insisted on also being appointed Chancellor of the Duchy of Lancaster for life on an additional salary of £4,000 p.a. (£400,000 today). This brought his Cabinet salary to a staggering £8,323 (£840,000 today) – he did, though, somewhat reluctantly agree to give up his legal practice.

In the ensuing 'No Popery' Election in April, Perceval was returned unopposed, and the Pittites secured a majority of sixty. Although widely considered completely ill suited for the Exchequer, he took up his new portfolio with alacrity. What he found when he entered the building was truly shocking. Many of the staff did not turn up until 11 a.m., and the whole place was riddled with complacency, incompetence and even corruption. For example, board minutes had never been taken, and the Royal Navy's accounts had been untouched since 1799.

With the Peninsular War now costing over £2.5 million annually (£250 million today), the new team launched into action: they needed to modernise the administration; they urgently had to prepare an innovative tax-raising Budget; the country's debt needed to be put onto a secure footing; and they needed to devise a clear policy to counter the growing demands for Britain to move onto the Gold Standard.

By the spring of 1809 the Duke of Portland had become completely incapable of transacting business. Perceval's big opportunity was getting closer. In early August the Duke suffered a stroke, and the leadership race began. Perceval was a strong contender, but the two favourites were Canning and Castlereagh. Everyone knew that Castlereagh was furious with Canning for trying to get him sacked. Their relationship did not just implode; they ended up fighting their infamous duel on Putney Heath that left Canning badly wounded in the leg. As public ridicule was heaped upon them, Wilberforce said that 'the news was totally humiliating, and both should be permanently excluded from office'.

Perceval's path to No. 10 was now clear, and on 4 October 1809 he kissed hands with the King. He then set about forming a ministry, but got off to the worst possible start when he offered the Duke a Cabinet seat without portfolio. Within a matter of days, though, he was dead.

The most immediate priority was the ongoing war. There was also the parliamentary fireworks that were about to go off over the ill-fated Walcheren Expedition. Of the 40,000 British troops landed near Antwerp, 4,000 had been killed, and the remainder faced a humiliating withdrawal. Recognising that this could bring down his government, Perceval ruthlessly dismissed the leader of the expedition, the Earl of Chatham, and on the back of some superb speeches, he won the final vote. In the words of Dennis Gray, 'he had pulled off a remarkable victory, and the Pittites now knew they had a leader of resolution and character'.

All of this character would now be needed in the Peninsular War, where British prospects of success seemed very distant. Not only was the war costing a fortune, but Sir Arthur Wellesley's forces were dug in behind the lines of Torres Vedras. Egged on by the Whigs, the press whipped up a vehement campaign for withdrawal. Even Perceval's own back-benchers were getting restless, but he held firm throughout, ever confident in the finances.

He also remained faithful to Wellesley, who turned out to be one of the country's most brilliant commanders. In early 1811 he broke out from Torres Vedras, won the Battle of Fuentes de Oñoro, and pushed Marshal Masséna into headlong retreat. Three months after Perceval's death, Wellesley triumphantly led British troops into Madrid. Within two years, just as Spencer Perceval was being airbrushed out of history, Sir Arthur had been created the 1st Duke of Wellington. Three years later he won his greatest victory of all at Waterloo. However, none of this would have been possible without the courage, total steadfastness, optimism and utter determination of the country's prime minister. Without him history would have been very different.

His conduct of the war certainly was not made any easier by the Regency Crisis. By the summer of 1810, the King's behaviour was becoming more and more erratic.

The Regency Bill was laid before the House on 19 December 1810. However, there was one major obstacle – the Prince Regent positively loathed Perceval, having never forgiven him for standing up for his former wife, Princess Caroline, when she was evicted from the Court. The bill was highly restrictive, and the Prince reacted with predictable fury. But by summoning the royal Dukes, and openly conspiring with the Foreign Secretary, he overplayed his hand. Perceval knew by now that this was a confidence issue, and stood firm. He made a number of brilliant speeches and eventually the bill received Royal Assent on 4 February 1811.

The Prince Regent took his oath two days later, but was in a filthy mood, and rather childishly displayed a bust of Charles James Fox on his desk. For Spencer Perceval this was a major triumph, and even the Whig opposition sang his praises. In his biography of Perceval, Dennis Gray describes this as a pivotal moment: 'He was heroic, and won a personal and Parliamentary triumph worthy of Pitt.' From now onwards, people would underestimate 'Little P' at their peril.

After a dismal start to his ministry, the Prime Minister's position was now secure. This mattered, as he tackled another personal priority, namely the illegal slave trade. In 1807 Wilberforce had finally succeeded in getting his bill through, but the illegal slavers used every cunning ploy to keep their trade going, including through British-registered vessels flying foreign flags. The Abolition Act needed teeth and required tougher penalties. It also needed both a Royal Navy presence off West Africa, and an effective court in Sierra Leone. The crusading Christian zeal of one man made all of this possible. One only has to look at what happened after his successor, Lord Liverpool, never a strong supporter of abolition, took over. The court was closed, the West Africa Squadron was downgraded, and the number of slaves being shipped went up by 12,000 a year. Perceval really did save thousands of lives, and few people who knew him well ever doubted that he regarded this as his greatest achievement.

With the nineteenth century producing so many extraordinarily brilliant and successful prime ministers, it is perhaps hardly surprising that Spencer Perceval's legacy ended up being largely forgotten and overlooked. That great American evangelist preacher, Jonathan Edwards, once said: 'By the manner of their departure, will ye know and remember them.' Maybe over two hundred years on, the time has now come to reappraise and revise our opinion of one of our most dogged, determined and principled statesmen.

In his history of the British army, 1910, J.W. Fortescue concluded that: 'His career was cut short by the hand of an assassin before he could share in the credit for having carried the war to a successful issue, but endured the dust and heat of the race without gaining the immortal garland.' Perhaps the time has now come urgently to award him that garland.

Lord Bellingham is a former minister and was Member of Parliament for North West Norfolk from 1983 to 1997 and 2001 to 2019.

18

Earl of Liverpool

8 June 1812 to 9 April 1827
Tory

By Peter Riddell

Full name: Robert Banks Jenkinson, 2nd Earl of Liverpool
Born: 7 June 1770, Westminster, London
Died: 4 December 1828, Coombe House, Kingston upon
Thames. Buried at Hawkesbury parish church, Gloucestershire
Education: Charterhouse; Christ Church, Oxford
Married to Lady Louisa Hervey (d. 1821), then Lady Mary
Chester; no children
Quotation: '(I consider) the right of election as a public trust,
granted not for the benefit of the individual but for the public
good.'

LORD LIVERPOOL IS both a largely unknown and an under-rated
prime minister. His reputation has permanently suffered from

Disraeli's typically pithy but unfair jibe in his novel *Coningsby* about 'the Arch Mediocrity who presided rather than ruled over this Cabinet of Mediocrities . . . In the conduct of public affairs his disposition was exactly the reverse of that which is the characteristic of great men. He was peremptory in little questions, and great ones he left open.' Liverpool was neither charismatic nor inspiring, and said little that was memorable. He opposed both Catholic emancipation and parliamentary reform. But not only did he have the political skills to survive as prime minister for fifteen years, surpassed only by Walpole and the Younger Pitt, and never since his death, but he oversaw the successful end to the Napoleonic Wars, and the fractious peace that followed. And though a constitutional conservative, in his final years his administration began the process of economic and social reform that came to fruition in the following decades. He also managed the very delicate and often trying relationship with George IV, both after his accession in 1820, and earlier when he was Prince Regent.

Liverpool was the consummate man of government, and held ministerial office over a period of thirty-four years for all but a year and a bit. He occupied all the then key offices of state, the Foreign Office, the Home Office, War and the Colonies, before becoming prime minister. In all he showed personal and financial integrity unusual for the time, assiduity, command of his brief and competence. He was more respected than liked since he could be brusque and awkward in his personal dealings, especially in his final years. While his early career was dominated by the Napoleonic Wars, he took a close interest in political economy and the sweeping industrial and commercial changes affecting Britain, though never neglecting the traditionally powerful agricultural interests. He was a cautious social and economic reformer.

As Norman Gash, his 1984 biographer, wrote, Liverpool's government was 'the last of the great eighteenth-century administrations in its structure and duration and the first of the great nineteenth-century administrations in its problems and achievements'. He operated in the transition between prime ministers, or chief or first ministers as they were still generally known, being dependent on the personal patronage of the Crown and the rise of party rule. General elections did not decide the fate of administrations, but rearranged the balance of factions, alongside many independent members. The House of Commons had, however, a growing influence during his period of power, though what mattered was manoeuvring between various personalities and their small bands of followers in what was still an era of aristocratic politics. It is anachronistic to put party labels on these essentially personal groups, and to talk of Liverpool heading a Conservative administration is premature. For much of his career he was seen, and saw himself, as a Pittite.

Liverpool, or Jenkinson as he was known until 1796, was born into an upcoming political and administrative family. His snobbish and pedantic father Charles held office under Lord North and the Younger Pitt and was raised to the peerage as Lord Hawkesbury in 1786, a title deriving from his Gloucestershire manor and land. He was a close adviser to George III, a link that subsequently helped his son. Aged forty-one, in 1769 he married Amelia Watts, the daughter of a former Governor of Fort William in Bengal and one of Robert Clive's protégées who made a fortune in India after the Battle of Plassey. The son, Robert, was born in June 1770 when his mother was still nineteen. But she died when he was only a month old. His father remarried twelve years later and Jenkinson had a much younger half-brother and half-sister.

At the age of thirteen he went to Charterhouse, his father's old school, then located close to Smithfield and the Old Bailey on the edge of the City. He was taught Latin and Greek, but, additionally and more unusually for the period, he had a knowledge of French, history and political economy. As a schoolboy, he had already met Pitt, Burke and Thurlow through his father.

In 1787, he went on to Christ Church in Oxford, where he first met George Canning, the start of a forty-year-long friendship and rivalry between the often plodding, worthy and invariably serious Liverpool and the brilliant, witty but unreliable Canning, who could never resist playing jokes on his friend. But, in rather a tortoise-and-hare way, Jenkinson had greater longer-term impact than the mercurial Canning, who was forever wavering about joining, or resigning from, successive administrations. Yet they were regarded then, and for many years afterwards, as the 'inseparables', featuring together in a cartoon by Gillray in 1796.

After just over two years at Oxford, Jenkinson went on a Grand Tour starting in Paris, where, a week after his arrival, he was in the crowd of Parisians watching the storming of the Bastille on 14 July 1789. This made a lasting impression, reinforcing his innate mistrust of radicalism. Leaving Paris three months later, he became a Master of Arts in May 1790.

His political career began almost immediately when the twenty-year-old was, thanks to his father, elected for Rye. Being under age, he did not take his seat immediately but resumed his European travels. On his return he was seen by some, understandably envious, friends as clever but self-important. He was an exceptionally young MP for any period, though it was not then that unusual for sons of peers to be elected in their twenties. A minority of them effectively became full-time, almost professional politicians, living both for and off politics, since ministerial salaries were then relatively high, even though MPs were not paid until 1911. Jenkinson finally made his maiden speech in February 1792, talking for more than an hour on the state of European politics in the light of the French Revolution, which attracted notice, not least from Pitt, the Prime Minister.

Liverpool's political career can be divided into three parts: first, 1793 to 1801, holding minor offices as a follower of Pitt; second, from 1801 until 1812, as a leading minister in several posts in successive administrations (apart from a short break in 1806–7 after Pitt's death); and then, third, as prime minister for fifteen years. He displayed increasing authority as someone who could be trusted to oversee the affairs of government. It made him the indispensable minister in the eyes both of the Crown and of his fellow politicians.

In the first phase, he was noticed less for the administrative tasks he performed than for being one of the government side's most effective speakers in the Commons, usually on the subject of relations with France. In February 1793, not yet aged twenty-three, he was the main speaker against a challenge to the outbreak of war from Charles James Fox. Pitt told George III it was 'a speech of uncommon ability and effect'. In April 1794 he became a butt of jokes for many years afterwards for urging a march on Paris. During the upsurge in patriotic sentiment in the mid-1790s, he became a colonel in Pitt's Cinque Ports Regiment of Fencible Cavalry, and, characteristically, took his duties very seriously. Canning wrote a parody of one of his recruiting posters – a joke that misfired at a dinner party when the long poem was read, leading Jenkinson to weep. In his turn, Canning was mortified. The two men were eventually reconciled, but the episode illustrates Jenkinson's sensitivity, and Canning's thoughtless mischief making.

At this period also, Jenkinson fell in love, and in March 1795 he married Lady Louisa Hervey, the youngest daughter of the Earl of Bristol, a colourful figure not unlike Lord Marchmain in *Brideshead Revisited* who spent much of his time travelling around Europe. Louisa grew up to be a rather prim, nervous and moralistic young woman. The courtship was not straightforward as a result of the opposition of his father, in part because of the absence of a dowry on her side, and it required the intervention of the King and the Prime Minister to secure the father's approval. They were a devoted couple. From the early 1800s their main home was Coombe House, at the end of Richmond Park, which had the advantage of being both secluded and only two hours travelling time from Westminster.

A year later, in May 1796, his father was created Earl of Liverpool and the son took the courtesy title of Lord Hawkesbury. During this period he slowly advanced up the political ladder as a loyal ally of the Prime Minister: in 1799, he became the Master of the Mint, which had some duties as well as a salary.

The second phase of his career and his decisive opportunity to move into the top rank of politics came paradoxically with the resignation of Pitt in February 1801. This followed a run of military failures, consequent war weariness and a row over Catholic emancipation. Hawkesbury urged Pitt to remain in office, but unsuccessfully. The main beneficiary from the formation of the Addington administration turned out to be Hawkesbury himself, who was unexpectedly promoted from Master of the Mint to Foreign Secretary since many other ministers had resigned with Pitt. Hawkesbury played a key role as the main spokesman in the Commons alongside Addington. Hawkesbury's elderly father was still in the Cabinet, though largely an absentee member due to ill-health, one of the rare father-and-son joint memberships of the same Cabinet (the Stanleys in the mid-19th century and Joseph and Austen Chamberlain in the 1900s being the other examples).

His main task was the peace negotiations with France, a demanding test of his limited experience. But he succeeded and the resulting Treaty of Amiens was widely welcomed after eight years of war, even though most saw it as a necessary truce rather than a final resolution of the conflict. Hawkesbury's robust defence of the treaty in the Commons enhanced his reputation, though, later, he was compared unfavourably with his long-serving predecessor Grenville. The peace did not last long, and hostilities broke out again in spring 1803. The resumption of war tested Hawkesbury's reputation and undermined his position. In late 1803 Addington asked him to move to the Lords to take over the leadership of the House to strengthen the weak team there. That move would have happened in any event five years later when his father died, but it complicated his remaining political career that he was not in the Commons.

In the spring of 1804, the unpopular Addington administration finally spluttered to a close with the return of Pitt. After the usual convoluted manoeuvrings characteristic of the time, Hawkesbury was reluctantly persuaded to move to the Home Office, while remaining Leader of the Lords. He became responsible for law and order, the ever-demanding question of relations with Ireland as well as measures to counter the feared invasion. But his period there was overshadowed by the declining health of Pitt and, despite the great naval victory at Trafalgar, by the defeat of the combined Austrian and Russian armies at Austerlitz. The death of Pitt in January 1806 prompted the King to offer Hawkesbury the premiership, but he rightly turned down the offer. It was time for a change of ministers. So an administration of all but the inner core of Pittites was formed with the nickname of the Ministry of All the Talents. Hawkesbury received the consolation of Pitt's old sinecure of the Wardenship of the Cinque Ports, which was both financially rewarding and brought with it Walmer Castle on the Kent Coast, which provided an attractive place for him to relax over the following two decades.

Hawkesbury's period in opposition lasted little more than a year as the Grenville administration was divided and fractious. The elderly Duke of Portland became prime minister in 1807 with Hawkesbury returning to the Home Office, and at the end of 1808 he became the 2nd Earl of Liverpool after the death of his father. This was another divided government weakened by personality clashes. Spencer Perceval emerged in 1809 as the fourth prime minister in less than four years, and Liverpool moved to the War Office. He showed steadiness and sure judgement in handling Wellington during the many ups and downs of the Peninsular War when many in Parliament doubted whether the campaign would succeed. The commander-in-chief in Portugal was, for all his formidable military reputation, touchy and a complainer, and Liverpool proved to be skilful in calming him and providing encouragement, support and warnings about what was happening back in London.

In the middle of all this came the assassination of Spencer Perceval in May 1812 in the House of Commons. Liverpool was the obvious successor within ministerial ranks, but little happened in a straight-forward way in that period, with a successful Commons motion calling for a 'strong and efficient administration' and the intervention of the vain and cantankerous Lord Wellesley, Wellington's elder brother. But after eighteen days, the Prince Regent appointed Liverpool, the safe choice, a man of proven administrative ability, solidity and trust-worthiness. His first, and lasting, act was to leave what was called Catholic relief, the extension of political rights, as an open question for ministers, as it remained for the whole of his premiership.

Liverpool's early years as prime minister were dominated by the end of the Napoleonic Wars. Wellington was the key, both in his military victories, notably from 1813 onwards, and in his refusal to join in the attacks on ministers by his elder brother and by Canning. After the abdication of Napoleon in 1814, Liverpool entrusted the detailed negotiations in Vienna to Castlereagh. The prime minister had to balance conflicting pressures at home over the future of Europe, and he showed a sure touch in keeping Parliament and the Prince Regent largely on side. The main British aims were ensuring the independence of the Netherlands, Spain and Portugal, and to keep France within her pre-war frontiers. There was also the distraction of the war with the United States, which no one really wanted and which was prolonged by the length of time it then took to commu-nicate across the Atlantic. The escape of Napoleon from Elba in March 1815 produced a dramatic interlude culminating in the British/Prussian victory at Waterloo, which decisively ended the Bonaparte era.

Yet, as often after a war, the main challenges became domestic. The long years of conflict had boosted public spending, taxation and national debt, while the transition to peace created social problems. Liverpool was by instinct and conviction a free trader, and, like his contemporaries, did not believe there was much the state could do directly to alleviate poverty and unemployment. But he was aware of, and responsive to commercial and industrial as well as agricultural interests. The immediate post-war challenge was over the price of food and the hardship among farmers, both tenants and landlords. The price of grain virtually halved in the two years to early 1815 and this led to calls for protection. Liverpool wanted a temporary measure and a sliding scale of duties, but he was forced by parliamentary pressure to agree to a fixed duty in what became known as the Corn Laws. Liverpool's speech on the Bill in the Lords was revealing about his economic philosophy: he had been bred in a school 'where he had been taught highly to value the commercial interest', but he could not sacrifice the agricultural interest to it – indeed, the two were not distinct but the same. He wanted to encourage agriculture, since if it was strong, the whole economy would benefit and it would 'render grain cheaper instead of dearer'. The motives of others in demanding protection were more self-interested and the Corn Laws became a recurrent, and divisive, issue of British politics for the following thirty years.

Liverpool's awareness of the increasing diversity, and complexity, of the British economy also emerged in his efforts to stabilise the nation's finances. He wanted to retain the wartime innovation of income tax to finance immediate spending and help address past debts. But, in face of opposition, all he could achieve was an extension for twelve months. While MPs did not want to approve higher taxes, they were keen to cut expenditure and there were big reductions in the budgets of the navy and army as well as domestically, similar to those achieved by the 'Geddes Axe' after the First World War. Liverpool had to tackle a huge gap between revenue of £12 million a year and expenditure of £20 million, and the result was even more borrowing. He can be criticised for accepting these largely parliamentary pressures, but he bided his time, showing calmness and clarity about what was wrong and what should be done. Eventually, in 1819, the opposition groupings in the Commons overreached themselves and Liverpool was able to win approval for a package, including a limited tax increase, which began to turn the tide on the public finances.

The post-war period also saw a trade recession, which, together with the demobilisation of troops, led to increased unemployment and widespread distress. Relief measures were introduced, such as support for loans for public works to be undertaken by local authorities, but they appear to have had limited impact as the state's administrative machinery was inadequate. Liverpool, in common with almost all mainstream politicians and economists of the time, believed there was a limited amount the state could do: as he argued in 1819: 'the evils inseparable from the state of things should not be charged on any government . . . by far the greater part of the miseries of which human nature complained were in all times and in all countries beyond the control of human legislation'.

The main problem was seen to be one of law and order. In an era where there were frequent fears among the propertied and professional classes about Jacobinism, there were plenty of conspiracy theories about secret societies and networks planning revolution. These fears were reinforced by a bungled attempt on the life of the Prince Regent in January 1817 as he opened Parliament. The response, via the suspension of habeas corpus, permitting summary arrest and detention, and the succeeding unrest, have subsequently been seen to define the Liverpool era, notably when the agitation and mass meetings in the summer of 1819 culminated in the suppression of the huge protest at St Peter's Fields in Manchester when a dozen were killed and hundreds injured in what has become known as the Peterloo Massacre. Liverpool and other ministers had reservations about the authorities' actions, but believed the magistrates were substantially right. His initial response was not to panic and not to recall Parliament. But his hand was forced when the issue was taken up by opposition leaders demanding an inquiry into what had happened in Manchester and reasserting the rights of public assembly. Liverpool then had to agree to the early return of Parliament and the government prepared what became known as the Six Acts dealing with big open-air public meetings, the banning of unauthorised military training and streamlining legal proceedings. These laws have subsequently been seen as draconian and repressive, but Liverpool was a voice of moderation and many of the government's supporters did not think the laws went far enough. In contrast to colleagues who invoked conspiracies, Liverpool said the measures were needed as a precaution. Recalling what he had seen in Paris in 1789, he argued that the best way of protecting liberty and the constitution was to put down the 'desperate conduct' of the few in order to protect 'the peaceable enjoyment of their rights' of the majority.

Any account of Liverpool's long premiership cannot ignore the challenges of dealing with the Prince Regent/George IV – as Wellington characteristically put it, the Royal Family was 'the damndest millstone around the neck of any government'. Placating, consulting and winning the approval of the monarch was time consuming, notably in the case of the Prince Regent over the adulterous behaviour of his estranged wife Caroline. The lengthy arguments over the royal divorce dominated public life in 1820–21, strained relations with the monarch, as George became in 1820, provided a cause for the parliamentary opposition and their allies to attack the government, and weakened the administration. The new monarch openly considered appointing a new prime minister, but, while being bruised and tired, Liverpool prevailed through patience, having a clear objective and being flexible tactically. So, despite widespread public support for her, Caroline was left a discredited figure, turned away at the door of Westminster Abbey at her husband's coronation, and without a royal residence or reinstatement in the liturgy of the Prayer Book, as she had sought.

The first two years of the new reign were also marked by an attempt on the life of the whole Cabinet (the Cato Street conspiracy of February 1820) and by the death of Liverpool's sickly wife Louisa in 1821. He remarried a close friend of his first wife in the following year. In 1822 came the suicide of Castlereagh, who had been the dominant figure in British foreign policy for a decade. He was replaced as Foreign Secretary by Canning, making one of his many comebacks.

Liverpool himself, though in his early fifties, was ageing and suffered from a bad leg. He was also seen as becoming increasingly testy and impatient. The leading historian of the period, Boyd Hilton, noted, in his authoritative *A Mad, Bad and Dangerous People?*:

'Nicknamed the "Grand Figitatis", Liverpool was mercurial, nervous, irritable, and even violent (at least with inanimate objects and when he thought no one was looking) . . . The calm competence which he contrived to display in public was more a question of tactics than of temperament.'

Yet the first half of the decade, until the financial crash of 1825–6 and later recession, was also a period of prosperity and improving public finances as well as an opportunity for economic and social reformers such as President of the Board of Trade William Huskisson and new Home Secretary Robert Peel. These laid the foundations for later social reforms in the early Victorian era. Liverpool understood the implications of the Industrial Revolution and specifically invoked the names of Watt, Boulton and Arkwright in a speech in the Lords. He was instinctively anti-Protectionist, but recognised that the complicated system of duties and tariffs could not be dismantled rapidly, not least because of the loss of tax revenue. But thanks to a combination of a series of parliamentary committee reports and ministerial initiatives, duties were reduced and trade opened up in order to make Britain the commercial hub of the world.

However, his final Cabinet after the reshuffles of 1821–2 was also noticeably more disunited than before. By 1826, ministers were arguing angrily with each other over economic policy and particularly Catholic emancipation. There was increased talk of Liverpool stepping down even before he suffered a cerebral haemorrhage in February 1827. He only partially recovered and had to resign two months later, living as an invalid until December 1828. The fractious Cabinet, which he had held together with increasing difficulty, then broke up, with half his senior ministers refusing to serve under his successor Canning, who himself died in August 1827. The political landscape then began to change dramatically, with Catholic emancipation coming in 1829 and the Reform Act in 1832. The political world that Liverpool had sought to maintain was no more.

Liverpool was not a great innovator in politics, though he was the first prime minister regularly to wear long trousers instead of knee breeches, and he was also the first to have a short haircut, as seen in the two fine Lawrence portraits of him. His personal legacy was limited to the naming of a major railway station in London and a road in Islington – though later generations should thank him most for his central role in providing the finance for the foundation of the National Gallery in 1824, authorising the expenditure of £57,000 for the purchase of thirty-eight pictures, still among the highlights of the collection, together with the lease of a house in Pall Mall.

Liverpool will never be seen as among the first rank of prime ministers. He manoeuvred around events and political pressures and was never able to dominate them. He did not seek to change the terms of the political debate. He counts rather among the influential, but nonetheless important, group of prime ministers who sought to be conciliators and to manage government efficiently and with integrity. He was always more than the passive chairman of Disraeli's dismissive jibe. He took a close interest in all matters facing his administrations. He once remarked that 'the first minister is necessarily the head of every department where important business is concerned'. And he showed his range in both his letters and his speeches in the Lords. There are parallels in his approach to politics with Baldwin in the 1920s and 1930s, and, more recently, with Callaghan and Major. For all their problems and failures, they were seen by contemporaries as sound managers of government business, unexciting perhaps, but committed to the public good.

Peter Riddell is the Commissioner for Public Appointments and was a political journalist and commentator for the Financial Times *and* Times.

19

George Canning

12 April 1827 to 8 August 1827
Tory/Whig coalition

By Theo Barclay

Full name: George Canning
Born: 11 April 1770, Marylebone, London
Died: 8 August 1827, buried at Westminster Abbey
Education: Eton; Christ Church, Oxford
Married to Joan Scott; 3 sons, 1 daughter
Quotation: 'The happiness of constant occupation is infinite.'

CUT SHORT BY his untimely death, George Canning's 119-day stint as prime minister stands as the shortest in British history. He was nonetheless granted the rare honour of a statue in Parliament Square, a privilege given to three other prime ministers: Disraeli, Lloyd George and Churchill. His presence in that company is a deserving tribute to his rise from humble beginnings, his extraordinary political talents, and to what might have been had he survived.

Canning was born in 1770 to Irish parents. His father was a penniless wine-seller who had abandoned his young family and was dead before his son was two years old. His desperate mother was forced to make ends meet by taking acting jobs in provincial theatres, bringing the infant George with her while lodging in boarding rooms across England.

During his political career Canning was often mocked for those lowly beginnings. Even when he was on the cusp of becoming prime minister, the leading Whig Lord Grey remarked that 'the son of an actress is, *ipso facto*, disqualified from becoming Prime Minister'.

Canning showed unusual intelligence from an early age, prompting family friends to persuade his newly wealthy uncle, the merchant Stratford Canning, to take charge of his upbringing. He was taken from his mother and raised with his cousins in relative comfort.

As a twelve-year-old boy, Canning arrived at Eton College as an outsider. Uncomfortable at the school, he struck his contemporaries as an isolated character and did not play games with them. Nonetheless, his teachers identified him as a talented classicist, skilled actor and ingenious debater.

His ambition was to pursue the career in politics for which his time at Oxford was invaluable training. He founded his own political discussion club, with members including the future Lord Liverpool, who, as prime minister, Canning would later serve as Foreign Secretary.

Throughout his time at university Canning was a staunch Whig. But full-time Whig politics was dominated by members of the landed aristocracy in league with rich industrialists; there was no room for a man of Canning's lowly origins, who had no steady income.

It was a combination of ideological drift and opportunism that caused Canning to become a Tory shortly after leaving Oxford. The French Revolution in 1789 split the Whigs between radicals who supported revolution, and liberals who were frightened that republican zeal would spread to Britain.

Canning concluded that his politics were far closer to those of the Prime Minister, William Pitt, than of his former Whig friends and that his talents were more likely to find favour with the Tories.

Having secured an introduction to the Prime Minister, Canning was soon established as Pitt's protégé and set about finding a parliamentary seat. With Pitt's support, by 1793 he had been elected to the rotten borough of Newtown in the Isle of Wight, and within the year he had been granted the honour of seconding the Address to the Throne.

Canning's eloquent parliamentary contributions focused on foreign policy. He became one of the most outspoken defenders of the government's approach to the war with France, using entertaining and witty speeches to focus attention on how much worse the crisis would be if the opposition were handling it. His caustic wit and unmatched oratory stood him apart from his peers. It was said that his rhetoric could 'lash the hind of a rhinoceros'.

The young MP swiftly developed an identifiable political position around which others could gather. Although anti-revolutionary and disdainful of extremism, Canning defied traditional High Tories by emphasising the moral imperative of addressing slavery and taking a liberal stance on Catholic emancipation. His beliefs were underpinned by a distaste for inherited privilege that was the product of prejudice he had suffered as a result of his own upbringing.

He was also happy in his personal life, having married the heiress Joan Scott in 1800 – a union that appears to have been born of genuine love. Pitt was a witness at the wedding and the pair's second child, William Pitt Canning, was named after him.

In 1801 Pitt resigned as prime minister due to the King's opposition to Catholic emancipation. Despite Pitt advising him to stay in office, Canning loyally followed his mentor into opposition. The following day, he wrote: 'I resign because Pitt resigns. And that is all.'

After four years on the back benches, Canning was brought back into government in a more junior role. He had to wait until 1807 to make his full return to front-line politics, entering the Cabinet as Foreign Secretary in the Duke of Portland's administration. He was in his element as Foreign Secretary, mastering complex diplomacy with insight and flair. His greatest triumph was arranging the confiscation of the Danish fleet at Copenhagen in September 1807, thwarting Napoleon's expansionary plans.

Canning's first stint as Foreign Secretary was defined, however, by his feud with his fellow Anglo-Irishman, Cabinet minister

Viscount Castlereagh, the Secretary of State for War. Canning and Castlereagh argued furiously over where to deploy Britain's troops, paralysing government policy. The ailing Prime Minister found himself powerless to stop the infighting.

Eventually Canning called for Castlereagh to be sacked, prompting his rival to challenge him to a duel. With characteristic impetuousness, Canning accepted.

The rivals met at 6 a.m. on 21 September 1809 on Putney Heath. Canning had never fired a pistol before, but refused to back down. The first shots both missed, but on the second attempt, Castlereagh, an expert marksman, hit Canning in the 'fleshy part' of his left thigh, passing straight through his leg. Remarkably, he made a full recovery in a matter of weeks.

A month later, the Prime Minister stepped down due to ill-health. Canning immediately offered himself to King George III as a replacement. His advances were rejected, largely as a consequence of the negative publicity caused by the duel, and the Chancellor of the Exchequer Spencer Perceval was selected instead. Canning left the government again, this time prepared for a long period in exile.

When Perceval was assassinated three years later, Lord Liverpool took over as prime minister. He asked his old university friend Canning to return to his previous role as Foreign Secretary. Spying the chance to build a power base at the apex of government, Canning demanded the additional position of Leader of the House of Commons. When Liverpool refused to cede so much power to one man, Canning elected to remain on the back benches, leaving the role of Foreign Secretary to his rival Castlereagh. This meant that it was Castlereagh, not the more talented Canning, who led Britain's delegation to the era-defining Congress of Vienna in 1814.

Canning returned to favour in 1822 when Castlereagh descended into depression and took his own life. He took back his former position as Foreign Secretary and, as he had demanded ten years before, was given the additional role of Leader of the House of Commons. Over the next five years he prevented South America from falling into French hands, promoted Greece's independence from Turkey, set up trade routes with new Central and South American republics, and signed the Anglo-Dutch treaty that set the current borders of Singapore, Malaysia and Indonesia.

When in April 1827 Lord Liverpool suffered a stroke and resigned after fifteen years in office, Canning was an obvious candidate to replace him. Gladly accepting the position from King George IV, he also handed himself the role of Chancellor of the Exchequer, centralising power and planning to dominate government policy.

The 'High Tories' like the Duke of Wellington and Sir Robert Peel were disgusted by Canning's liberal views, Whiggish sympathies and humble origins. They refused to work with him, splitting the party between the 'Ultras' and the 'Canningites'.

In a daring riposte to those internal critics, Canning invited a team of Whigs to join the Cabinet, forming a coalition government of liberals that cut across the extremes of both parties and foreshadowed the Liberal Party that would emerge decades later.

The stage was set for Canningites and their coalition partners to transform British politics and, perhaps, to reshape the Tories in their image.

But it was not to be. Canning's health had been in slow decline since early 1827, and, by July – only three months after his appointment as prime minister – he was too ill to continue in office. He died of pneumonia on 8 August 1827.

Just after his death the *Annual Register* published the following opinion of Canning, which stands the test of time:

Europe lost in him the ablest statesman, and the Commons of England the finest orator of his day . . . As a practical statesman, his views were always clear and manly. He was the most unyielding opponent of all the schemes which, for more than thirty years, had thrown the world into confusion under the name of reform: and he had done his country much good service in maintaining the integrity of her existing institutions . . . The later acts of his public life, before he became Prime Minister, had, in an equal manner, strengthened his hold on the admiration and favour of his country.

Theo Barclay is a barrister at Hailsham Chambers and is the author of Fighters and Quitters: Great Political Resignations.

20

Viscount Goderich

31 August 1827 to 8 January 1828
Tory/Whig coalition

By Gordon Pentland

Full name: Frederick John Robinson, 1st Viscount Goderich
and 1st Earl of Ripon
Born: 1 November 1782, Newby Hall
Died: 28 January 1859, Putney Heath, London. Buried at
Nocton, Lincolnshire
Education: Harrow; St John's College, Cambridge
Married to Sarah Albinia Louisa Hobart; 2 sons, 1 daughter
Quotation: 'There was no one good in this life that had not
with it some concomitant evil.'

IN POLITICAL LIFE any nickname framed around an evasive and
changeable quality is apt to become something of a hostage to
fortune. So it was for Frederick 'Prosperity' Robinson, who forged

a reputation as a pioneer of free trade as President of the Board of Trade and Chancellor of the Exchequer before embracing the unenviable task, as prime minister, of trying to hold together the fissile materials of Canning's ministry and stay on the right side of an increasingly irritable monarch. Viscount Goderich (as Robinson had then become) was not up to the task and so to this day bears the dubious distinction of being the only prime minister to have begun and ended his tenure without having to face Parliament. He also earned the right to a Disraeli barb, dismissed as a 'transient and embarrassed phantom'.

Though not as prime minister, in other regards Goderich was a great political survivor. Between joining Lord Liverpool's ministry in 1818 and exiting with Peel's in 1846, he was a member of every government except those of Wellington and Melbourne. Some biographers have shrewdly pinned both features of his career – the longevity as a minister and the brevity as prime minister – on a single character trait. 'Goody' Goderich was simply too nice.

Robinson was born in 1782 at Newby Hall in Yorkshire, the second son of a diplomat father and a mother from the Yorke family, Earls of Hardwicke. The hand he was dealt at birth ensured two things. As a second son, bereft of an independent fortune until 1830, Robinson would have to find some place in the world. As a member of the elite of the elite, his connections would smooth his path to doing so.

The accident of birth also provided him with what appears to have been a generally happy upbringing. Though his father died when he was three years old, Robinson's doting and supportive mother nurtured the quiet but unflashy intelligence that distinguished his time at Harrow and Cambridge. It won him, at the latter, the prize for the best Latin ode, a patriotic celebration of the conquest of Malta by Nelson. He remained a poet, and an admirer of Coleridge in particular, for the remainder of his life, becoming President of the Royal Society of Literature in 1835.

Any literary ambitions he might have had took a back seat to the need to forge a career for himself. The 3rd Earl of Hardwicke (his mother's cousin) gave him an easy entrée, taking him on as private secretary during his time as Lord Lieutenant of Ireland and arranging for a parliamentary seat through the tried-and-tested means of a close Irish borough, Carlow, which boasted thirteen electors. He promptly switched this for a close Yorkshire borough, Ripon, whose electorate was at least ten times the size of Carlow's and whose representation was determined by a pair of sisters who his mother claimed as kin.

The beginning, highpoint, and end of his political career were all marked periods of political realignment. He entered Parliament in 1806, a year that witnessed the deaths of two era-defining political colossuses, Pitt and Fox. This fluid situation presented opportunities that suited Robinson well. First, his broadly Pittite politics put him somewhere in the squidgy middle of the contemporary spectrum, well placed to offer support to a variety of ministries. He was also busily storing up political capital for the future, socialising with a group of other up-and-coming Pittites (which included Peel, Palmerston and Croker) at the Alfred Club. Second, he carried forward his patriotic credentials from Cambridge, penning a pamphlet in support of the Peninsular campaign in 1810 and making a well-received speech in 1812 advocating an offensive 'war of hope'. Third, and most importantly, he quickly made powerful friends, most notably Lord Castlereagh, whose protégé he became in 1809. Thereafter, his political fortune rose alongside that of his chief, and in 1814 he had the foresight to marry Sarah Albinia Louisa, heir to the 4th Earl of Buckinghamshire, a friend and kinsman of Castlereagh.

The relationship with the older statesman was not without its challenges. Castlereagh was both Foreign Secretary and Leader of the Commons. The continental touring required of the first post meant it fell to Robinson to present and support one of the most infamously unpopular pieces of nineteenth-century legislation, the 1815 Corn Law. Though he had been involved, through his position at the Board of Trade, in framing the legislation, it was not a task Robinson, whose instincts were for liberalisation, relished. He strained to present it as a pragmatic measure, a choice between two evils, but speaking for it identified him as its sponsor and the London mob took its revenge. His London home was attacked on subsequent nights and he moved his frantic and pregnant wife to his father-in-law's. Soldiers drafted in to keep order killed two of the crowd, circumstances that prompted a serious debate in the Commons, during which Robinson tearfully related his experiences (a defining moment, in tandem with later tears, in the creation of another nickname: Robinson 'the Blubberer').

Such political service was not, however, readily or easily forgotten. Despite a growing reputation in some quarters for indolence and nerviness, Castlereagh ensured Robinson's elevation to the Cabinet in 1818 as President of the Board of Trade. In that post he entrenched his credentials, whether deserved or not, as a powerful advocate of free trade, most notably by dismantling the navigation laws that had been the hallmark of 'protection' of Britain's global trade. He thus stood – along with Canning, Huskisson and others – as a herald of the kind of 'liberal Toryism' that would mark the second half of Liverpool's long premiership.

Castlereagh was inadvertently and tragically of service one final time in 1822, when his suicide prompted a substantial Cabinet reshuffle. This allowed Liverpool to bump the unpopular Baron Vansittart – 'the real blot and sin of the government' according to Huskisson – from the Exchequer and elevate Robinson. There was good fortune involved here. 'Van' had endured an atrocious hand during his time as Chancellor, administering the economy at the end of a long and expensive global war and during the painful transition to peace. Robinson inherited an economy energetically breaking free of these restraints. And he made the most of it in what were undoubtedly the most successful years of his career. He set the tone in his first Budget speech in February 1823, striking an optimistic 'you've never had it so good' note with a quote from Addison's *Cato*: 'The wide, the unbounded prospect lies before me [. . .] We have seen the opening of a brilliant dawn, and we may anticipate without hesitation the steady and glowing splendour of a meridian sky.'

It was the first of three Budgets that triumphantly removed or reduced taxes (many of them legacies of war finance), gloried in apparently endlessly increasing domestic consumption, and psychologically marked Britain's emergence from the difficult post-war years. Robinson attracted widespread praise for his management of the economy in these years.

But while he made hay in the boom, Robinson was unfortunate enough to still be in post for the bust. It came in 1825 when the frantic speculation and easy credit abruptly ended in the summer. By Christmas, bank and business failures and accelerating depression provided a very different canvas for Robinson's chancellorship. He was not well suited to such moments of crisis. The Bank of England survived, issuing notes and gold, despite rather than because of any guidance from the Exchequer. When a more sober Robinson met Parliament in February and boldly declared, 'I am not afraid or ashamed to use the word "prosperous"', he provided a much richer target for Hume and the political economists. The 'Prosperity' of Robinson's nickname gained its second edge.

Other headwinds made for a more challenging politics at this point. The issue of civil liberties for Catholics – a deep but relatively subterranean division within Liverpool's governments – was dramatically and destructively brought into the open by the insurgent Catholic Association and its charismatic leadership. The sort of liberalising economic policies advocated by Robinson and others, eventually reached far enough (especially with efforts to liberalise the Corn Law that Robinson had so uneasily introduced) to provoke organised reaction from the older, illiberal, parts of the Tory Party. Lord Liverpool's great achievement had been keeping together a ministry composed of such materials. When a serious stroke took him out of the game in early 1827, and his more divisive successor, Canning, died in August, the Whig–Tory coalition he had fabricated badly needed leadership that could fuse together, or at least paper over, the different competing factions.

In some ways, Robinson, ennobled by Canning as Viscount Goderich and leading the government in the Lords, seemed the right man for the job. He was well liked and widely respected, and had not been the kind of political streetfighter who had marked his card with any of the powerful personalities on which a viable ministry might be built. He had long been in favour of Catholic claims, but not in such a way or so vociferously as to make himself generally obnoxious to the 'Protestant' Tories or the prejudices of George IV. Indeed, it was no small feat in itself to tiptoe around the combustible materials Canning had left behind and the demands of an increasingly gouty and irascible monarch to reconstruct a ministry that even *looked* to be remotely sustainable. Goderich did so.

Nonetheless, an amiable chairman was not well fitted to the political moment, and Goderich was overwhelmed by stronger personalities and the increasing political trenchancy of the dawning age of reform. Troubles beset him on the domestic front as well, his 'all but crazy wife' being a general topic of discussion among Cabinet ministers. Resignations and recriminations ensured that the ministry was dead by January 1828, before Parliament had met. Goderich, unaware that he had resigned, was informed of the fact by George IV, who apparently handed him a handkerchief to soak up the inevitable waterworks. A long ministerial career and an earldom were still to come, but Goderich's overall reputation as prime minister has suffered, especially because of the very different estimation of the character and personality of his immediate successor Wellington. The 'Tearful Sisyphus' gave way to the 'Iron Duke'.

Gordon Pentland is professor of political history at the University of Edinburgh.

21

Duke of Wellington

9 January 1828 to 16 November 1830;
17 November 1834 to 9 December 1834
Tory

By Jacqueline Reiter

Full name: Arthur Wellesley, 1st Duke of Wellington
Born: 1 May 1769, 6 Merrion Street, Dublin
Died: 14 September 1852, Walmer Castle, Kent. Buried at St Paul's Cathedral
Education: Eton
Married to Hon. Catherine 'Kitty' Pakenham; 2 sons
Quotation: 'Nothing except a battle lost can be half so melancholy as a battle won.'

FEW PRIME MINISTERS have arrived at No. 10 with as much standing as the Duke of Wellington. As the man who defeated Napoleon at Waterloo, he was an international celebrity – 'every one knew him by sight . . . the conqueror of conquerors'. He held honours from nine different countries. His name was commemorated in countless different ways: as an item of clothing (the Wellington boot); as a tree (the *Wellingtonia*, a giant redwood); as a public school; as the capital of New Zealand.

Wellington was Britain's second prime minister to have been a soldier (the Earl of Shelburne was the first), and this has strongly coloured narratives of his government. After his first Cabinet as premier he supposedly said (but almost certainly didn't), 'An extraordinary affair. I gave them their orders and they wanted to stay and discuss them!' But Wellington never wanted to run his government like an army: he simply wished to maintain 'the prerogatives of the Crown, the rights and privileges of the Church and its union with the state' – in other words, to be a steady, calming influence through the difficult conditions of the late 1820s, when party identities and international conditions were in flux. Unfortunately, his government never appeared quite in command of the political agenda and eventually fell victim to its own weakness.

The Viscount, Earl, Marquess, and Duke of Wellington was born the Hon. Arthur Wesley in Dublin in 1769, third surviving son of the 1st Earl of Mornington. An unpromising child, his mother concluded he was 'food for powder and nothing more'. In 1787, Arthur obtained an ensign's commission and a post as aide-de-camp to the Lord Lieutenant of Ireland. There followed a rapid series of purchases and exchanges so that, by 1793, the twenty-four-year-old was a lieutenant colonel. War with France gave Arthur Wellesley, as he spelled his name from 1798, a chance to prove he was more than just 'food for powder'. His big break came in India at Seringapatam and Assaye; by the time Wellesley returned to Britain in 1805, he was a rising military star.

From 1808 Wellesley commanded a British force sent to help liberate Spain and Portugal from French domination. He demonstrated the ability to fight and the imperative to preserve his troops, along with an extraordinary grasp of logistical detail that complemented his strategic and tactical genius. Victories – and honours – followed fast. In 1809 he became Viscount Wellington; in 1812 he became first an earl, then a marquess. In October 1813, at roughly the time Napoleon was being crushed at Leipzig, Wellington crossed the Pyrenees into France. Following Napoleon's abdication, Wellington climbed the final rung of the peerage ladder and became a duke. He was appointed ambassador to France and briefly represented Britain at the Congress of Vienna, where the major powers were rearranging the post-war map of Europe. Here, in 1815, he learned that Napoleon had escaped from the island of Elba.

Napoleon's unexpected arrival near Brussels took Wellington, in command of the Allied army, by surprise. He later described the battle that followed near Waterloo as 'the nearest-run thing you ever saw in your life'. It was also the moment Wellington graduated from hero to almost mythical figure. Being a celebrity naturally affected the way he viewed himself in relation to others: 'I am the Duke of Wellington, and *bon gré mal gré*, must do as the Duke of Wellington doth.'

In 1818 Wellington accepted the post of Master General of the Ordnance in Lord Liverpool's Tory Cabinet. Liverpool had been Prime Minister since 1812, keeping the peace among his heterogeneous following through compromise and canny statesmanship. This appearance of harmony concealed growing ideological divisions between 'Liberals' – anti-oligarchy, pro-public opinion, pro-liberty – and 'Ultra' Tories emphasising the aristocratic, Anglican, property-based nature of Britain's polity. Wellington was somewhere in the middle, his conservatism tempered by a refusal to conform to labels: 'We hear a great deal of Whig principles, and Tory principles, and Liberal principles . . . but . . . this country was never governed in practice according to the extreme principles of any party whatever.'

Cracks in Liverpool's Tory hegemony appeared after George Canning became Foreign Secretary in 1822. Canning, a brilliant but divisive figure, soon alienated most of his colleagues, including Wellington. When Liverpool suffered a stroke in 1827 and Canning became prime minister, Wellington and five Cabinet colleagues resigned (followed by thirty-six junior ministers). Wellington defended his actions by claiming he was a soldier, not a politician, and ruled out becoming prime minister himself: 'I should have been worse than mad if I had thought of such a thing.' Within three months, however, Canning was dead, in Rory Muir's brilliant phrase, 'leaving the eggs broken but the omelette unmade'. The successor government under Lord Goderich lasted only six months, and on 9 January 1828, the Duke of Wellington did indeed become prime minister.

Wellington wanted to reconstruct the Liverpool consensus of the 1810s and 1820s. On that basis, William Huskisson, leader of Canning's following, remained in office, along with three colleagues; other government members fell at various points along the Tory scale. Probably Wellington's most talented recruit was Home Secretary Sir Robert Peel; but, despite Wellington's best efforts at conciliation, the Cabinet's key feature was its discordance (the Lord Privy Seal described his colleagues interacting with 'the courtesy . . . of men who had just fought a duel').

Ironically, Wellington's government is best remembered for repealing the Test and Corporation Acts excluding non-Anglicans from civil and military office and passing Catholic emancipation. Few among the ruling class doubted that the relationship between Church and State was fundamental to British liberties. Industriali-sation, however, spurred the rise of a prosperous, non-Anglican class of influential men who were barred from full political participation. The incorporation of Ireland following the 1801 Anglo-Irish Union also introduced a large Catholic population. Faced with these re-alities, many believed that allowing non-Anglicans full citizenship was vital to preserve the status quo.

Although reluctant to break up the Anglican settlement, Wel-lington knew he would have to face it eventually; but in February 1828 the Whigs forced his hand by introducing a Test and Corporation Acts repeal bill that reached the House of Lords. There seemed no reason to split the new government and force a consti-tutional crisis, so Wellington and Peel brokered a deal with the Anglican Church to secure the bill's passage in suitably amended form. Many, however, interpreted this sensible compromise as tacit acknowledgement that Wellington was not in control. More seri-ously, it revealed deep divisions within Wellington's political support. The Tory Ultras had hoped Wellington would stand as firm in defence of the Anglican settlement as he had against Napoleon; many now turned against him. This was particularly significant because Wellington's fragile alliance with the Canningites had finally broken down. Several of the men brought in to replace Huskisson's following had served with Wellington in Spain, which allowed the Whigs to claim he was trying to govern by military despotism (an accusation exacerbated by the 1829 London Metropolitan Police Bill establishing the capital's first official police force). Wellington now had to fend off the Whigs, the Tory Ultras, *and* the Canningites, even as his government faced the next big issue: Catholic emancipation, the logical sequel to the Test and Corporation Acts repeal.

The shock victory of Daniel O'Connell – who, as a Catholic, could not sit in Parliament – in the 1828 County Clare by-election opened sectarian wounds and pushed emancipation to the top of the agenda. This time Wellington was determined his government would not wait for the opposition to introduce such a vital measure, but there were problems. Without the Canningites, the government was more markedly 'Protestant' – particularly Peel, who now threatened resignation. Given that Peel was the government's most talented orator, his departure would leave Wellington exposed in the Commons. 'I do not see the smallest chance of getting out of these difficulties if you should not continue in office,' Wellington begged him. Eventually Peel relented, but George IV remained recalcitrant, his resolve stiffened by his Ultra brother, the Duke of Cumberland. In Ireland, the indiscretions of the pro-emancipation Lord Lieutenant, Lord Anglesey, worsened an already volatile situation. None of this made Wellington appear in control.

Naturally, the Ultras were appalled. Wellington reminded the bill's opponents that Ireland was in turmoil: 'If I could avoid, by any sacrifice whatever, even one month of civil war in the country to which I am attached, I would sacrifice my life in order to do it.' But as the bitter fight continued, Wellington's temper frayed. On 16 March 1829, the Ultra Lord Winchilsea accused Wellington of acting 'under the cloak of some outward zeal for the Protestant religion [to] carry on his insidious designs, for the infringement of our liberties, and the introduction of Popery into every department of state'. These intemperate words caused the two men to meet at Battersea Fields on 21 March (Winchilsea fired in the air; Wellington missed) – the last time a serving prime minister fought a duel.

Catholic emancipation became law on 13 April 1829. The most immediate effect of the measure was to tear Wellington's Tory Party apart. Many Ultras were so incensed they began to believe a truly representative Parliament would never have passed such an Act. When, therefore, the Whigs pushed for parliamentary reform, many Ultras supported them.

Reform and the economic problems that paved the way for it were the last straw for Wellington's beleaguered government. A financial depression in 1829 caused widespread agricultural rioting. These 'Swing Riots' were alarmingly reminiscent of the run-up to the 1789 French Revolution – a parallel sharpened by France's July Revolution of 1830, driving Charles X into British exile. Wellington's reaction to the crisis did little to inspire confidence. He reduced government spending and cut taxes, but insisted distress was only 'partial', which made him seem callous and out of touch.

A General Election had to take place in summer 1830 following William IV's accession to the throne. Wellington's government lost considerable support in the county constituencies, which reflected the opinions of landed property – the government's base. Wellington knew he would not survive another controversy, but there was now little chance of escaping parliamentary reform. Talks with the Canningites came to nothing, and when Parliament reassembled on 2 November 1830, Wellington immediately faced the issue he had hoped to avoid. His defiant boast that the British legislature 'possess[ed] the full and entire confidence of the country' was startlingly ill-advised; it fuelled pro-reform rioting in London and caused Wellington to cancel his appearance at the Lord Mayor's banquet on 9 November (apparently confirming his total loss of authority). A week later, a minor opposition motion on the civil list passed by twenty-nine votes. This was so unexpected that Wellington did not believe it, expressing disappointment at what he thought was a tiny majority: 'What, *no more*! I don't understand it. There must be some mistake.' Faced with reality, however, Wellington admitted defeat and resigned. It was the first time a government had been brought down by a Commons vote since Lord Shelburne's resignation in 1783.

Wellington truly believed reform would lead to the collapse of the constitution; it was the one issue on which he was not prepared to compromise. When Grey's Reform Act passed in 1832, Wellington was categorical: 'The government of England is destroyed.' To his credit, however, he did not despair and adapted to the new political conditions. Within a decade Wellington had helped heal the breach with the Ultras, strengthened Tory ties with the King, and assisted his party in surviving the realities of post-1832 politics. In 1834 he technically served again as prime minister, holding Peel's seat warm until his return from Italy, when Wellington himself became Foreign Secretary. Over the next two decades Wellington's reputation as a safe pair of hands was restored; he was again the hero of Waterloo rather than the man who nailed his reactionary colours so firmly to the mast he brought his own ministry down. But he was getting older. His hearing deteriorated, and in the early 1840s he suffered a series of strokes. Although he served in Peel's 1841 government as minister without portfolio, he did not hold office again after 1846. Still, he remained a celebrity. When he died in 1852, contemporaries likened it to the passing of an era: 'We all felt as if we lived, now he was dead, in a different England.'

In the last assessment, Wellington was not one of the most successful prime ministers. Many considered him a great man whose gifts lay in another field; others thought him an old soldier too thoroughly set in his ways. To some extent Wellington himself courted this: 'I am *Nimmukwallah*, as we say in the East; that is, I have eat[en] of the King's salt, and, therefore, I conceive it to be my duty to serve . . . when and wherever the King or his government may think proper to employ me.' As Rory Muir notes, however, this represented what Wellington *wanted* to be rather than what he actually *was*. Recent historians stress his ability to back down, negotiate and listen, essential qualities in the treacherous political waters of the 1820s. Although Wellington presided over a significant dismantling of the old order (the repeal of the Test and Corporation Acts and Catholic emancipation), this was not a sign of commitment to change. Rather, it showed Wellington's ability to read a battlefield, remain flexible, and occasionally steal a march on his opponent – useful assets in politics, as in war.

Jacqueline Reiter is a historian of the eighteenth and early nineteenth centuries and is the author of The Late Lord: The Life of John Pitt, 2nd Earl of Chatham.

22

Earl Grey

22 November 1830 to 9 July 1834
Whig

By Gerry Hassan

Full name: Charles Grey
Born: 13 March 1764, Falloden, Northumberland
Died: 17 July 1845, Howick Hall, Northumberland. Buried at Howick Hall
Education: Eton; Trinity College, Cambridge
Married to Mary Elizabeth Ponsonby; 10 sons, 7 daughters
Quotation: 'No man can subscribe more cordially than I do to the maxim that in government practical good is infinitely preferable to speculative perfection.'

CHARLES GREY, 2ND Earl Grey, is one of the great names of nineteenth-century British politics; a prime minister remembered for his deeds and immortalised via a blend of tea.

He was one of the leading figures of the Whigs for over thirty years, leader of the Whig Party for an astounding twenty-seven years – leading them in opposition for twenty-three of those, and became prime minister in November 1830 at the age of sixty-six. He then presided over an administration that began the slow march towards the British democracy we know today, the creation of Victorian liberalism and the nineteenth-century electoral dominance of the Liberal Party.

Grey's career is most remembered for the four years he spent as prime minister, but the nature of his calling to office was marked. As prime-ministerial chronicler Andrew Gimson observed, his arrival in office in his mid-sixties after decades in opposition was unparalleled: 'To find a comparable comeback from the wilderness, one has to turn to Churchill, who became Prime Minister in 1940 at the age of sixty-five to save Britain from invasion.'

Grey is a transitional figure who oversaw the shift from politics run by aristocrats to the fledgling beginnings of a politics that took more account of, first, upper-middle-class sentiment, then the wider middle classes, contributing to the creation of more formal party politics.

In style, demeanour and background he came from the former age, his leadership widely seen then and since as arrogant, aloof, 'cold and shadowy', and in his long period of opposition as simply not present. Despite this, when crisis arose he showed genuine leadership qualities, which led historian T.B. Macaulay to state he was 'the sole representative of a great age which has passed away'.

Charles Grey was born to a landed family; his father, Charles Grey, a general, and his mother, Elizabeth Grey, daughter of George Grey of Southwick. Educated at Marylebone, then Eton, he spent three years at Cambridge, where he failed to complete his degree – not unusual at the time. He became a student at Middle Temple in 1783 and the following year embarked upon a Grand Tour of Europe, which included visiting the cultural highlights of Italy.

On 18 November 1794, aged thirty, Grey married Mary Elizabeth Ponsonby. This brought Grey fully into the 'Whig cousinhood' of which the Ponsonby family were a part, with the marriage producing sixteen children (with another child born to Georgiana Cavendish in an affair before his marriage) – the most children of any UK prime minister.

Grey was first elected to the Commons at the age of twenty-two in September 1786 when a vacancy occurred in Northumberland. The main political issue of the times was soon to be the French Revolution of 1789, the resulting Napoleonic Wars, and pressure and expectations in the UK for reform. The country's political arrangements had barely altered since the 'Glorious Revolution' of 1688 and the union between England and Scotland in 1707, and had grown ossified and anachronistic in an increasingly capitalist country with a rising middle class.

Despite this, many in the ruling elites saw any concession to reform as tantamount to encouraging revolution and sedition, while an emerging movement of political unions was attracted to republicanism and the ideas of Tom Paine's *The Rights of Man*. Between these two currents, in 1792 Grey became a founding supporter of the Society of the Friends of the People – a Whig group advocating for reform – a move seen by many fellow parliamentarians, such was their conservatism, as far too radical and daring.

In February 1806, following the death of William Pitt the Younger, a new government was formed known as 'the Ministry of All the Talents' – a loose coalition led by William Grenville in which Grey served as First Lord of the Admiralty in the year after Trafalgar. He then became Foreign Secretary and Leader of the House of Commons in September 1806 before the government fell the following March due to disagreements over Catholic emancipation.

In 1807, following the death of Charles James Fox, Grey became the leader of the Whigs, a post he had to undertake from the Lords following the death of his father, the 1st Earl Grey in November of that year. This resulted in what he had always feared and knew he could not avoid – being forced to the second chamber at a relatively early age. He showed his displeasure at this turn of events in a letter to his wife after his first speech in the Lords in January 1808: 'What a place to speak in! with just light enough to make darkness visible, it was like speaking in a vault by the glimmering light of a sepulchral lamp to the dead. It is impossible I should ever do anything there worth thinking of.'

How wrong Grey's judgement eventually turned out to be. In

the long years of Whig opposition and Tory government there was a gathering climate of authoritarianism and suppression of due process, which did not aid the cause of reform – parliamentary or social. Twice, Grey advocated for widening the electoral franchise from the Lords, only to be empathically defeated. Similarly, any route back to power was blocked for as long as George IV remained on the throne, as he held a personal dislike of Grey and refused to countenance him as a minister.

All of this changed in the summer of 1830. The King died in June, and this event was followed by the Paris revolution in July, while Belgium emerged from Dutch rule with its independence subsequently guaranteed by Britain – a move that would have momentous consequences at the outset of the First World War.

There then followed the 1830 General Election, after which Grey again made the case for reform, while the Tory leader, the Duke of Wellington, made the case that the British constitution in its current arrangements could not be improved. This led to the Duke's administration being defeated in a vote on the civil list, and on 22 November 1830 Grey was appointed prime minister by William IV.

Nine of the thirteen members of Grey's Cabinet were Lords – alongside an Irish peer, the heir to a peerage and a baronet. This was, in Grey's words, government by the upper class: 'I admit that I should select the aristocrat, for that class is a guarantee for the safety of the state and of the throne.' However, his mission was to bring about reform.

The first English Reform Bill was presented to the Commons on 1 March 1831 (there being separate Scottish and Irish legislation). It proposed the enfranchisement of major industrial towns and cities, and the expansion of the electorate. This was cautious reform, yet met with furious opposition from Tories, with the bill only passing in the Commons by a single vote on 22 March.

Seeing parliamentary storms ahead, Grey requested a dissolution, which the King refused, but after an opposition wrecking amendment was passed on 20 April – by 299 to 291 – Grey resigned from office and called an election.

The 1831 election became a single-issue election – for or against reform. The result was a sweeping Whig victory and majority, with 370 seats to the Tories' 235. A second Reform Bill was introduced, which passed easily through the Commons but was opposed in the Lords. Despite a powerful intervention by Grey, in a passionate debate on 8 October, the peers voted down the bill by forty-one votes.

The Cabinet made amendments and introduced the third Reform Bill, which passed through the Commons, but again hit trouble in the Lords. Grey knew that to get it through he would have to threaten to create many new peers to overcome resistance, while those opposed to change knew that the King was resistant to such action.

On 14 April 1832, the Lords passed the second reading by nine votes, a portent of difficulties to come, and on 7 May a wrecking amendment was carried in the second house by thirty-five votes. The next day, the Cabinet agreed to support the creation of new peers, which led to Grey briefly resigning, Wellington trying and failing to form an administration, and then Grey returning as prime minister.

There subsequently followed the breakneck passing of the third Reform Bill, with Wellington withdrawing his supporters from opposition to allow the bill to pass smoothly, judging it better to retain his support and strength in the Lords for another day. Royal assent was given on 7 June 1832 to the English Act (with Scotland and Ireland following shortly afterwards).

Grey's tenacity, refusal to back down, combined with his tactical agility, all contributed to the passing of the Great Reform Act (actually three separate Acts – for England and Wales; Scotland; and Ireland) – a milestone in the history and politics of Britain. He held to a carefully considered moderate but principled position while surrounded by crisis, pressure and political unrest, as well as by those wanting no change and more radical currents pushing for far-reaching reform.

The 1832 election was fought against the backdrop of reform and the expansion of the electorate into the middle classes, resulting in an emphatic Whig victory – with 441 Whigs returned to 175 Tories.

Grey's administration had other achievements – the abolition of slavery in the British Empire in 1833, alongside the 1833 Factory Act, which restricted child labour. But not all was enlightenment, and the 1834 Poor Law Amendment Act created a brutal workhouse system of poor relief for England and Wales, Scotland following in 1845, which became one of the most shameful aspects of nineteenth-century Britain. Few remember this was initiated by Earl Grey's government – reaching the statute book the month after he resigned as prime minister.

As with any administration, Ireland proved divisive (over Irish tithes in relation to the Church) and Grey did not feel he had the wherewithal to address Cabinet disagreements. On 9 July 1834, at the age of seventy, he resigned as prime minister and never played an active part in politics again – dying aged eighty-one in Howick, Northumberland, in July 1845. He stated on his last day in office:

> I leave the government with the satisfaction, at least, that in having used my best endeavours to carry into effect those measures of reform that the country required, I have not shrunk from any obstacles, nor from meeting and grappling with the many difficulties that I have encountered in the performance of my duty.

Making Charles Grey human and 'relatable' in the modern age is complex, as with many politicians from a very different age. Grey had many qualities and strengths, as well as shortcomings. He was a powerful, convincing orator who could command the attention of the Commons or Lords, and exude authority. He was someone who could chart a course and keep to it through storms and difficulties, and work in a collegiate way shaping and leading a broad spectrum of parliamentary opinion.

His biographer E.A. Smith offered this judgement:

> He was a man of principle and integrity, though not always successful in execution. His bearing and attitudes were aristocratic, and his instincts were fundamentally conservative. He was a Whig of the eighteenth-century school, most at home among his deferential clients, tenants, and labourers at Howick, and he never came to terms with the new industrial society which was coming into being during his later years.

From today's vantage point, for someone of privilege and virtually born to rule, Earl Grey had an ability to see how social forces were bending and changing the country, and did not resist but cautiously embraced incremental reform. In this he was a successful prime minister and statesman in his day, while remaining firmly rooted in the old world that he contributed to ending.

Gerry Hassan is a political commentator, academic and author and editor of more than two dozen books on Scottish and UK politics including The Strange Death of Labour Scotland *and* The People's Flag and the Union Jack: An Alternative History of Britain and the Labour Party.

23

Viscount Melbourne

16 July 1834 to 14 November 1834;
18 April 1835 to 30 August 1841
Whig

By Robert Buckland

Full name: William Lamb, 2nd Viscount Melbourne
Born: 15 March 1779, London
Died: 24 November 1848, Brocket Hall, Hertfordshire. Buried at Hatfield church
Education: Eton; Trinity College, Cambridge
Married to Lady Caroline Ponsonby; 1 son
Quotation: 'If a thing is very urgent you can always find time for it, but if a thing can be put off, why then you put it off.'

IN SUMMING UP the life and career of William Lamb, 2nd Viscount Melbourne, Home Secretary and twice prime minister, it is best described as starting with huge promise, turning to sadness and disappointment, followed by the achievement of ministerial office, and finally an Indian summer in the form of his stewardship as prime minister of the young Queen Victoria. There were two distinct phases to his life; from his birth in 1779 to 1828, when his wife died and he succeeded to his father's peerage, and then the remaining twenty years during which Melbourne served in high office, including his terms in office as prime minister that totalled over six years.

A study of his life reveals several distinct images. Which image of Melbourne predominates? Undoubtedly, it is the kindly, worldly-wise 'Lord M' of Victoria's private journals who is chiefly remembered now. Indeed, it is this version of Melbourne that I first encountered as a boy when I began my lifelong fascination with Victoria, her reign and her contemporaries.

Yet there was a long and turbulent life before those times, which shaped a prime minister who is not seen as having been driven by an underlying ethos or ideology and is therefore not as well remembered as others who served far shorter terms in office.

The Lamb family was anything but aristocratic. William's grandfather, Peniston Lamb, was a Nottinghamshire attorney who amassed a fortune and acquired a baronetcy. His unremarkable son became the first Lord Melbourne. It was his wife, William's mother, who was the mover and shaker, whose popular presence in London society meant access to George, Prince of Wales, and others in that set. The Melbournes' first son, Peniston, was born in 1770, but such was the reach of Lady Melbourne's charms that it may well be that William, the second son and the subject of this essay, was fathered by Lord Egremont, whom he was said to closely resemble. It may have been aristocratic Wyndham blood that coursed in his veins, rather than something more humdrum, therefore.

William's childhood passed happily, and after Eton and Cambridge, he was called to the Bar and practised for a while. In these years as the second son, with no immediate prospects of wealth, William had enjoyed the salons of London Whig society, which meant a constant shuttle between Holland House, Devonshire House, Carlton House and Brooks's Club. William was developing his skills of diplomacy, civilised conversation and handling royalty to boot. Then, his elder brother died and William became heir to the Melbourne title and fortune. This meant one important thing: politics and Parliament would now be open to him, and so it was that William Lamb entered the Commons in 1806 as MP for Leominster, which proved to be the first of the many constituencies that he represented. By this time, he had married the love of his life and the woman who was to undermine and shatter his innate confidence, the petite, brittle and brilliant Lady Caroline Ponsonby.

Nestling between the Cabinet Office and the Admiralty, Dover House is a rather lovely eighteenth-century mansion that nowadays houses the Scotland Office, but during the Regency, it was in part the setting for one of the most notorious love affairs of all time, which enveloped and helped to shape William Lamb. This elegant home, with its panoramic views of Horse Guards Parade, was then known as Melbourne House, having been the London residence of the Melbourne family from the 1790s, which after their marriage, included William and Caroline. After initial matrimonial bliss, the couple experienced sadness; their son, Augustus, was born with learning difficulties, and they went on to lose a daughter in childbirth. As their sorrows multiplied, Caroline's sharp intellect, her strongly held views and her fiery nature met with passivity and avoidance by her husband, and they grew apart.

It was against this troubled background that Lady Caroline Lamb met the young, handsome, limping extrovert George Gordon, the 6th Lord Byron, who was basking in the huge success of the publication of the first part of his narrative poem, *Childe Harold's Pilgrimage*. Their intense, open and ultimately unhappy *grand passion* shocked London society, and was followed by her progressive exclusion from the great salons of the West End, made even worse by the publication of her scandalous and semi-autobiographical novel *Glenarvon* in 1816. Whether her affair with Byron was anything more than intensely platonic is something of a moot point, but it scandalised fashionable London, precisely because it was conducted so openly. It had even involved a mock marriage ceremony. All the rules of polite society were being trashed by such wanton theatricality.

What of William in all of this? He most certainly was no cuckold, but his innate passivity meant that he did not protest his honour or issue any challenge to Byron. It was clear that the marriage was in terminal decline, with both husband and wife conducting extra-marital affairs, designed to cause each other the maximum pain possible. Caroline ended up in near-seclusion at the Melbournes' country seat, Brocket Hall, as the mental health issues that had beset her from youth worsened. Caroline's death in 1828 marked the end of the first phase of William Lamb's life. She had been the object of his deep love and affection, but also the source of his self-doubt, pessimism and loss of self-confidence.

During these years of personal strife prior to 1828, Lamb's political career in the Commons meandered along an uncertain course, punctuated by periods of complete political inertia when he did not sit as an MP. The generally held view in Whig society was, however, that he was an extremely able prospect for ministerial office, being gifted in the art of conversation and debate. Lamb retained a developed and sophisticated sense of humour and had accumulated an increasing sense of wisdom, even cynicism, that impressed both his political allies and his adversaries.

Lamb was an admirer, friend and follower of George Canning, and although he always identified himself as a Whig, he joined Canning's Whig–Tory administration as Chief Secretary for Ireland in 1827. '*William Lamb! William Lamb* – put *him* anywhere you like!' exclaimed George IV to his new prime minister, recalling a happy conviviality with the younger Lamb at Carlton House when the King was Prince of Wales.

In August 1827, Lamb arrived in Dublin and immediately took a different approach to the Chief Secretary's role. Rather than clinging to Irish Protestant circles as his predecessors had done, he made the acquaintance of many Catholics, including those who noisily opposed the prevailing dispensation. His tenure, however, was all too brief as Canning had died in August 1827 and the Canningites, including Lamb, finally broke with the Wellington administration in May 1828. His father died in July 1828 and William Lamb became the new Viscount Melbourne, selling Melbourne House in the process and choosing to live in Mayfair instead.

The next few years saw the Tory administration wrestle with and pass the Catholic Emancipation Act, which Melbourne supported, and then founder on the rocks of the growing Reform movement that propelled the Whigs to power in November 1830 under Earl Grey, who appointed Melbourne to his Cabinet as Home Secretary.

Chief among Melbourne's immediate tasks was how to deal with the upsurge in rural unrest, caused by low wages and increased mechanisation. The so-called Swing Riots were in full flight across rural England when he took office. The air of insurrection was also abroad in London itself. Melbourne had to maintain the balance between inaction and heavy-handedness. The trials, executions and deportations that were meted out by the courts in response to the riots were savage, even by the standards of the day. They took place against a backdrop of parliamentary struggle over the reform bills, in which Melbourne did not play a principal role.

Even after the Great Reform Bill finally got through in 1832, unrest continued. The labourers of Tolpuddle were sentenced to deportation by the Dorset magistrates, causing a huge outcry that resulted in a march down Whitehall by a quarter of a million people in support of a pardon for the Tolpuddle Martyrs in April 1834. Melbourne watched the demonstration from the Home Office, smiling and unperturbed, and promptly refused to see the petitioners. The protests died down, and he was widely credited as having defused a potentially explosive situation. This may well have been a question of luck rather than judgement, however. What was undoubtedly a local decision by the Dorset magistracy became a national issue, but one that frankly did not excite his interest. His insouciance in the face of rural anxiety was seen by many at the time as a virtue, but his lack of imagination and true understanding of the plight of rural workers, and his lack of real interest when he gave in to demands to pardon them a year later, tell us a lot about the full character of the man and his upbringing.

At the age of fifty-five, Melbourne was first asked to form a government by William IV in 1834, after the fall of Earl Grey's administration over the issue of coercion in Ireland. Frankly, his appointment was more about who he wasn't, rather than who he was, as the other available alternatives were either too inexperienced or beyond the pale. Melbourne was definitely not a radical, but was able to work with this faction, despite his difficulties with the often-histrionic Lord Chancellor, Brougham, who left his government in 1835. His Commons leader, Viscount Althorp, was a key member of the new administration, but when Althorp succeeded his late father as Earl Spencer and left the Commons, precipitously, and for the last time in our history, a reigning monarch dismissed a government entirely of their own volition.

William IV's reason to act was, he said, that Melbourne had told him that Althorp was the rock upon which his government was founded. Peel and the Tories formed an administration and called an election, which they failed to win. Within months, Melbourne had formed his second government. This administration, led in the Commons by Lord John Russell, implemented the reforms to the Poor Laws, modernised local government, set up a county police framework and took further action to strengthen the use of inspectorates in a range of areas. The Whigs won the 1837 election caused by the death of William IV with a reduced majority, and as the 1830s ended, politics was conducted against the background of an increasing agricultural depression, rising food prices and political agitation in the form of the Chartist movement in England and Wales, and the Rebecca Riots of rural Wales.

However well intentioned their reforms might have been, there is no doubt that the Whig Poor Law reform caused widespread misery and attached increased stigma to those in dire poverty and in need of help. The workhouses, so memorably and rightly excoriated by Dickens, were the product of this Whig attempt to concentrate provision for the poor. They represent a shameful episode in our history, and blame has to be laid at the feet of Russell, Melbourne and the Whigs for their lack of understanding as to the baleful effect on family life and the community that these reforms engendered.

The tumults of Chartism and rural discontent were a world away from the primary preoccupation of this prime minister, however. Without Melbourne acting as her de facto personal secretary, the eighteen-year-old Queen Victoria, who had no other effective means of support, would have struggled. Victoria's own journal gives us a fascinating window into their close relationship. The ageing premier was a kind of father-confessor to the teenage Queen, who was forty years his junior. He helped to strengthen the Queen's determination to exclude her mother, the Duchess of Kent, from any involvement in the running of the Court, thereby removing the sinister Sir John Conroy, the Duchess's adviser, from any influence.

Victoria's voluminous journals about her relationship with her prime minister tell us much that is of political importance and much that is, frankly, ordinary or extraordinary, depending on how you look at it; conversations with Melbourne about the way they respectively lay in their beds to sleep, for example. This was not, it would seem, merely a working relationship. He became her confidant and, to all intents and purposes, the person she looked to above all others for approval and emotional support. This did not always occasion benign results. In 1839, Melbourne and the Queen's unthinking behaviour in failing to prevent Royal Household gossip about the alleged unmarried pregnancy of the Tory lady-in-waiting Lady Flora Hastings (her 'pregnancy' was, in fact, a tumour of the liver that led to her tragic and early death), enraged the Hastings family, damaged public perceptions about behaviour at Court and led to race-goers hissing at the Queen at Ascot.

In May 1839, after Lord John Russell and the Commons Whigs narrowly survived a knife-edge vote on anti-slavery measures in Jamaica, Melbourne tendered his resignation to an alarmed Queen and advised her to send for the Tory leader in the Commons, Sir Robert Peel. The Queen had been somewhat naïve, even reckless, in revealing her public partiality for Melbourne and the Whigs; she found Peel, in her words, to be 'a cold unfeeling disagreeable man' and made no secret of her distrust of the Tories. These sentiments undoubtedly contributed to what became known as the Bedchamber Crisis, during which Victoria misrepresented the refusal of Peel to allow some of her Whig ladies-in-waiting to continue serving in the Royal Household as a refusal to allow any of them to continue, meaning that Peel was not able to take office as prime minister and form a new Tory administration.

In this regrettable saga, Melbourne can be criticised for not having pushed the matter vigorously enough in Peel's favour when he discovered the true position, and by then allowing himself to be reappointed as prime minister by a triumphant Sovereign who was keen to maintain his company, advice and correspondence, he placed the Crown in a position of having a perceived party preference. The fact that the Queen had, within two years of her accession, become so identified with the Whig Party and the Whig faction at Court was perhaps Melbourne's greatest failure of statesmanship, and could have endangered the future of the monarchy itself had not others later intervened.

This uniquely close relationship between Queen and Prime Minister was not to last. After the concerted efforts of Victoria's uncle, King Leopold of the Belgians, Victoria met Prince Albert of Coburg and a love-match ensued, beginning the process that resulted in the new Prince Consort developing a role as her chief adviser and influence, and helping Victoria onto a path of careful distance from either of the great parties.

As for the Whigs, they had now been in office for over a decade, but after the government lost a vote on sugar duties in May 1841, they were decisively beaten by Peel and the Tories in the ensuing election that August. Melbourne tendered his resignation to the Queen and was now out of office for good. Victoria, supported by her new young husband, soon learned to work with and even get to like Peel, and his predecessor was, fairly quickly, forgotten by the Court. Melbourne's retirement was not helped by a serious stroke in 1842 that heralded a rather sad twilight, spent mainly at Brocket Hall, ending in his death in that year of revolutions, 1848.

Melbourne had the intellect and the ability to communicate that are the necessary elements to make a great prime minister, but as is often the way of these things, there were no events of the greatest magnitude during his term in office against which he could definitively have been tested.

The emergence of Melbourne as prime minister suggests that when he took office, there was no further call for a radical reforming pair of hands, and that the air of insouciant inertia that he projected was a reflection of the prevailing political climate at Westminster. It was mere good fortune that resulted in Melbourne being the prime minister who went to kiss hands on the morning of young Victoria's accession to the throne. His handling of the Accession, and then the coronation of 1838, despite the number of inadvertently hilarious mistakes made during the ceremony itself, support the safe contention that he was a dedicated steward of our constitution, rather than an iconoclast. No burning radical, he harboured doubts about the Great Reform Act, for example. He can best be characterised as a centrist, instinctively tacking towards the middle and seeking to bring as wide a group of support with him as possible.

I have described the late 1830s as a transitional period, but storm clouds were already gathering as an agricultural recession took hold and the spirit of radicalism and rebellion began to rise, despite the best efforts of the Whig government to avert their eyes and ignore the problem.

Melbourne was definitely not a Victorian, and yet he guided and supported the young Queen in the earliest years of what came to be known as the Victorian era. Melbourne was a product of late eighteenth-century Whiggery; one who adapted to the rapidly changing world of the nineteenth century reluctantly, but more readily than is often acknowledged. He will be remembered as a figure who helped to usher out the spirit of eighteenth-century Whiggery and herald the arrival of what was later called the Liberal Party.

His biographer David Cecil summed it up well:

> The difficulties of his private, the disappointments of his public life, so far from hardening him, had taught him to be tolerant in practice as well as in theory. Further, the unsatisfactory spectacle of his own career disposed him to look kindly on the shortcomings of others. Profoundly unegotistic, he judged the rest of the world as he would judge himself.

Melbourne will not be remembered as a truly great prime minister, but as a steady hand on the tiller at a time of change, doing his best to guide a new Queen as the most successful phase in Britain's history was beginning.

Robert Buckland is Lord Chancellor and Secretary of State for Justice and has served as a Member of Parliament since 2010.

24

Sir Robert Peel

10 December 1834 to 8 April 1835;
30 August 1841 to 29 June 1846
Conservative

By Robert Saunders

Full name: Sir Robert Peel
Born: 5 February 1788, Chamber Hall, Bury, Lancashire
Died: 2 July 1850, 4 Whitehall Gardens, London. Buried at
Drayton Bassett parish church, Staffordshire
Education: Harrow; Christ Church, Oxford
Married to Julia Floyd; 5 sons, 2 daughters
Quotation: 'Do you not think that the tone of England – of that
great compound of folly, weakness, prejudice, wrong feeling, right
feeling, obstinacy, and newspaper paragraphs, which is called public
opinion – is more liberal – to use an odious but intelligible phrase
– than the policy of the Government?' (Letter to JW Croker)

Two years after the death of Sir Robert Peel, Walter Bagehot asked his readers: 'Was there ever such a dull man? Can anyone, without horror, foresee the reading of his memoirs?' Peel was not one of the great characters of British politics. He was not flamboyant, like Disraeli, or charismatic, like Gladstone. He wrote no novels, published no diary and articulated no new or elevating ideas. His oratory was functional, rather than elegant: as Disraeli memorably sneered, Peel 'soared with the wing of the vulture', not 'the plume of the eagle'.

If imagination were the test of statesmanship, Peel would not rank highly. Disraeli thought him 'a burglar of others' intellect', a man who 'traded on the ideas and intelligence of others'. For Bagehot, he was a follower of political fashion: 'a placid, adaptive intellect', content to paddle along behind 'the practical intelligence of his time'. To his critics, Peel's infirmity amounted almost to disease, indicative of a mind that was seriously disembarrassed of conviction. No other statesman made so many changes of policy, or proved, in Lord John Russell's caustic jibe, such a 'pretty hand at hauling down his colours'.

Yet Peel was both one of the most important prime ministers of modern times and one of the most intriguing. His premierships would shatter the party system, transform the relationship between government and governed, and reset the course of British politics. His placid exterior concealed a burning sense of political and religious mission, and his career offers a seething mass of contradictions. Peel was a passionate anti-democrat, who became a hero to the popular Chartist movement. He rebuilt the Conservative Party out of the ashes of the Great Reform crisis, only to shatter it for a generation in 1846. He was the champion of the Protestant ascendancy, who admitted Catholics to Parliament and endowed the Catholic seminary at Maynooth.

When Peel died in 1850, he was hailed both as a champion of the poor and as the saviour of the aristocracy. Historians have identified him variously as 'the founder of modern Conservatism' (Gash), as 'the progenitor of Gladstonian Liberalism' (Hilton), and as an 'anomaly', who was 'profoundly unrepresentative of British politics' (Ghosh). So what animated Peel's politics, and what was the legacy of his time in office?

Peel was born in 1788, the son of a Lancashire industrialist who employed more than fifteen thousand people in his factories. His political training began early: as a little boy, he was encouraged to stand on the table during dinner parties and make speeches to his father's guests. A more orthodox education followed at Harrow and Oxford, where he won an unprecedented 'Double First' in Classics and Mathematics. When he turned twenty-one, in 1809, his father bought him a seat in Parliament for a corrupt Irish borough. 'Bob, you dog,' he growled, 'if you don't become prime minister one day, I shall disinherit you.'

Peel grew up under the shadow of the French Revolution, and was perhaps the last British statesman to hear the whirr of the guillotine in his dreams. Even François Guizot, who dominated French politics in the 1840s, was struck by Peel's obsession with the Revolution and 'the ideas and social forces which it has called into play'. Peel collected more than two hundred volumes on the revolutionary era, one of the largest collections in Britain, and French politics provided a reference throughout his life.

For Peel, the 'Dantons, and the Marats, and the Robespierres' of revolutionary history were not 'monsters peculiar to France'. They were 'the foul, but legitimate spawn of circumstances', born of the same volcanic passions that boiled beneath British society, too. At any moment, a breakdown of political authority could produce 'the same consequences, the same men, and the same crimes, here as in France'.

This was reinforced by a 'gloomy view' of industrial society. As the son of a wealthy industrialist, Peel had seen at first hand the transformative power of modern industry. The results, he told MPs, had been 'extravagant wealth and deplorable penury', inflicting 'acute and undeserved suffering' on the poor. Vast cities had grown up around a single source of employment, only for a collapse in demand to see 'thousands . . . deprived of the means of existence'.

Like his younger contemporary, Karl Marx, Peel saw in industrial society a world cycling towards its own destruction. Rising prosperity, he feared, would simply 'increase . . . inequalities'; poverty was 'a necessary consequence of mechanical inventions', and no legislation could offer 'an effectual remedy'. Talk of de-industrialisation, favoured by the more eccentric on the Tory benches, risked 'drying up the sources of our prosperity' and devastating the very people it was intended to protect. 'If you had to constitute new societies,' he acknowledged, 'you might on moral and social grounds prefer corn-fields to cotton factories, an agricultural to a manufacturing population. But our lot is cast, and we cannot recede.'

From 1812 to 1818, Peel served as Chief Secretary for Ireland, in charge of the Irish administration. The experience left a lasting imprint on his thought. Even more than in England, Irish govern-ance centred on the maintenance of order over a turbulent and discontented population, and Peel's official correspondence, with its daily diet of arson, cattle-maiming and murder, entrenched a nat-urally volcanic conception of the social order. Peel was not unique in believing that 'an honest despotic government would be by far the fittest government for Ireland'; Lord John Russell once suggested that Ireland was better suited to Czarism than to freedom. What was less common was his fear that England might follow where Ireland led; that, 'when the storm rises – when the passions of the people are excited', England might face 'the same consequences . . . that have followed in Ireland'.

Peel's obsession with French politics, his view of industrial society and his experience in Ireland shaped a politics that was dominated by the fear of revolution. Like the poet, John Webster, Peel 'saw the skull beneath the skin'. The first responsibility of government, he believed, was to check 'the unruly passions and corrupt nature of human beings', for 'no Government can exist which does not control and restrain the popular sentiments'.

The maintenance of order animated his most lasting achievement at the Home Office in 1829: the creation of a Metropolitan Police Force, staffed by 'Peelers' or 'Bobbies'. It was a task that would become harder still with the passing of the Great Reform Act in 1832: the moment, above all others, that would shape his time as prime minister.

Peel was not hostile to electoral reform in principle. He had suggested in 1820 that 'public opinion' was growing 'too large for the channels that it has been accustomed to run through', and had hinted at a cross-party alliance to settle the question without contro-versy. Yet he was horrified by the Whigs' reform proposals in 1831, which he thought embodied three very dangerous errors.

First, the sheer scale of the measure had stripped the constitution of its surest protection: 'the magic influence of prescription'. The ignorant and unstable population of Peel's imagination was governed, not by reason, but by an unthinking recognition of authority and tradition: those 'unseen prompters of loyalty' that served 'to correct and fortify the feeble contrivances of reason'.

Second, the Whigs had 'sent through the land the firebrand of agitation, and no one can now recall it'. One of Peel's most basic instincts was a horror of agitation, when those 'embittered hearts' and 'uncultured intelligences' exploded into public life. The Whigs, he believed, had awoken a monster that would quickly turn on its creator. Prefiguring his analysis of Chartism, Peel warned that the 'bribe' offered by the Whigs would hold only for a short time.

Peel's third concern was for the stability of government finance. Unlike some of his followers, Peel did not expect a reformed Parliament to strip the upper classes of their property. He did, however, fear a decline in financial responsibility, as Chancellors sought popularity by lowering taxes without diminishing expenditure. It was no surprise to Peel that the first decade of the reformed Parliament produced an accumulated deficit of more than £10 million – at a time when the entire revenue was less than £50 million.

The Tories paid a heavy price for their resistance to reform. In the elections that followed, they were reduced to a rump of 150 MPs. Yet Peel never regretted the course he had taken. The purpose of resistance, he told a colleague, was not to stop the Reform Bill but to make its passage as difficult as possible; 'to teach young, inexperienced men charged with the trust of government that . . . they shall not override on the first springtide of excitement every barrier and breakwater raised against popular impulses'. 'These', he concluded, 'are salutary sufferings.'

The decade that followed was one of extraordinary volatility, marked by industrial depression, the Chartist insurgency and an increasingly chaotic Parliament. As so often, Peel's thoughts turned naturally to France. Reading a memoir of the Revolutionary Terror, he 'could hardly believe' that he 'was not reading the Annual Register of 1836'. What most alarmed him was the lack of a strong Parliament, capable of resisting any 'temporary storm of passion'. Without such a ballast, governments would be at the mercy of small knots of MPs, compelled 'to gratify their constituents by popular measures'. From this perspective, Peel's task after 1832 was not simply to rebuild a shattered party. At a deeper level, it was to close the revolution that had been opened by the Whigs and to restabilise the politics of the reformed era.

The first task was to build a moderate force in Parliament, capable of resisting 'further encroachments of democratic influence'. This was to be the function of the new Conservative Party. In a series of speeches around the country, Peel promised to accept the Reform Act as a final settlement and even to support the Whig administration in moderate, pragmatic reform. But he would resist any further democratic changes. This was a manifesto for moderate, progressive Conservatism, undertaking 'the correction of proved abuses and the redress of real grievances', while saying 'to the restless spirit of revolutionary encroachment, "Here are the bounds by which thy vibrations shall be stayed."'

Peel intended this as a manifesto for opposition, yet he found himself plunged sooner than expected into office. Barely two years after the Reform Act, in November 1834, William IV dismissed his ministers and sent for Peel – the last time a British monarch would remove a government. Peel was in Italy at the time; it took three weeks to track him down and two more to bring him back to London. Though he accepted the King's commission, forming his first government in December, Peel knew that his prospects were grim. Fresh elections improved the Conservatives' position – almost doubling its representation to 290 seats – but it was no surprise when the government fell after barely a hundred days in power.

Peel's first spell as prime minister left few legislative achievements, but it laid the foundations for future success. The elections established the Conservatives as the largest group in Parliament, well placed to profit as the reforming parties fell out among themselves. Peel's own performance won general admiration, and his 'Tamworth Manifesto' made him the flagbearer for a politics combining moderate reform with the defence of Church and State. Over the next five years, his party would consolidate its position both in the country and in Parliament, with at least fifty Whigs and Liberals crossing the floor to support him.

Peel might have formed a second minority government in 1839, had Queen Victoria not refused to change her ladies-in-waiting in a public rebuke to the proposed Conservative government. Instead, the elections of 1841 returned a handsome Conservative majority, establishing Peel in power as well as in office. The result would be one of the most significant governments of the century.

Peel took office in the summer of 1841, amid some of the worst economic conditions of the century. A prolonged industrial depression was producing horrifying levels of suffering: in just one Scottish town, Paisley, 17,000 workers were at risk of starvation. Chartism was resurgent, and in 1842 an attempted general strike swept across the north. A year later, Peel's secretary was shot dead by an assassin, who had mistaken him for the prime minister. Across the Irish Sea, Daniel O'Connell was preparing his last great campaign for repeal of the Union, drawing huge crowds in support of Irish self-government. Public debt continued to grow, with expenditure outstripping revenue by more than £2 million a year. This, Peel insisted, was not a 'casual deficiency' but a financial disease, with its origins in the Reform Act.

For Peel, the three main goals of his premiership were to stabilise the public finances, tackle the economic emergency and end what his Home Secretary, Sir James Graham, called 'the mad insurrection of the working classes'. The 'great object' of his ministry, he told a friend, would be 'to keep out of view all topics calculated to disturb the public mind'. Rather than agitating constitutional questions, the government would seek to 'make this country a cheap country for living'. This was a *conservative* policy, not just a humanitarian one, for 'landed property would not be safe during this next winter with the prices of the last four years'.

Peel began with a daring financial stroke: the reintroduction of the income tax. This had previously been thought of as a wartime measure, and its introduction in time of peace was hugely controversial. Since it was only levied on the highest earners, it marked a significant shift in the burden of taxation towards the government's own supporters. Yet Peel insisted that it was 'for the interest of property that property should bear the burden'. The goal was not simply to close the deficit, but to send a signal about the willingness of the propertied elite to make sacrifices for the public good.

Accepted 'voluntarily and with a good grace', the tax would 'be a cheap purchase of future security'.

Peel expected a revenue of nearly £4 million from the income tax, allowing him not just to bring down the deficit but to experiment with tariff reductions. The goal, as ever, was counter-revolutionary: if the masses could 'consume more by having more to spend', they would be less drawn to revolutionary politics. Tariff reductions could not, of course, abolish poverty, but they would make it harder to blame government for the price of food. By taking government out of the marketplace, Peel hoped to break the golden thread between hunger and radical politics.

In his first great Budget, in 1842, and in subsequent Budgets, Peel either lowered or abolished tariffs on hundreds of different items, from food and raw materials to clothing and finished products. Like the income tax that made them possible, these reductions were not merely a fiscal alteration: they were part of a larger counter-revolutionary strategy. The goal, as he put it in 1846, was that 'thoughts of the dissolution of our institutions *should be forgotten* in the midst of physical enjoyment'.

A similar strategy underpinned his Irish policy. In Ireland, as in Britain, Peel sought to combine firm policing – including the arrest of O'Connell in 1845 – with concessions designed to take the heat from popular protest. He launched a commission into Irish land conditions, sought to extend access for Catholics to university education, and, in a bid for the loyalty of the Catholic clergy, increased the grant to the Catholic seminary at Maynooth. The latter, in particular, shook his party to its foundations. Even the loyal Gladstone resigned, in a letter of such tormented logic that Peel confessed himself at a loss to understand what it meant.

As Chartism declined and the level of popular protest fell away, Peel was confident that his actions had been vindicated. Tariff reductions, he claimed, had 'extinguished agitation and discouraged sedition', fostering a 'disposition to confide in you, and not to agitate questions that are at the foundation of our institutions'. The failure of his party to understand this, or to appreciate the 'functions and duties of a Conservative Government', was infuriating. As Peel complained in 1845, 'the people are contented', 'Chartism is extinguished' and 'any wish for organic change in the Constitution – for addition to popular privileges – is dormant'. 'But we have reduced protection to agriculture, and tried to lay the foundation of peace in Ireland; and these are offences for which nothing can atone.'

As relations with his party deteriorated, Peel became increasingly contemptuous of his own back-benchers: 'men with great possessions and little foresight . . . whose only chance of safety is that their counsels shall not be followed'. After a collision with his party in 1845, he boasted privately that 'people like a certain degree of obstinacy and presumption in a minister. They abuse him for dictation and arrogance, but they like being governed.' It was an approach that would soon bring the destruction of his government.

By the autumn of 1845 a new crisis was brewing in Ireland, where the failure of the potato crop threatened a catastrophic famine. Over the coming years, more than a million people would die of starvation. A million more would emigrate. While Protectionists, like Lord George Bentinck, mocked 'the pretended potato famine in Ireland', Peel began buying up foreign grain. That immediately opened the question of the Corn Laws: the rock on which his premiership would founder.

The Corn Laws (or 'the Bread Tax') were import duties on grain, imposed at the close of the Napoleonic Wars. They were of doubtful relevance to a subsistence economy – Ireland was a net *exporter* of grain – but the famine gave a new impetus to radical politics in Britain. The Anti-Corn Law League had been campaigning for years for repeal, deploying the tax as a battering ram against aristocratic government. The potato blight gave it a propaganda weapon of extraordinary power, forcing ministers to defend a tax on food at a time of mass starvation.

The League began at once to prepare a new campaign, and Graham warned Peel in October that 'it will be the most formidable movement in modern times'. Such a movement, Peel feared, would endanger not only the Corn Laws but the political system that imposed them. As he told Prince Albert, a conflict that pitted 'the manufacturers, the hungry and the poor' against the landed proprietors and the aristocracy could 'only end in the ruin of the latter'.

For Peel, it was axiomatic that 'the *worst* ground on which we can fight the battle of true Conservatism is on a question of *food*'. Maintaining the Corn Laws, 'in the state of things which Ireland *will present*', would trigger 'a desperate conflict between different classes of society', plunging the aristocracy into 'a bitter and, ultimately, an unsuccessful struggle'. Any rise in prices that was attributable to the Corn Laws would pose a 'serious danger' to the state. It was 'not safe' any longer to maintain Protection.

Peel had not been converted to the constitutional programme of the League. As he told MPs in 1846, he remained convinced 'that land is the safest basis of political power'; but MPs would better 'fortify and maintain the influence of the land' by giving up an unpopular privilege. This gave repeal a peculiarly conservative cast. A critic who likened Peel to Turgot, the reformist minister blamed by some for triggering the French Revolution, received a characteristic rebuke: it was the 'maintenance of bygone privileges that led to the revolution', not 'the doctrines of Turgot'.

For Peel, who had long been persuaded of the economic case for free trade, the only *conservative* course was to launch a preemptive strike against the Corn Laws, sidelining the League and depriving it of a pretext for agitation. For that reason, he refused calls to submit the Corn Laws to a General Election. Even in the 1820s, when fighting an increasingly lonely battle against Catholic emancipation, Peel had refused to contemplate a 'Protestant' election that would exploit the anti-Papalism of the masses. A dissolution on the price of bread, he believed, would stir public opinion to boiling point. Victory for free trade would reinvigorate popular radicalism, while defeat might discredit the electoral system altogether, fuelling demands for a more democratic franchise.

Repealing the Corn Laws split the Conservative Party down the middle. Peel himself was sick and exhausted, suffering agonies from tinnitus and nose-bleeds. Mocked and belittled by Disraeli, he cut an increasingly isolated figure. His young apprentice, William Gladstone, had lost his seat in 1845, and had to watch helplessly from the gallery as his master was cut down before him. When the House divided on the second reading of the Corn Bill, only 114 Conservatives voted with their leader; 241 backed Bentinck and Disraeli in opposing repeal. The measure only passed with the support of the Whigs, and as soon as repeal was secure they united with the Protectionists to expel him from government. Peel would never hold office again.

Peel embraced his defeat with the satisfaction of martyrdom, convinced that the repeal of the Corn Laws had prevented 'a convulsion endangering the whole frame of society'. He was vindicated, in his own eyes, at least, by the continental revolutions of 1848, when governments across Europe collapsed under popular pressure. Peel never doubted that repeal had saved Britain from a similar fate. 'The part that I have taken has been very grievous; but I believe that it has been the better.'

The circumstances of his fall helped shape Peel's reputation. His was a culture saturated in the theology of the atonement: the belief that Christ died to atone for the sins of a fallen people. For his supporters, Peel himself became a Christ-like figure: a man of sorrows, crucified by his party to give his people the bread of life. When he walked to the House for the last time as prime minister, crowds lined the streets cheering his name. A Chartist newspaper issued his portrait in a series of popular heroes, alongside revolutionaries like George Washington and Lajos Kossuth. When he died in 1850, *Punch* magazine suggested as his monument a pile of cheap loaves, while 400,000 working men subscribed to a 'Poor Man's Memorial'.

The Chartists may have respected Peel, but he made their task more difficult. As he had intended, repeal weakened the link between hunger and radical politics: free trade did not banish poor harvests, but it made it harder to blame misgovernment. '[B]y the repeal of the Corn Laws,' wrote *The Times*, 'Government has for ever emancipated itself from the unpopularity which used to follow a bad harvest, and effectually removed one of the most prominent and frequently-recurring causes of discontent and sedition.'

Peel's career, then, ended as it had begun: in a nest of paradoxes. The man who had built the Conservative Party broke it for a generation. A staunch anti-democrat became a pin-up for radical politics. The dominant parliamentarian of the early nineteenth century ended his career leading an isolated rump detached from the major parties. Yet he succeeded in his primary objective: to close the revolutionary politics of the reformed era. In that respect,

Peel was neither the father of modern Conservatism nor the founder of Gladstonian Liberalism. He did, however, help to create the conditions in which those creeds could thrive.

Robert Saunders is reader in modern British history at Queen Mary, University of London.

25

Lord John Russell

30 June 1846 to 21 February 1852;
29 October 1865 to 26 June 1866
Whig/Liberal

By Duncan Brack

Full name: Lord John Russell, later 1st Earl Russell
Born: 18 August 1792, Hertford Street, London
Died: 28 May 1878, Pembroke Lodge, Richmond Park, Surrey.
Buried at Chenies, Buckinghamshire
Education: Westminster School; University of Edinburgh
Married to Adelaide Lister (d. 1838), then Lady Fanny Elliot; 3
sons, 3 daughters
Quotation: 'I have made mistakes, but in all I did my object
was the public good.'

LORD JOHN RUSSELL was the last Whig prime minister: 'the last
Doge of Whiggism', as the late nineteenth-century Liberal leader

William Harcourt described him. Scion of one of the most powerful aristocratic Whig families, he held firm throughout his life to the Whig view of the aristocracy as the natural leaders of society, occupying a middle place between Crown and people and holding their great estates in trust for the preservation of the constitution. As a propertied class, the aristocracy possessed the standing and the security to be able effectively to hold the executive to account.

The defining moment in Russell's politics, which occurred nine years before he was born, was King George III's dismissal of the Whig leader Charles James Fox's government in 1783. Throughout his life he worked with a statue of Fox on his desk, and like Fox he believed that even in an age of revolution a wilful monarch posed a greater threat to Parliament than the people. But he was always aware that public opinion required managing and leading, and Tory misgovernment posed a threat in terms of the likelihood of fomenting revolutionary pressures.

He saw the British constitution as a magnificent achievement that had secured tolerably effective representation and respect for order: the conditions for Britain's progress in wealth, civilisation and morality. His main concern was to further that progress by using the power of government to replace bad law with good. This included parliamentary reform, to prevent Parliament acting solely on behalf of narrow factions, a wider provision of education, so that all could understand their moral purpose in society, and tolerance for Catholics, Nonconformists and Jews, to prevent the Church of England taking an excessively narrow view of its place in the nation. He believed that reform would advance liberty, the power of reason and hence national harmony. And he believed also that he himself, because of his Whig inheritance and his beliefs, deserved to play a leading role in bringing all this to pass.

He had, indeed, a fine reforming record. He was the main architect of the Great Reform Act of 1832, the first major reform of the representative system in two centuries. He championed the cause of religious freedom, democratised the government of large towns, reformed criminal justice, began the system of state inspection and support of public education, established the ten-hour day for factory labour and founded a national board of public health.

He also played a vital part in harnessing the many parliamentary and public groups that contributed to reform: Whigs, reformers, radicals, Dissenters and Irish Catholic supporters of repeal of the 1801 Act of Union. While political parties during this period were very far from cohesive, Russell played a key role in the slow transition to a more disciplined party system through a protracted period of confusing debate and realignment. He was also clearly aware of the perpetual tendency of progressive parties to shake loose their supporters: 'That very old difficulty of Whig administrations, that their friends expect them to do more than is possible; so that if they attempted little, their friends grow slacker, and if they attempt much, their enemies grow strong.'

But he was not necessarily the man best equipped for the task. In many ways he was a very able politician: intelligent, decisive and a good (though not compelling) public speaker. He was never afraid of taking the initiative and generally displayed shrewd judgement about the measures that opinion could be persuaded to adopt. He became an effective parliamentarian; in 1841 Joseph Parkes, his Chief Whip, consoled himself at the prospect of defeat with the thought that: 'Johnny counts for 25 himself, which so balances parties.'

But he had two major drawbacks. The third son of the Duke of Bedford (a Whig minister from 1806 to 1807), he had been born prematurely, and, as a result, was not only slight of stature but frequently in delicate health; he sometimes lacked the physical stamina necessary to carry through his impulses. More serious was the consequence of his belief that a Russell's place must always be in the lead. Intensely ambitious and self-confident but naturally shy, he rarely consulted others and never flattered subordinates, often appearing abrupt and indifferent. After 1852, facing eclipse as Liberal leader, first by the Peelites, and then by Lord Palmerston, he became selfish, petulant and unpredictable.

On top of this, although he had a fine ministerial record, as prime minister he never commanded a solid majority. Holding together the coalition of Whigs, radicals and reformers while at the same time needing support from either Peelites or Irish or both was a challenging task, and helps to explain why Russell has more achievements to his credit as a minister under Grey and Melbourne than he does as prime minister.

Russell's poor health – which led to him largely being taught by private tutors – did not prevent him from attending university in Edinburgh or travelling to the Iberian Peninsula and Italy during the Napoleonic Wars, and to France after them. He became an MP early, for a family-controlled borough, but for the first seventeen years of his political career the Whigs were in opposition. This provided him with the opportunity to start a literary career, which was eventually to feature a play, a novel, biographies of Charles James Fox and his ancestor William, Lord Russell (a protagonist of the exclusion crisis of 1678–81 from which the Whigs derived their origins), *An Essay on the History of the English Government and Constitution* and works on European history.

In Parliament he argued for reform and toleration. He opposed many of the Tory prime minister Lord Liverpool's repressive measures, and condemned the massacre at Peterloo, which he thought might never have taken place had Manchester had a voice in Parliament. He was an early proponent of redistributing seats from the smallest boroughs (which often had a tiny electorate, frequently in the pocket of a local landowner) to the counties and large towns. In 1828 he successfully moved the repeal of the Test and Corporation Acts, which, in theory (although frequently ignored in practice), restricted official positions to Anglicans.

In 1830, Wellington's resignation, under pressure over political reform, finally brought the Whigs back to power under Lord Grey. Russell was offered office as Paymaster General and, although outside the Cabinet, a place on the committee of four that drafted the Reform Bill; it was largely his proposals that the Cabinet accepted. Since Althorp, the Whig leader in the Commons, was a poor speaker, it was Russell who introduced the bill – and a second and a third bill over the following fifteen months of political turbulence. It was this third effort that became the Great Reform Act of 1832, both redistributing seats and enlarging the franchise. While in retrospect this can be seen as paving the way to full democracy over the following century, that was certainly not Russell's intention; he aimed to forestall what he called 'reform upon a principle' and the 'fanatics' who called for universal suffrage and annual parliaments. To the end of his career he opposed the secret ballot on the grounds that the people had a right to know how those privileged enough to possess the vote had cast it on behalf of their community.

The huge Whig majority bequeathed by the 1832 election created opportunities for Russell to demonstrate both his skills as a leader, energising the government and steering the measures through the Commons, and his deficiencies, unnecessarily creating crises through impulsiveness and ill-chosen initiatives. Under-occupied as Paymaster General, in 1833 he visited Ireland at the behest of his brother, and concluded that even after Catholic emancipation (in 1829), the country remained unjustly ruled by the minority Protestant ascendancy. His impetuous declaration in the Commons in support of using surplus (Anglican) Church of Ireland funds for Irish education or the payment of Catholic priests split the Cabinet (driving Lord Stanley to resign and join the Tories; as Lord Derby, he was later to become prime minister) and led to Grey's retirement. When Grey's replacement Lord Melbourne appointed Russell as Leader of the Commons, Russell's support for church funds appropriation was so unpopular with King William IV that he dismissed the ministry.

Although the Tories recovered some of their losses in the election that followed, they did not gain a majority, and Russell negotiated the Lichfield House Compact between Whigs, radicals and Irish to return Melbourne to power. He was appointed as Home Secretary as well as Leader of the Commons, and between 1835 and 1839 oversaw a wave of reforms. He limited the range of crimes for which the death penalty applied, established a prison inspectorate, separated young offenders from adults, and obtained a pardon for the Tolpuddle Martyrs, who had been transported to Australia for trade union activity. He dealt calmly and effectively with the first wave of Chartist activity without resorting to repression.

Through the Municipal Corporations Act he rationalised local government, creating ratepayer-elected councils with powers to establish police forces, install drainage and undertake street cleaning. Although, like the Reform Act, this was a moderate measure dealing mainly with the worst abuses and leaving considerable room for further improvement, like that Act it was highly partisan, designed to undermine the Tory near-monopoly of local corporations. Russell was proving himself not just a reformer but an effective leader of the Whig/Liberal cause.

Although the Tory majority in the Lords destroyed most of

Russell's efforts to legislate for Ireland, he ameliorated the Catholic position through measures such as the appointment of Catholic magistrates and policemen, and a new Poor Law. He did rather better for the English Nonconformists, commencing the reform of tithes, legalising marriage ceremonies in Nonconformist chapels, and instituting a national register of births, marriages and deaths to replace the purely Anglican parish registers. He attempted to bring in a national system of primary education, but was defeated by the vested interests of the Anglican schools. Nevertheless, he introduced school inspectors and created a committee of the Privy Council to oversee the distribution of (modest) government funds; this was the predecessor to the first education ministry, created in 1856.

As Secretary of State for War and the Colonies, from 1839 to 1841, Russell annexed New Zealand, ended the role of New South Wales as a penal colony, and steered the union of Upper and Lower Canada through Parliament. By the time Melbourne's ministry fell, in 1841, Russell was clearly established as his successor as leader of the Whigs. He also put down a marker to those radicals who followed Cobden and Bright – the founders of the Anti-Corn Law League – by tabling proposals to reduce the corn duty (and therefore cut the price of grain) as one of the final acts of the Melbourne government.

Four years later the same issue was to provide Russell with his first, abortive, bid for the prime ministership. In late 1845, with poor harvests in England and the failure of the potato crop in Ireland, pressure mounted for the repeal of the Corn Laws; it was opposed by the bulk of the Tories, on behalf of the landowners who benefited from high grain prices. In November, without consulting any of his colleagues, Russell declared for total abolition. After the Tory prime minister Peel failed to carry his Cabinet for repeal, he resigned as prime minister and Queen Victoria sent for Russell, but he was unable to persuade enough of his colleagues to serve and Peel returned to office. In fact, Russell's failure was providential; the following year, with Whig and radical support, Peel reformed the Corn Laws against the opposition of his own party, led by Disraeli and Bentinck. The resultant fracturing of the Tories kept them mostly out of power for a generation and was instrumental in the formation of the Liberal Party, which eventually absorbed its Peelite free-trade component and was to hold to free trade as an article of faith for the rest of the century and beyond.

Peel's government fell soon afterwards. By then, Russell had conferred with his colleagues and was able to construct a Cabinet; he took office for the first time as prime minister on 30 June 1846.

Russell as prime minister, however, was not as successful as Russell as minister. Not only did external circumstances turn unfavourable, with a financial crisis in 1848 and a resurgence of Chartism and revolutionary activity on the Continent and in Ireland, but Russell's administration never enjoyed a majority in Parliament, despite some gains in the 1847 election. Alongside the Whigs, Russell could only hope for intermittent support from the independent Liberals (a variety of radicals, who often disagreed among themselves), Irish supporters of repeal and the followers of Peel. While the Peelites theoretically held the balance of power, in practice their leader gave no clear sense of direction beyond his desire to prevent the protectionist Tories from taking office. Even after Peel died in 1850, the Peelites did not resolve to take sides.

Consequently, Russell's legislative record was slim, and he often took advantage of bills put forward by back-benchers, for example to limit factory hours for women and children. In education, he was able to negotiate some state funding for Catholic and Nonconformist schools, and grants towards the funding of teachers (rather than just school buildings) and improved teacher-training arrangements. The government completed the abolition of the Corn Laws, rationalised the sugar duties, and, in 1849, abolished the Navigation Acts (which had restricted the use of foreign shipping for British trade), extending further the commitment to free trade. Central control over the administration of the Poor Law was rationalised, though it was never made as humanitarian as its critics would like or as cheap as economists hoped. The government established a central board of health in 1848, and encouraged the establishment of local boards with powers to provide paving, water and drainage and to inspect food quality and lodging houses. This prepared the way for future action, but the legislation was only permissive, and few local authorities seized the opportunity, given that no central funding was available.

Russell's government can be cleared of the exaggerated claims by some of genocide in Ireland, but its response to the great famine of 1845–49 was inadequate. Repeated failures of the potato crop meant starvation on a mass scale; possibly one million people died and a further million emigrated. Russell aimed to provide relief without creating dependency, to ensure that the better-off Irish landlords fulfilled their responsibilities, and to guarantee that reforms would prevent any future recurrence of famine. But different parts of the government took different views of how this could be achieved, Parliament vetoed aspects of the programme, and inadequate administration within Ireland, in both the public and charitable sectors, thwarted even the best of intentions. Direct food relief through soup kitchens was provided on a temporary basis, but inadvertently helped to spread disease. Land reform was intended to bring in new capital to farming, but respect for property rights frustrated the proposals, and the approach was too long-term to deal with the immediate problem of starvation.

Russell's biographer, John Prest, criticises his inability, as prime minister, 'to apply himself regularly and steadily to the problem at hand'. He 'tried to guide his colleagues by hasty judgements, whose limitations were exposed by the first objection', though he 'handled his Cabinet as a committee of friends and equals, and good humour predominated'. Such traits left him vulnerable when mistakes were made, and his authority began to weaken. In the 1850 Don Pacifico debate, Foreign Secretary Lord Palmerston's oratorical assertion of Britain's right to protect its citizens anywhere in the world not only positioned the Whigs well to capitalise on pride in nation and empire, but caused his own stock to rise and reinforced his tendency to act independently of colleagues or convention.

In the same year, Russell sought to reinforce the government's Protestant popularity, writing a letter to the Bishop of Durham attacking the decision of the Pope to restore a diocesan Catholic structure in England. This was a mistake, alienating his own latitudinarian Whig colleagues (whom he had not consulted), the High Church Anglicans among the Peelites, and the Irish Catholic MPs; it undermined his reputation for support for toleration. His next mistake, though an unavoidable one, was to sack Palmerston in December 1851 for officially recognising Louis Napoleon's coup in France without consulting either Russell or the Queen. In February

1852, Palmerston enjoyed his 'tit for tat with Johnny Russell' by organising Russell's defeat on an amendment to the Militia Bill. The government resigned, and Russell's first premiership came to an end.

Lord Derby's minority Conservative administration was rapidly destroyed by the Peelite Gladstone's attack on Disraeli's Budget, so the Liberals (as by then they mostly called themselves) returned to office. Thanks to the Durham letter, Russell was unable to form a government, which needed to include Irish and Peelite support. Persuaded by his brother, he agreed to accept office as Leader of the Commons and Foreign Secretary under the Peelite Lord Aberdeen.

Although the Aberdeen coalition brought together the forces that were to form the Liberal Party in 1859, the fusion of 1852 proved premature. The government proved unable to withstand the strains of the Crimean War, which it had drifted into without clear objectives or competent military leadership. By the time the ministry's failings had been exposed in *The Times*, and the radical MP Roebuck had tabled a critical motion in Parliament, Russell had been rebuffed in his attempts to remove the Peelite Newcastle from the War Office. Since he was unwilling to defend the government against Roebuck, he resigned. Once again, Russell was right in his intentions but clumsy in his actions. His desertion of the ministry made it impossible for him to construct a replacement government from the same colleagues, and made it unavoidable for Palmerston to become prime minister in 1855.

For the next few years, the rivalry between Russell and Palmerston persisted. After accepting Cabinet office as Colonial Secretary in February 1855, Russell was forced to resign five months later, finding himself caught in the political cross-currents of negotiating the Crimean peace settlement. Embittered and hostile, he nursed a lingering resentment against his former colleagues. When Palmerston gagged his education reform proposals in April 1856, Russell became, as one Whig observed, 'a concentrated essence of lemon'. In 1857 Russell had his revenge, combining with radicals and Peelites to defeat Palmerston over the Second Opium War, helping to force his resignation the following year and colluding to prolong the life of Derby's second minority Tory government.

When the 1859 General Election saw an improvement in Derby's position, however, it was clear that the Liberal forces needed to unite. The outbreak of war between France and Austria over the future of Italy, and Derby's apparent sympathy for Austria's position against Italian nationalism, provided the pretext. On 6 June 1859 Russell and Palmerston declared to the famous meeting of Whigs, Peelites and radicals in Willis's Rooms their mutual willingness to serve under one another in order to bring down Derby; this meeting is generally held to mark the formation of the Liberal Party.

The Queen attempted to avoid the choice between these 'two terrible old men' by sending for Lord Granville, but, in the end, chose Palmerston as the lesser evil; Russell agreed to serve as Foreign Secretary. For the following six years Palmerston and Russell worked together surprisingly well. Together, they avoided the calamity of backing the wrong side in the American Civil War, though neither was blameless for Britain's impotent posturing over Prussia's invasion of Schleswig-Holstein in 1864. In 1861 Russell was elevated to the House of Lords as Earl Russell, to relieve the stresses to his health inherent in serving in the Commons.

When Palmerston died in 1865, Russell took office as prime minister for the second time, on 29 October. His career ended as it had begun, with parliamentary reform. While in the 1830s he had defended the Great Reform Act with such vigour that he had earned the nickname 'Finality Jack', he had long since concluded that further expansion of the electorate was both desirable and safe; he had made unsuccessful attempts to bring in new reform bills throughout the 1850s.

The 1865 election bequeathed the Liberals an increased majority, but support for reform was not unanimous; a rebel group was concerned about the implication for taxation of an extension of the franchise into the working classes and were also antagonised by Russell's haste in introducing the measure, impatient for one last great achievement. The bill was defeated and on 26 June 1866 Russell left office for the second time, just eight months after becoming prime minister.

In the end, the Liberal rebels were betrayed by Disraeli, whose own Reform Act of 1867 was more radical than Russell's – though his attempt at 'Tory democracy' did not prevent the Liberals decisively winning the 1868 election. Russell did not officially retire and may have been disappointed not to have been included in Gladstone's first Cabinet. He remained active in the Lords, proposing universal primary education and discussing reforms to the Church of Ireland with Gladstone, both issues the Liberals took up after 1868. He died in 1878.

Lord John Russell had many qualities – and many defects. Looking over the whole of his career, the historian Jonathan Parry was surely right to conclude that: 'the ultimate fact about Russell is that a combination of name, achievement, talent, fearlessness and principle left him without serious rivals as the greatest Liberal statesman of the age.' But although his achievements for the reform and modernisation of the British state were considerable, his nature was too impulsive and erratic to be able to rank him as a truly great Prime Minister.

The Whig cleric Sydney Smith left a picture of Russell that well captures his courage and his commitment to the Liberal cause but also the impatience and disregard for his colleagues that often frustrated his ambitions. As he wrote: 'There is not a better man in England than Lord John Russell; but his worst failure is that he is utterly ignorant of all moral fear; for there is nothing he would not undertake. I believe he would perform the operation for the stone, build St Peter's, or assume (with or without ten minutes' notice) the command of the Channel Fleet; and no one would discover by his manner that the patient had died, the church tumbled down, and the Channel Fleet had been knocked to atoms . . . [He wants] to shake the world, and be the Thunderer of the scene!'

Duncan Brack is an Associate Fellow at Chatham House, and editor of the Journal of Liberal History.

26

Earl of Derby

23 February 1852 to 17 December 1852; 20 February 1858
to 11 June 1859; 28 June 1866 to 25 February 1868
Conservative

By Nigel Fletcher

Full name: Edward Smith-Stanley, 14th Earl of Derby
Born: 29 March 1799, Knowsley Hall, Lancashire
Died: 23 October 1869, Knowsley Hall, Lancashire; buried at St
Mary's Church, Knowsley
Education: Eton; Christ Church, Oxford
Married to Emma Bootle-Wilbraham; 2 sons, 1 daughter
Quotation: 'The duty of an opposition was very simple – it
was, to oppose everything, and propose nothing.' (Citing George
Tierney, 1841)

TAKE A WALK around Parliament Square, and you will be
confronted by a host of statues of prime ministers from the
last two centuries whose names echo with familiarity: Churchill,

Lloyd George, Disraeli. Standing among them in the north-west corner, under the shade of the trees, is a tall bronze figure depicted in his robes, on a plinth inscribed 'Derby'. Few visitors will have much idea who he was, still less what he achieved. It is for good reason that one of the very few biographies to have been written of him is entitled *The Forgotten Prime Minister*.

Even to a curious reader of history, Derby's ministries may appear as mere temporary interludes between the achievements of more famous prime ministers. If he is mentioned at all, it is usually as the slightly obscure figure under whose nominal leadership Disraeli rose to fame. But this neglect appears on closer examination to be unjust. He was, in his time, a major player amid the shifting sands of mid-nineteenth-century party alignment, with his journey from traditional Whig to reforming Conservative embodying a fundamental realignment of both the party system and the tenets of modern Conservatism.

He remains the longest-serving leader of the Conservative Party in its history, and made it to No. 10 not just once but on three separate occasions – the first person to do so. For these achievements alone, he is worthy of note. But a proper appraisal of the achievements of his long career cannot simply be restricted to the crude measure of his time in the top job. As a true Victorian statesman, his life and work reward more nuanced study.

The Hon. Edward Stanley was born at the family seat of Knowsley Hall in Lancashire at the very end of the eighteenth century. Politics was in the blood. The Stanleys had been at the centre of power for centuries, and young Edward's grandfather and father both served as Whig Members of Parliament before succeeding to the earldom. It was therefore into a solidly political household that the future prime minister was born and raised. He attended Eton and Christ Church, Oxford, before declaring himself ambitious to pursue a distinguished career in what he now considered to be his 'profession': politics and public life.

That career began properly in 1822, when at the age of twenty-three he was elected to the Commons for the rotten borough of Stockbridge. Joining his father in the Commons, he voted in support of an early bill for parliamentary reform, a growing campaign that would define the politics of the next half-century. In 1825 he married Emma Bootle-Wilbraham, daughter of Lord Skelmersdale, a near-neighbour to the Knowsley Estate. Their marriage would endure for the rest of his life, with Emma providing a loving and stable family life for the aspirant statesman.

Stanley rose quickly to prominence during the 1820s, and in 1830 became Chief Secretary for Ireland in the government of Earl Grey. He enacted a number of significant measures, including reform of the controversial system of church tithes and establishing a Board of Commission for Education to standardise provision and help desegregate Protestant and Catholic children. During this period he also consolidated his position as a leading voice in favour of parliamentary reform, the central issue facing the government, winning him promotion first to the Cabinet, then later to the post of Secretary of State for War and the Colonies in 1833. In this role he devised and enacted a truly historic measure: the abolition of slavery across the British Empire.

Stanley was now a major figure in the government, but increasingly worried by what he considered to be a growing radical influence on Whig policy. He resigned his post in May 1834, and began vocally opposing the government, now under the leadership of Viscount Melbourne. When the King dismissed Melbourne's government later that year, it briefly appeared that Stanley might succeed in forming a new centrist coalition around himself, based on the 'Knowsley Creed' that he set out in a keynote speech in Glasgow. The bid failed, however, with Tory leader Sir Robert Peel pre-empting Stanley by issuing his own appeal for moderate, responsible reform in the form of the Tamworth Manifesto, and taking office himself. Following the election of January 1835, Stanley and his band of supporters (dubbed the 'Derby Dilly' by mocking observers) briefly held the balance of power, but when Peel's government fell and Melbourne returned to office, Stanley was marginalised. His moment had passed – and the prospect of a new centre party of moderates was, not for the last time in British politics, thwarted.

The next six years of Whig government were marked by Stanley's continuing move away from his Whig roots towards the new moderate Conservatism espoused by Peel. When Melbourne's government fell and Peel returned to office, Stanley was recalled to his previous cabinet post of Colonial Secretary. But he felt increasingly peripheral, with other senior colleagues in the Commons gaining greater prominence, and in 1844 he asked Peel to elevate him to the House of Lords by a writ of acceleration to help lead the party there.

The following year, Peel's proposed reform of the Corn Laws provoked civil war within his own ranks, and prompted Stanley's resignation from the Cabinet. The Conservative Party was now fatally divided, and while Benjamin Disraeli and Lord George Bentinck led the Protectionist faction of Conservatives in the Commons, Stanley somewhat reluctantly took on the role of leading the equivalent group in the Lords. After Peel passed the repeal of the Corn Laws with Whig votes in May 1846, Disraeli and Bentinck mounted a coup that forced him from office and led to the return to office of the Whigs under Russell.

Shortly afterwards, at a dinner for Conservative peers and MPs at the Trafalgar Tavern in Greenwich, Stanley was hailed by Bentinck as the leader of the Protectionists in both houses. With Peel now leading his own band of supporters, Stanley had become de facto leader of the Conservative Party, a position he would hold for the next twenty-two years. Having been an unwilling rebel, he nurtured hopes that in opposition the Conservative factions could be reconciled, but this proved a painfully slow process.

Opposition to Russell was made more difficult by the lack of clear leadership of the party in the Commons. Stanley had a tense relationship with Disraeli, whom he distrusted, and only reluctantly allowed him to take on the role of leader after a number of other candidates proved unequal to the task. Gradually, however, their combined efforts helped erode support for Russell's government, and in 1851 Stanley was asked to form a replacement administration, but was unable. That summer, as Stanley awaited his next chance for political advancement, he suffered a personal loss, with the death of his father. The sad news did, however, provide a poignant foreshadowing of his likely rise in national status. Succeeding to the title as 14th Earl of Derby, he was now one of the richest landowners in the country, and one of the most senior peers of the realm.

The Whig government finally collapsed in 1852, and Russell advised the Queen to send again for Derby. This second attempt

at forming a government was more successful, but the new ministers were notably inexperienced, with the elderly Duke of Wellington
famously asking 'Who? Who?' as the list of names was read out.
Queen Victoria herself privately described it as 'a very sorry
Cabinet'. Besides Derby himself, the central figure was Disraeli,
who was appointed Chancellor of the Exchequer and made Leader
of the House of Commons. Expressing doubts about his ability to
manage the Treasury, he was reassured by Derby that 'You know
as much as Mr Canning did. They give you the figures.'

While the government performed better than many had expected,
its minority status gave it an air of being a temporary innovation.
Derby kept to a holding position of retaining his party's opposition
to free trade, while agreeing with Disraeli on the need to abandon
Protectionism as a policy. An election in June was disappointing for
Derby, who had hoped to win a majority, but it helped settle the
vexed issue, delivering another Commons majority for free trade.
Disraeli duly planned to use his autumn Budget to bury Protectionism
for good, with bold measures to cut duties and demonstrate the
Conservatives had adapted to the new spirit of the age. While
received enthusiastically by Conservatives, it soon encountered implacable resistance from the combined opposition in the Commons,
and was defeated, whereupon Derby resigned and advised the Queen
to send for the Peelite Earl of Aberdeen. The latter took office at
the head of a coalition that Derby expected to quickly unravel.

Just over two years later, Aberdeen was forced to resign after
losing a vote on a motion criticising the government's handling of
the Crimean War, and Derby was again asked to form a government.
As before, however, he proved unable to win over the support of
either Palmerston or the Peelites, and he was reluctant to take office
as another minority administration. Instead, Palmerston himself took
office, and remained in power for another three years. When that
government fell after a defeat in the Commons in 1858, Derby was
again recalled to power, and this time consented to rule as a minority
Conservative government.

Lasting just under a year and a half, this second government
enacted some significant measures, the most prominent of which
was the establishment of the British Raj, as administration by the
East India Company was replaced by direct Crown Rule under the

Government of India Act. This created a new Secretary of State for India, the first incumbent being Derby's son, Lord Stanley (later the 15th Earl).

A General Election in 1859 showed an increase in Conservative support but failed to give them the elusive majority that Derby had sought. When the new Parliament assembled, the opposition passed a vote of no confidence and forced the government to resign, with Palmerston returning to office. Many observers might have assumed this would mark the end of his time in high politics, and the Queen's personal recognition of his service through the award of the Order of the Garter certainly suggested an imminent retirement from public life. However, he remained at the helm of his party in opposition for the next seven years, with Disraeli again leading in the Commons. Free of office, Derby also made time for writing, publishing in 1864 a translation of Homer's *Iliad*, which won him much praise and sold well.

During this time, as in previous periods, Derby exhibited a determinedly restrained attitude to opposition, believing in the virtue of patience. He once told his son: 'Wait – don't attack ministers – that will only bind them together – if left alone they must fall to pieces by their own division.' This passive approach often caused friction with Disraeli, whose instincts were far more activist, but in the politics of the time it undoubtedly had some wisdom to it.

Palmerston died in 1865, and while the Liberal government briefly continued under Russell, this only lasted eight months before divisions brought about its collapse in June 1866. Derby was duly recalled to the premiership for an unprecedented third time. By now, however, he was old and increasingly suffering from gout, leaving Disraeli to shoulder much of the burden of administration. He did, however, devote considerable attention to overseeing the drafting and passage of the Second Reform Act in 1867, which doubled the electoral franchise, and neatly ended his ministerial career on the issue that had first made his name.

In February 1868 Derby bowed to ill-health and tendered his resignation for the last time. Despite his continuing misgivings about the suitability and credibility of Disraeli, he nonetheless advised the Queen to send for the Chancellor as his successor. He lived another year and a half, dying at Knowsley in October 1869. When asked in his final days how he felt, he is reported to have replied: 'Bored to the utmost power of extinction.'

Disraeli, unveiling the Parliament Square statue to his predecessor in 1874, pithily summed up his career as: 'He abolished slavery, he educated Ireland, he reformed parliament.'

In physical terms, he has left his mark on the world in a number of ways, with further statues erected on the façade of the Colonial Office on Whitehall, in Miller Park, Preston, and at St George's Hall, Liverpool. He has also been kept firmly on the map in the form of the capital of the Falkland Islands, which was named Stanley in his honour while he was Colonial Secretary in 1843.

In assessing his political character, Derby emerges as a genuine moderate and pragmatist. At a time of huge division and turmoil, he sought conciliation, unencumbered by rigid dogma, and was concerned primarily to preserve stability and order in society. Although accused of lacking principle, he had twice broken from his leadership and party, sacrificing his personal prospects for what he believed to be the right course. He is as notable for the occasions when he resisted office as for those when he took it.

He also possessed a genuine social conscience and liberal instinct. His concern for the landed interest extended to diligent care for the welfare of working people, and despite a lifelong commitment to preserving the pre-eminence of the Anglican Church, he opposed the religious bigotry of many in his party. In later life he championed the first law to combat industrial air pollution, the Alkali Act 1863, making him an early pioneer of the environmental movement.

While his whole range of achievements and qualities are worthy of reappraisal, it is his role as a modern Conservative that perhaps deserves most attention. He inherited the wreckage of a divided Tory faction, and over two decades restored and rebuilt it into a united party of power. There was nothing inevitable about this revival, and without a respected and patient conciliator at the helm the party could well have fractured further and ceased to exist. Credit for forging the modern Conservative Party is too often allocated solely to Peel and Disraeli, while the man who held it together between their tenures for so long is dismissed as a mere placeholder. He deserves much better than that.

By modern standards his reforming views might appear modest, but he believed steadfastly in the virtues of political moderation, making incremental changes to address specific grievances while resisting destabilising radicalism. In this, he can be considered a true Conservative moderniser.

Nigel Fletcher is a Teaching Fellow in Politics and Contemporary History at King's College London, and co-founder of the Centre for Opposition Studies.

27

Earl of Aberdeen

19 December 1852 to 30 January 1855
Coalition

By Jonathan Parry

Full name: George Gordon (Hamilton-Gordon from 1818)
Born: 28 January 1784, Edinburgh
Died: 14 December 1860, Argyll House, St James's, London.
Buried at St John the Evangelist parish church, Stanmore,
Middlesex
Education: Harrow; St John's College, Cambridge
Married to Catherine Elizabeth Hamilton (d. 1812), then
Harriet, widow of Viscount Hamilton, née Douglas (d. 1833); 4
sons, 4 daughters
Quotation: To Clarendon about Gladstone: 'You must keep that
d—d fellow always in office, give him plenty to do, else he is
sure to do mischief.'

GEORGE GORDON SUCCEEDED his grandfather as 4th Earl of Aberdeen when he was just seventeen and took his seat in the House of Lords when he was twenty-two, in December 1806. As a result, he, together with the Earl of Rosebery, was the only prime minister since the 1832 Reform Act who never sat in the House of Commons. It was not impossible to be an effective prime minister from the Lords. However, in Aberdeen's case the narrowness of his political experience helps to explain why his career and his premiership were not more successful.

Aberdeen was, first and foremost, a landed proprietor who believed in aristocratic rule. He preferred life on his Aberdeenshire property to London society. When he inherited the 50,000-acre estate from his grandfather, it was indebted, neglected and backward. He turned it round, drew up model leases for most of his thousand tenants, and planted an estimated 14 million trees in order to aid housebuilding, diversify production and beautify the area.

He was not a man of fashion; his dress style was compared to that of a Methodist parson. Between 1802 and 1804 he used an unusually serious Grand Tour to develop a classical and archaeological expertise, and produced some learned articles.

His formative years were defined by the horror of the French Revolution, which left him equating democracy with disorder and made him a Tory. Though by 1830 he accepted the need for some parliamentary reform, he maintained, when the Reform Act was passed in 1832, that 'the country is thoroughly revolutionised at heart'.

He hated canvassing for votes: the only elections he faced in his life, between 1806 and 1812, were for one of the sixteen places in the House of Lords allocated in each Parliament to the representatives of all the Scottish peers, of which he was one. Fortunately for him, his peerage was upgraded to a United Kingdom one in 1814.

As a result, to an extent that is difficult to credit, Aberdeen was not interested in most of what passed for parliamentary politics: that is to say, day-to-day debates on MPs' grievances and campaigns. He rarely discussed such issues. In fact, he was never comfortable making speeches, even in the comparatively decorous atmosphere of the Lords. He failed to deliver his maiden speech owing to nerves. Subsequent orations were sometimes mumbled to the point that *Hansard* could only observe that 'The Earl of Aberdeen said a few words.'

After a brief diplomatic mission in 1813–14, he half-retired from politics until 1828. At that point, he was tempted by the Duke of Wellington's promise that he could be Foreign Secretary, and this post, which he held in 1828–30 and 1841–6, seems genuinely to have interested him. He was briefly Colonial Secretary in 1834–5, but found colonial affairs tawdry.

His first wife, whom he married in 1805, died in 1812 leaving him with three young daughters. In 1815 he married again and had four sons and a daughter, though he was a widower again from 1833, and by 1834 all four daughters had died.

Aberdeen's two main political principles were old-fashioned ones. The first was a standard Tory loyalty to the King's, or Queen's, government, as the fount of order. His premiership, when it came in 1852, was actively promoted by Victoria and Albert, whose private secretary helped to negotiate it. The second principle was 'men, not measures' – a loyalty to political leaders who upheld Crown authority honourably, rather than to issue-based party campaigns that were likely to foment division. In Aberdeen's case this meant loyalty to William Pitt and then Sir Robert Peel.

When he left the Foreign Office on the collapse of Peel's government in 1846, Aberdeen was sixty-two and rationally could not have expected further office. He had no popular following, had held no domestic post, was universally regarded as reserved and morose, disliked society, and had alienated most Tory peers by supporting Peel. He had been troubled by persistent headaches for years, as well as sciatica. In 1839 his hair fell out and he resorted to wigs and dyed whiskers. Nonetheless, one of the fascinations of politics is the way in which old principles can be reworked and modernised in new circumstances, and Aberdeen became a great beneficiary of that process.

This was, first, because he had considerable talent and intellectual self-confidence. Managing the Foreign Office at the height of Britain's world power required administrative ability, commitment and energy, and Aberdeen, so different from his rival Lord Palmerston in many ways, matched him in that. He mastered his briefs, got quickly to the heart of issues, and had great mental calmness. His scholarly temperament allowed him to see questions from all sides; his judgements were detached and solid.

In 1813 the politically savvy army officer Robert Wilson, soon to be a radical MP, was surprised to discover that Aberdeen was a man like his friends, 'a Liberal politician', with none of the Tories' disabling religious and social prejudices that obstructed clear-headed rational policy making. Like Peel, Aberdeen thought that responsibility in government meant the freedom to make executive judgements without being obstructed by the opinions of those less knowledgeable and dispassionate than himself, whether these were radical orators or Tory backwoodsmen. He may have doubted his talents at public speaking, but he did not doubt his ability to govern.

Second, Aberdeen came to be in the right place at the right time because of the collapse of the old party system between 1846 and 1850 and the desire to find a leader who could rise above enfeebled party divisions.

After the 1848 revolutions on the Continent, it was not plausible for Britain to be governed by landed Tories who wanted to revert to the class-based Corn Laws, or by the old aristocratic Whig family network. More mundanely, neither of these groups could get a majority in the House of Commons at either the 1847 or 1852 elections.

In 1850, Peel dramatically died after falling from his horse. All his remaining followers agreed that Aberdeen was now their senior spokesman. From 1850, he was playing the political game as much as the other party leaders, and after Lord John Russell and the Earl of Derby had each failed to keep their Liberal and Conservative governments together, the choice settled on him as the next prime minister, in December 1852.

The government that Aberdeen formed needed to be a coalition of his own small Peelite group with the bulk of the Whig or Liberal Party. The coalition defined itself largely in terms of what it was not. First, it rejected partnership with the backwoods Conservative Party led by Derby and Benjamin Disraeli, although they had now abandoned their flagship policy of protection for agriculture – because to prejudice they had now added insincerity. Both leaders seemed lightweight, untrustworthy, and hence unstable coalition allies. Second, it rejected Palmerston's bombastic foreign policy, which had created great tensions within the two previous Liberal governments, had annoyed the courts of Europe, had added to international instability, and had triggered economically damaging defence spending increases at home.

Aberdeen's great aim as Foreign Secretary from 1828 to 1830, and again from 1841 to 1846, had been to smooth over differences with the European powers, to defuse tensions and thus to lighten the taxpayer's burden. In fact, it was at his house in 1843 that the phrase 'entente cordiale' was coined to describe the relationship he was seeking with France.

Third, the coalition sought to defuse radical discontent, but to do so by actively managing and disciplining the House of Commons to some useful purpose, so as to show that the existing political system was capable of providing 'good government', or what Aberdeen's Peelite lieutenant William Gladstone called 'efficiency'.

There were two standard ways of disciplining the Commons to support efficient government – the Whig tradition, which prioritised inclusive legislative reforms, especially on constitutional and religious issues; and the Peelite one, which prioritised fair-minded and competent economic policy – but they were not at all incompatible and Aberdeen sought to marry them up. It was obvious, however, that all the key battles would be in the Commons. Therefore, while Gladstone as Chancellor of the Exchequer would facilitate a Peelite economic policy, the most important appointment of all was Russell as Leader of the House of Commons. Russell was the lynchpin of the coalition, driving the legislative agenda that would satisfy Liberal MPs and thus make it work. He had *carte blanche* on domestic policy, which is why Aberdeen now, for the first time, supported his call for a moderate parliamentary reform bill, and a state education bill. In other words, Aberdeen would chair the Cabinet from the Lords, as a cross between Lord Liverpool and Lord Melbourne, while Russell would reprise the dynamic role he had played from 1835 to 1841.

Aberdeen wanted to govern under the label of 'Liberal Conservative', and insisted on a balance at Cabinet level to signify the equal input of both traditions, so that five of his twelve colleagues were Peelites (though there were only forty-five Peelite MPs). His key relationship, and difficulty, throughout the government was with Russell, who had so recently been prime minister for five and a half years, led 270 MPs, and at the age of sixty still had considerable energy and dynamism, but whose various mistakes between 1850 and 1852 made it impossible for him to head the ministry.

Aberdeen was the only person senior enough for Russell to accept as his leader. He also made a verbal promise to step down in Russell's favour at some point. Russell's expectations of the succession were to be a continuing problem for the coalition, but only in combination with much greater difficulties, which ensured that its promise was not delivered. One of these was that the government lacked a majority for a bold agenda. Thus while Gladstone's Budget turned into a great success of the 1853 session, Russell's plans for educational and parliamentary reform had to be deferred, though Aberdeen continued to support them in principle. The ministry instead filled up the session with relatively uncontentious measures generated by the increasingly professional Victorian administrative machine. A good deal of Commons time was also occupied with the reform of Indian administration, including the introduction of competitive examinations into the Indian Civil Service.

By far the government's greatest problem, however, was the worsening international situation caused by Russian pressure on the Ottoman Empire and Napoleon III's determination to combat this in order to increase France's global weight. This was a completely debilitating conundrum, not only because Britain was placed in an unenviable position as between Russia and France, but also because it made Aberdeen himself a politically contentious figure rather than the eirenic elder statesman that he intended.

Aberdeen had sought to marginalise Palmerston by removing him from the Foreign Office, but Palmerston was still a senior Cabinet minister, and anxious to assert his political virility. A strong anti-Russian policy was irresistible for him, but also for most Liberals, for whom Russia was the enemy of liberal nationalism all over central and eastern Europe. Conversely, everyone knew that Aberdeen wanted to maintain good terms with Russia, and to do so by old-school private diplomacy.

This position was half-sustainable in 1828–9, before the increased politicisation produced by the Reform Act, but even from 1844 to

1846, when much less was at stake, Aberdeen's reluctance to confront Russia (or France) had led to coolness with Peel and a lot of press criticism.

It is often said that Britain was dragged into the Crimean War because Cabinet divisions prevented it from following either Aberdeen's or Palmerston's policy consistently, giving Russia fatally mixed messages. There is some truth in this, but it exaggerates Aberdeen's chances of ever getting the Cabinet to support him. The pressure from the Commons in favour of a more assertive policy became overwhelming, especially when it appeared, in September 1853, that Russia's proposed compromises were insincere. Russell as well as Palmerston now succumbed to it. Moreover, the Cabinet's choices were limited by Napoleon's forwardness. It was more logical to work with him in the hope of restraining him than to risk a Franco-Russian partition of Ottoman spoils. Thus, three times in 1853, in June, early October and December, Aberdeen could not prevent the Cabinet from ratcheting up its anti-Russian stance, and already by September he was privately resigned to the inevitability of war. In December, Palmerston's threats to resign from the Cabinet made his position even weaker.

The beginning of the war in March 1854 was the beginning of the end for Aberdeen, though he would not see it. Just as he had failed to speak at the beginning of the 1853 session, leaving Russell to announce the government programme in the Commons, so he continued now not to use the Lords to project any sense of national leadership. Three days after the declaration of war, on 31 March, he made a disastrous reply to a vicious assault by Derby on his weakness towards Russia in 1853; he said that peace remained his main object. He was in no way a war leader. The *Daily News* called him a wet blanket dousing the national fire. Increasing deafness added to his woes. In June he kept his protégé the Duke of Newcastle at the War Office despite press coverage of army maladministration; by the autumn this was in full flood.

Newcastle also became the symbol of Aberdeen's arrogant imposition of Peelites on the Cabinet. As was conventional during the grouse-shooting season, Aberdeen held no cabinets between mid-August and mid-October 1854, to widespread criticism. He was one of very few prime ministers until then who was still in post at seventy; by January 1855, at seventy-one, he was within months of beating the oldest, the Duke of Portland, who had died in office. He clung on mainly because both he and the Queen wanted to keep the objects of the war conservative – limited to ending Russian pressure on Constantinople – rather than liberal, for wider European purposes such as the restoration of Poland. But this decision was hardly within his gift: it would depend overwhelmingly on the course of the fighting, on Napoleon III, and on the peace efforts of the Austrians.

At the beginning of the 1855 parliamentary session, Russell pulled the plug on the government. The radical MP J.A. Roebuck had tabled a motion of inquiry into the conduct of the war effort. Russell jibbed at whipping his Liberal MPs against it. He resigned; the motion passed by 305 to 148; the government fell. Russell's detractors have held the field with their assertion that he acted out of selfishness, but it was surely asking too much to expect him to lead the Commons through a whole parliamentary session amid sensational press exposés of Crimean mismanagement, no prospect of military breakthroughs, and no changes of regime.

As in 1804, 1916 and 1940, Parliament demanded a change of leader in order to prosecute a vigorous war. Aberdeen's defence was the classic one of the competent establishment administrator: that the glaring abuses had been tackled, affairs were on the mend, and nothing would be gained by populist gestures. He also saw – though it is difficult to believe that Russell did not equally see – that MPs would turn for their new leader not to Aberdeen's restless assassin but to Palmerston, who had cannily professed loyalty to the premier while repeatedly burnishing his own popular credentials.

At the end of 1856 Aberdeen wrote to Russell's brother lamenting that Russell had not kept him in place for longer so that peace could have been secured. Russell could then have inherited the coalition intact, preventing the rise of Palmerston, whom they both distrusted, and facilitating a reformist peacetime agenda. This was self-deluding. Aberdeen's tantalising hints about resigning the premiership to Russell had become a clear delaying tactic, a tactic later to be turned into an advanced art by his pupil Gladstone.

After he left office, Aberdeen felt some responsibility for the war, and in the last few months of his life, when his mind gave way, this started to weigh on him acutely. In retrospect, it is difficult to deny that he failed completely as a wartime prime minister. This was due even more to his unenviable position, lacking anything near a majority of like-minded MPs, than to his undoubted short-comings as a speaker and self-publicist. His defenders have always suggested that both Palmerston and Russell behaved in underhand ways by undermining him, but arguably they were the more respon-sible politicians because they were the more responsive to public complaints.

In terms of overall governing strategy, Aberdeen could be seen as the founder of a new Liberal approach to politics. But in truth this would give him more credit than he deserves, since he never articulated this approach well, and many other centrist figures were toying with the same combination of ideas. He played conscien-tiously the main prime-ministerial role now left to a peer, that of Cabinet chairman charged with soothing the great egos of the leading Commons performers. In an era of unthreatened peace, the coalition he put together might have worked, at least for long enough to make future cooperation among its members more likely. If so, it would have generated some impressively 'efficient' govern-ment – though, as Aberdeen's personal traits show, its overall effect would have been to uphold a system of propertied politics that was fundamentally and profoundly conservative.

Jonathan Parry is Professor of Modern British History at the University of Cambridge and a Fellow of Pembroke College.

28

Viscount Palmerston

6 February 1855 to 19 February 1858;
12 June 1859 to 18 October 1865
Liberal

By Roy Hattersley

Full name: Henry John Temple, 3rd Viscount Palmerston
Born: 17 October 1784, Westminster
Died: 18 October 1865, Brocket Hall, Hertfordshire. Buried at
Westminster Abbey
Education: Harrow; University of Edinburgh; St John's College,
Cambridge
Married to Emily Lamb; no children
Quotation: 'The Schleswig-Holstein question is so complicated,
only three men in Europe have ever understood it. One was
Prince Albert, who is dead. The second was a German pro-
fessor who became mad. I am the third and I have forgotten all
about it.'

LORD PALMERSTON WAS almost certainly the most popular politician in British history. It was not a distinction for which he worked or even wanted. To him, the opinions of the common people were of no account. It just so happened that for most of his sixty years in the House of Commons he said and did what most Englishmen would have said and done. He spoke for England and, in consequence, England loved him.

At least, most of England did. Palmerston was the hero of the disenfranchised masses who, before the great reform bills of 1867 and 1884, played no part in determining the government of Great Britain. He was, his stepdaughter ruefully confessed, 'not popular except out of doors among the people'. And, since the choice of government was made 'inside' by the 'quality', Lord Palmerston had to wait to become prime minister until he was seventy-five. Even then, Queen Victoria offered the seals of office to Lord Derby, Lord Lansdowne, Lord John Russell and Lord Clarendon before she sent for 'Old Pam'. He 'kissed hands' on 5 February 1855 and began to rebuild the government that had disintegrated after the House of Commons carried, by 305 votes to 157, a vote of censure on the conduct of the war in the Crimea.

His elevation was greeted by the establishment with a mixture of apprehension and incredulity. John Bright called him an 'aged charlatan', and William Gladstone said that he was the worst minister with whom he had ever worked. Benjamin Disraeli, in a letter to Lady Londonderry, described him as 'an imposter. Utterly exhausted, and at the best only ginger beer not champagne and now an old Pantaloon, very deaf, very blind and with teeth which would fall out of his mouth when speaking if he did not hesitate and halt so in his talk.' But although Palmerston suffered from all the symptoms of old age that Disraeli so cruelly identified, he possessed a remarkable resilience. There were times when he fell asleep in the House of Commons and meetings with ministers had to be cancelled because of his exhaustion. But there were days when his energy seemed undiminished by the years. So – if his response to the vote of censure was a guide – did his arrogance.

There was no escape from the admission that the campaign in the Crimea had been a catastrophe. And Palmerston had no choice but to accept the demand for an inquiry. But even as he announced its creation, he set out what the government was *not* prepared to do. The purchase of commissions would continue as a necessary protection against the creation of a professional officer corps, which, continental experience proved, was inclined to mutiny. There would be no purge of senior officers. Flogging – regular punishment for minor military offences – would not be prohibited. The House of Commons expressed its grudging acquiescence. Parliament took note and the Prime Minister moved on.

The peace talks had begun while the war was still in progress and at a time when it was by no means certain that the Franco-British alliance would win a clean-cut victory. Nevertheless, the Prime Minister already knew the terms of settlement that he wanted to impose on Russia. Palmerston was determined that the Crimea – annexed by Catherine the Great in 1774 – should be returned to Turkey. France and Russia had grown weary of the war and, after the fall of Sebastopol, both governments wanted a quick settlement. Russia was ready to make concessions, though not to surrender. France was willing to sign a peace treaty that did little more than guarantee the end of further Russian expansion. When Palmerston persisted in the demand that the Tsar be humiliated, Napoleon III responded with an ultimatum. France – which supplied two-thirds of the troops fighting in the Crimea – was dissatisfied with the allies' limited war aims and would only fight on if they were extended to include the liberation of all the European vassal states – starting with freeing Poland from Russian rule. Palmerston was cornered. He wanted to contain the Tsar's territorial ambitions, not to depose him. He had no choice but to sign the Treaty of Paris and end the war with the Crimea still an offspring of Mother Russia. *Civis Britannicus* – which Palmerston had done so much to create – was, like the Prime Minister himself, beginning to look outdated.

Then, on 25 October 1856, there occurred one of the unanticipated 'events' that, a hundred years later, another prime minister identified as the nemesis of over-confident politicians. Chinese coastguards stopped and boarded the *Arrow*, a pirate ship that was pillaging merchantmen in the Canton delta. The incident, in itself, was neither unusual nor controversial. But the *Arrow* was different from the other pirate ships that stalked the delta. It was captained by an Ulsterman, registered as British in Hong Kong and flew the Union flag.

Sir John Bowring, the Governor of Hong Kong, and Harry Parkes, the British Consul in Canton, combined in demanding the immediate release of the ship's Chinese crew and a public apology for insulting the British flag. The prisoners were released, but the demand for an apology was ignored. Whereupon Bowring, acting on his own authority, ordered ships of the Royal Navy, which were harboured in Canton, to bombard the town. The local population responded with attacks on British property and British citizens. Five nights of mayhem followed. In London, ministers came to the reluctant but unanimous conclusion that, although the Governor had behaved unwisely, the government had no choice but publicly to support him. Palmerston's defence of Bowring's misplaced belligerence reflected none of the Cabinet's reservations. It included the allegation that critics of the Governor's conduct were willing to 'abandon a large community of British subjects at the extreme end of the globe to a set of barbarians – kidnapping, murdering poisoning barbarians'.

As he expressed his pride in the Royal Navy – ready to sail to the rescue of British citizens anywhere in the world – Palmerston must have remembered his maiden speech in the House of Commons, which sought to justify another naval bombardment – the 1807 assault on neutral Copenhagen that had preceded Britain's illegal 'confiscation' of the Danish fleet. He had believed, for as long as he could remember, that cordite was an essential instrument of diplomacy.

Harry Temple, the 3rd Viscount Palmerston, was born on 20 October 1784. By then the Temples were established at Romsey in Hampshire, but their fortune had been made in Ireland and it was to the Irish peerage that the 1st Viscount Palmerston was elevated in 1723. Irish peers did not sit in the House of Lords and were in consequence eligible for election to the Commons. And it was in the Commons that Harry Temple – who succeeded to the title in 1802 – made his name. He was still a Cambridge undergraduate in 1806 when he fought, and lost, a by-election in the university city. From then on, Lord Palmerston had only two interests in life: politics and women. In Regency England – where preferment depended more on social status than on talent – the two obsessions fitted neatly together.

Palmerston became an independent-minded Tory whose opposition to the government's refusal to extend the franchise to Manchester and Birmingham was described by Wellington as 'mutiny'. The young Harry Palmerston was a follower of George Canning and, despite his regular excursions to the wilder shores of foreign policy, the moderate Canningite within him often slept but never died.

The possession of influential friends did not save Palmerston from languishing in the lower reaches of government for twenty-three years. He was appointed a Junior Lord of the Admiralty in anticipation of his election in 1807 and held that sinecure until 1809. Then he was made Secretary at War, a job that mostly concerned army estimates, pay and rations, while decisions about strategy and deployment of forces were taken by the Secretary of State for War and the Commander in Chief. He was heartily disliked by the War Office clerks, on whom he imposed a strict code of discipline, and was in constant conflict with the Commander in Chief, the Duke of York, who accused him (usually with good reason) of exceeding his authority. Yet, despite its obvious uncongeniality, Palmerston made no attempt to escape the War Office. Offers to make him Irish Secretary and Governor General of Jamaica (with the promise that India would follow) were declined without explanation. His detractors put it about that he was unwilling to be separated from London society, in which, thanks to his amorous adventures, he was known as 'Lord Cupid'. But he also rejected the chance to become Postmaster General, with a seat in the Cabinet. Then Lord Grey, a Whig, offered him the Foreign Office. He accepted and was Foreign Secretary for sixteen of the next twenty years.

Despite the shifting alliances that were a feature of early nineteenth-century politics, a Tory Foreign Secretary in a Whig-led government still excited accusations of desertion and betrayal. In fact, Palmerston's Tory principles were fraying at their edges. He was no longer an implacable opponent of Catholic emancipation, an extension of the franchise or free trade. More important, his foreign policy was, in large part, more progressive than anything that had gone before. Britain's interests, he argued, would be best served by the stability that democracy guaranteed. In consequence, British governments were entitled to 'interfere' – he rejected the term 'intervene' as 'non-English' – when the old autocracies opposed the establishment of representative government in the provinces within their empires. Austria, which Palmerston regarded as an essential bulwark against Russian expansion, was spared the consequences of that policy. But its mere expression made him the hero of Europe's liberation movements. It was a very different philosophy that made him a hero at home.

Palmerston set out the principle on which his foreign policy was based in a speech by which he justified the blockade of the Greek coast during the winter of 1850. 'A British subject, in whatever land he may be, shall feel confident that the watchful eye and strong arm of England will protect him against injustice and wrong.' The 'British subject' in question was, in fact, Portuguese. But Don Pacifico – a money-lender based in Athens – claimed that, having been born in Gibraltar, he was entitled to British help in obtaining compensation for damage done to his property during disturbances in the city that he temporarily called home. Palmerston agreed and accepted, without question, both the justice of the claim and its size as calculated by the claimant. For good measure he informed the Greek government that Greece would be in economic quarantine until all its debts to British subjects were paid. The British government insisted that its Foreign Secretary abandon the blockade. Palmerston remained unrepentant.

Repentance – indeed the acceptance of error as well as the admission of guilt – was not in Palmerston's nature. That was one of the reasons why he lived dangerously in the Foreign Office. But he survived on self-confidence and good fortune. He was lucky when the lady-in-waiting whom he attempted to seduce during a soirée at Windsor Castle decided not to complain to Queen Victoria, and lucky – though he did not think so at the time – when he was forced to resign from the Foreign Office after endorsing, without consulting his colleagues, the *coup d'état* that elevated Louis Napoleon from President of the French Republic to Emperor of France. Palmerston returned to the Cabinet. But he returned as Home Secretary. In consequence, he escaped all blame for the catastrophe of the Crimean War and was ready, in February 1855, to become prime minister. Even then, the highest office almost escaped him. Queen Victoria disliked him. She disapproved of his promiscuity, resented his *hauteur* and believed, not without reason, that he felt it beneath his dignity to serve a woman. He had shown Foreign Office telegrams to William IV before they were dispatched. Queen Victoria was not afforded the same courtesy.

Palmerston's first administration lasted for barely three turbulent years and even that brief tenure was interrupted by a General Election. Britain rejected China's claim for compensation for lives lost and damage done in Canton, and the fighting that followed was fierce enough to be called a war. During the debate on the inevitable vote of censure, the moral outrage expressed by Gladstone and Cobden combined with Disraeli's blatant opportunism to contrive a government defeat by 263 votes to 247. The Prime Minister had ended the debate by describing Yeh Ming Chin, the Chinese leader, as 'guilty of every crime which can deface human nature'. It was the sort of speech that troubled his intellectually fastidious colleagues. But not the British people. According to Lord Shaftesbury, the General Election that followed was fought on a single issue: 'Are you or are you not for Palmerston?' A large majority was 'for'.

Palmerston did not believe that Parliament should waste its time arguing about domestic issues, which he regarded as none of its business. Yet the new government chose to legislate on a subject that provoked unparalleled controversy: divorce law reform. Until 1857, divorce in England and Wales required the applicant to promote an Act of Parliament that ended the marriage. The new bill provided for divorces to be awarded in court after the applicant had proved that a 'matrimonial offence' had been committed. The Church of England was, of course, deeply opposed to relaxing the rules by which couples brought together by God could be rent asunder. But Palmerston was unexpectedly determined that the bill became law. Six years later, at the age of seventy-eight, he was cited as the co-respondent in an application for divorce by Fergus O'Kane, a radical Irish journalist. Folklore credits Disraeli with predicting that news of Palmerston's adultery would double his vote. In fact, Disraeli made a better joke. He compared the alleged liaison to the Fall. 'About Cain we can be certain. But was Palmerston Abel?'

On 8 May 1857 – while the Matrimonial Causes Bill was going through Parliament – ten Hindu sepoys revolted against the use of cartridges that they believed to contain animal fat. They were court-marshalled and imprisoned. Two days after their conviction, an entire sepoy regiment revolted, shot its British officers and marched on Delhi. What Britain calls the Indian Mutiny had begun. The fighting was confined to half a dozen garrison towns, but both the garrisons and the insurgents behaved with unrestrained barbarity. British women and children were brutally murdered. Sepoys were indiscriminately tortured and executed – often by being tied to the mouth of a cannon and blown to pieces. Palmerston remained strangely detached from both the threat to British effective rule of India and the savagery of the conflict. Confident that British arms would prevail in any battle against native levies, he first refused to send reinforcements to India and when, at last, he accepted that they were needed, would not accept the 'indignity' of saving time by sending them overland through France as far as Marseilles. Clarendon, the Foreign Secretary, wrote in his diary: 'Confidence and courage are fine things and contain in them elements of success, but they are bad when, as with Palmerston, they lead to neglect of the means by which they can be attained.' At first, the British press and public applauded the brutal vengeance that followed the suppression of the mutiny – the massacre of sepoys at Cawnpore and the execution of any Indian who turned his back, in a gesture of contempt, on a marching column of British soldiers. Then the tide turned. And Palmerston turned with it. The whole tragedy was blamed on the inefficiency and corruption of the East India Company – the effective government of India. Palmerston revoked the Company's charter and proposed to make India a Crown Colony ruled directly from London. Lord Malmesbury – who had been Foreign Secretary in Lord Derby's Tory Cabinet – confided his frustration in his diary: 'The people talk of our victories in India as being proof of Palmerston's glorious administration.'

Palmerston certainly enjoyed a popularity that was out of all proportion to either his achievements or his ability. But it was based on the single supposition that he spoke for England strong and free, and was, in consequence, as fragile as it was irrational. As soon as it seemed that he no longer represented limitless patriotism, the esteem in which he was held began to crumble. The feet of clay first became visible in 1858 as the result of another of the damaging 'events' that politicians can neither predict nor prevent. A bomb was thrown through the window of the carriage in which Napoleon III and the Empress Eugenie were travelling to the opera. Neither of the royal passengers was hurt, but there were two deaths and many injuries in the surrounding crowd. National outrage followed the discovery that parts of the bomb were 'made in England'. France made an official protest, which ended with the familiar demand that 'something be done'. French army officers petitioned the Emperor with the request that they be allowed to mount a punitive expedition on London. An invasion of the Channel Islands would have been more effective. For it was there that refugees from The Third Republic had gathered. The British government had no doubt that some of them were potential assassins. A letter from the Prime Minister to the Home Secretary began with a request for the invention of an order that could be awarded to Florence Nightingale and ended with the proposal that the Channel Island refugees should be deported to London, where they could be kept under surveillance and measures taken to prosecute any of their number found plotting to overthrow the government of France. The outcome of the request was the Conspiracy to Murder Bill.

For once Palmerston failed to understand, and therefore did not reflect, in either word or deed, the mood of the British people. Disraeli did. The Prime Minister was accused of accepting orders from the hated French and calling into question the ancient right of asylum that proud Englishmen had always believed exemplified the difference between 'this throne of kings' and 'less happier lands'. Palmerston was caught in a trap of his own making. He had encouraged the meaningless patriotism that fuelled the allegation that he was 'toadying' to foreigners. When the Conspiracy to Murder Bill was debated in the House of Commons, radical members proposed the removal of clauses that extended the jurisdiction of British courts to crimes committed abroad. The Tories, who had originally welcomed the bill, caught the mood of the moment and voted with the radicals, and the government was defeated by 215 votes to 254. Palmerston could have attempted to survive in office by moving a vote of confidence. But on the day following the amendment to his bill, he was booed when he rode in St James's Park. He had lost the confidence of the country. So he resigned.

He was not out of office for long. In the spring of 1859, Derby's proposals for electoral reform were rejected by the House of Commons and in the General Election that followed, the Tories could not, alone, command a majority in the House of Commons. By June, Palmerston was back in office. But it was a chastened Palmerston, who looked more cautiously upon Britain's place in the world. There had been years of argument about the status of two duchies – Schleswig and Holstein – which the Treaty of Vienna had guaranteed independence under their Dukes, and the King of Denmark. The Duke of German-speaking Holstein had become a member of the recently formed German Federation. The Duke of mostly Danish-speaking Schleswig had not. Nationalist movements in both Denmark and Germany demanded the recognition of the duchies' true nationality and their incorporation within their culturally parent country. Frederick VII of Denmark proposed a division of the dukedoms between Germany and Denmark. Germany was not satisfied and Bismarck suggested that a settlement would not be reached by diplomacy but by 'blood and iron'.

On 23 July 1863, Palmerston told the House of Commons that if attempts were made to change the status of the duchies by force, the aggressor would find that 'it would not be Denmark alone with which they would have to contend'. On 1 February 1864, Prussian and Austrian forces invaded Schleswig-Holstein. The Danish government waited for Britain to keep what had been accepted as the promise of help. It never came. The Cabinet discussed it, but prudence prevailed. A House of Commons motion, accusing Palmerston of betraying Denmark, was defeated by 313 votes to 295. Palmerston had defeated attempts to resuscitate Palmerstonian foreign policy.

There was another year of life left in 'Old Pam' and another General Election to be fought and won. Then, on 18 October 1865, two days before his eighty-second birthday, he died, still in office. William Ewart Gladstone, who deeply disapproved of both

Palmerston's character and political philosophy, was horrified to discover that no preparations had been made for an appropriate funeral. Gladstone believed that a life of service qualified for a place in Westminster Abbey. So he telegraphed Windsor Castle. And it is in Westminster Abbey that Palmerston rests.

Lord Hattersley is a historian, biographer and former Deputy Leader of the Labour Party. He served as a Member of Parliament from 1964 to 1997.

29

Benjamin Disraeli

27 February 1868 to 1 December 1868;
20 February 1874 to 21 April 1880
Conservative

By Edward Young

Full name: Benjamin Disraeli, later 1st Earl of Beaconsfield
Born: 21 December 1804, 6 King's Road, Bedford Row, Holborn
Died: 19 April 1881, 19 Curzon Street, London. Buried at
Hughenden church, Buckinghamshire
Education: Eliezer Cogan School, Walthamstow; Miss Roper's
School, Islington, and John Potticary's School, Blackheath
Married to Mary Anne Lewis; no children
Quotation: 'Though I sit down now, the time will come when
you will hear me.' (House of Commons, 7 December 1837)

DISRAELI WAS IN bed when news of a General Election reached
him. All his life, Disraeli had been a late riser, but now,
approaching seventy, the idleness was no longer a mere matter of

choice. He was afflicted by gout, which ailed all parts of his body. Each winter, he was worried by asthma and bronchitis. Two years earlier, Disraeli had lost his wife and companion, Mary Anne, to cancer. Without her, he no longer had a London residence. He lived large parts of his days in solitude at Edwards's Hotel in Hanover Square.

It was here, that morning – Saturday 24 January 1874 – that Disraeli, still in his bedclothes, read Gladstone's appeal to his constituents in Greenwich. He stirred himself to work through the weekend. His election address was completed in time for publication in Monday's newspapers. Here at last was Disraeli's opportunity. After almost thirty years without a Conservative majority, the prospect of victory was real.

Six years earlier, Disraeli had enjoyed a brief foretaste. Having outwitted the Whigs to pass the Second Reform Act, he finally climbed, in his own words, 'to the top of the greasy pole', becoming prime minister of a minority Conservative government. But the taste had soon soured. Within a year, the Liberals had regrouped and resumed their rightful place on the mountaintop of British politics. At the 1868 General Election, the Tories suffered their worst defeat in over ten years.

Now the mood had changed. In an age long before opinion polls, insights were unearthed at public gatherings. Two years earlier, at the service to mark the Prince of Wales's recovery from typhoid, Disraeli had been cheered as he made his way down from St Paul's Cathedral. Gladstone, the great reforming prime minister, had been received in silence, punctuated by a few grumpy jeers.

In these ways and others, the political weather had turned. Britain was exhausted after years of Gladstone's hectoring. Disraeli had used the time in opposition to build up the Conservative organisation. Together with John Gorst, he had established a new Conservative Central Office and a fresh apparatus of Conservative associations. Over the coming weeks, the party fielded more candidates and had more money than ever before.

The first votes were cast on 1 February. It soon became clear that the Wilderness Years were at an end. The Conservatives won their first majority since the days of Sir Robert Peel in the 1840s. In all, 350 Tories were elected, compared to 245 Liberals and 57

Irish Home Rulers. Gladstone complained about the immoral forces that had conspired against him. But Disraeli at last had a majority and a moral mandate to rule.

Disraeli never had been given to outward rejoicing, but he found time to celebrate this success. Over the coming weeks, he hosted a series of dinner parties with friends and supporters. It was not then, but two years later, that he made the confession: 'Power has come to me too late. There were days when on waking I felt I could move dynasties and governments, but that has passed away.'

Disraeli's problem was twofold. The first was physical. Years of ceaseless manoeuvring had withered him. At dinner parties and meals, Disraeli would sit in silence – sometimes taking breaks between courses to read extracts from his favourite books. As he had written in his novel *Coningsby* thirty years earlier, 'when men are young, they want experience, and when they have gained experience, they want energy'. So it proved for Disraeli's own career.

There was also another challenge. This was the lack of a plan. Forty years of politics and campaigning had not equipped Disraeli with anything as humdrum as a set of practical policies. The absence became obvious when the new Cabinet met. In the words of Disraeli's Home Secretary, Richard Cross: 'From all his speeches, I had quite expected that his mind was full of legislative schemes; but this did not prove to be the case. On the contrary, he had to rely on the various suggestions of his colleagues, and as they themselves had only just come into office, there was some difficulty in framing the Queen's Speech.'

Yet the gap was more than a mere oversight. For Disraeli, real power was not about anything as prosaic as preparing a Budget or passing bills. To be Prime Minister had always been Disraeli's aim. The trappings of office, the privileges of patronage, meetings with a monarch and manoeuvring an empire – these were the real tasks of any self-respecting prime minister. Occasionally a cartoon captures the truth better than an essay. So it was with one published by *Punch* in 1872. A deputation arrived to speak to Disraeli; they wanted to enquire about the Conservative leader's programme for government; Disraeli responded: 'Eh? – Oh! – Ah! – Yes! – Quite so! Tell them . . . with my compliments, that we propose to rely on the Sublime Instincts of an Ancient People!!'

Years before, as a young man, Disraeli had developed a dazzling set of ideas about the country. These ideas stopped short of an ideology, but he returned to them throughout his career. They were like a collection of family silver – proudly polished, genuinely cherished, rarely used, but always on display. It is hard to argue that any were realistic. On the contrary, they were preposterous, based on three ahistorical themes – like the Cavaliers, Disraeli believed in the potential of a reawakened English monarchy; like a medieval knight, he believed in a chivalrous alliance between the rich and the poor; and as Palmerston and Canning had done before him, Disraeli believed in national prestige as the only solid basis for foreign policy. Every so often, these ideas would be taken out of the cupboard and put to practical use – perhaps as an epigram in a novel, or as the inspiration for a speech. In a similar fashion, these ideas were now taken out of the cupboard and prepared for service.

The first outing was Disraeli's elaborate, almost ironic, courtship of the Queen. All his life, Disraeli believed that kings and queens retained an inner magic. This magic, in his view, rendered pointless the modern trend to restrict royal power. Indeed, he once said, mischievously, that if Prince Albert had not died, the nation would soon have gladly restored an absolute monarchy. On taking office, Disraeli therefore told the Queen that whatever she wanted would be done, 'whatever the difficulties might be'. The Queen in these days was at her most unhinged and erratic. But she was taken in by Disraeli's attention. He took to calling her the 'Faerie Queen' and 'Queen Titania', and in his own words, laid the flattery on 'with a trowel'.

It took time for this flattery to bear fruit. In 1876, Disraeli brought forward the Royal Titles Bill. This made Victoria the Empress of India. Disraeli was pleased because 'it is only by the amplification of titles that you can often touch and satisfy the imagination of nations'. The Queen was pleased because her daughter was married to the son of the German Emperor, which meant that one day she herself would become an Empress, and therefore take precedence over Victoria at dinner.

The second area where Disraeli's youthful ideas gave a boost to policy was in reforming society. The government's efforts here were undeniable, although they stopped short of a full-blown alliance between the rich and the poor. As the years went on, a belief grew that Disraeli's government had done more to help the working poor than any other Victorian administration. This belief had powerful sponsors; one radical MP told his constituents that the 'Conservative Party have done more for the working classes in five years than Liberals have in fifty'. Disraeli himself told one correspondent that his legislation would 'gain and retain for the Conservatives the lasting affection of the working classes'. It is important therefore to examine the legislative record carefully.

Disraeli's first government in 1868 had brought in a number of domestic reforms, for example abolishing public executions and setting up a Royal Commission on Sanitary Laws. Four years later, Disraeli made two significant speeches, the first at Manchester's Free Trade Hall, and later at the Crystal Palace to the National Union of Conservative Associations. Both placed a clear emphasis on social reform. Although the bulk of both speeches was an assault on the Whig government, there were hints of new policies ahead. Remarkably for a Victorian prime minister, Disraeli claimed that the 'first consideration of a minister should be the health of the people'. He invoked the classics to reinforce his argument: '*Sanitas Sanitatum, Omnia Sanitas*'.

Now in office with a clear majority, for a brief period these sentiments seemed to surface. Within a few years, the government had passed a Public Health Act, two pieces of trade union legislation, an Act to protect Friendly Society funds, the Artisans Dwellings Act, the Agricultural Holdings Act, two Factory Acts, the Merchant Shipping Act, an Education Act, the Rivers Pollution Act and a Sale of Food and Drugs Act. Of all the bills passed, perhaps the most important were the Employers and Workmen Act, and the Conspiracy and Protection of Property Act. In effect, the second of these legalised peaceful picketing. 'We have settled the long and vexatious contest between Capital and Labour,' Disraeli observed.

Except behind the record lies a flaw. The Home Secretary, Richard Cross, not Disraeli, was the driving force. On the whole, the pattern of policymaking tended to be that Cross and his patron Lord Derby would come up with a proposal; they would bring it to Cabinet, where a number of ministers would complain – but Disraeli would step in and give Cross permission to proceed. From then on, the Cabinet would work through the details. Disraeli meanwhile would fall asleep.

Foreign policy was the exception that proved the rule. Here Disraeli was highly active. His motivation was essentially literary rather than geopolitical. All his life, Disraeli believed that the world should be divided into empires, each one underpinned by a cast of bankers, priests, princesses and secret societies. Moreover, this was a field of policy that suited Disraeli's own skills. In nineteenth-century diplomacy, the pen did appear mightier than the sword. As Disraeli wrote in his final novel, *Endymion*: 'Look at Lord Roehampton – he is the man. He does not care a rush whether the revenue increases or declines. He is thinking of real politics: maintaining our power in Europe.' Disraeli barely understood European geography, but this reinforced rather than reduced his self-belief. 'I really believe that the "Eastern Question" that has haunted Europe for a century . . . will fall to my lot to encounter – dare I say settle.' And so he thrust himself into the scene.

Two thoughts guided him. The first was that Britain was an imperial country. For Disraeli this did not simply mean a collection of colonies. He meant that Britain was an Asiatic power, focused particularly on India, but also on British interests in the Near and Middle East. The second thought was about prestige. Prestige in Disraeli's mind was a solid asset. It should be preserved and accumulated at every opportunity. Prestige was the true single currency of international politics.

There is no space here to replay the Cabinet drama that ran for two years during the Eastern Crisis. Nor is there scope to tell the story of Disraeli's crowning moment, the Congress of Berlin and the jubilant return to Charing Cross in July 1878. In both cases, it is hard in retrospect to see exactly what Disraeli's policies achieved in terms of refashioning the balance of European power. A more solid success was the purchase of a minority share in the Suez Canal two years earlier. This had all the characteristics of a typically Disraelian intrigue – the flattery of the Queen, the urgent Cabinet meeting, the diligent emissary, and above all Lord Rothschild and an enormous commercial loan. The purchase itself gave Britain little practical power in the short term, but as a signal of intent in the region, it bolstered British confidence and ultimately made Britain some money.

The real challenge came in the last two years of Disraeli's government. His domestic reforms had petered out. Abroad he was unable to extract Britain from a series of spectacular failings in South Africa and Afghanistan. Gladstone meanwhile once again was at the forefront of politics through his Midlothian campaign. Worst of all was the harvest. Disraeli had built his Conservative career on his performances during the Corn Law crisis in the 1840s, but as prime minister he encountered his own agricultural catastrophe. Faced with the prospect of bringing back protection or relying on cheap imports, Disraeli chose the latter, annoying many farmers but also completing his own reverse from the champion of protection to supporter of free trade.

Disraeli ran down the clock before calling a General Election. When the moment finally came in March 1880, he made no attempt to campaign on his record. His election address warned of the emerging dangers in Ireland. In his campaign headquarters at Hatfield House, Disraeli sustained the belief that he would prevail. But Gladstone's campaign had proved effective. The result was almost a mirror image of Disraeli's success six years earlier: 353 Liberals were elected, 238 Tories and 61 supporters of Home Rule.

A few weeks later, Disraeli wound up his government and returned to his solitude as leader of the opposition. For the rest of the year, he lived a strange existence. Lytton Strachey described him as an assiduous mummy – moving from dinner party to dinner party, saying little and largely detached from politics. At the end of March 1881, Disraeli caught a chill which turned into bronchitis. 'I am blind and deaf. I only live for climate and I never get it.' His last twenty-four hours were acutely painful as he struggled to breathe. He died at half past four in the morning on 19 April 1881.

Disraeli after his death became the subject of an extravagant posthumous mythology. The first flowering was quite literally a flower. In the years after 1881, people came together on 19 April and pinned primroses to their coats to remember Disraeli. The custom grew into a club, which became a cult across the country, as Lord Randolph Churchill and Henry Drummond Wolff established the Primrose League in Disraeli's memory. Within six years of Disraeli's death, 500,000 had enrolled in the organisation. By 1910, two million were members. No other political organisation has had success like it in British history.

A few decades later came Hollywood films. Even Disraeli's quotations have endured. Eighty-eight appeared at our last count in the *Oxford Dictionary of Political Quotations* – more than any other prime minister, then or since. Many remain in common use: 'England does not love coalitions'; 'I have climbed to the top of the greasy pole'; 'A range of exhausted volcanoes'; 'The Right Honourable Gentleman caught the Whigs bathing, and walked away with their clothes.' In death, Disraeli has also been hailed as the author of a small library of aphorisms with which he seems to have had no actual link. Wit has its own magnetism it seems.

But the largest cloud of confetti has been thrown by generations of Conservative politicians. Tributes to Disraeli have been almost like a rite of passage for any aspiring Tory MP. Over the last two centuries, Conservatives have hailed him variously as the man who invented Tory Democracy, a progressive Conservative, a supreme parliamentary tactician who dragged the party from the doldrums, and the inventor of something called 'One Nation' Conservatism.

Yet the closer one looks, the more unsteady these achievements seem. How do you piece together a fair judgement of Disraeli? There are clues in his youthful exploits and early career. Unlike other Victorian prime ministers, many of whom emerged almost effortlessly from school and university into politics and public service, Disraeli's early years were unimpressive. He was consumed by a destructive desire for fame. 'I am one of those to whom a moderate reputation can give no pleasure', he wrote on one occasion. And on another: 'Fame, although not posthumous fame, is necessary to my felicity.'

The search for fame drove Disraeli down different paths. He was articled as a solicitor's clerk, but soon came to the conclusion: 'To be a lawyer, I must give up my chance of being a great man.' Literature provided a more interesting opportunity. Much has been made of Disraeli as the first novelist to become prime minister. The truth is that most of Disraeli's novels don't work. Many were an exercise in self-analysis. As he wrote in 1833: 'My works are the embodification of my feelings. In *Vivian Grey* I have portrayed my active and real ambition. In *Alroy*, my ideal ambition.' *Contarini Fleming* meanwhile was the 'development of my poetic character'. He concluded: 'This Trilogy is the secret history of my feelings – I shall write no more about myself.'

It was while writing these novels that Disraeli decided on politics. But here, too, was a difference. Other prime ministers described politics as lofty service or a divine calling. Not so Disraeli. For him, politics was an almost physical craving. As he wrote in *Vivian Grey*: 'And now everything was solved! The inexplicable longings of his soul, which had so often perplexed him, were at length explained. The want, the indefinable want, which he had so constantly experienced, was at last supplied . . . He paced his chamber in an agitated spirit, and panted for the Senate.'

As it turned out, it took Disraeli five elections before the panting ended and he entered the senate. But throughout that time, there was another guiding theme.

On 31 July 1817, Disraeli aged twelve was baptised into the Church of England. Born a Jew, it is unlikely he would have ever become an MP if not for this chance event. Curiously, Disraeli, who expended huge energy describing his upbringing, made no mention of this moment in later writings. But he remained fascinated by race and religion throughout his career.

His views were consistent but unique. It is hard to detect any deep religious conviction in Disraeli, but nonetheless he believed strongly in the social utility of belief. 'The connexion of religion with the exercise of political authority is one of the main safeguards of the civilisation of mankind,' he explained. At the same time, Disraeli developed his own ranking of the Abrahamic religions. These can be found most starkly in his writings and speeches. For example: 'The Jews are humanly speaking the authors of your religion.' 'God never spoke to a European.' Arabs are merely 'Jews on horseback'. In this hierarchy of faiths and religions, Disraeli himself held a notable position. 'I am the blank page between the Old Testament and the New.'

These beliefs underpinned the one conviction on which Disraeli never wavered. Equivocal and evasive on so many issues, Disraeli never faltered in his support for the rights of practising Jews to sit in Parliament. He did so even when it damaged his political interests.

But the way he made his case often undermined the argument. While others appealed to the growing trend of religious toleration, Disraeli argued that Jews should be admitted because of their superiority. 'Where is your Christianity if you do not believe in their Judaism?' he asked his fellow MPs.

Disraeli himself was always viewed as an outsider and at times tolerated enormous abuse. When he stood for election, he was invariably welcomed with cries of 'Shylock' and 'Ole Clothes'. At Shrewsbury when he stood for election, a man arrived on a donkey saying he had come to take Disraeli back to Jerusalem. It was partly in response to these barbs that he developed his famous sense of self-control. He learned a trick of delivering jokes without showing any flicker of emotion. The stream of cutting comments simply flowed out of his mouth. This was the skill that at last made Disraeli famous when, during the Corn Law crisis in the 1840s, night after night, his speeches proved lethal to Sir Robert Peel.

It was also around the time of the Corn Law crisis that Disraeli finished his novel, *Sybil, or The Two Nations*. It is one of his finest works and reads more fluently than novels by many of his peers. Out of that book arose the most powerful myth about Disraeli. This is the notion that he invented 'One Nation' Conservatism.

The flaws in the theory are plentiful. The first is pedantic but important. So far as we can tell, Disraeli never used the phrase 'One Nation'. It was invented fifty years later by Stanley Baldwin. The second weakness is the plot of *Sybil*. This is a love story, in which an aristocratic Tory falls in love with a working-class girl. Much of the book is therefore about why the two cannot be together. Yet at the end the problem is magically solved – Sybil turns out to be an heiress after all. The plot therefore disproves the philosophy; the heroine ends up not crossing, but confirming, the class divide.

Then there are Disraeli's own notebooks and private jottings. These contain evidence about what was in his cupboard of ideas. Two extracts in particular are revealing. The first mention of 'Two Nations' by Disraeli is not in fact in *Sybil* but in his commonplace book three years earlier. In the book, he sets out the idea of 'The Two Nations' but links it to 'The Five Great Forces' of political power. These were 'Dynasties and Governments', 'Nationality', 'Religious Opinions', 'Political Principles' and 'Material Interests'.

There is nothing here, however, to suggest that these forces or facts could be collapsed or eroded. They were simply a description of an underlying truth about the world. A few pages further on in the notebook, we find another example: 'The fusion of manners, classes & peoples diminishes national & individual character.' The last thing Disraeli would have wanted was to diminish national character by levelling up, or levelling out, society.

And so we are left with a set of contradictions. The novelist who inspired One Nation Conservatism never shared its ambitions. The politician with no strong religious feeling nevertheless believed strongly in the utility of belief. The Conservative who rescued his party from opposition had wrecked it himself in the 1840s. The parliamentarian who bewitched his peers found it hard to hold down any lasting coalition. The campaigner who became one of the greatest leaders of the Conservative Party only won one General Election and lost six. The Prime Minister who became a favourite of Queen Victoria never really behaved like a Victorian at all.

Oscar Wilde later wrote that Disraeli hadn't earned a place in Parnassus, but he would be quoted in Piccadilly. This is indeed a fair summary of what he achieved.

Consider Disraeli's career. By any standard, he ought never to have had political success. He lied and cheated repeatedly. He was mired in debts and threw off any relationship that no longer suited him. And yet, over time, he soared past these problems. He did so because he breathed life into politics.

Disraeli deserves to stand on a different summit to other prime ministers. There is no doubt that Disraeli attained considerable achievements as prime minister – not least becoming the first Jewish politician to hold the position. But when the ledger is looked at, and all sides accounted for, it is hard to sustain the view that Disraeli was one of our greatest prime ministers. The legacy he left the country was mixed and his political achievements were, by and large, not lasting. Instead, Disraeli deserves a different accolade. Over the course of forty years, he almost single-handedly raised the esteem in which Parliament was held by the people it represented. He was therefore the greatest Member of Parliament our country has ever seen.

Disraeli would not have been downcast at this verdict. He held no truck with traditional claims about what prime ministers were meant to achieve. The fact that he had made it, and enjoyed it, and dazzled in office, was enough of a legacy. As Disraeli lay dying on 19 April 1881, his friend and private secretary, Monty Corry, observed that Disraeli enjoyed a final moment of calm just before he passed away. We do not know what he was thinking, but Corry's account is perfectly plausible: 'as I looked on his dear face, just at the moment when his spirit left him, I thought that I had never seen him look so triumphant and full of victory'.

Edward Young is a Partner at Headland Consultancy and stood as the Conservative Candidate for York Central in 2017. His book Disraeli, or The Two Lives *co-written with Douglas Hurd was published in 2013.*

30

William Ewart Gladstone

3 December 1868 to 17 February 1874;
23 April 1880 to 9 June 1885; 1 February 1886 to
20 July 1886; 15 August 1892 to 2 March 1894
Liberal

By Simon Heffer

Full name: William Ewart Gladstone
Born: 29 December 1809, Liverpool
Died: 19 May 1898, Hawarden Castle, Flintshire. Buried at
Westminster Abbey
Education: Eton; Christ Church, Oxford
Married to Catherine Glynne; 4 sons, 4 daughters
Quotation: 'All the world over, I will back the masses against
the classes.' (Liverpool, 28 June 1886)

GLADSTONE'S REPUTATION ALMOST a century and a quarter
after his death relies too much on folk memory and too little

on the hard facts of history. He was an unbending religious zealot who used to flagellate himself; he took prostitutes into Downing Street and sought to reform them; he spoke to Queen Victoria as though she were a public meeting; he saw the means of settling Ireland's differences with Britain but was thwarted by reactionary Tories; he was a rigid economist who believed in the small state; he was a fanatical chopper-down of trees (what is less well known is that he was an equally fanatical planter of them) and he spent much of the mid nineteenth century sparring with Benjamin Disraeli, his Tory counterpart. There is enough truth in all those statements to make one understand why so many people hold them to be entirely accurate, but as with all aspects of a man as complex, brilliant and long-lived as Gladstone, they are nowhere near the whole truth. And his is a life about which we know a great deal; from the age of sixteen he kept a diary, which runs to fourteen published volumes, and left behind a vast correspondence.

Gladstone is the incarnation of nineteenth-century liberalism, yet he started his privileged political career (he was given a pocket borough by the Duke of Newcastle at the age of twenty-two, fresh from Eton and Oxford, where he took a Double First in *Literae Humaniores* and mathematics) as a Tory, and as a Tory fiercely opposed to one of the main political movements of his youth: the abolition of slavery. This was not least because the Gladstones were a family of slave owners; when slavery was abolished, the family received over £100,000 in compensation: more than £15 million, tax free, in today's values. He had grown up in an intensely politically minded family, and his interest in politics had driven him to become President of the Oxford Union. The wealth of his mercantile family meant he did not need to work for a living; a political career, if he could find a patron, was the obvious next step. Newcastle was that patron. In his first election at Newark, Gladstone demonstrated his power as a stump-orator and campaigner, qualities that would mark him out throughout his political career. In a further irony, given the direction of his later career, he argued forcefully in his first campaign against Whig plans for parliamentary reform, as he had in his career in the Oxford Union. Even then, he was not against a measure of reform; he just feared the Whigs wanted too much too soon.

Gladstone's immense talent was spotted as soon as the Whigs left office, when Sir Robert Peel – his first and most important political influence – gave him a junior position in the Treasury at the end of 1834. Within a month he was moved sideways to a job at the War Office, but soon Peel left office. In opposition, Gladstone's main cause became to attack British encouragement of the Opium trade in China, which Britain fought to ensure could continue. His sister Helen had suffered as a result of taking the drug, and Gladstone considered the Whig government's support for the trade immoral. It would not be the last time he would savage a government for what he considered its ethical shortcomings.

Gladstone had not only imbibed Tory politics as a young man: he had also imbibed Christianity, a creed that, unlike Toryism, would stay with him for life. It underpinned his ethic of public service, even if it made him, in the eyes of some of his critics, priggish or, at times, messianic; some of his Oxford contemporaries found him so insufferable that, in 1830, they went to his rooms and beat him up. He considered offering himself for ordination, but his family talked him out of it. However, religion would increasingly inform his political decisions and, in many respects, necessitate in his estimation his move from Toryism to Liberalism. In 1839 he published *The State in its Relations with the Church*, his first great intellectual treatise, which caused him to be denounced by Macaulay as 'the rising hope of those stern and unbending Tories'. When Peel returned to office in 1841, Gladstone was reluctant to join his ministry, because of what he saw as the Tory Party's equivocation over the opium trade, but he accepted the post of Vice-President of the Board of Trade; he was promoted to President, and the Cabinet, in 1843. This would have a seismic effect on the future of Britain, in more ways than one.

Gladstone's first legislative priority was also morally driven: it was to ensure some degree of security for the large number of men employed as 'coal-whippers', the name given to those who moved coal from vessels to barges at docks. There was not only no security, but the men, in order to get work, had to frequent dockside pubs and have the approval of the landlord, which meant they spent most of their earnings on alcohol, and were frequently drunk. This appalled Gladstone. He intervened in what he considered to be the most 'socialistic' act of the era, and set up central employment exchanges for them.

However, his main job at Trade was to manage the outbreak of 'railway mania' – the desire to link up towns and cities across the country by the revolutionary new means of the steam train. He streamlined legislation to assist the construction of long stretches of line; he also laid the foundations of the modern regulatory state, by forcing railway companies to provide cheap fares. This had an immense effect on the British economy, enabling greater physical mobility of labour and establishing around London and other major cities a commuter belt, allowing the expansion of those cities and the growth of a clerical, middle class. Gladstone ensured two other important by-products of the railway boom: he ensured that the equally novel invention of the telegraph could run on wires and poles alongside the new network of railways; and he put a contingency in the rail legislation that, in times of emergency, the network could be commandeered by the state. Long after Gladstone's death, in the Great War and the Second World War, this contingency would prove invaluable.

Yet the most influential and far-reaching act of Gladstone's time at the Board of Trade was his advice to Peel that, if Ireland were not to starve during the potato famine of the mid-1840s, the government should repeal the Corn Laws to enable the importation of cheaper grain. The laws had been passed by Lord Liverpool's administration after the Napoleonic Wars to safeguard the income of Tory landowners; tariffs placed on imports of cheap grain from overseas kept the price of home-grown crops artificially high. But it also caused immense hardship to poorer people, and when the potato crop failed in Ireland, there was no chance of most of the starving population being able to afford grain, and therefore bread, as a substitute. Gladstone succeeded in convincing Peel that basic humanity demanded a reversal of thirty years of Tory policy; the process of repealing the Corn Laws followed in the teeth of opposition from Peel's own party, and was completed only with the help of what was now called the Liberal Party. The internal opposition was led by Disraeli, in a series of morally shameful speeches made in his capacity as a client of the landed Cavendish-Bentinck family: it confirmed Gladstone's dismal opinion of the man who would soon become his main political adversary. No one at the time could realise just what a profound effect Gladstone's advocacy to Peel of free trade in cereals would have on British prosperity. When prices fell and people felt their purchasing power, and therefore their standard of living, increasing, it became apparent that free trade in all commodities – not just in grain – was likely to improve prosperity. More fundamentally, as Britain removed tariffs from all sorts of imports, so did other countries lift their taxes on goods imported from Britain. At a time when Britain was the leading manufacturing nation in the world, this was hugely significant. From 1846 to 1873, when an agricultural depression started, the country enjoyed almost three decades of non-stop growth. This was Gladstone's triumph as much as Peel's, and one of his greatest legacies.

But before the repeal could happen, Gladstone had left the Cabinet, for the most abstruse moral reasons. The government made an annual grant to a Catholic seminary at Maynooth in Ireland; Gladstone had long objected to the taxpayers of a country with an established Protestant church funding a training school for clergy of what he saw as an alien religion. So when the government decided to increase the grant in 1845, he voted for it, under collective responsibility, but then resigned in case anyone should think he had done so out of hypocrisy in order to keep office and further his ambitions. Later in the year Peel restored him to office as Colonial Secretary. Under the law at the time, he had to resign his seat and fight a by-election on receiving his new office, but because of his support for the repeal of the Corn Laws, the Duke of Newcastle (an avid Protectionist) removed his patronage. Gladstone kept his post while searching for another seat, but soon the search lost its urgency, as Peel's government was defeated within weeks on a measure unrelated to the Corn Laws.

The behaviour of the Tory Party over the repeal ended Gladstone's affiliation with the party: but he did not yet join the Liberals. He became, after Peel himself, the most prominent member of the Peelite faction, a group that can now be seen as 'transitioning' from the Tory Party to a Liberal Party, which, under the growing influence of men such as William Cobden and John Bright, was becoming increasingly associated with free trade in all its forms. Gladstone managed to get elected for Oxford University in 1847, and would never be without a parliamentary seat again.

While out of office in the late 1840s, Gladstone continued to do important work. He lived on his wife's family's estate at Hawarden in Flintshire, and applied his mind to making it profitable, in which he succeeded. He was a founder of a school at Glenalmond in Scotland – this was an era of the establishment of numerous private schools – rooted in the principles of Anglicanism. He also, in 1848, founded the Church Penitentiary Association for the Reclamation of Fallen Women: from the following year he started to encounter prostitutes on the street, and would take them back to the kitchens of his house in Carlton House Terrace where he would sit, often with his wife, and talk to them, and try to persuade them to end their life of vice. He helped support institutions for them, and to find work for them, often overseas in the colonies. This work brought ridicule and suspicion upon him, but in his papers after his death was found a sworn declaration by him that he had never been unfaithful to his wife. He did, however, feel severe temptation, and between 1845 and 1860 often flagellated himself as a punishment, noting the act in his diaries.

Peel died in 1850, but Peelism lived on, and when Aberdeen formed a government in 1852 it was with a coalition of Whigs, Liberals and Peelites, and the free-trading strict economist Gladstone – who had already exhibited, in his attitude towards Maynooth, an almost religious zeal in spending taxpayers' money responsibly and frugally – was the obvious choice as Chancellor of the Exchequer. Gladstone had dismissed with predictable distaste an approach by Disraeli, his predecessor as Chancellor, on behalf of the Tories to swallow his principles and bring the Peelites back to the Tory Party. Disraeli was desperate to cling to office, Gladstone desperate to cling to his principles; the twain would never meet, and the cynicism of Disraeli's approach further disgusted Gladstone, and lowered his opinion of the latter still further.

Once in the Treasury, Gladstone proceeded in a familiarly Peelite way. His first priority was further tariff reform. He also made a strategic plan to cut government spending so that, in time, he could abolish the income tax, and put more weight on indirect taxes. In his 1853 Budget he cut the threshold on income tax from £150 to

£100, believing that the more people he forced to pay it, the more they would demand its abolition by supporting an administration that promised to cut public spending; and the sudden increase in revenues helped make up for what was lost from import duties, until rising consumption of goods bearing indirect taxes made up the shortfall. The 1853 Budget, and the five-hour speech in which it was delivered, was regarded as one of the greatest financial measures ever introduced, and one of the finest parliamentary performances ever heard. Again, the moral underpinning of the speech was profound: Gladstone believed, plainly and simply, that the state had no right to help itself to a share of people's income, and that the fairest form of taxation was levied on goods such as alcohol, tobacco, sugar and other luxuries that people chose, but did not need, to buy.

His determination to eliminate income tax was thwarted by the outbreak of the Crimean War in 1854, when he had to raise the rate from 7d in the pound to 1s 2d in the pound over two Budgets in two months. When the conduct of the war led to a demand for an enquiry, all the Peelites in the government resigned, and from 1855 to 1859 Gladstone was out of office. It was during this respite that he discovered the pleasures of forestry, not merely felling trees (principally as part of generating income for his estate) but also extensively planting them. In 1858 Lord Derby formed a Conservative government in which, once more, the Peelites refused to serve because of Derby's and Disraeli's rigid commitment to Protectionism. When Palmerston returned to power in 1859, the Peelites went in with him, and Gladstone was once more Chancellor.

The underlying principle of his seven years at the Treasury – he would be there until the Liberals went out of office after the defeat of their Reform Bill in 1866 – was a refusal to borrow to cover the deficit he had inherited from the Tories. So income tax, which had been cut to 5d in the pound, was raised to 9d, with a 1s 1d rate for those on higher incomes. Gladstone continued to promote free-trade arrangements with countries resistant to them, his first success being with France. He had a further moral purpose in this, believing that countries who traded with each other would not fight each other, and so Europe would continue to be at peace.

In the 1860 Budget, Gladstone abolished 85 per cent of the

remaining duties on imported goods, and by 1865 he had cut income tax to 4d in the pound. It was in this period that he talked of preferring to allow money to 'fructify in the pockets of the people' rather than have it wasted by the government. In 1861 he encouraged the spread of knowledge by removing the duty on paper; this was the era in which he became 'the people's William', being credited with making the essentials of life, notably food, more affordable, and fuelling the rise of British industry through his deregulatory policies. Working people came to see Gladstone as a man who believed – to use a phrase from a later era – in social justice. In less than twenty years since the repeal of the Corn Laws, wealth in Britain had, slowly but unmistakeably, come to be shared more evenly; and Gladstone was celebrated for having been the main agent of this.

It was a natural progression from this belief in enriching the working man to enfranchising him; and by 1864 Gladstone firmly believed there should be another measure of reform, and argued for it passionately in Cabinet – not least because he believed that by giving the working man a stake in the country's future he would rise to his responsibilities, and above all would support the Liberals for having given him the vote. Palmerston, the prime minister, violently disagreed: but when he died in 1865 his successor, Lord Russell, was more amenable. The bill he and Gladstone tried to get through Parliament in 1866 failed because of opposition from Whigs, led by Robert Lowe, who doubted the ability of the lower classes to cope with the challenges of enfranchisement, and who joined forces with the Conservatives to defeat it. Disturbances broke out around Britain in the autumn and winter of 1866–7, terrifying the Tories so much that Disraeli ended up piloting through the Commons a Reform Bill far more liberal than Russell and Gladstone had tried to secure. Lord Derby handed over the leadership of his party to Disraeli, and Russell to Gladstone: the peak of the rivalry of the two men thus began in 1867, and when Disraeli was forced to call an election in 1868, Gladstone's chance to hold the highest office came at last.

In that era, elections were held over several days, and Gladstone, famously, was cutting down a tree at Hawarden in December 1868 when he had word that General Grey, the Queen's private secretary, was on his way to him to invite him to an audience with the Queen, to kiss hands and become prime minister. It was at this point that, somewhat ahead of the game (though there had been Fenian outrages during the 1860s, notably some bomb attempts in London in 1868 itself), he said that 'my mission is to pacify Ireland'. The Queen, a few years later, equally memorably told her daughter, the Crown Princess of Prussia, that Gladstone spoke to her as if she were 'a public meeting'. The two of them would never get on, especially after 1880 when the Queen had had six years of Disraeli fawning and grovelling to her in a way she was too stupid to see through. Disraeli told Matthew Arnold at this time that, when flattering royalty, the secret was 'to lay it on with a trowel'; no one had a bigger trowel, or laid it on more lavishly, than he did. Gladstone, who quite probably had more genuine respect for the Queen than Disraeli did, demonstrated it by treating her with sincerity rather than with flannel, and speaking to her as someone on his intellectual level (which she plainly was not) rather than patronising her.

Gladstone's administration of 1868–74 was one of the greatest, perhaps *the* greatest, of the nineteenth century. It was informed by his profound sense of morality and belief in justice and meritocracy. He did not believe in the latter – the word itself would not be coined until a hundred years later – for its own sake, but because he saw how acting on its principles would enrich the country. The measure whose effects still echo today was the 1870 Education Act. It did not provide a free school place for every child; but it did ensure that every child up to the age of twelve had access to such a place. This accelerated the opportunities for working-class children to be educated, and to enhance social mobility and prosperity in Britain, and was fundamental to the development of society.

His administration did two other things that brought radical change to Britain. He abolished the purchase of army commissions, which meant that promising men could become army officers without having a fortune behind them. And he ensured that admission to all senior jobs in the home civil service was secured by examination rather than by patronage – the diplomatic service finally followed suit after the Great War. He also brought the secret ballot into parliamentary elections, began the reorganisation of the English courts system, and introduced a Licensing Act that regulated the sale and content of alcoholic beverages. The main policy front on which Gladstone made no advances during his first administration, ironically, was Ireland, where matters largely pacified themselves during the period; though Irish politics were changing, and matters would not remain quiet for long.

He had, through his Chancellor Robert Lowe, maintained a determination to cut spending and taxation, and with nearly two years of what was then a seven-year mandate still to run, he called an election in the winter of 1874 to seek a mandate for the complete abolition of income tax. He lost. The main reason for his defeat was that Disraeli, in opposition, had developed a serious organisation for the Conservative Party, which was mobilised to enlist the support of what was still a relatively new electorate. The Liberals had made no such provision. The result was that Gladstone, having lost, gave up the leadership of his party, and departed mainly to Hawarden to fell trees and pursue his intellectual interests, notably in theology and classical studies. His first task was to write and publish a pamphlet attacking the doctrine of papal infallibility. His antipathy to the Roman Catholic Church, which he regarded as a repository of superstition, was deep-seated and lifelong. At the time of his death he had a library of 32,000 books, and consumed information greedily.

His adherence to Christianity led him to denounce the Disraeli administration's toleration of attacks by Ottoman Muslims on Bulgarian Christians: what became known as the Bulgarian atrocities. At the same time, Russia was persecuting the Jews, and British Jews waited in vain for Gladstone to speak up against this. However, he felt motivated to attack the morality of the Conservative Party's foreign policy between 1878 and 1880, not merely over Bulgaria, but also over the war it was conducting in Afghanistan and in southern Africa against the Zulus. This vigorous assault on the government has come to be known as the Midlothian campaign, after the constituency he was contesting: and it is regarded as having been a template for election campaigns for decades to come. It was in any case obvious to the electorate that the Conservatives had run out of ideas, and lacked vision; the Liberals won the ensuing election comfortably.

However, Gladstone had not led the party in the campaign, whatever had seemed to be the case: since his 'retirement' in 1874, it had been led in the Lords by Lord Granville and in the Commons by the Marquess of Hartington, the heir to the Dukedom of Devonshire. Queen Victoria, who regarded Gladstone as some sort of madman – a word she used frequently to describe him – pleaded with each man separately to form her government, but each said, quite accurately, that the country would only accept Gladstone as leader; and thus it was, with immense reluctance, that she invited him to become her prime minister for a second time.

This administration, though, was to endure far more problems than its predecessor. It coincided with the start of the 'land war' in Ireland and the rise of Parnellism – the demand by the Irish to be rid of absentee landlords, to be allowed a greater stake in their country and to have an element of self-rule. Gladstone was also sufficiently concerned about the neglect of sound economic principles under Beaconsfield (as Disraeli had become in 1876, with the acquisition of his earldom) that he was, until 1882, his own Chancellor of the Exchequer. But his workload became so fraught that he had to give up his second job; and Ireland became increasingly the main cause of his anxiety.

The disturbances there, notably the rise of the boycott – named after the County Mayo land agent ostracised by his local town over his policy of evictions – led to Gladstone's having to pass a Coercion Act in 1881 that, among other things, allowed detention without trial. However, matters got worse rather than better, and in May 1882 the new Chief Secretary for Ireland, Lord Frederick Cavendish, was assassinated alongside the country's most senior civil servant as they walked through Phoenix Park in Dublin on his first day in the country. This initiated a period of increased tension and repression that was entirely at odds with Gladstone's intentions. Further afield, there were other challenges. Gladstone himself was no imperialist, and his party was mostly against the expansion of Empire; but in 1882 the government decided to intervene in Egypt because of a nationalist uprising that threatened Britain's rights to the Suez Canal and the passage to India. It led, however, to a British presence in Egypt for the best part of half a century. Gladstone's main achievement in this otherwise difficult administration, however, was to extend the franchise to the rural working class, and to secure a redistribution of parliamentary seats in 1884–5.

Yet it was events, again, far from home that brought down the administration. Matters remained restive on Egypt's southern border, with the Sudan, and in 1884 General Charles 'Chinese' Gordon, one of the most remarkable soldiers in the Empire, was asked by Gladstone to go out there and take control of the situation. Gordon was a religious maniac with a death wish; he did not expect to come back from Khartoum, and he did not. Communications were poor, and Gordon was slow in asking for reinforcements. They were sent eventually, but by the time they arrived Gordon had been killed. The public were outraged, and Gladstone's reputation collapsed; no one voiced the outrage better than the Sovereign herself, for whom this represented a superb opportunity to vent years of spleen at her prime minister. Normally telegrams between her and her ministers were sent encrypted; the one she sent to Gladstone expressing her disgust at his casual treatment of Gordon was sent from Balmoral to London *en clair*, which meant it was read by every telegraph operator between whom it was relayed. Her views were soon public knowledge and printed in the newspapers. She did, though, offer Gladstone an earldom when he resigned in June 1885, in a state of demoralisation, which he refused.

Salisbury then came to office, but relied on Parnell's Irish nationalists to keep him in power. Gladstone saw a natural comity between the Liberals and the Parnellites, and in December 1885, having thought about the question extensively, sent out his son Herbert to suggest to the press that a measure of Home Rule should be offered to the Irish – what history has called 'flying the Hawarden kite'. The Conservatives – who quickly became the Unionist party, as the question came to define British politics – were horrified, as were a number of Liberals, including Gladstone's leading lieutenant Lord Hartington and the charismatic Joseph Chamberlain. With Gladstone offering Home Rule, the Parnellites defeated Salisbury, and Gladstone's third, and briefest, administration began in February 1886. The measure had little hope of reaching the statute book; even if it got through the Commons (which, thanks to the Liberal Unionists, it did not), there was no chance of its being approved by the Lords, where the Tories predominated and absentee landlords were thick on the ground. When the Commons threw it out, Gladstone had no choice but to resign, and this time Salisbury was back in power for six years.

Many of Gladstone's contemporaries thought that the Grand Old Man (as he had become known, before the abbreviation was reversed and he became the Murderer Of Gordon) would retire: but the fires of righteousness still burned within him, and he planned to do nothing of the sort, despite being in his seventy-seventh year. He used the years of opposition to step up his crusade for social justice. He wanted more civil rights for the Irish; he supported the London Dock Strike of 1889 on the grounds that the wages dockers were paid were exploitative; and he began to make the case for a country so wealthy as Britain to consider old-age pensions, rather than consigning the indigent elderly to the workhouse after a life-time of labour. In this way he set out the intellectual agenda for successors such as Campbell-Bannerman, Asquith and Lloyd George. He did, however, raise hackles: his radicalism having been too much for the Liberal Unionists, he now found himself accused by some of veering towards socialism in his old age, in his attacks on the greediness of capitalists.

Gladstone went to the country at the 1892 election on a pro-gramme spearheaded by a promise of Irish Home Rule and the disestablishment of the Scottish and Welsh churches. The Liberals won fewer seats again than the Tories, but the Tories lacked a majority, and were soon defeated in a vote of confidence; thus Gladstone, in August 1892 and to the Queen's horror, found himself prime minister for the fourth time. This time Home Rule passed the House of Commons, but was heavily defeated in the Lords in September 1893. By now it was clear not only that Gladstone's considerable powers were failing, but that his doctrinaire refusal to countenance greater public spending put him greatly out of step with the rest of his party. For example, his Cabinet wanted expan-sion of the navy to help keep growing German sea power in check; Gladstone would not have it, sticking to the principles he had exercised as Chancellor forty years earlier. He was also horrified by the proposal of his Chancellor, Sir William Harcourt, to impose death duties that would lead to the break-up of Britain's network of landed estates, and threaten the stewardship of that land. Similarly, he felt it was immoral to inflict a burden of taxation on so small a group of people: the rich, in his view, were as entitled to justice as the poor. His Cabinet opposed him on that too, and by February 1894 he recognised, at the age of eighty-four, that it was time for him to go. He was the oldest man ever to form a government in British history, and remains the oldest ever prime minister.

He left the premiership on 2 March, two days after his last audience with the Queen, who made a point of not thanking him for his services. Nor, having turned down an earldom, was he offered a peerage again. In his papers after his death was found an exasperated memorandum in which he expressed his bemusement about why the Queen was so relentlessly hostile to him; but then part of his Christian charity was that he never brought himself to see what an incipiently stupid, vain, narrow-minded and ignorant woman Victoria was.

He left Parliament at the 1895 election, and maintained the vigour of his mind as best he could, amid his massive library at Hawarden. He was well enough to travel to Cannes in 1897, where he encountered the Queen, who, like him, was there for her health: and civilities were observed to the extent that she shook hands with him for the first time, he thought, in fifty years. Friends who visited him found that his main political concern, in the era of Joe Chamberlain as Colonial Secretary, was the growth of jingoism and imperialism; he died months before that movement reached its nadir in the prosecution of the Second Boer War. His faculties gradually declined, and he died, aged eighty-eight, on 19 May 1898, after the extensive ministrations of the Church. To the Queen's disapproval he was accorded a state funeral in Westminster Abbey, and to her horror her son and grandson – the future kings Edward VII and George V – atoned for her beastly behaviour towards Gladstone by acting as pallbearers.

Gladstone has a claim to be the greatest of all our prime ministers, despite the failures of his second administration. He was certainly morally titanic, in a way that puts him beyond equal. His greatness consists not just in the sincerity of his belief in public service, but in the correct application of his immense intellect. His most profound achievement came before he held the highest office, in persuading Peel to reform the Corn Laws, and thereby laying the foundations of Britain's prosperity for the rest of the nineteenth century. His first administration directed society away from advancement by patronage and towards advancement by merit, recognising the moral and economic imperative to maximise the potential of the country's human capital. The second administration expanded the franchise, recognising the inevitability of social progress; the third and fourth recognised the inevitability of Irish Home Rule. What a later prime minister called 'the forces of Conservatism' thwarted Gladstone in his aims, but this visionary's ideas for the extension of democracy and liberty were all achieved within a quarter-century of his death, and together comprise his legacy.

Simon Heffer is professorial research fellow at the University of Buckingham, the author of many books on modern British history. He also writes for the Telegraph.

31

Marquess of Salisbury

23 June 1885 to 28 January 1886; 25 July 1886 to
11 August 1892; 25 June 1895 to 11 July 1902
Conservative

By Tony Little

Full name: Robert Arthur Talbot Gasgoyne-Cecil Later
Viscount Cranborne, then the Marquess of Salisbury
Born: 3 February 1830, Hatfield House, Hertfordshire
Died: 22 August 1903, Hatfield House. Buried at Hatfield
Church
Education: Eton; Christ Church, Oxford
Married to Georgina Caroline Alderson; 5 sons, 3 daughters
Quotation: 'No lesson seems to be so deeply inculcated by the
experience of life as that you never should trust experts. If you
believe the doctors, nothing is wholesome: if you believe the
theologians, nothing is innocent: if you believe the soldiers
nothing is safe.'

No VISITOR TO Hughenden is left in any doubt that its owner had been Benjamin Disraeli, later Lord Beaconsfield. But at Hatfield House, there are far fewer signs that its previous owner, the 3rd Marquess of Salisbury, had been one of the most successful Conservative prime ministers, serving for thirteen years at the end of the Victorian period.

Robert Cecil was the last peer to be a premier and the last prime minister to sport a full beard. But few who observed him as a youth would have thought it likely that he could aspire to lead a political party. An academically bright but intensely shy child, Cecil was a younger son of the 2nd Marquess of Salisbury. He did not enjoy Eton, where he was bullied and spent the holidays avoiding contact with fellow pupils. As an adult he dreaded recognition by members of the public and had no appetite for the club life of his party colleagues or the country house entertainment common to the leading members of both Liberal and Conservative parties. His outlook was pessimistic and throughout his life he was subject to what he called 'nerve storms', suffering what would now be diagnosed as depression. Despite his academic prowess he was advised to safeguard his mental health by not completing his competitive finals examinations at Oxford. Instead, between 1851 and 1852, he toured Australia, New Zealand and South Africa, leaving him much better informed about the practicalities of colonial life than most Victorian politicians.

On his return, Cecil needed to choose an occupation suitable to his aristocratic status. The Church was rejected, but not for want of belief. His commitment to High Church Anglicanism, based on the Oxford Movement, remained firm throughout his life. Unlike Gladstone, also a strong Anglican, Cecil felt no need to discuss his religion; it was not a matter of rational debate but of faith. He began reading for the Bar, as favoured by his father, but despised the profession. He was rescued by the chance to stand unopposed for the pocket borough of Stamford in an 1853 by-election. The same year he also became a fellow of All Souls, Oxford.

Through his stepmother, Cecil met Georgina Alderson, the daughter of a legal family. Serious and similarly interested in church affairs, they were well suited. Despite the strong opposition of his father, they married in 1857. Over the next dozen years they had eight children. Georgina proved a valuable partner for him both personally and politically, sharing a sharp sense of humour, lifting his mood and compensating for his lack of sociability by organising the political hospitality he would rather have avoided. Nevertheless, in the short term, the parental disapproval posed a problem. His father refused to fund his career at a time when MPs were not paid. The income from the capital left by his mother, about £300 a year, was inadequate for the growing family. To supplement it, he became a journalist publishing in *Bentley's*, the *Quarterly* and *Saturday Reviews* and the *Standard*. His output included both book reviews, especially of German books, and lengthy political essays.

Although these were supposedly anonymous, contemporaries detected his authorship of many pieces from the similarities between his written style and mordant humour and his speeches in the Commons. The essays gave the young politician the opportunity to develop and refine his views. In sharp contrast to Disraeli, his Conservatism was not based on any romantic notions of the past but on pessimistic utilitarian views of his own time and fears for any future influenced by Liberal reformist policies. The ineffectiveness of Whig bluffing on Schleswig-Holstein and his distaste for ambitious nationalism informed his foreign policy outlook. He advocated realistic objectives, within the constraints on British military spending, and frank diplomacy to avoid war in Europe. Scepticism about the moral purpose and ambitions of the colonists coloured his imperialism. He maintained that commercial speculation caused colonial expansion rather than the policy of British governments, which were then lumbered with the costs of imperial defence. He especially feared the expansion of democracy. Many of his articles were written in the first half of the 1860s when reform agitation revived in Britain and the US fought its civil war, which Salisbury attributed to the tyranny of a democratic (Northern) majority. While the roots of Salisbury's mature policies may be found in his early gloomy journalism, his views mellowed and adapted to political circumstances. Liberalising legislation could be resisted but rarely reversed.

Naturally, his articles attacked his political opponents, especially the radicals among the Liberals and Lord John Russell's bombastic foreign policy, but he was also highly critical of his own side, particularly Disraeli's unprincipled flirting with radical ideas in the hopes of dividing the Liberals. His antagonism to Disraeli won him friends among the more old-fashioned Tories, but did not unduly upset the victim of his barbs. The leaders of the party, Derby and Disraeli, recognised his developing talents and, from 1864, he participated in what would now be considered the shadow cabinet. At about the same time, relations with his father began to thaw and he was invited back to Hatfield House with his wife. In 1865, on the death of his elder brother, he became the heir to the estate with the courtesy title of Lord Cranborne.

The death of the Liberal prime minister Lord Palmerston, shortly after his 1865 General Election victory, brought Earl Russell into office determined to enlarge the electorate. The moderate Liberal bill was clumsily handled by the novice Liberal leader in the Commons, William Gladstone, bringing down the government. In the resulting minority Conservative administration under Lord Derby, Disraeli was Leader in the Commons and Cranborne entered the Cabinet as Secretary of State for India. The appointment was short-lived. When Derby and Disraeli sought to 'dish the Whigs' by taking on reform themselves, Cranborne resigned; he would no more tolerate democracy promoted by Conservatives than by Whigs. The manoeuvres, by which Disraeli constructed a majority for what proved to be a much more radical extension of the franchise than he had intended, were probably his finest but confirmed Cranborne's view of Disraeli as a dishonest adventurer. The Whigs remained undished; the 1868 election gave the Liberals a substantial majority and provided Gladstone with the platform for a great reforming government.

The resulting period in opposition proved valuable to Lord Salisbury, as Cranborne became when his father's death elevated him to the Lords in April 1868. Salisbury's principled opposition to the Second Reform Act meant that he arrived in the Upper House as the keeper of traditional Tory values and he cemented that position by his defence of Anglican values against Gladstone's flagship policy to disestablish the Church of Ireland. In one of the early Lords' disestablishment debates, he formulated the convention that still bears his name and governs the Lords' relations with the Commons. While rejecting the 'humiliation of being a mere echo and supple tool of the other House', he counselled his colleagues that 'when the opinion of your countrymen has declared itself, and you see that their convictions – their firm, deliberate, sustained convictions – are in favour of any course, I do not for a moment deny that it is your duty to yield'. His careful use and abuse of that convention preserved the Lords' veto for the rest of his life.

The following year Derby died, exposing weaknesses in the Conservative leadership in the Lords. Derby's immediate successor was Lord Cairns, an austere Ulster Protestant lawyer, whose flaws were quickly evident. When Cairns resigned in 1870, Salisbury and Derby's son (the 15th Earl) were both offered his job. Both declined, Derby citing lack of experience and Salisbury want of confidence in Disraeli. Consequently, the Tory peers were led by the Duke of Richmond, a more representative substantial landowner but dismissed by Disraeli's biographer, Lord Blake, as 'an amiable but ineffective nonentity'. Nevertheless, Richmond retained Cairns as an adviser, a role for which he was better suited, and persuaded Salisbury to join the front bench, though he was unable to stop him pursuing an independent and generally combative line whenever it suited.

When, in 1874, the nation tired of Gladstone's reforms, Disraeli returned to office with the first Conservative majority government in a generation. With some reluctance on both sides, Salisbury accepted Disraeli's offer of the India Office – Disraeli hoped to restrain a critic by Cabinet responsibility, Salisbury feared confinement to a political wilderness. Differences between the two men persisted. Salisbury did not support elements of the schools policy, was cynical about proclaiming Queen Victoria Empress of India and publicly declared his hostility to Disraeli's bill to curb 'ritualism' in the Church of England. This earned an equally public rebuke from Disraeli, describing Salisbury as 'a great master of gibes and flouts and jeers' in the Commons. But none of these disputes provoked him to resign. During the 1870s Eastern Crisis, Disraeli and Salisbury combined to force a vacillating Derby from the Foreign Office and face down Russian aggression against Turkey. As the new Foreign Secretary, Salisbury quickly brought rigour and clarity to policy, and in partnership with Disraeli, at the subsequent Berlin Congress, resolved the immediate crisis and incorporated Cyprus into the Empire to strengthen British naval dominance of the eastern Mediterranean.

After Disraeli's death in 1881, the Conservative leadership was divided between Salisbury in the Lords and Stafford Northcote in the Commons, as the party was in opposition and the succession was not obvious. Throughout Gladstone's second government (1880–85), Northcote's position weakened and Salisbury's strengthened. Northcote had been Gladstone's private secretary and, in debate, his reasoned approach showed his old master too much deference for the liking of his more bellicose party colleagues. Unfortunately for Northcote, a ginger group of younger Tory back-bench MPs, led by Lord Randolph Churchill, was only too willing to take the fight to the Liberal leader. Brilliantly exploiting the rules and Gladstone's excessive respect for the House, they obstructed government business and hogged the headlines. Unfortunately, Churchill's sallies were aimed as much at his leader as at his opponents and Northcote had no effective answer. By contrast, no one ever accused Salisbury of dodging a fight, though at times his temper might have been better controlled and the Lords were not always as willing as he to man the barricades. In addition, emulating Gladstone's Midlothian campaign, Salisbury overcame his inhibitions to platform oratory, raising his profile with the party faithful. He delivered more than seventy fully reported public speeches between 1881 and 1885, mostly in the major cities, though he remained disparaging about their impact. 'As a rule I observe that the places where we win seats are the places where no Tory leader has spoken.' In reality, his efforts broadened the Conservative appeal beyond the traditional rural interests to include the urban business and professional classes who were anxious about Liberal ineffectiveness and Joseph Chamberlain's pressure for extensive state intervention.

The flagship achievement of the Gladstone government was the 1884 Reform Act, but Salisbury used the Lords' veto to secure its modification, ensuring a simultaneous redistribution and the introduction of single-member constituencies. The switch to single-member seats meant that Conservative areas in the boroughs/cities formed separate constituencies rather than being lost within city-wide districts. Without multi-member seats, Liberals could no longer gloss over splits between Whigs and radicals by running balanced slates. Salisbury proved to be the major political beneficiary of the Act.

A Budget revolt brought down Gladstone's government in 1885, much to the relief of its squabbling Cabinet ministers. The Queen had no hesitation in sending for Salisbury, rather than Northcote, though he exercised considerable brinkmanship to achieve a smooth transition for the resulting minority government to prepare for the inevitable election on the new franchise.

The other beneficiary of the enlarged electorate was Charles Stewart Parnell's Irish Home Rule Party, which ended the 1885 election narrowly holding the balance of power in a hung parliament. Gladstone hoped that Salisbury would emulate Peel over the Corn Laws and enact devolution for Ireland, in the national interest. Although Churchill and Lord Carnarvon had cosied up to the Irish during the minority government, Salisbury declined to fall into this trap. Taking up the challenge, Gladstone split his party, managing to lose most of the moderate or Whig wing, under Lord Hartington, and those radicals associated with Joseph Chamberlain. Gladstone pressed his case to a General Election, in 1886, and lost.

Salisbury offered the rebel unionist Liberals a non-compete agreement with the Conservatives that allowed most to retain their seats and hardened the Liberal split. Building on this foundation, he formed another minority government loosely supported by the Liberal Unionists, which retained office until 1892.

The worst of the government's political challenges occurred in its first year. Churchill's sparkling, pugnacious forays in the House, his campaigns promoting a nebulous 'Tory Democracy' to the new electorate, and his performance at the India Office in 1885 earned him promotion as Chancellor of the Exchequer. But he proved as disruptive in Cabinet as he had been in the Commons. At Christmas 1886 he put forward Budget proposals demanding cuts in military spending, forcing Salisbury to choose between his Chancellor and his Minister of War, W.H. Smith (of news-vending fame). Frustrated by the government's failure to accelerate the reforms he favoured, Churchill's challenge for dominance was mistimed and on the wrong issue; his tactics were ill judged. Fatally, Churchill offered his resignation, expecting its refusal, but Salisbury accepted. Churchill never held office again. When Salisbury reshuffled his Cabinet, he brought in George Goschen, a Liberal Unionist, as Chancellor of the Exchequer. He made Smith Leader of the House through his own office of First Lord of the Treasury and took on the Foreign Office himself. This entailed the demotion of Lord Iddesleigh, as Northcote had become, but at a meeting of the two men in 10 Downing Street, Iddesleigh died of a heart attack. Initially, the loss of Churchill caused problems for the Unionist alliance. Chamberlain had been close to Churchill, seeing him as a kindred reformer, and he reacted by opening talks with his former Gladstonian colleagues, but they demanded too complete a surrender; thereafter, he gradually drew closer to both Hartington and Salisbury.

In looking at Salisbury's record, three factors should be borne in mind. First, he always led minority or coalition governments. Retaining both Liberal Unionist and Conservative support required arbitrating the demands for honours, office and policies of both parties. Salisbury's ability to accommodate Chamberlain's anxiety to preserve his radical credentials by generating imaginatively innovative policies demonstrated the premier's skill in arts he found deeply unattractive. Second, Salisbury controlled and managed a foreign policy that was still adapting to the unification of Germany and the complex competition among European powers for new colonies. Third, and partly explained by Salisbury's immersion in foreign affairs, he allowed ministers a fairly free hand to implement departmental agendas. His continued conviction that change was usually for the worse was tempered by electoral necessities and the duty of the aristocracy to alleviate social problems.

Opposition to Home Rule for Ireland was the force holding the Unionist alliance together and Salisbury was implacable in his hostility. He had little respect for Irish nationalists, who used rural intimidation and rent strikes as political weapons – plundering the property of others. But for all his tough rhetoric, he employed the standard Victorian combination of coercion mitigated by conciliation to deal with Ireland. Tough reaction to violent land campaigns alternated with efforts to kill Home Rule by kindness through subsidising tenants to buy their land. This reduced the risk to Anglo-Irish landlords and met Irish ambitions for a peasant propriety. Entrusted with the task of Chief Secretary for Ireland was Salisbury's supposedly dilettante nephew, Arthur Balfour. Balfour proved surprisingly resolute in pursuing coercion and resilient in the face of Irish vituperation. He was rewarded with the Leadership of the Commons after Smith's death. Cynicism about Salisbury's promotion of his nephew and, later, other relatives led to the government being called the Hotel Cecil and may be the origin of the phrase 'Bob's your uncle'.

The government's domestic achievements were by no means negligible. Some were the usual modest accretions to previous reforms, such as extending government regulation of coal mining, taking the government into technical education and making it easier for local authorities to clear and replace slums. Others, which were more substantial and of greater value to the alliance, included providing land for allotments, making schools free for pupils through better educational funding arrangements, and the 1888 County Councils Act, a much overdue and long-lasting reform. Although these had all formed part of Chamberlain's Radical Programme of 1885, Salisbury discouraged Chamberlain from praising his liberality in case it antagonised Tory back-benchers.

Despite these successes, Salisbury lost the 1892 election, but only by a narrow margin. Gladstone's second attempt at Home Rule legislation passed the Commons, but was quickly vetoed by Salisbury, in the Lords, on the basis that there was no English majority for the abandonment of the Ulster Protestants. The Liberals declined to follow Gladstone in an attack on the Lords, and when the Cabinet would not back him in cutting defence expenditure, he resigned.

His replacement, Lord Rosebery, proved unequal to the job and the Conservatives won the 1895 election with a majority of 152. Liberal Unionists were now willing to accept office and were generously treated by Salisbury: Hartington, after 1891 the Duke of Devonshire, had oversight of defence, while Chamberlain asked for and was given the Colonial Office rather than a domestic ministry. Somewhat unexpectedly, the government worked well, with Chamberlain, as a colleague, proving less troublesome than anticipated though still capable of creating problems through his imperial aspirations.

The scale of the government's majority was not matched by its ambitions. Useful legislation was passed, but given Salisbury's scepticism about government interference in social and economic conditions, nothing constituting a memorable landmark. In 1896 a bill was passed allowing the Board of Trade to arbitrate in trade disputes, and in 1897 the government introduced an insurance scheme for compensating workmen for industrial accidents. Local

government, on the English model, was extended to Ireland, and London was provided with boroughs as well as the London County Council. One big opportunity was missed. Earlier in the decade, Chamberlain had been among the first arguing for old-age pensions. But despite some technical investigation, nothing was done, leaving the opportunity to be seized by the Liberals after 1906.

When Salisbury advised Lord Lytton that 'English policy is to float lazily downstream, occasionally putting out a diplomatic boat-hook to avoid collisions', it suggests a lethargy commensurate with his bulk in later years, but it is a misleading judgement on his tenure as Foreign Secretary. He feared that technological improvements in armaments and the logistical advances demonstrated by the Prussians had increased the risk of war, the 'supreme evil'. Although warning of 'splendid isolation', he was unwilling to commit Britain to military alliances, believing that democratic governments could not bind their successors in the face of public opinion. Consequently, the boathook was regularly employed to avoid confrontation by ensuring that the other powers clearly understood British intentions and that Britain's actions matched her words.

His principal objectives, largely attained, were to restrain Russian ambitions within Europe and in the frontier areas of the British Empire, to delay the break-up of the Ottoman Empire, to maintain Austria's ability to counter Russian influence in the Balkans, and to use Italy as a counterweight to France while preventing German dominance of France. In response to signs of an entente between France and Russia, his government adopted the two-fleet navy standard by which the Royal Navy was enlarged to match the fleets of its next two rivals combined. No similar effort was made to develop an army comparable to the conscripted continental forces. While fully committed to safeguarding the Empire, Salisbury was relaxed about its expansion. This facilitated good relations with the other powers by accommodating their colonial ambitions, particularly in Africa.

Other ministers, and Chamberlain in particular, entertained greater imperial ambitions and were not always scrupulous in their methods. A crisis came in 1899, in South Africa, when British determination to re-establish authority over the Transvaal clashed with Boer efforts to prevent their territory being swamped by British migrants. The resulting war exposed serious deficiencies in the army and the widespread antipathy of our continental neighbours. Despite Salisbury's fears that the Powers might conspire to 'treat the English Empire as disposable booty', none acted. When, in 1900, the British appeared to have won the Boer War, Salisbury called and won an election against a still-divided opposition. In reality, General Roberts required increasingly repressive measures to defeat a Boer guerrilla campaign lasting until 1902.

Shortly after the beginning of the Boer War, Salisbury's wife died. Increasingly showing his age and becoming less capable of meeting the demands made upon him, Salisbury assigned the Foreign Office to Lord Lansdowne, in 1900, but soldiered on as premier until after the death of Queen Victoria. He resigned in the summer of 1902 to be succeeded by his nephew, Balfour. He died at Hatfield, the place of his birth, the following year.

Salisbury never offered Conservatives an attractive vision of the future comparable to that of his predecessor, Disraeli, or of his youthful rival, Churchill. His legislative record was as good as, if not better than, Disraeli's and his electoral record far superior. He never enjoyed Disraeli's tactical flexibility but neither was he ever described as an unscrupulous adventurer. Rather he offered true conservative principles, resistance to change, and support for the Church and established institutions. But while he consolidated the landed interest by absorbing the bulk of the Whig peerage into the Conservative ranks, he broadened his party's base to include the business and associated professional classes, leaving it prepared for the class-based politics of the twentieth century. His skill in holding together the Unionist alliance is demonstrated by the fate of his nephew. Balfour failed to control Chamberlain's campaign for an imperial federation held together by tariff reform, splitting the party and losing the 1906 election.

Perhaps a more valuable comparison is with Gladstone. Opponents for over thirty years, both were educated at Eton and Oxford, and were driven by the same Anglican faith. Both were intellectuals in politics, though Gladstone's interests were in the classics while Salisbury's were in science, tinkering in his laboratory at Hatfield. They both had the conservative intentions of enabling the individual to achieve sturdy self-reliance, of preventing 'socialistic' state intervention

and encouraging the elite to perform their traditional duties. Where they differed was in outlook. Gladstone was optimistic that the working classes could be incorporated into active citizenship by reforming the state, while Salisbury resisted because he feared that the envious masses would abuse state power to seize what others had earned. Gladstone's over-energetic reforms fractured his party; Salisbury, always realistic, prepared his for the class politics of the twentieth century. Gladstone, often a guest at Hatfield, judged his opponent to be a 'model of political integrity . . . a most amiable, a most able man'.

The place to find a monument to Salisbury is where he was most engaged in government, the Foreign Office, which now incorporates the Durbar Court from the old India Office. On Open House weekends, the space where he worked may be visited, a magnificent portrait admired, and his statue, aptly, found near the staircase designed to impress visiting ambassadors with British imperial power.

Tony Little is chairman of the Liberal Democrat History Group.

32

Earl of Rosebery

5 March 1894 to 22 June 1895
Liberal

By Leo McKinstry

Full name: Archibald Philip Primrose, the 5th Earl of Rosebery
Born: 7 May 1847, Mayfair, London
Died: 21 May 1929, The Durdans, Epsom. Buried at Dalmeny parish church
Education: Eton; Christ Church, Oxford
Married to Hannah Rothschild; 2 sons, 2 daughters
Quotation: 'The Empire is a Commonwealth of Nations.'

THE PREMIERSHIP ALWAYS seemed the certain destiny of the 5th Earl of Rosebery. A fabulously rich Scottish aristocrat, he appeared to have all the right attributes for the highest office, including a brilliant intellect, a brooding magnetism and a potent eloquence. His Liberal colleague John Morley described him as 'the

most natural born leader I have ever met'. The writer J.M. Barrie called him 'the uncrowned King of Scotland'. In an age when political oratory was a form of mass entertainment, he was perhaps the biggest box-office star of the late nineteenth century, drawing huge crowds for his platform speeches. His striking phrases, like his description of the Empire as 'a Commonwealth of Nations', entered the political lexicon.

Before he succeeded William Gladstone as Liberal prime minister in March 1894, he had built an impressive political record. Two successful spells as Foreign Secretary had won him a reputation for both decisiveness and a determination to uphold Britain's imperial interests. According to one diplomat, he was 'the ideal master to serve'. Though his inheritance of his title in 1868 at the age of just twenty-one meant that he had never served in the House of Commons, he was elected to the newly created London County Council in 1889, where he served as its first chairman. His assured management of the body attracted widespread praise across the political spectrum, the dockers' leader Ben Tillett asserting that Rosebery's 'was pioneer work in the great revolutionary effort in municipal life'. His claim on the succession to Gladstone was re-inforced by his shrewd performance as a mediator in settling the national coal strike of 1893, just as his democratic credentials had been burnished by an innovative role in organising Gladstone's great Midlothian campaigns, using techniques imported from the USA.

Indeed, one of the keys to Rosebery's popularity was the breadth of his support, which reflected not only his image as a statesman above the partisan fray but also his capacity to embrace often contradictory positions. During the peak of his career, he was able to present himself as an Irish Home Ruler and a robust imperialist, a friend of labour and an enemy of socialism, a distinguished peer and a passionate advocate of Lords reform, a moderate and a radical. In 1893, the French writer Augustin Filon expressed his wonder at Rosebery's 'remarkable' gift for facing in several directions: 'How can the same individual please so many people, advance so many causes, play so many parts?'

Rosebery's political prestige was further enhanced by his celebrity status. He was the object of constant fascination to the public and the press, because of both his patrician charisma and his colossal wealth, augmented by his unorthodox marriage in 1878 to the Jewish heiress Hannah Rothschild, the richest woman in England. His fortune, which included an annual income of £140,000 a year (well over £1.5 million annually in today's money), enabled him to possess a string of stately homes and a villa in Italy, as well as racehorses, two of which won the Derby in the 1890s.

His promise ensured his rise to the top in 1894, as the Liberal Cabinet preferred him to his only rival, the Chancellor Sir William Harcourt, who was disliked for his rudeness and bad temper. Yet, after he reached No. 10, Rosebery proved a sorry disappointment. Lasting just sixteen months, his premiership turned out to be one of the shortest and least accomplished in modern British history. Far from displaying his mastery, he was overwhelmed by the position. 'I think the poor fellow knows what a terrible mess he has made of it', wrote Morley, who had previously been one of his strongest supporters.

His problems began as soon as he took over from Gladstone. From the start, he had a fractious relationship with Harcourt, who believed that the premiership should rightfully be his and was contemptuous of Rosebery. 'A rogue and a liar', was one of his descriptions of the Prime Minister. Sir William's seething hostility was fed by his son Lewis, or 'Loulou', a feline political intriguer who acted as his secretary and, because of thwarted ambition for his father, came to loathe Rosebery with an almost neurotic intensity. Apart from Harcourt, the construction of his Cabinet proved difficult, especially because Morley, a radical reformer, fiercely objected to the appointment of Lord Kimberley as Foreign Secretary, since that meant both the top posts were in the Lords. There were also early rows with Queen Victoria, increasingly reactionary in her old age, over plans for Scottish and Welsh disestablishment.

Rosebery's first address as prime minister in the Upper House was a disaster. Speaking to a packed chamber in the debate on the Queen's Speech, he declared that Irish Home Rule could not proceed until England, 'as the predominant member' of the United Kingdom, had been convinced of the case for the measure. His remark may have been a statement of political reality, but it appalled many of the Liberals and their partners, the Irish nationalists. They exacted their revenge in the subsequent Commons vote on the

Queen's Speech, inflicting a humiliating defeat on the new government.

Rosebery's nerve was badly shaken by the episode, and his authority was further weakened by an explosive dispute with Harcourt over the 1894 Budget, which proposed a radical expansion in death duties. Rosebery felt that property was dangerously threatened by the scheme, but Harcourt was dismissive of the Prime Minister's objections, calling them nothing more than 'a fine old Tory doctrine'. With his far deeper grasp of economics, Chancellor prevailed over Rosebery, who suffered more embarrassment when his proposal for a secret agreement with Belgium about territory in the Congo was overturned by the Cabinet.

In the autumn of 1894, Rosebery tried to recover by launching a campaign for the reform of the House of Lords. But after opening with a powerful speech in Bradford, he failed to capture the imagination of the public or pursue the policy with any dynamism. Rather than reviving his leadership, the initiative only further diminished him. 'Did ever the head of a great party speak in a more helpless or hopeless strain?' asked *The Spectator* after a flat Rosebery speech on Lords reform. By February 1895, the Prime Minister felt under such siege that he issued a threat of resignation to the Cabinet. 'No one wants me. Everyone will be glad when I am gone,' he wailed. After the Cabinet expressed its support, he continued in office, but by now he was a broken man, so plagued by anxiety and insomnia that he had to be given large quantities of morphine to help him sleep, though the drug had only a limited effect. His doctor was worried that his condition might lead to 'a fatal termination'. With morbid relish, Loulou Harcourt thought he might commit suicide. 'I am crucified to my place and it is damnable,' Rosebery himself complained.

His release came at the beginning of June 1895, when the government lost a Commons vote on the supply of cordite to the British army. It was a minor issue, but Rosebery was determined to use it as an excuse for resignation. In the General Election that soon followed, the Unionists emerged with a crushing majority, while the Liberals fell to just 177 MPs. Rosebery was still nominally the party leader, but, to the dismay of his colleagues, he went on a yachting trip around Scotland instead of campaigning. Reluctantly and distractedly, he hung on to the Liberal leadership until October 1896, when he resigned with another melodramatic flourish. He never held senior office again.

There were political reasons for Rosebery's failure as prime minister, such as the fissures in the Liberal Party, the absence of a parliamentary majority and the incoherence of its programme. But his own character was also to blame. He was too prickly, self-enfolded and sensitive to criticism for the demands of No. 10. There was an air of wounded narcissism about his tenure, an excessive awareness of his own dignity. He was drawn to men of strong will but lacked the fibre or the energy to emulate them. 'You will never undertake the continuous effort and drudgery that is essential to success,' he was told by one disillusioned associate. Rosebery regularly complained that he was not consulted by his colleagues, yet he made little attempt to see them. His Education Minister Arthur Acland said his leadership was 'intolerable' because he was 'shy, huffy' and gave himself 'the airs of a little German King'. Rosebery himself wrote that 'pride' was 'my besetting sin, the blight at the root of my life'.

That characteristic reflected the privilege into which he had been born in 1847, the son of a Scottish MP and grandson of a peer. From his earliest years, he was accused of being 'spoilt'. At Eton, his tutor William Johnson said that, despite his 'genius', he wanted 'the palm without the dust'. At Oxford, he left without a degree because of his refusal to comply with an official instruction to give up his ownership of a racehorse. One guest to Mentmore, the vast Buckinghamshire palace that came with his marriage to Hannah Rothschild, wrote that 'truffles are treated here as potatoes are elsewhere'. Cocooned by his fortune, Rosebery was obsessed throughout his political career with maintaining his independence. Despite his ambition, two of his favourite activities were refusing office and resigning from it, traits that exasperated Gladstone. 'It is marvellous how a man of such gifts can be so silly,' said the Grand Old Man.

In fact, Rosebery's whole personality was bound up with paradox. He could be aloof yet charming, flippant yet stern. He collected pornography but had a streak of seventeenth-century Calvinism. He craved bookish solitude yet complained of loneliness. The sense of mystery and contradiction that enveloped Rosebery has led to claims that he harboured a dark secret, one that would have created a sensation if it had been revealed. According to some critics, the real explanation for the enigma of Rosebery is that he was a clandestine homosexual, despite his devotion to Hannah and his grief at her early death from typhoid in 1890, a tragedy that exacerbated his habitual reserve. His alleged proclivities were the subject of whispers during his lifetime, as highlighted by the author George Ives, who claimed in his diary that 'Rosebery was said by everyone to be homosexual'; the Metropolitan Police, though, were under orders never to arrest him 'on the principle that too big a fish breaks the line'. Rosebery's strange, solitary ways, like his habit of opening his own post, even as prime minister, added to the suspicion that he had something to hide.

Further ammunition for this charge came from the downfall of Oscar Wilde in 1895. Rosebery's name was dragged into the scandal because one of his secretaries, Lord Drumlanrig, was the elder brother of Wilde's lover, Lord Alfred Douglas, and the son of Lord Queensberry, the deranged homophobic, anti-Semitic Scottish peer. Queensberry was convinced that Rosebery and Drumlanrig were having an affair, his fury prompting him to pursue the Liberal statesman to the German resort of Bad Homburg with a dog whip. When Drumlanrig was killed in a shooting accident in October 1894, Queensberry believed his death was either suicide or a cover-up. Having supposedly lost one son to an illicit liaison, he was determined not to lose another, hence his vendetta against Wilde that ended up in the courts. Rosebery's insomnia and breakdown at the height of the trial are sometimes said to have been caused by his terror at the thought of exposure. But, as Rosebery's biographer, who spent years studying his papers, observes, there is little evidence to support this claim. In fact, all the insinuations about him are unsubstantiated. They remain nothing more than gossip.

Rosebery's collapse in 1895 was probably due to political strains rather than the Wilde trial. In fact, Rosebery was so scarred by the experience of the premiership that he never dared accept responsibility again, 'like a burnt child dreading fire', in the words of Algernon Cecil. There was no lack of opportunities for a return, since he continued to mesmerise the public. During the crisis of the Boer

War, his name was touted as a possible saviour of the nation, particularly after a barn-storming speech he gave in Chesterfield in 1901. Winston Churchill and the Northcliffe press wanted him to lead a new centre party at the height of the Edwardian era, while as late as 1916 Lloyd George sought to add Rosebery's lustre to his government. But he remained in political isolation. In a memorable essay written in 1909, the journalist A.G. Gardiner described Rosebery in his twilight as 'the Flying Dutchman of politics, a phantom vessel floating the wide seas without anchor and without a port'. He died in 1929, the last Liberal peer to serve as prime minister.

Leo McKinstry is a journalist, historian, broadcaster and author.

33

Arthur Balfour

12 July 1902 to 4 December 1905
Conservative

By Jack Brown

Full name: Arthur James Balfour
Born: 25 July 1848, Whittingehame, East Lothian, Scotland
Died: 19 March 1930, Fisher's Hill House, Hook Heath,
Woking. Buried at Whittingehame churchyard, Lothian
Education: Eton; Trinity College, Cambridge
Unmarried
Quotation: 'Nothing matters very much, and few things matter
at all.'

A T FIRST GLANCE, Arthur James Balfour, Conservative prime
minister from 1902 to 1905, appears an unremarkable former
occupant of No. 10. Inheriting his premiership from his uncle
Robert Gascoyne-Cecil, the 3rd Marquess of Salisbury (hence the

phrase 'Bob's your uncle'), Balfour was a man of aristocratic privilege whose path to Downing Street was apparently almost effortless. Once he arrived, he made for a fairly unspectacular prime minister. His premiership was short, and his greatest achievements at 10 Downing Street generally far from eye-catching. But dig a little deeper and we find a complicated figure and, in some respects, an impressive statesman, who led in remarkable times.

First, the case for the prosecution. The list of significant legislation brought forward under Balfour is short and mixed in its legacy. The Education Act of 1902 established a truly national education system in the longer term – a rare triumph – but met with religious controversy and had serious political and religious consequences for Balfour's government. Most of Balfour's legislation was defensive, attempting to appease or stall changing sentiments in the country. Much of it worked for Balfour, but would ultimately fail in the long term: the Unemployed Workmen Act of 1905 sought to appease the growing working class and the unemployed; the Aliens Act of the same year limited immigration in an attempt to calm anti-migrant sentiments; and the Land Purchase (Ireland) Act of 1903 saw the British state intervene to help Irish tenants buy out their landlords, in an attempt to calm pressures towards Irish Home Rule.

Balfour's greatest successes as prime minister were arguably in defence and foreign affairs. He ended the South African War, played a key role in delivering the foundations for the Entente Cordiale with France, and developed the Anglo-Japanese alliance. At home, he established the Committee of Imperial Defence to better coordinate Britain's military endeavours, a machinery of government innovation that significantly outlasted his premiership.

Yet the one historic event that bears his name, the 'Balfour Declaration' of 1917, which expressed British support for a 'national home for the Jewish people' in Palestine, was the product of his time as Foreign Secretary, a job he held subsequent to the premiership. His conduct during and after the First World War, in this role and as First Lord of the Admiralty, was impressive. He was sent to the United States to ease their entry into the war, and then, when it was won, Balfour played his part in the peace, arguing for more measured treatment of Germany, and advocating for the League of Nations. But all of this arguably suggests a man more suited to foreign than domestic affairs, and a prime minister whose peak of achievement came after departing No. 10 Downing Street.

Balfour's electoral record, which is an important but slightly crude single measure for rating prime ministers, was spectacularly poor. His premiership lasted for under three and a half years, and was defined by struggles within an almost unmanageable Cabinet (and Conservative Party), which was slowly being torn apart over the issue of tariff reform. Having the premiership passed down to him through the family, Balfour never had his own mandate from the electorate. When he finally sought one, at the General Election of 1906, an election that he himself called by resigning at the end of the previous year, he achieved the notable feat of losing both the national election (by a landslide) and his own seat in Manchester East. Brought swiftly back into politics as MP for the City of London, Balfour then led the Conservatives to two further defeats in 1910, albeit by tight margins.

Balfour could be considered an extremely privileged loser, then. But there are several counterpoints that make him worthy of study, and perhaps reappraisal. Despite his short reign as prime minister, he would serve at Cabinet rank for longer than Churchill, Gladstone or Palmerston. While his initial entry into politics was at the gift of his uncle, successive leaders of differing parties felt him talented enough to repeatedly offer him influential roles in their governments. His foreign and defence policy was influential. And no assessment of prime-ministerial performance can claim to be complete if it does not acknowledge the external pressures, national and international, political and cultural, that a premier faces.

This was especially true of Arthur Balfour's time at Downing Street. The mitigating circumstances of this 'rather louche public schoolboy' being tasked with managing a tremendous shift in the tectonic plates of British politics are substantial and important. In addition, his orthodox, privileged background should not obscure Balfour's unusual personal qualities, which made for an intriguing manager of change. Nor should we overlook his limited but notable innovations as premier.

Arthur James Balfour's *fin de siècle* premiership took place at a time when many old assumptions were being challenged, both at home and abroad. The country was becoming more democratic and less deferential. An expanded franchise and an emerging and increasingly organised working class saw the Liberals in the ascendancy and the early elements of what would become the Labour Party (formally established the year after Balfour lost the premiership) emerging as a new political force. As the last member of his own great political family to rule, Balfour must have felt this change acutely.

At first glance, it is hard to think of a prime minister less suited to these changing times. An Old Etonian, part of a ruling class family (the Cecils) whose roots could be traced back to a key adviser to Elizabeth I, Balfour could be forgiven for thinking that he was literally born to rule. At the turn of the century, Balfour found himself alongside his brother in a Cabinet appointed by his uncle, with positions in the government found for three further family members. Arthur Balfour's premiership, like his initial seat as a Member of Parliament, were effectively family inheritance, with the two intersected by a series of interesting Cabinet roles, including dealing with local government, Scotland, and Ireland. He had even lived at No. 10 Downing Street for two periods prior to becoming prime minister: briefly, between 1891 and 1892, as First Lord of the Treasury and Leader of the Commons; and again from 1895 in the build-up to his premiership, until his defeat as prime minister in 1905.

But Balfour proved a generally astute manager of change. His Education Act achieved a lasting impact that endured beyond his premiership. As Chief Secretary for Ireland, he focused on placating pressure for Irish Home Rule with a series of measures that used both carrot and stick, continuing this approach as prime minister. Holding his party together over the tariff question was an immense task and a great consumer of his time. Balfour himself was sympathetic to some form of reform, but attempted to stay neutral in Cabinet, proclaiming himself a free trader in the Commons. Ultimately, as historian E.H.H. Green notes, 'It could be said that Balfour fudged, fudged, and fudged again to save the Party he loved.'

His record was not perfect. Post-premiership, as leader of the opposition, Balfour blundered over the Conservative-dominated House of Lords' response to Lloyd George's 'People's Budget' of 1909. The Budget, which contained several measures felt to hit the aristocracy particularly hard, elicited strong feelings among many of the Tory Lords. Balfour failed to persuade enough Tory members that their opposition was not only futile, but actively counter-productive. Their rejection of the Budget, which would eventually pass following the General Elections of 1910, which Balfour lost, can be argued to have played a substantial part in the build-up to the 1911 Parliament Act, effectively ending the Lords' veto over legislation. In this area, despite his awareness of the damaging implications of opposition, Balfour failed on his own terms, with his leadership left irreparably damaged.

It did not help that he had publicly remarked that, regardless of who ran the House of Commons, the Conservative Party still ran the Empire, through its domination of the Lords. Given that Lloyd George was to describe the Lords as 'Mr Balfour's poodle' (despite his eventual inability to control them), this was an uncharacteristically unwise piece of political positioning. While Balfour generally proved an adaptable and astute leader, he could have blind spots. He displayed an unappealing class prejudice, albeit privately, in his early years. Writing to his uncle in 1891, recommending Leeds businessman W.L. Jackson be appointed to the Cabinet, he demonstrated his own snobbishness when describing Jackson's 'tact and judgement – middle-class tact and judgement I admit, but good of their kind. He justly inspires great confidence in businessmen and he is that *rara avis* – a successful manufacturer who is fit for something besides manufacturing.'

Given the times, and his background, this snobbery is perhaps unsurprising. As the 'last grandee' in a time of social transformation, Balfour generally kept his true feelings on the rise of British democracy private, with his public positioning much more savvy. In fact, he kept a great deal private. To an unusual degree, Balfour's personality remains an enigma.

He is easily caricatured as entitled. Brought up on the impressive Whittingehame estate in East Lothian, which he subsequently inherited, the young Balfour read voraciously, but in a manner that was entirely undisciplined. He achieved only a second-class degree at Trinity College, Cambridge. Even as a politician, he never really appears to have learned the skill of taking in and retaining information that did not intensely interest him.

In the late 1800s, he was a prominent member of 'The Souls', a group of aristocratic 'aesthetes', and he had a passion for the arts, alongside golf, tennis and croquet. His bookishness and delicate physicality earned him the nickname 'Pretty Fanny' in his younger years, and Winston Churchill, while praising his conduct over the Boer War, noted that critics would describe him as 'a ladylike dilettante dialectician'. Balfour was a slow starter in Parliament, biding his time to make his maiden speech in order to ensure the smallest possible audience, and initially contributing little to debates.

But the real Arthur Balfour was far from a straightforward toff. He published works of philosophy: his first, *A Defence of Philosophic Doubt*, offered a sceptical defence of belief in the age of science. His books were not bestsellers, but indicate that Balfour was an original thinker. He was (quietly) an early sceptic of unqualified free trade, and an enthusiast for 'bimetallism' (introducing silver alongside the Gold Standard). For an establishment Conservative, Balfour regularly seemed to find himself associating with ideas and people from differing traditions: the Prime Minister was, at various points in his career, fairly close (but not too close) to Randolph Churchill and his rebellious 'Fourth Party' group in the Commons; to Joseph Chamberlain's advocacy of some form of tariff reform; and to David Lloyd George, in whose coalition government Balfour continued to serve after the First World War had come to an end.

And, despite his image as a disinterested figure, sprawled across the benches of the Commons, his casual indifference was to some extent manufactured, useful in leading to his being underestimated by his opponents. His private life remains a mystery to this day: Balfour never married, and his sexuality, or apparent lack thereof, can only be speculated on. In trying to understand Balfour, it does not help that the man himself had a personal disinclination towards being analysed: 'I am more or less happy when being praised, not very comfortable when being abused, but I have moments of uneasiness when being explained.' But in remaining unknowable, Balfour was able to be many things to many people – an important quality in a time of great division.

Balfour also achieved a few significant 'firsts' while occupying the top job in the country. His biographer, R.J.Q. Adams, compared his enthusiasm for acquiring the latest technologies for his home to that of Toad of Toad Hall; Balfour had electrical and telephone services installed in his London residence as soon as possible, and was among the first to own a gramophone in Scotland. In 1900, he became the first inhabitant of No. 10 to bring a motor car to Downing Street.

Balfour also left his mark on the premiership itself. He was the Prime Minister who set the precedent that modern premiers would actually live and work at No. 10 Downing Street. Prior to this, he was the last politician to hold the title of First Lord of the Treasury without also simultaneously serving as prime minister. He has also been credited with firmly establishing the precedent that it was the prime minister's sole and absolute right to hire and fire cabinet ministers, when engineering the departure of several free traders from his Cabinet, while holding Joseph Chamberlain's resignation secretly in his pocket. Establishing the Committee of Imperial Defence was another innovation that outlasted Balfour, and was widely regarded as a success; recent events may suggest that committing his party to a referendum to settle an issue that was tearing it apart (namely the question of tariffs) when leader of the opposition was setting perhaps a less successful historical precedent, albeit one that two lost elections ensured he never needed to implement.

Balfour's political life arguably improved in the years after his premiership. He became close to Lloyd George, and proved an able and influential First Lord of the Admiralty, and then Foreign Secretary, in the coalition government. On the occasion of his eightieth birthday, the Commons and the Lords teamed together to buy the automobile enthusiast a Rolls Royce as a token of their admiration.

His private life, by way of contrast, was a story of riches to rags. Bad investments saw him lose his largely inherited fortune, including the Whittingehame estate that he had hoped to leave to his family. He died with his memoirs incomplete, having begun them in the hope that they would generate some income.

Balfour did not seek to change his country radically, but rather to steer it carefully and safely ahead. His record as prime minister was mixed, but there were some notable successes. And, perhaps most impressively, he has managed to retain for himself a private life that remains an unsolvable riddle. His funeral, like his love life, was a private affair. He remains an unknowable enigma, and in this he is among the more fascinating individuals to have held the office of prime minister.

Jack Brown is a lecturer at the Department of Political Economy at King's College, London. He was the first Researcher in Residence at Number 10 Downing Street.

34

Sir Henry Campbell–Bannerman

5 December 1905 to 3 April 1908
Liberal

By David Campbell Bannerman

Full name: Henry Campbell–Bannerman
Born: 7 September 1836, Kelvinside House, Glasgow
Died: 22 April 1908, 10 Downing Street, London. Buried at
Meigle parish church, Perthshire
Education: The High School of Glasgow; Glasgow and
Cambridge Universities
Married to Charlotte Bruce; no children
Quotation: 'When is a war not a war? When it is carried on by
methods of barbarism in South Africa.' (Speech at the Holborn
Restaurant, 14 June 1901)

THE NAME OF Sir Henry Campbell–Bannerman is probably best
known today among quiz aficionados, as the first politician to
be given official use of the title 'prime minister', not just 'First

Lord of the Treasury', and he is one of the most unfairly forgotten prime ministers of all.

Yet Campbell-Bannerman, known as 'CB' for short, led a popular, radical, free-trading, modern Liberal government driven by electoral reform; one that formed the keystone of the Welfare State, initiating the first state pensions, won a landslide election in 1906 and spearheaded a government lasting nine years.

It vies with the 1945 Labour government and 1979 Thatcher government in radical significance. Three future prime ministers were in his administration – Asquith, Lloyd George and Churchill – and his Cabinet is regarded as one of the strongest in history.

Other firsts include the dubious honour of being the only prime minister to die in No. 10 – in the White Room on 22 April 1908, aged seventy-one, having resigned on 3 April in favour of Asquith. His last words were intriguingly, 'You haven't seen the last of me!' CB called No. 10 'a rotten old barrack of a house' while his adored wife Charlotte thought it a place of doom.

He was also the only prime minister to combine the office with being 'Leader of the House' – the longest-serving MP – and his short tenure as PM was in large part due to his coming to the premiership late in life and to sheer exhaustion as he devotedly nursed his unwell wife.

CB was rare as a prime minister to serve in one constituency throughout all his thirty-nine years – the five Stirling burghs (boroughs). Gladstone had five different constituencies.

He was also one of the first with commercial experience – as a 'Glasgow draper' – in an era when the Cabinet was dominated by Lords and unpaid MPs (until 1911).

Born as plain Henry Campbell on 7 September 1836, he became 'Campbell-Bannerman' in 1871 under the terms of his uncle's, Henry Bannerman of Manchester, will, which left him a life interest in the delightful Hunton Court, Kent, on the condition that he took on the name 'Bannerman'. His wife hated the resulting long name, so CB was preferred. He lived at Gennings, on the estate there, until 1887, when they moved to Belmont Castle, Scotland.

Sir Henry had no children. The Bannerman link comes through his mother Janet Bannerman, who he resembled: 'Mr Henry's no a Campbell – he's just a Bannerman!' said a contemporary.

But the Bannerman legacy helped set him up to be well-off, if not rich. He lived longest at 6 Grosvenor Place, from 1887 to 1904, which now bears a blue plaque commemorating his time there, but became premier while residing in 29 Belgrave Square, moving to No. 10 in 1906. These are massive houses, ideal for the entertaining he enjoyed, hosting there, for example, Gladstone, Asquith, Princess Alexandra and Mark Twain.

Distinguishing Campbell-Bannerman's political achievements from his personal qualities, Roy Hattersley's biography is correct that 'much more was begun than was concluded. But his premiership marked a turning point in political and parliamentary history.'

His administration should be seen as a continuous programme that he initiated, but that was carried on by Asquith and Lloyd George.

Conservatives respect CB for supporting free trade against Protectionist Jo Chamberlain's 1903 Imperial Preference. His government abolished Balfour's 1902 import corn duty, putting half a penny on a loaf. CB retorted: 'Are our free ports to be shut up by preferential duties? . . . [by] this innocuous, little, imperceptible, intangible duty on corn.'

Free trade helped win the 1906 election, his own election manifesto declaring: 'Nothing in their experience lends me to suppose that by limiting our imports we shall increase our exports, or that by raising prices, no matter by what kind of tariff expedients, we shall assist in equalising the conditions of international competition.' There are questionable 1906 posters offering (tariff-) 'free food'.

CB was not a fan of Germanic Customs Unions such as the Brussels Sugar Convention. His 1902 damnation could apply to the EU's Customs Union today:

It means that we abandon our fiscal independence, together with our free trade ways; that we subside into . . . a Vehmgericht which is to direct us what sugar is to be countervailed and . . . the British Chancellor of the Exchequer in his robes obeys the orders he receives from this foreign convention in which the Britisher is only one in ten, and the House of Commons humbly submits to the whole transaction. Sir, of all the insane schemes offered to a free country as a boon this is surely the maddest.

It was free trade that won over a 'furious' Winston Churchill, who was given his first government job by Sir Henry and first chance to shine presenting CB's lasting self-government plan for South Africa.

Campbell-Bannerman was also a social reformer. His December 1906 Cabinet approved a non-contributory means-tested pension for the elderly poor, funded from general taxes. His government introduced free school meals in 1906 and children's medical inspections in 1907.

He strengthened parliamentary democracy by reforming Commons procedures, by challenging the House of Lords, and promoting self-government – whether over Irish Home Rule, his favoured four UK national parliaments, or in the Empire, where South African self-determination was extended to the Dominions.

He stunned old Boer War enemies by granting self-government to Transvaal and Orange Free State, a 'miracle' of magnanimity according to General Smuts, that led to vital support in both world wars, and Smuts serving in the British War Cabinet.

Campbell-Bannerman delivered one of the most powerful putdowns ever of the posturing Balfour, who had just lost both the election and his seat: 'I say enough of this (tom)foolery . . . (it) is altogether out of place in this Parliament.'

On the Lords blocking five acts, CB said: 'The resources of the British Constitution are not wholly exhausted . . . a way will be found, by which the will of the people expressed through their elected representatives will be made to prevail.'

He supported global parliamentary democracy too. As prime minister, he criticised the Tsar's arbitrary dissolution of the Duma. Speaking in French, CB's address to the Inter-Parliamentary Union (IPU) from twenty-two parliaments ended: '*La Douma est morte – Vive la Douma!*'

Campbell-Bannerman also left a strong legacy as secretary of state, and earlier Financial Secretary, of the War Office and Admiralty. He helped create a reformed army and a strong but not exorbitantly spending navy – for he was a keen administrator with an eye to costs. He fully backed Cardwell's (and later Haldane's) vital modernisation of the army, including ending the sale of commissions and delicately uprooting the anti-reform Duke of Cambridge as commander. This helped create the 1914 British Expeditionary Force. He introduced the Territorial and Reserve Forces Act 1907, which formalised the Officers Training Corps (OTC) and created the Territorial Force.

But CB was neither a jingoist nor a warmonger. He thought the Boer War avoidable, sought to replicate the 1904 UK–France Entente Cordiale with Germany, and favoured armament control at the 1907 Hague Conference, earlier saying, 'I hold that the growth of armaments is a great danger to the peace of the world.' CB unilaterally cut military expenditure, ending the 2:1 commitment (that the Royal Navy be twice the size of the next two powers) to help fund social spending, while leaving the UK dominant with its Dreadnoughts.

One of his bravest speeches condemned the 'concentration camps' in South Africa, when the military countered Boer guerrilla tactics by destroying their bases and incarcerating their occupants – these were not Nazi death camps, but disease led to 50 per cent adult death rates. Moved by first-hand accounts from campaigner Emily Hobhouse in June 1901, he damned these as 'methods of barbarism'.

He received much opprobrium, appalled Asquith, Grey and Haldane, and inspired Kipling's ditty: 'Mildly nefarious, Wildly barbarous, Beggar that kept the cordite down.' But he embarrassed the Balfour government into forming a committee chaired by suffragette Millicent Fawcett, which led to life-saving improvements. The cordite vote refers to when Campbell-Bannerman resigned after the government miscalculated and lost a motion to cut his salary by £100 for not storing enough cordite. Given the army had plenty of reserves, and that cordite is unstable, it was a distraction, but poor work by the whips brought down the short-lived Rosebery government.

CB remained a true believer in Irish Home Rule throughout his political career. He backed Gladstone's bills in 1886 and 1893, and introduced his own, all tragically defeated by landowner Lords, before finally being forced through in 1912 under the 1911 Act. The Irish nationalists' leader John Redmond, on seeing CB on his deathbed, said: 'it will never be forgotten by Ireland that no stress of circumstances induced him to lower the Home Rule flag'.

CB only became Irish Secretary in 1884 after his predecessor Lord Cavendish and the top official Burke were murdered in the terrible Phoenix Park episode. CB later remarked that he was more in danger at the official residence from sewage running into the fresh water supply than from Fenians. The bitter consequence of the murders was the loss of Cavendish's brother Lord Hartington's support for Home Rule, the formation of the Liberal Unionists working with Conservative Lord Salisbury, and a twenty-eight-year delay.

Intriguingly, CB stood on a UK manifesto of a wider 'Home Rule, All Round' – four national parliaments for domestic matters, including an English Parliament. One could argue that Scottish Home Rule (devolution) did just enough to stop full independence. On the 200th Anniversary of the Act of Union in 1907, CB called the British Union a 'mighty combination' with its 'profound effect for good upon the world'. But he also acknowledged that 'In every sort of union there must be some give and take; but . . . Scotland is Scotland still, and the Scot, so far from being de-Scotticised, still loves his country, has in him the old, stubborn, ever-turbulent spirit and is still devoted to things of the mind.'

Campbell–Bannerman also brought extraordinary party unity. Contemporary historian Goldwin Smith summed up CB's challenge: 'A very motley Government it is: Home Rulers and anti-Home Rulers; Imperialists and anti-Imperialists; Capitalists and Labour men: Feminists and anti-Feminists; moderate Liberals and extreme Radicals, looking for anything but favour on each other.'

The selfish agendas of Rosebery, Grey and Asquith, the 'half mutinous crew' as Chamberlain put it, were cannily redirected by CB into strong government. In the 1906 Relugas Conspiracy, these three plotted to put Asquith in as Commons leader, while pushing CB up to the Lords. But he saw them coming, and when Asquith met to propose this, CB replied that the Lords was 'a place for which [he had] neither liking, training nor ambition' and collapsed the plot by offering the ambitious Asquith the position of Chancellor of the Exchequer.

Balfour made the calamitous mistake of resigning his government in December 1905 on the basis that the Liberals would be too divided after Rosebery's attack on Home Rule and would quickly collapse. He realised too late that Rosebery was 'abandoned' even by Asquith and Grey.

On the debit side, in terms of failings, could Sir Henry have delivered Home Rule? Fear of party splits, and political exhaustion, pushed the matter back to a second term.

Could he have done more for 'Votes for Women'? His advice as prime minister to 300 suffragettes was that they had 'a conclusive and irrefutable case' and 'should go on pestering!' He voted for the 1907 Women's Enfranchisement Bill, saying 'the exclusion of women . . . is neither expedient, justifiable nor politically right'. His government did legislate to allow widowers and single women householders to stand as council candidates. But his Cabinet – including Asquith – and the Commons were against more concessions, as was King Edward VII, who rebuked CB for speaking up for 'these dreadful women' suffragettes.

Possibly his biggest failure was loss of attention to his brief owing to having to nurse his adored dying wife in person. While admirable, one consequence was not keeping a firm grip on the highly independent Foreign Secretary Lord Grey, who encouraged secret military talks with France. This gave the French a false picture that Britain would automatically get involved in another Franco-German war. When CB later told Prime Minister Clémenceau in person that the UK had made no such commitment, it came as a severe shock. The history of the First World War may have been different, though it was the attack on Belgium that triggered British involvement.

CB's fine biographer John Wilson concluded: 'Sir Henry was one of the nicest and most sensible men ever to be leader of a political party or Prime Minister.' This was echoed in Lloyd George's own tribute: 'He was not merely respected; he was loved by all . . . He was truly a great man. A great head and a great heart. He was absolutely the bravest man I ever met in politics.'

His private secretary Arthur Ponsonby summarised CB as 'absolutely unspoilt by high office. He wears it like an old well-fitting coat . . . no trace of vanity or conceit, no symptom of affectation . . . and will reject . . . all meanness and pettiness.'

Even the plotter Grey testified to CB's power of forgiveness: 'He made no distinction in personal relations, in intimacy and sympathy between those who had helped him and those who had made difficulties for him . . . the Cabinet was peculiarly free from personal differences and restlessness.'

CB appears to have been neither jingoistic not imperialist. Interestingly, he found love of Europe was not inconsistent with love of Nation. He had a lifelong love of France, its literature, culture, furniture, language – but that did not mean he was unprepared for Britain to fight France, if need be.

Campbell–Bannerman's relations with the monarchy were also helpful to his success. He managed to win King Edward VII around from anger at his 'methods of barbarism' speech, and later berated Sir Henry for the brevity of his Cabinet reports – incredibly, in those days the Prime Minister would hand-write these for the King.

On personal character failings, CB did have a tendency not to consult with senior colleagues. Amusingly, on one occasion, attending a debate as prime minister, he was so persuaded by an opponent's arguments over the Trade Disputes Bill that he immediately accepted the amendment, which his Attorney General had just dramatically rubbished.

Did he even want the job? The minister John Morley found that 'He had no wish that he should be Prime Minister, but was like a man in an express train. He could not alight.'

It was Charlotte who had the ambition for him. She was the one who made him take the post of Irish Secretary, which he initially refused and nearly lost out on. She insisted too that he veto moving to the Lords and receive his just reward of prime ministership.

Indeed, we nearly lost him as prime minister several times. After resigning over the cordite vote, as a lover of the Commons he put himself forward for Speaker. He was nearly Viceroy of India in 1894, but Gladstone wouldn't spare him, and he nearly joined the Lords in 1895.

Sir Henry Campbell-Bannerman was a good man – principled, courageous, kind, resilient and humorous – who achieved a great deal more than history has credited him with, and initiated many of the vital reforms that helped shape today's modern world. He deserves to be better remembered.

David Campbell Bannerman is a former Conservative Member of the European Parliament. He was chairman of the Bow Group and served as deputy leader of UKIP.

35

Herbert Asquith

5 April 1908 to 5 December 1916
Liberal

By David Laws

Full name: Herbert Henry Asquith
Born: 12 September 1852, Morley, Yorkshire
Died: 15 February 1928, The Wharf, Sutton Courtenay,
Berkshire. Buried at Sutton Courtenay parish church
Education: City of London School; Balliol College, Oxford
Married to Helen Melland (d. 1891), then Margot Tennant; 5
sons, 2 daughters
Quotation: 'We are fighting to vindicate the principle that small
nationalities are not to be crushed, in defiance of international
good faith, by the arbitrary will of a strong and overmastering
power.' (House of Commons, 6 August 1914)

H ERBERT HENRY ASQUITH has fair claim to be one of the best-known prime ministers. In modern times, only Margaret Thatcher and Tony Blair exceeded his 8 years and 243 days in office – and neither had previously served in great offices of state, as Asquith had.

Asquith was appointed by Gladstone as Home Secretary, aged only thirty-nine. Then, as Chancellor, he ushered in his country's first old-age pensions – the beginning of the modern Welfare State. As peacetime prime minister, he skilfully saw off an attempt by the House of Lords to stymie Liberal Party social legislation, and embarked on a carefully calibrated attempt to deliver Irish Home Rule. In 1914, he led a largely united country into the First World War, and helped put in place the foundations of victory.

Nor was Asquith an uninteresting personality. Behind the seemingly reserved and even dull Edwardian exterior, was a man of passion, dry humour and human fallibility. While prime minister, he fell deeply in love with a young lady, Venetia Stanley, who at just twenty-five was less than half his sixty years. To Miss Stanley, he wrote almost six hundred letters over five years. Sometimes he composed these while chairing important meetings of the Cabinet or War Council.

Like Churchill, he drank to excess. But he had none of Churchill's flair and appetite for the limelight. He dispatched government business with extraordinary efficiency, and even took on temporarily the jobs of War Minister and Foreign Secretary. But to many he seemed hopelessly detached and disengaged – in the early months of the war, he would sometimes walk over to the Athenaeum Club on Pall Mall, to read a light novel, without risk of disturbance. And when he was asked by Lady Tree in 1915: 'Mr. Asquith, do you take an interest in the War?', he regarded it as an amusing joke. In fact, it was a dangerous one, and the impression that he was not sufficiently energetic in pursuing 'total war' sealed his fate, and robbed him of the reputation that he would otherwise deserve. That may explain why one of Britain's most significant prime ministers is relatively unknown and unappreciated.

Asquith was born in Yorkshire, in 1852. His family had strong Nonconformist traditions – and from the earliest days, Asquith possessed a mainstream Liberal outlook.

In 1860, his father died, and he moved to London to live with his uncle. He was sent to the City of London School, where he thrived. Fascinated by politics, he frequently visited the House of Commons, to listen to debates.

In November 1869, Asquith secured a classical scholarship at Balliol College, Oxford. Having cultivated his debating skills at the Union, he became its President in 1874.

After university, he opted for the law, but his ultimate ambition was a political career. In 1883 he joined J.S. Wright's chambers at the Inner Temple – and was asked to prepare a memorandum for the Prime Minister – Gladstone – on the status of the parliamentary oath. Asquith's clearly argued paper was well received by Gladstone – further encouraging him.

His chance came at the General Election of 1886. He was elected in East Fife, by almost four hundred votes. At the age of just thirty-three, Asquith was a Member of Parliament. His eloquence, impressive intellect and natural authority were quickly recognised, and he was marked out as a future star. In 1877, he had married Helen, and they now had five children. This seemingly perfect life was shattered in September 1891, when Helen contracted typhoid and died. In reality, their interests and aspirations had begun to diverge, and within a short period of Helen's death Asquith was in a new relationship with Margot Tennant, daughter of a wealthy Liberal baronet. They married in 1894.

Asquith's personal life was happy again. His career was going well. But he was not a contented man. He would later write that 'of all human troubles the most hateful is to feel that you have the capacity of power and yet no field to exercise it . . . no one who has not been through it can know the chilly, paralysing, deadening depression of hope deferred and energy wasted and vitality run to seed'.

Asquith's career now took a sudden turn for the better. In the 1892 General Election, the Liberals returned to office. Gladstone was again prime minister – and elevated Asquith from the back benches to become Home Secretary. He soon set about finding pragmatic solutions to tricky problems, such as rights of protest in Parliament Square. He demonstrated an interest in social reform – pressing the case for legislation to protect employees injured at work. But he could be tough too – sending in the Metropolitan Police to deal with striking miners. In general, Asquith's approach was rational, progressive, but otherwise even-handed between radical and conservative extremes. In modern parlance, he was a Blairite, before Blair.

In 1894, Gladstone retired, and Lord Rosebery became prime minister. But the Liberals lost office in 1895. For Asquith, it was back to juggling politics and the law.

Out of office, the Liberal Party suffered from splits. These were exacerbated by the Boer War. Asquith was a somewhat lukewarm supporter of the war, which put him at odds with its many passionate Liberal opponents.

But the party was soon able to reunite to fight Conservative plans that threatened 'free trade' – Asquith playing a high-profile role in demolishing Chamberlain's case.

In 1905, the Liberals returned to government. Campbell-Bannerman became prime minister, and offered Asquith another big job – Chancellor of the Exchequer. Asquith was a careful steward of the public finances. His first Budget was unremarkable, but his second involved a little fiscal radicalism – higher rates of tax for unearned, rather than earned, income. In spite of this innovation, however, Asquith came across as solid, unthreatening and impressive – he championed progressive social measures behind a veil of fiscal orthodoxy.

His third Budget was more radical still – it paved the way for the introduction of a new state pension. Meanwhile, Asquith advanced the case for a progressive income tax structure, in the face of Treasury orthodoxy.

By the time Asquith came to present this 1908 Budget, he was no longer Chancellor. Campbell-Bannerman had died in early April 1908, and Asquith was regarded by all as the obvious successor. On 6 April, he drove to Charing Cross Station, and took the 9 p.m. boat train for France. He travelled completely alone. On 8 April, at the Hotel du Palais, Biarritz, he knelt and kissed the hand of King Edward VII. He had climbed the greasy pole. There would be no more 'vitality run to seed'.

His first task was to appoint a Cabinet. Asquith had to accommodate some big political 'beasts': the first of these – Lloyd George

– was sent to the Treasury. The second – Winston Churchill – became President of the Board of Trade.

Asquith took easily to the job of prime minister. He was commanding in the House of Commons, respected around the Cabinet table, and assumed easily the burdens of high office. Dealing swiftly with government business, he still found time for leisure pursuits – including evening bridge, late-night reading, and a growing output of letters to Venetia Stanley.

Asquith brought to his role the sharpness of a first-class lawyer's mind. He also possessed the patience, calmness and shrewdness necessary to heal divisions and unite his talented but diverse Cabinet.

Confronting him were three major issues with the potential to divide country and party. A dispute about naval expenditure threatened to split his Cabinet. A division over Lloyd George's 'People's Budget' risked a constitutional crisis. Splits over Irish Home Rule could even bring civil war.

The first of these proved the easiest to fix. Germany had embarked on a significant programme of naval construction, threatening Britain's naval supremacy. The new 'Dreadnought' battleships had at a stroke made Britain's earlier dominance less secure. Some in Cabinet wanted more money to build more ships. The 'economists', including Lloyd George and Churchill, saw in this a threat to their social and economic plans. Asquith patiently negotiated a sensible compromise.

The second challenge proved much trickier, and eventually required two General Elections, a near constitutional crisis, and a pledge from the new King (George V) to flood the House of Lords with Liberal Peers.

The Liberals had, in 1908, a decisive majority in the Commons, and used this to force through major economic and social reform. But in the House of Lords, there continued to be a deeply entrenched Conservative majority, resistant to radical measures. Campbell-Bannerman had considered curbing the power of the Lords, but this was unfinished business.

Asquith and Lloyd George, however, believed that the Lords would not dare impede a so-called 'money bill' – this had not happened since the reign of Queen Anne. So they included their radical measures in the 'Finance Bill' that implements each Budget.

However, the Lloyd George 'People's Budget' of 1909 proved far too much for the Lords. They hated the big increases in direct and indirect taxes. There was to be a 20 per cent tax on unearned increase in the price of land, along with a graduated tax on incomes, and higher tax on alcoholic beverages. Even some senior Liberals objected, former prime minister Lord Rosebery describing it as 'inquisitorial, tyrannical and Socialistic'.

The Budget was attacked in the press, and was overwhelmingly rejected by the Lords. Asquith was determined to prevail, through a calm, reasonable and measured approach. This was not the Lloyd George way – the Chancellor made some provocative speeches, asking why 'five hundred men, ordinary men, chosen accidentally from the unemployed' should be able to impede the will of the people. The King, fearing revolution, was furious.

In November 1909, after the Lords had rejected the Budget, Asquith asked the King to dissolve Parliament. In the resulting election, the Liberals lost many seats – but continued in government with the support of the Irish nationalists and the Labour Party.

But the Lords continued to exercise their power and influence – prompting another election. Asquith led the Liberal campaign – and was a model of calm and measured good sense. The result was little changed. This time, understanding that Asquith had extracted a promise from the King to flood the Lords with Liberal Peers, the Upper House fell into line and the Budget passed. The Cabinet also backed a bill that would eventually become the Parliament Act of 1911 – preventing the Lords from blocking money bills, curbing their powers of veto of other bills, and reducing the maximum length of a Parliament from seven to five years.

It had been a dangerous moment for the country and for the Liberal programme of social reform. But Asquith had steered his government through treacherous waters, and had secured all of his objectives. It was his finest hour. As his biographer, Roy Jenkins, concluded, Asquith had given a 'masterly display of political nerve and patient determination'.

There now followed other progressive legislation – Labour exchanges, the introduction of state insurance for unemployment and health, trade union protections, and the payment of MPs. Only in the area of votes for women was Asquith determinedly conservative in outlook. He did not understand the issue of 'equal rights'. To him, it was a question of whether change would lead to better government, and of this he was unpersuaded.

Parliamentary arithmetic, as well as Liberal conviction, now required attention to be given to Irish Home Rule. Typically, Asquith presented Home Rule as a moderate and pragmatic solution – in which the Irish would be given control of their 'domestic' affairs, but the 'Imperial Parliament' would continue to exercise control over other matters.

The Conservatives were both opposed in principle and passionately against including Protestant Ulster. The new Conservative leader, Bonar Law, pursued a particularly extreme and uncompromising line – warning of 'Rome Rule'.

While Asquith was publicly resistant to giving Ulster a special status, he was pragmatic enough to recognise that this might eventually be necessary.

In March 1914, with the Home Rule Bill proceeding through the Commons, there occurred the so-called 'Curragh Incident', when around sixty British army officers announced that they would rather resign their posts than uphold Home Rule. The Secretary of State for War, Jack Seeley, made an unauthorised promise that force would not be used against Ulster. A furious Asquith repudiated the statement and forced Seeley's resignation – taking control of the War Office. An all-party conference at Buckingham Palace failed – a solution 'lost in the muddy by-ways of Fermanagh and Tyrone', in Churchill's vivid phrase.

It now seemed as if Asquith was 'between a rock and a hard place'. He could not retreat, without potentially bringing down his government. He could not advance, without risking division and bloodshed. For the best part of six years as prime minister, he had been the great unifier. But Ireland seemed too much for even his skills.

Then, on 28 June 1914, the Archduke Franz Ferdinand was shot dead in Sarajevo. Everything changed. Home Rule was now put into the deep freeze.

Until late in the day, Asquith and his Cabinet were convinced that they could avoid joining the war. Indeed, when – as late as 24 July – Austria delivered its ultimatum to Serbia, Asquith wrote that:

'Happily there seems to be no reason why we should be anything more than spectators.'

As the risk of conflict grew, Asquith was confronted with a deeply divided Cabinet – with at least ten ministers being determined against war, including Lloyd George. Germany's blatant violation of Belgium's neutrality changed all this – uniting the country and the Cabinet. By the eve of conflict, the streets of London were massing with crowds baying for war. Asquith observed: 'I have never before been a popular character with the "man in the street".'

At 11 p.m. on 4 August, the British ultimatum to Germany expired, unanswered. The peace-loving, mild-mannered, moderate Asquith was now to lead his country into the bloodiest war in its history – in which almost 900,000 men would die and 1.6 million would be wounded.

The early months of the war saw Asquith at his sure-footed best. His address to the House of Commons rallied the nation. His selection of the revered military leader, Lord Kitchener, was astute – politically and militarily. Kitchener did not fall for all the talk about a war that would be 'over by Christmas' – he immediately planned for a mass army and a war of three or four years. Meanwhile, the tiny British Expeditionary Force was dispatched to Belgium, where it helped hold the left flank of the Allied line. So far, so good.

And then, the problems started to pile up. The war in the west was soon bogged down in trench warfare. The enormous increase in the army, and the unprecedented increase in the use of shells and equipment, caused bottlenecks and shortages. This should not have been a surprise – in the whole three years of the Boer War, just 273,000 shells were fired. In the first six months of the First World War, the figure was 1 million shells. But governments in power will always be held accountable for current problems.

A mass assault on the 'western front' in France seemed bound to fail, but some other attack on Germany and her allies was necessary to relieve the pressure on Russia. Not wishing to remain idle, but fearing to remove troops from the main front, Asquith agreed eventually to a hare-brained scheme devised by Churchill to force the Dardanelles – with a purely naval force. Unsurprisingly, the plan was a disaster – leading to the resignation of the First Sea Lord, Fisher.

This disaster, along with newspaper stories about shell shortages, forced Asquith to form a coalition government with the Conservatives, in May 1915. He was not to know it, but he had just led the last majority Liberal government.

That this was a difficult stage of the war was no fault of Asquith's. The tiny pre-war British army would take time to expand, as would arms production. The French and British armies faced a large and formidable foe. Barbed wire, trenches and machine guns gave a marked advantage to the defender. But Asquith's war leadership was increasingly questioned by politicians and the press.

The problem was not just the stalemate in France – it was about Asquith's style of leadership. The unflappable, laid-back style that worked so well in peacetime was not fit for total war. It was a style as different as could be imagined from that which Churchill would adopt in the Second World War. Meetings of the Cabinet and the War Committee would go on for hours without seeming to reach clear solutions. The approach to fixing supply bottlenecks seemed to lack urgency. Meanwhile, British attacks continued on the western front, with tens of thousands of casualties, but without any material gains on the ground.

Asquith took many months to move from a voluntary system of recruitment to compulsory enlistment – as he struggled to unite his party.

His personal behaviour grated too – he continued to attend weekend parties, often appeared inebriated at night, played bridge in the evenings, and was spotted writing letters to Venetia Stanley during crucial government meetings. It was perhaps fortunate that his colleagues did not know that these letters often shared the most confidential of military secrets – even of operations yet to take place.

Lloyd George complained privately that Asquith had 'no plan, no initiative, no grip, no driving force'. He was now emerging as Asquith's greatest rival.

The Prime Minister now also suffered a series of severe personal blows. On 12 May 1915, Venetia Stanley wrote to tell him she was going to marry Edwin Montagu – one of Asquith's closest political friends. In spite of the enormous age gap, Asquith was in love with Stanley and hugely emotionally dependent. In February 1915, he had written to her: 'Sometimes a horrible imagination seizes me that you may be taken from me . . . with you would vanish all the colour and "point" of my life . . . these last two years the love of you and trust in you . . . have made life worth living.' On 4 March, he told her: 'All that I do and try to do, I do with the hope of earning your praise.'

That now all ended, along with the letters, Asquith describing it as a 'death blow'. Not many months later, in mid-September 1915, came the news that his eldest son, Raymond, had been killed in action.

It was not only Liberal rivals who doubted whether Asquith had the required character and drive to lead the war effort. In February 1916, Conservative leader, Bonar Law, warned Asquith that 'In war, it is necessary not only to be active but to seem active.'

On Easter Monday 1916, there was an outbreak of Irish nationalist violence in Dublin. Asquith sent Lloyd George to find a solution. The Chancellor had been planning to join Kitchener on a secret mission to Russia, on HMS *Hampshire*. The ship hit a mine on 5 June – Kitchener and most of the crew were lost. But the last-minute change of plan saved Lloyd George's life, and sealed Asquith's fate.

By December, Lloyd George had joined with the Conservative leadership to force Asquith from power. Asquith did not expect the new government to last for long and refused to join it. Lloyd George's actions and Asquith's response split the Liberal Party, and in the 'Coupon election' of 1918, many Liberal MPs who did not support the new Lloyd George coalition lost their seats – including Asquith. He was re-elected to Parliament in 1920, but lost his seat in 1924. In 1925, he accepted a peerage. He remained Liberal leader until October 1926 – a serious mistake. The Liberal Party never recovered from the divisions of 1916.

Asquith suffered a series of strokes in 1926 and 1927. His last visit, in autumn 1927, was to see the widowed Venetia. He died, aged seventy-five, on 15 February 1928. He was buried, with simplicity and without show, in the graveyard of All Saints' parish church at Sutton Courtenay.

Asquith was a prime minister of formidable intellect, strong commitment to public service, and high standards of behaviour. Even his critics recognised his 'unrivalled gifts of lucid and logical statement' (Lloyd George). He was skilled in listening to arguments, analysing their strengths and weaknesses, and coming quickly to a conclusion. Lord Morley once said of him: 'Asquith ought to have been a judge. He would have made a great one.'

He dealt swiftly and efficiently with the heavy burdens of office – possessing, as he once wrote, 'energy under the guise of lethargy; a faculty for working quickly; patience; a temperate but persistent ambition; a clear mind; a certain faculty and lucidity of speech . . . a natural tendency to understand and appreciate the opponent's point of view'. Taken together, these were formidable assets.

Asquith was deeply liberal in his convictions, but moderate and consensual when it came to implementing them. The essence of his belief was the supremacy of national interests over factional considerations, combined with a commitment to extending oppor- tunities across society: 'Liberalism means two things – the pres- ervation and extension of liberty in every sphere of our national life, and the subordination of class interests to the interests of the community.'

In contrast to Liberals of the nineteenth century, Asquith believed that 'the time [had] come for the State to lend a helping hand'. He believed in 'liberty in its positive as well as in its negative sense'.

The case against Asquith is made most brutally by Lloyd George:

> He never drove or initiated . . . He dealt with questions not as they arose but as they were presented to him . . . He was always essentially the judge . . . He gave dignified but not rousing and vigorous leadership to the nation. But a War Minister must also have vision, imagination and initiative . . . Asquith's will became visibly flabbier, tardier, and more flaccid under the strain of war.

Churchill held a similar view: 'The agonised nation demanded a frenzied energy at the summit; an effort to compel events rather than to adjudicate wisely and deliberately upon them.' It was exactly this style of leadership that Asquith could not offer.

Asquith's record must be assessed in two parts – peacetime prime minister and wartime leader.

As peacetime prime minister, there seems little to fault and much to praise. He held together at critical moments both his Cabinet and the country. He advanced progressive social legislation. He got the better of the deeply Conservative House of Lords without provoking a constitutional crisis. He did his best to advance a peaceful and pragmatic solution to the problems of Ireland. He ensured the British navy was predominant when the war of 1914 began. He led the nation united into a war that could probably not have been avoided, given the German breach of Belgian neutrality.

Had that war never occurred, Asquith might now be seen as one of the greatest of British prime ministers – the Edwardian gentleman who paved the way for a typically low-key and peaceful British 'revolution' – the Welfare State. Given time, he might also have secured a settlement of the Irish question, just as he had resolved the position and powers of the House of Lords.

But by interests, temperament and personality, Asquith was not cut out to be war leader, in the first industrial-scale conflict. His laid-back style – such an asset in dealing with peacetime problems – was no longer what was required.

Asquith did not offer the visible and energetic leadership that is expected in wartime, but there is little to suggest that his replacement by Lloyd George had much impact on the course of the war. Had Asquith possessed the political strength to hold off Lloyd George's challenge, the war would likely still have ended in November 1918 with an Allied victory, and Asquith might have retired with the reputation of one our greatest prime ministers. As it is, after Gladstone, Asquith surely still ranks next as the greatest ever Liberal prime minister.

David Laws is Executive Chairman of the Education Policy Institute. He served as a Member of Parliament from 2001 to 2015 and was a minister in the 2010 coalition government.

36

David Lloyd George

6 December 1916 to 19 October 1922
Liberal

By Damian Collins

Full name: David Lloyd George
Born: 17 January 1863, Chorlton-on-Medlock, Manchester
Died: 26 March 1945, Ty Newydd, Llanystumdwy. Buried by the River Dwyfor, near his house at Ty Newydd
Education: Llanystumdwy National School
Married to Margaret Owen (d. 20 January 1941), then Frances Stevenson; 2 sons, 4 daughters
Quotation: 'What is our task? To make Britain a fit country for heroes to live in.' (Speech following the end of the First World War in Wolverhampton, 24 November 1918)

'BIGGEST CROWDS IN New York streets since home coming of US Troops greet the "Wizard of Wales",' exclaimed the Pathé newsreel. It was 5 October 1923, nearly five years since the end of the First World War, and twelve months following David Lloyd George's resignation as prime minister. Dressed in a morning coat and silk top hat he was greeted with thunderous applause from a large crowd of New Yorkers when he landed with his party at Pier A on the Battery in Lower Manhattan. Accompanied by the State Governor Al Smith and the Mayor of the city John Hylan, they were swept away in a cavalcade of more than thirty open-top motor cars for the mile-long parade along Broadway to the City Hall. Every window along the route, even from fifty-storey skyscrapers, was filled with people cheering and throwing down ticker-tape.

To the Americans, Lloyd George was not just the man who had won the war, but someone who embodied their national dream. Like his hero Abraham Lincoln, Lloyd George had risen from the simple origins of a remote cottage home, and was as he described himself, a 'ranker . . . who had not passed through the Staff College of the old Universities'. The editorial column in the *New York Times* that morning exclaimed:

> Was there ever a more romantic rise from the humblest beginning than this? Has any statesman of our time combined in himself so many diverse and fascinating qualities as those which have made Mr Lloyd George known to the whole world? His versatility, his eloquence, his uncanny ability to read the public mind almost before it has formed itself.

Lloyd George's arrival in New York was reminiscent of the hero's welcome he'd received when returning to London in 1919, following the signing of the Treaty of Versailles that officially ended the First World War. Then King George V had greeted him at London's Charing Cross station and they had ridden together in an open carriage through cheering crowds. Years later, the press baron Lord Beaverbrook would recall that, 'it is not now possible to realise the immense position of this man Lloyd George'. Even his great political rival, the Conservative Party leader Andrew Bonar Law, then believed that Lloyd George could be 'Prime Minster for life if he likes'. Yet divisions between the members of his post-war Liberal and Conservative coalition government brought about its collapse in 1922 and, although just fifty-nine years old at that time, Lloyd George would never hold public office again.

His nickname of the 'Welsh Wizard' was born of his fame, but also marked the seal of his fate. Lloyd George was at times magical, but also mercurial. As a boy he was brought up in the Nonconformist Free Church movement, but as a man he became a serial woman-iser; a social reformer, who also courted the financial support of wealthy businessmen; and an anti-Boer War campaigner, who later perfected the organisation of total war and extended conscription into the British army. He was 'a dynamic force', concluded the future Conservative prime minister Stanley Baldwin in 1922, which in his opinion was a 'terrible thing' that had 'smashed' the Liberal Party, and that, left unchecked, would do the same to his own. Lloyd George did not feel constrained by political or social ortho-doxies if they held him back from achieving his goal, and felt free to change his own positions as the situation demanded. This made him a risk taker, in both his political and private lives. As a man of action, he saved Britain during the war, laid the foundations of the modern Welfare State, and created structures for government that are still followed to this day. Lloyd George redefined the role of prime minister, and, after Winston Churchill, could claim to rank alongside any of the holders of that office in the twentieth century.

'The Tories have not yet realised that the day of the cottage-bred man has at last dawned,' David Lloyd George told a public meeting in 1890 during his successful by-election campaign to be elected as the MP for his home constituency of Caernarvon Boroughs. He was born David George, on 17 January 1863, at 5 New York Place, in Chorlton-on-Medlock, an industrial area to the south-east of central Manchester. His father William was a teacher from a Pembrokeshire farming family, whose 'restless ambition' had led him away from home. However, poor physical health took his life when he died of pneumonia in June 1864, having previously suffered from tuberculosis. His thirty-six-year-old widow Elizabeth, then expecting their third child, sold all that the family had and moved with David and his elder sister Mary Ellen, to live with her brother Richard Lloyd at Llanystumdwy in north-west Wales. This would be the village that raised the future prime minister.

Llanystumdwy, located near Criccieth and nestled between Cardigan Bay and the Snowdonia mountain range, was Welsh speaking, and this would be David's first language as he grew up. Richard Lloyd, a shoe maker and a minister in the local chapel of the Disciples of Christ, would have the strongest influence on the early life of his nephew, so much so that David altered his surname to Lloyd George as a mark of affection and respect.

The chapel would also be a big influence on the life of the young Lloyd George, which he attended three times on Sundays and where he would listen to his uncle as well as many other great Welsh preachers of that time. At the age of nineteen he made his first appearance before the congregation, with Uncle Lloyd noting in his diary, 'O! my dear boy, he did speak so well! Never was anything more striking and profitable.' This experience greatly influenced Lloyd George's early speaking style, which according to his aide and fellow Welshman Thomas Jones, 'was much closer to [the] Welsh pulpit model'.

Lloyd George's first step in his journey from Llanystumdwy came when, aged sixteen, he was articled to a firm of solicitors in nearby Porthmadog, where he also joined the local debating society and became involved with the Liberal Party. While staying in London in order to take the Law Society's intermediate exam, he visited the House of Commons for the first time and noted in his diary, 'I eyed the Assembly in a spirit similar to that which William the Conqueror eyed England on his visit to Edward the Confessor, as the region of his future domain. Oh, vanity!' He qualified as a solicitor in 1884 and immediately started his own practice in Criccieth, making his name when in 1888 he successfully represented the Nonconformist Roberts family against Richard Jones, the Church of England vicar at Llanfrothen. Believing an 1880 Act of Parliament gave them the right to bury their father in consecrated ground, Lloyd George advised the family to break into the church-yard at night to do so, despite the objections of the vicar, who had locked the gate. The following morning, the latter applied for a court summons against the family, but Lloyd George won the case, taking his argument ultimately all the way to the Royal Courts of Justice. This victory also helped him secure the Liberal Party nom-ination to stand for Parliament in Caernarvon Boroughs, an opportunity that would come sooner than expected when on 19 March 1890 the Conservative MP for the seat died. Lloyd George won the by-election by just eighteen votes, beginning an unbroken period of fifty-five years in Parliament representing the same constituency.

Lloyd George entered a House of Commons where William Gladstone still led the Liberals, and he considered him even years later to be 'the best of all parliamentary speakers'. He also greatly admired the Irish nationalist MP Charles Stewart Parnell, who had led the battle in Parliament for Home Rule, and David believed that the Welsh MPs should similarly organise themselves to act in the interests of their nation. Lloyd George was elected to Parliament in the year of Parnell's fall, when his affair with the wife of fellow Irish MP, William O'Shea, was exposed in court. Yet this case did not appear to influence the risks the young Welshman was prepared to take with his own private life. He had married Margaret Owen in 1888, the daughter of a respectable Criccieth farming family, and they would go on to have five children. Yet, she preferred to keep their home in Wales, leaving Lloyd George on his own in London when Parliament was in session. He pursued a number of affairs, including one in 1913 with Frances Stevenson. She had been a school friend of his daughter Mair, and was later hired by Lloyd George as a governess for Mair's younger sister Megan, which was when their affair began. Frances was persuaded to take up the dual positions of being both private secretary and mistress to Lloyd George, and they then effectively lived and worked together in London for the next thirty years, until Margaret's death in 1943, after which they married.

The campaign that established Lloyd George as one of the leading radical Liberals was his opposition to the initially popular Boer War, and his direct challenge to the Colonial Secretary, Joseph Chamberlain, one of the stars of late Victorian politics. In December 1901 he even agreed to speak against the war at a public meeting in Birmingham, the home city of Chamberlain. Tens of thousands of protesters successfully broke up the meeting and started a riot in which one man was killed and forty others were hospitalised. Lloyd George was forced to flee for his life with the help of the police and disguised in one of their uniforms.

Lloyd George's first position in government came in 1905 when he was appointed President of the Board of Trade, in Sir Henry Campbell-Bannerman's administration. There he first demonstrated his great skills as a negotiator, by brokering the deal between the railway companies and the trades unions that avoided a national strike. When Herbert Asquith succeeded Campbell-Bannerman in 1908, Lloyd George was appointed as Chancellor of the Exchequer, and would soon prove to be one of the great reforming holders of that office. In Lloyd George's 1909 'People's Budget', he told the House of Commons that it was 'a War Budget. It is for raising money to wage implacable warfare against poverty and squalidness.' He proposed raising taxes by over £14 million, then an unprecedented measure in peacetime, to build eight new Dreadnought battleships for the Royal Navy, and to fund Britain's first national scheme of old-age pensions. Yet his method was deeply political, for while he proposed increases in income taxes, and 'death duties', the most controversial measure was a new tax on undeveloped land, and a 20 per cent capital gains tax on land sales. If Lloyd George believed in redistributing wealth, it was from the landlords, rather than the new men who had earned money through their industry.

When the Budget was eventually passed in April 1910, a year after its introduction and following a great constitutional stand-off with the House of Lords, Lloyd George sent a bound copy to Uncle Lloyd inscribed, 'To the real author of this budget with his pupil's affectionate gratitude.' The introduction of old-age pensions would be followed by the 1911 National Insurance Act, providing a scheme of health insurance from contributions made by the employer, the employee and the government. Later in 1920, Lloyd George's government would bring forward an Unemployment Insurance Act, to provide financial support to people while they were looking for work.

In the summer of 1914, the world 'unexpectantly plunged', as Lloyd George later remarked, into the First World War. His friend the businessman and owner of the *News of the World* Lord Riddell, noted that Lloyd George was being 'bombarded with telegrams from friends like [C.P.] Scott of the *Manchester Guardian* who had wired him to say that any Liberal who supported war would never be allowed to enter another Liberal Cabinet'. Lloyd George would have supported British neutrality if Germany had agreed to respect the independence of Belgium, but he told his wife Margaret that if that small country was attacked, 'all my traditions and even my prejudices will be engaged on the side of war'. He would prove to be one of the most innovative and effective ministers in prosecuting it.

In 1915, Lord Northcliffe's *Daily Mail* newspaper ran a campaign focused on how the shortage of shells and ammunition for the British troops was contributing to a series of military setbacks on the western front and a growing concern that the government hadn't got a grip on the war. In May, pressure for a change in direction led the Prime Minister, Herbert Asquith, to bring leading Conservatives into a national government, and he created a new Ministry of Munitions, to be led by Lloyd George, to solve the 'shells crisis'. This new role showcased his powers of invention and love of unorthodox solutions; it would also put him at the forefront of Britain's organisation for war on the home front.

Lloyd George brought in 'push and goes' from industry, whom he called the 'leading hustlers' of their day. These included Sir Eric Geddes from the North East Railway Company, to drive forward the process of increasing production and improving supply to the front. He encouraged women to work in the munitions factories and in turn ensured that for the first time they would receive the vote at the next General Election. Lloyd George told Asquith in December 1915, 'You sent me to France to see what was wanted. I have seen for myself what the troops need . . . and I'm going to keep my promise to them, experts or not.' This made him dismissive of the estimates of the British commander General Sir Douglas Haig and Lord Kitchener, then the Secretary of State for War, as to what the army's actual equipment needs were. Kitchener thought that four machine guns per battalion were more than sufficient, which prompted Lloyd George to tell Geddes to 'Take Kitchener's figure. Square it. Multiply by two. Then double again for good luck.' The army began the war with 1,330 machine guns and, thanks to the work of the Ministry of Munitions, 240,506 more were manufactured.

In his *War Memoirs* Lloyd George protested against the war of attrition on the western front, with soldiers being thrown at the enemy trenches with 'unintelligent hammering against the impenetrable barrier'. In the summer of 1916 he visited Haig at the British General Headquarters in France, in the town of Montreuil-sur-Mer about twenty miles south of Boulogne. Lloyd George's sense of mission in war was, as it had been in peace, to challenge authority on behalf of those who suffered, without the power to do so themselves; in this case, the soldiers at the front. This led to complaints from the generals at growing interference from ministers, but for Lloyd George it was born of a real concern, as he expressed to Maurice Hankey, the secretary to the War Council, that 'We are going to lose this war.'

As 1916 drew to a close, Britain's position looked bleak. Germany was the dominant power in Europe, France exhausted and Russia edging closer to collapse. America's president Woodrow Wilson was still committed to neutrality and British shipping was under constant U-boat attack in the Atlantic, which was creating shortages and hardship at home. A powerful coalition of senior politicians, including Andrew Bonar Law, the leader of the Irish Unionist Party, Sir Edward Carson, and former prime minister Arthur Balfour, as well as the leading press barons, concluded that the direction of the war should come under the leadership of Lloyd George. He was, as the *Daily Mirror* proclaimed, 'The man the nation wants.'

The withdrawal of their support led to Asquith's resignation on 5 December and the formation of a new coalition government. This was the closest thing the modern British constitution has seen to a palace coup. Without an election, a division in Parliament, or even a vote of the MPs of the governing party, one prime minister was forced out and replaced by a new coalition under the command of a man who wasn't even the leader of one of the main parties. As the former Conservative prime minister Arthur Balfour exclaimed, 'if he wants to be a dictator, let him be. If he thinks he can win the war, I'm all for his having a try.'

So fell a prime minister, regarded by some as 'the last of the Romans', to be succeeded by the only Welshman to hold the office. His nationality defined him in the eyes of some of his critics, including the economist John Maynard Keynes, who dubbed him 'this siren, this goat-footed bard, this half-human visitor to our age from the hag-ridden magic and enchanted woods of Celtic antiquity'. Lloyd George was proud of his heritage, and would from time to time during meetings confer in Welsh to his aides and compatriots Thomas Jones and J.T. Davies.

From the start as prime minister, Lloyd George transformed the structure of government, creating a small War Cabinet of five members to aid decision making. Maurice Hankey was appointed as the first Cabinet Secretary, responsible for ensuring accurate minutes were kept of meetings; something that had never happened before. A new secretariat of policy experts and civil servants, known initially as the 'Garden Suburb', grew up in temporary buildings in the Downing Street garden; a precursor to the modern-day Cabinet Office. In 1917, Lloyd George successfully pushed for the creation of a unified Allied War Council to better coordinate military action on the western front. He also required that the Admiralty adopt the convoy system to protect transatlantic shipping and defeat the U-boat attacks; one of the most significant actions of the war.

When victory came in November 1918, Lloyd George was the most powerful man in Europe, and led his coalition government to a landslide victory in the 'Coupon' election (the term 'coupon' was coined by Herbert Asquith as a dismissive reference to the endorsement letters sent to candidates by Lloyd George and Bonar Law the following month). Yet the balance of power greatly favoured the Conservatives, with 379 MPs to Lloyd George's 127 Liberals. The Tories could have governed by themselves, and there would always be those who questioned why they did not. Yet as long as they believed in Lloyd George's popularity with the returning soldiers, and the newly enfranchised working classes, whom they feared would otherwise support the Labour Party, they would back him.

Lloyd George became the dominant politician at the Paris Peace Conference in 1919, which redrew the boundaries of Europe, striking down ancient empires and giving birth to new states. Yet the nation he returned to after the signing of the Treaty of Versailles on 28 June 1919 was one weary from the war and suffering from the ravages of the Spanish flu pandemic, which would claim the lives of more than 200,000 people in the UK alone. Lloyd George had nearly succumbed in September 1918, when he fell ill with the virus after speaking at a public meeting in Manchester.

During the General Election campaign he had promised 'a fit country for heroes to live in', and had created a new Ministry for Health to oversee the building of homes, as well as the improvement of the physical health of the nation, and the creation of a national strategy to more effectively respond to viral infections like the flu pandemic. Yet the progress of recovery was slow, and in 1920, as a result of a global economic crash, the unemployment rate went up to 23.4 per cent from 2.7 per cent a year earlier.

Serious industrial disputes with the coal and railway trade unions had threatened to bring the country to a standstill, and the still-rising national debt following the war was creating mounting political pressure to cut government spending. There were growing concerns about Lloyd George's working style as well. He had devoted considerable time to international conferences to settle the affairs of the post-war world. Versailles had been followed by meetings at Cannes, San Remo, Spa and a series of intimate summits with the French government at the luxurious home of his wealthy parliamentary private secretary, Sir Philip Sassoon, at Port Lympne on the south Kent coast. Maurice Hankey observed after visiting the Prime Minister at Lympne that he had a 'disagreeable feeling' he was getting 'too fond of high living and luxury'.

In Ireland, the war of independence against British rule had led Lloyd George to approve the use of the 'Black and Tan' armed force to carry out brutal reprisals against the IRA. The situation reached a crisis point following the shooting on 21 November 1920 of innocent spectators at Croke Park stadium in Dublin by the Royal Irish Constabulary, in reprisal for the murder of British intelligence agents by the IRA earlier that day.

There were growing tensions with Lloyd George's Conservative colleagues in the Cabinet, which were made worse by Bonar Law's resignation from the government in March 1921, on grounds of ill-health. As the Tory grandee Lord Derby noted, the government was held together by the 'extreme loyalty' of Conservative MPs to Bonar Law, and problems could be avoided only for as long as Lloyd George and Bonar Law stuck together. On 30 May, Sassoon hosted a dinner for the Cabinet at his mansion at 45 Park Lane, where, as Lord Beaverbrook recalled, the Prime Minister would try to exert 'his charms. That was the object of the Sassoon parties.' Over dinner, Lloyd George set out his case for a negotiated settlement on Ireland, and shortly afterwards there occurred what Churchill described as the most 'complete and sudden . . . reversal of policy . . . In May the whole power of the State and the influence of the Coalition were used to "hunt down the murder gang": in June the goal was a lasting reconciliation with the Irish people.'

For the rest of the year, until the Treaty was signed on 6 December, the Irish negotiations dominated the work of the government. They brought Lloyd George face to face with another cottage-bred man, the IRA leader Michael Collins, who was not seduced by the Welshman's charms; 'He is all comradely, all craft and wiliness – all arm around the shoulder . . . not long ago he would have had me joyfully at the rope end.'

The final settlement required a masterful balancing act by the Prime Minister between the conflicting interests of the Irish nation-alists, a Conservative Party that had opposed Home Rule, and the Ulster Unionists. The treaty creating the Irish Free State, but preserving six northern countries in Ulster within the United Kingdom, was seen as a temporary solution, but remains fixed to this day. Lord Beaverbrook noted that,

> The achievement of the Irish Treaty revealed in full what it was that LG possessed which other men lacked, in the understanding of human nature, in the art of tenacious negotiation, to a degree which few men in history have exhibited. If one way closed, he opened up another; he was, in the words of one of his friends, who presented him with a lovely piece of silver to mark the signing of the Treaty, 'the solver of the insoluble'.

Yet many Conservative MPs remained unreconciled to the Irish Treaty and there was the growing whiff of scandal around the Lloyd George political fund, created to finance future election campaigns, but resourced through the selling of honours and peerages. Amid the mounting pressure, there was a sense that the Welsh Wizard was losing his magic touch.

In April 1922 he had been the driving force behind the Genoa Conference, designed to be a second Versailles, at which Lloyd George wanted to create a new strategy to support the reconstruction of Germany and negotiate a relationship with the Soviet Union; another issue that many Conservatives opposed. The arrival of Lloyd George for the conference impressed a young Ernest Hemingway, who was covering the event for the *Toronto Star*. He wrote, 'The hall is nearly full when the British delegation enters. They have come in motorcars through the troop-lined streets and enter with élan. They are the best-dressed delegation.' Yet they would leave empty-handed.

The final straw for many Conservative MPs was a government statement on 16 September threatening war with Turkey if it violated one of the neutral zones at Chanak on the Asian side of the Dardanelles Straits. As Thomas Jones noted, 'The outcry in war-weary Britain was immediate and widespread.' Shortly afterwards, at a meeting of Conservative MPs at the Carlton Club on 19 October, they voted by 185 to 88 in favour of a motion that the party should fight the next election as an independent force with its own manifesto and leader. Lloyd George resigned, but the King wrote in his diary, 'I am sorry he is going, but some day he will be Prime Minister again.'

Andrew Bonar Law returned to lead the Conservatives and formed a new government, one dismissed by Churchill as being made up of a 'second eleven' of Cabinet ministers. Lloyd George expected to return to office and, in the aftermath of the Conservative General Election victory in November 1922, thought about how he could create a new centre party, comprising his coalition Liberals and moderates from Labour and the Conservatives.

In a presidential system of government, Lloyd George could have used his profile and reputation to mount a serious challenge, but in Parliament the Liberals were divided and had been pushed into third place by Labour. It speaks volumes for the political significance of Lloyd George even out of office that both Stanley Baldwin and Ramsay MacDonald, who would go on to share the office of prime minister between them from 1923 until 1937, consistently manoeuvred to keep him out of government. Even when the Liberals under his leadership held the balance of power after the 1929 General Election, and later when the National Government was formed during the Great Depression, Lloyd George was excluded.

He nevertheless maintained an active political life as an advocate of government investment as the solution to the unemployment problem. He called for the National Government to create a 'New Deal' for Britain, as President Franklin Roosevelt had in the USA, and was critical of the policy followed in the 1930s of appeasing the dictators in Europe, despite the terrible error of judgement he showed in visiting Adolf Hitler at Berchtesgaden in 1936. His last significant speech in the House of Commons came during the famous Norway debate in May 1940, which led to Neville Chamberlain's resignation as prime minister. There, Lloyd George, summoning up the experience of his own wartime premiership, stated that,

> The nation is prepared for every sacrifice so long as it has leadership, as long as the Government show clearly what they are aiming at and so long as the nation is confident that those who are leading it are doing their best. I say solemnly that the Prime Minister should give an example of sacrifice, because there is nothing which can contribute more to victory in this war than that he should sacrifice the seals of office.

He was invited by Winston Churchill to join the Cabinet in 1940, but declined despite being urged to accept by his friends. In a letter to Frances Stevenson's daughter Jennifer, he gave his reason as, 'I do not believe in the way we entered the war – nor the methods by which it has been conducted . . . I do not believe in the way or in the persons with which the War Cabinet is constituted.' Perhaps Lloyd George believed that the call to high office would come again, if it became clear that the new government would likely fail in its aim to deliver 'victory at all costs'. However, his long-serving aide, A.J. Sylvester, had a different theory: 'His amazing gifts of genius were denied the nation in her hour of dire need, not because he was too old to serve, but because he would not enter the Cabinet in a subordinate position . . . he acted like the spoiled child he was.'

Lloyd George would spend his last year back home in Llanystumdwy, where he died from cancer on 26 March 1945, missing by a few weeks the final triumph of Britain and her Allies over Nazi Germany. Despite the Welsh Wizard's many personal flaws, Churchill stated of him in his eulogy in the House of Commons that, 'As a man of action, resource and creative energy he stood, when at his zenith, without a rival.'

Damian Collins has been a Member of Parliament since 2010 and is the author of Charmed Life: The Phenomenal World of Philip Sassoon.

37

Andrew Bonar Law

23 October 1922 to 20 May 1923
Conservative

By Keelan Carr

Full name: Andrew Bonar Law
Born: 16 September 1858, Kingston, New Brunswick, Canada
Died: 30 October 1923, 24 Onslow Gardens, Westminster;
buried at Westminster Abbey
Education: The High School of Glasgow
Married to Annie Pitcairn Robley; 4 sons, 2 daughters
Quotation: 'If I am a great man then a good many great men
of history are frauds.'

A s the owner of a memorably strange name, as the shortest-
serving prime minister of the twentieth century, and (until
the New York-born Boris Johnson robbed him of the distinction)
as the only one to have been born overseas, Bonar Law is prob-

ably more familiar today as the answer to a pub quiz question than for his political achievements. But what W.H. Auden said about books applies equally to politicians: none is undeservedly remembered, but many are undeservedly forgotten. Bonar Law is one.

He played, as his friend and wartime comrade Lloyd George said, 'a great part in great events'. He led the Conservative Party for more than a decade – longer than anyone but Thatcher, Churchill and Baldwin in the twentieth century. As much as any of them, he redefined what it meant to be a Conservative leader and set the political course that his party would follow for a generation. He was also a modest and decent man.

Bonar Law's coda-like 209-day premiership, in the final illness-ravaged year of his life, is better understood as a tribute to his prior career than as its fulfilment. That career began in as remote a spot as any prime minister's, before or since.

Bonar Law was born in 1858 in the riverside village of Kingston, New Brunswick, in what is now Canada. He was the fourth son of James Law, an Ulster Scot and local minister of the Free Church of Scotland, and Eliza Kidston, of an established local family with strong ties to the West of Scotland. Bonar Law did not spend long in New Brunswick. His mother died when he was two, and his aunt Janet Kidston came over from Dumbartonshire to keep house and look after the children. When James Law remarried a few years later, Aunt Janet returned to Scotland and took young Bonar with her.

The move transformed Bonar Law's prospects. The Kidstons owned a thriving bank in Glasgow and lived a comfortable life in genteel Helensburgh. They sent Bonar to the High School of Glasgow, trained him in the family business and set him up in the iron trade. By his early forties he was a successful businessman, the happily married head of a growing family, and a good speaker: a selection committee's dream. The Unionists of the Blackfriars and Hutchesontown division of Glasgow duly adopted Bonar Law as their candidate and in the 'khaki election' of 1900 he defeated the incumbent Liberal.

In just over a decade he would be leader of his party. He became so by being on the right side (as his party saw it) of the two biggest political issues of pre-First World War politics: 'tariff reform' and Irish Home Rule.

The brainchild of Joseph Chamberlain, 'tariff reform' was a plan to bind the British Empire together by giving a customs preference to imperial imports. That meant tariffs on goods coming from outside the Empire – anathema to the free-trade element of the party. Bonar Law was a keen supporter of Chamberlain and tariff reform. His colonial origins made him sympathetic to imperial unity, and his time in the Glasgow iron trade exposed the downsides of unilateral free trade in an increasingly Protectionist world. An effective Commons debater, Bonar Law's views carried weight. According to one contemporary, 'he seemed to speak with the full practical knowledge of a man of business but with the detached theoretical method of a Scottish metaphysician'.

Within two years he was the junior minister at the Board of Trade. His rise coincided with sliding Conservative fortunes. Balfour, the donnish prime minister, was trying and failing to unite his divided party around a policy of studied vagueness on tariff reform. In the election of 1906, the government went down by a landslide. Bonar Law was swept away in Glasgow Blackfriars, but he was not out for long, winning safe Dulwich in a by-election a few months later.

The tariff reform debate raged on as the party suffered two further election defeats in 1910. In the second of those, Bonar Law was persuaded to sacrifice his safe berth at Dulwich to contest the marginal Manchester North West (in free-trade Lancashire) on a tariff reform platform. It is a mark of his enthusiasm for the policy and his loyalty to his party that he agreed. He won plaudits for a spirited campaign, but was narrowly defeated. Treated as a hero nonetheless, he was again brought quickly back, his star on the rise.

Balfour finally threw in the towel and resigned the leadership in 1911, setting up a contest between two frontrunners: the former Chancellor (and son of Joseph) Austen Chamberlain, a tariff reformer representing the urban, commercial section of the party; and the former Chief Secretary for Ireland Walter Long, a Wiltshire land-owner, representing the Old English squirearchy and a leading voice for Unionism.

Bonar Law, the outside bet, benefited from the party's divisions and the personalities of his rivals. Chamberlain's filial devotion to tariff reform made him unattractive to free traders. Long was regarded by many as temperamentally unsuited to leadership. Both withdrew to avoid a bitter contest and Bonar Law – enough of a tariff reformer for the Chamberlainites to live with, and as impeccable a Unionist as any Long-supporter could wish for – was elected unopposed.

The most pressing political question he faced was Ireland. Bonar Law gets a bad press from historians for his approach to the crisis prompted by Asquith's decision to bring forward a third Irish Home Rule Bill. The Conservative Party at this time was more commonly known as the Unionist Party, reflecting its implacable opposition to Home Rule. Bonar Law learned his Unionism at his father's knee. The Rev. James Law retired to Ulster in 1877 and for the remaining five years of his life Bonar visited him most weekends. For him it was personal. He felt horror at the prospect of his beloved Ulster being forced out of the United Kingdom against its will.

In his trenchant opposition to the Home Rule Bill, Bonar Law has been accused of coming close to advocating insurrection. He certainly regarded civil war as inevitable if any attempt were made to coerce Ulster into accepting 'Dublin rule' through 'a corrupt Parliamentary bargain' between a minority Liberal government and their Irish nationalist allies. In civil war, he remarked, 'soldiers are citizens like the rest of us'. That as sober and pragmatic a man as Bonar Law was willing to go so far reflects not just his passion for Ulster, but also his approach to political leadership.

He had watched Balfour be outflanked on both sides in a doomed effort to broker compromise on tariff reform. Bonar Law was determined that no one should be more royal than the King – his would be the loudest and clearest voice speaking for the Union. That would both minimise the threat of a challenge to his leadership from Unionist die-hards like Long and Edward Carson, and allow him to exert a moderating influence, keeping a lid on the party's passions.

In fact, Bonar Law's position was nuanced. Home Rule was a transformation of the nation state for which he believed the Asquith government had no mandate. Unlike the die-hards, however, Bonar Law conceived circumstances in which Home Rule would be inevitable. If the British people expressed a clear desire for it, through either a referendum or a General Election fought on the issue, Bonar Law said his message to Irish Unionists would be, 'you have got to submit'. In the end, he felt that partition was the only viable solution, and one of the few Acts of Parliament passed during his short premiership was ratification in 1922 of the Anglo-Irish Treaty, which did just that.

The Home Rule crisis was suspended only by the outbreak of war in 1914. The Conservatives initially tried to be a 'patriotic opposition' – suspending normal political hostilities. This soon proved unsatisfactory. Asquith continued to bring forward controversial legislation. Many Tory MPs, too old to enlist, yearned to serve their country; sitting unemployed on the opposition benches did not feel like much of a contribution to the war effort. Finally, the political fallout from the Asquith government's blunders – from a shortage of shells to the debacle in the Dardanelles – rendered coalition inevitable if a divisive election was to be avoided. Taking his party into coalition in June 1915 was the first of several decisive interventions by Bonar Law in the political conduct of the Great War. The next came eighteen months later.

Perhaps because of his own melancholic temperament, Bonar Law enjoyed friendships with more ebullient characters: one such was Lloyd George. When the Welsh Wizard became Chancellor in 1908, Bonar Law wrote to congratulate him: 'it always gives me pleasure to see success attained by merit done and without any outside aids'. Bonar Law's relations with the Prime Minister were chillier. Asquith treated him with barely disguised contempt. As ambitious as anyone else who makes it to the top of the greasy pole, Bonar Law was unusually modest and generous in his opinions of others. Despite the provocations, he regarded Asquith as the indispensable leader the country needed and, despite heading the largest party in the government, was willing to accept the relatively minor office of Colonial Secretary if that was what it took to make coalition work.

In December 1916, Bonar Law decided that Asquith had ceased to be indispensable. The forces ranged against the Prime Minister – intense Unionist hostility and the machinations of Lloyd George – were only held in check by Bonar Law. Asquith's underestimation of his opposite number was his undoing. Lloyd George was now the indispensable man.

Attlee's wartime role supporting Churchill is well known, but Bonar Law's even more substantial contribution as de facto deputy to Lloyd George is now largely forgotten. Unlike Attlee, Bonar Law led by far the largest party in the 'second coalition' (the Liberal Party being now split). He served simultaneously as Chancellor of the Exchequer, responsible for financing the war effort, and Leader of the Commons, managing Parliament virtually single-handedly. It was a crippling workload. Part of its appeal was as a distraction from loss. After the untimely death of his much-loved wife Annie in 1909, work provided a refuge from intense grief. It did so again when, like many fathers of all social classes, he lost dear sons on active service. Charlie, an infantry officer, was killed at the Battle of Gaza in April 1917. His eldest, James, a Royal Flying Corps fighter pilot, was shot down in September. Bonar Law went to France to meet James's fellow officers. After sitting alone for two hours in the cockpit of a plane that had made it back from the battle, he returned to London and resumed his punishing duties.

After the Armistice, Bonar Law felt Lloyd George's talents were as indispensable to the challenges of peace as they had been to those of war. Bonar Law gave up the Treasury in 1919, but (much to the chagrin of incoming Chancellor Austen Chamberlain) continued to reside in Number 11. Each morning Lloyd George would wander through the connecting door to talk shop with his friend and partner. They decided to fight the General Election of 1918 as a coalition, issuing the famous 'coupon' to approved candidates. Bonar Law returned to Glasgow and won the Central division with 79 per cent of the vote. The Conservatives won 379 seats (up 108). Lloyd George's Coalition Liberals came second with 127. Asquith lost his seat.

Years of gruelling work had taken their toll on Bonar Law's health and in 1921, on medical advice, he retired from government and leadership. The dramatic announcement by Lloyd George of this news on the floor of the Commons provoked shocked dismay from friend and foe alike.

His successor, Austen Chamberlain, proved a less skilful leader.

Unlike Bonar Law in 1916, he could not read the writing on the wall. Conservatives had grown weary of Lloyd George and the coalition's days were numbered. A meeting at the Carlton Club in 1922 delivered the *coup de grâce*. Once again, the decisive intervention was from Bonar Law. His decision to attend and speak against the coalition was taken as a sign of his willingness to lead again. Lloyd George resigned the premiership, and Austen Chamberlain the leadership of the party. At sixty-four Bonar Law was at last prime minister.

It came too late. Although he did not know it, he was already suffering from the throat cancer that would kill him a year later. Aware that his health remained delicate, he toyed with announcing that he would only serve a year in office, but wisely thought better of making himself a lame duck from the start. In forming his Cabinet, he faced the challenge that many of his party's most experienced figures (Balfour, A. Chamberlain, F.E. Smith) were disgruntled coalitionists, unpopular with the bulk of the party and unwilling to serve under him. Bonar Law was keen to rehabilitate them, but knew it would take time. His Cabinet, the smallest of the twentieth century, drew heavily from the Lords, placing a greater burden on Bonar Law to provide leadership in the Commons. A beneficiary of the decision of senior figures to stand aside was the new Chancellor, the Bonar Law protégé Stanley Baldwin.

Parliament was immediately dissolved and Bonar Law led the Conservatives to their first solo-election victory for twenty-two years. His message to an electorate greatly expanded by the 1918 Representation of the People Act to include working-class men and middle-class women played to his strengths. He wrote in the manifesto: 'The crying need of the nation at this moment – a need which in my judgement far exceeds any other – is that we should have tranquillity and stability both at home and abroad so that free scope should be given to the initiative and enterprise of our citizens.'

The implicit contrast was with Lloyd George's manic hyperactivity. Bonar Law offered a more conservative statecraft. His personal maxim was 'do not touch anything unless you are quite certain that you are going to improve it'. His 'idea of the work of a Prime Minister', he told a party audience, was 'that of a man at the head of a big business who allows the work to be done by others and gives his general supervision'. That supervision was also close and commanding. He was the dominant figure in his government, chairing brisk, business-like cabinets.

The most urgent issue facing that government was the refinancing of Britain's enormous war debt to the United States. The UK had drawn heavily on American loans to finance the war effort, with much of this borrowing channelled into French and Italian coffers. Neither country could repay its debts to Britain until Germany began paying reparations. In the meantime, Britain wanted America to forbear calling in the loans. Baldwin was sent to Washington to negotiate a deal. The Americans, back in isolationist mode, drove a hard bargain. Regarding their terms as the best he could get, Baldwin landed back at Southampton and promptly blurted out as much to gathered journalists. The problem was, Bonar Law disagreed. At a tense Cabinet meeting, just two of his colleagues sided with the Prime Minister. Bonar Law dropped the bombshell that he would rather resign than accept usurious terms. Cabinet adjourned for the night and by the next day he had thought better of it, accepting the deal as a *fait accompli*.

It was a demoralising episode. Added to his political worries was a lingering pain in his throat that for months had weakened his usually fluent speaking voice. Hoping that warmer air would aid recovery, Bonar Law took a cruise to the Mediterranean. His condition worsened and he was diagnosed with inoperable throat cancer, a probable legacy of his only vice: prolific cigar-smoking. By now gravely ill, he immediately resigned and declined to recommend a successor to the King. Against expectations, George V selected the former iron merchant Baldwin over the more experienced aristocrat Lord Curzon.

That decision was in a sense a tribute to Bonar Law – the first modern Conservative leader. His leadership marked the end of aristocratic dominance in the Conservative Party. From 1911 to 1940 the party was led not by the sons and grandsons of titled men, but by middle-class businessmen. Churchill disrupted this line, and Douglas-Home was a throwback, but the leadership template established by Bonar Law remains intact to this day.

Four years after Bonar Law's death, Baldwin paid a visit to New Brunswick. The Prime Minister told a local audience that 'the judgement of posterity' would be that their native son 'played a part unselfish, of the highest importance, which in the circumstances no one but he could have played' and that 'his figure will emerge amongst the statesmen of that period as one of the greatest of that time'.

Unfairly, it is a prediction that has yet to come to pass.

Keelan Carr is a former speechwriter to Theresa May.

38

Stanley Baldwin

22 May 1923 to 22 January 1924;
4 November 1924 to 4 June 1929
Conservative

7 June 1935 to 28 May 1937
National

By John Barnes

Full name: Stanley Baldwin, later Earl Baldwin of Bewdley
Born: 3 August 1867, Lower Park House, Bewdley
Died: 14 December 1947, Astley Hall, Stourport-on-Severn.
Buried at Worcester Cathedral
Education: Harrow; Trinity College, Cambridge
Married to Lucy Ridsdale; 3 sons, 4 daughters
Quotation: 'Four words, of one syllable each, are words which
contain salvation for this country and for the whole world. They
are "faith", "hope", "love" and "work".' (16 February 1923, Speech
on the Address)

BALDWIN RANKS WITH Thatcher, Attlee and Asquith as a peace-time prime minister. However, his standing has been obscured by widespread acceptance of Churchill's charges that he failed to avert a wholly unnecessary war and concealed the need to rearm his country in order to win a further term in office for his party in 1935.

In making these accusations, Churchill gave legs to a myth deliberately created in 1940 to bring about a change of government, and to obscure the fact that the Labour Party before the summer of 1937 had opposed rearmament. Most historians would now accept that Baldwin, in Churchill's own words, 'fought, and largely won, the General Election' on the issue of rearmament and that he successfully rearmed his country.

Whether the policies he followed made sense will be explored in due course, but the part he played in determining the future shape of the British polity is too considerable to be obscured by the ongoing debate about appeasement.

The critical moment in Baldwin's career was his decision to break with Lloyd George and break the coalition. Not only did he organise the rebellion that came to a head at the Carlton Club meeting of Conservative MPs in the autumn of 1922, but he persuaded Bonar Law to attend the meeting, and made a devastating speech on the destructive force Lloyd George represented. Within days, Bonar Law was prime minister and Baldwin Chancellor of the Exchequer. Significantly, he had not expected to win. He put his political future on the line again when he reached a settlement of Britain's wartime debt to the USA: Law was against it, but all but two of his Cabinet backed Baldwin. When Bonar Law retired in May 1923, the King insisted that his successor could not be a peer since Labour was now the major opposition party, but it is probable that Baldwin would in any case have been the Cabinet's choice. He had already displayed his mastery of parliamentary debate and his sensitivity to the moods of the House of Commons. Although he had limited Cabinet experience, he had many years behind him on the Boards of Baldwins Ltd, the Great Western Railway and the Metropolitan Bank; and a lengthy spell as Financial Secretary in the Treasury gave him insight into the civil service and the sinews of government.

Baldwin was to be the dominant figure in British politics for the next fourteen years. The public sensed correctly that he was in politics out of a profound sense of duty. As a Christian, he thought himself bound to serve wherever God seemed to call on him, and to that was added a deeply felt obligation to those who had lost their lives in the Great War. He was quietly convinced that he was God's instrument to help heal a divided nation.

He has been considerably underestimated as a prime minister, largely because he approached the task as team leader rather than chief. He believed that a key part of the job was over within a day or so of taking office: the choice of those who were to run the departments of state, the mix of the Cabinet cocktail. If his role thereafter was to manage men rather than measures, that does not diminish his importance to the outcome. His reputation has also suffered from his preference to transact business in conversation rather than on paper.

Baldwin kept no diary. His relations with ministers 'were always personal and informal', a close colleague recalled. 'To him "come and have a word" meant speedier and easier despatch of business.' Deft in handling his Cabinet, knowing whom to call and when, he was 'always quietly but definitely in control'. Some thought him too indulgent a chairman, especially when the rows between Churchill and Amery about how far the government should pursue protection were at their height in 1928–9, but few doubted that Baldwin would have the final word. His unobtrusive skill generated an atmosphere that was conducive to constructive debate. Within months of bringing them together in 1924, as Birkenhead noted, he was able to turn a Cabinet made up of men who, only two years earlier, had been fiercely at odds over terminating the Lloyd George coalition, into 'a band of brothers'.

After his retirement, Neville Chamberlain's more overt dominance 'seemed to crystallise all the fluid forces in the Cabinet' and a senior minister noted what had been lost as opinion polarised. Although at first somewhat diffident about throwing his weight around, Baldwin proved increasingly adept at doing so as year succeeded year in his 1924–9 administration. That he could, when he chose, deploy silencing authority was already clear as early as March 1925 when, in the absence abroad of its author, he exerted himself to save a proposed quadrilateral pact, which became the Locarno

Treaties, from the combined opposition of Churchill (Treasury), Amery (Dominions), Birkenhead (India), Salisbury (Lords), Bridgeman (Admiralty) and Hoare (Air). He also 'astonished' Austen Chamberlain 'by the power that he showed in a Cabinet discussion . . . on the political levy'. Resolved not to fire the first shot where the trade unions were concerned, he not only secured Cabinet backing to resist a back-bench member's attempt to make the levy voluntary, but secured a parliamentary triumph when he did so.

In his 1924–9 administration, he had the benefit of supremely creative policy makers in Churchill (Treasury) and Neville Chamberlain (Health). An interesting dynamic developed. While rarely at odds over the long-term goal, the two were in frequent dispute about pace and detail. It fell to Baldwin to mediate, to ensure that detailed criticisms were properly addressed, and then to throw his weight into the scale to determine which of the two should carry the day. Where they continued at odds, as over the extent to which industry and agriculture should be relieved of rates, or on the decision to derate the railways (1928), Baldwin's voice was decisive. Although he did not always side with his Chancellor, he was in daily conversation and close to Churchill in these years. Churchill's private secretary was adamant that Baldwin had the measure of his master. While he deferred to Churchill's determination that safeguarding should not be extended to basic industries like steel, that was not, as some thought, because he was under the Chancellor's thumb, but a matter of political calculation. Baldwin was determined as far as possible to bring the Liberal vote into the Conservative camp, and the prominence of Churchill in his counsels burnished the government's national credentials.

Acutely sensitive to the moral challenge posed by socialism, Baldwin knew that there had to be a positive response on the part of his own party. Sound finance had to be accompanied by policies of social welfare and the creation of a property-owning democracy. Towards the end of his first administration, he commissioned from officials a report on a plan for comprehensive social insurance, and in opposition asked Neville Chamberlain to develop a scheme. When the Conservatives returned to power in November 1924, Churchill agreed to make it the centrepiece of his first Budget. Paradoxically, that meant that the Widows, Orphans and Old Age

Pensions Act (1925), although of immense importance in shaping the architecture of the Welfare State, was less comprehensive and less generous than its progenitors had wished. Nevertheless, it was a major step towards what has been characterised as 'the welfare state in scaffolding' in place before the Second World War; and in 1937 the scheme was extended to 'black-coated workers'.

Baldwin wanted his party to 'win by the hardness of their heads and the largeness of their hearts', and a substantial body of legislation was testament to both. His first administration saw Chamberlain's Housing Act onto the statute book, and in the years that followed, local government and its finance were remodelled, unemployment insurance put on a sound footing, provision made for the unemployed outside its scope by the creation of the National Assistance Board, and the local authorities given the task of extending the supply of hospital services to complement those offered by the voluntary sector. Major legislation to update public health provision and children's services was enacted, and midwifery and maternity services were strengthened. As a result, absolute poverty was more than halved and inequality considerably reduced.

Although his interest in developing prefabricated housing brought few results, the fall in building costs, coupled with low interest rates in the 1930s, led to a remarkable housing boom, taking the total number of units from 8 million in 1921 to 11.3 million in 1939. The government was able to reduce the level of subsidy in the late 1920s and switch subsidies to slum clearance in 1933. Legislation to deal with overcrowding followed in 1935, and areas of redevelopment were designated under the 1936 Act. By 1939, social housing had risen tenfold to constitute 10 per cent of housing stock, but owner occupation had also expanded from about a quarter of the whole in 1921 to just under a third by 1938. If Labour looked to build the Conservatives out of London, Baldwin's political dream was being realised in the expanding suburbs around Britain's major cities.

Less recognisable as an achievement, but of great prospective importance, was Baldwin's acceptance of the need to expand both the size and scope of the state's activities at a time when large segments of society, a major part of his own party, and even large parts of the trade union movement were sceptical about the desirability of such a move. Grappling with the problem of unemployment, the Baldwin government and its national successors were increasingly involved in managing the economy. Industrial protection, imperial preference and Empire settlement were Baldwin's favoured goals. However, when he failed to secure a mandate for protection in December 1923, he knew that it would take time, in fact nine years, before the electorate could be brought to recognise the benefits of the 'imperial vision'.

Forced into a pledge against a General Tariff, Baldwin's second administration nevertheless reinstated the duties that protected the fast-growing motor industry and introduced further safeguarding measures, but only to the extent thought compatible with his promise. It was inevitable therefore that Baldwin and his free-trade Chancellor, with widespread approval, should return Britain to the Gold Standard in 1925, looking for a revival in world trade, and to the benefit of the City. But it was evident that Britain's staple industries would never regain their former markets, and their inability to do so left around a million men out of work.

Initially, the government sought to transfer unemployed workers from the 'necessitous areas' to places where there was employment, whether through inducements to local authorities to employ out-of-work miners on road building or the more structured activities of the Industrial Transference Board (1928). In addition, the government relieved industry and agriculture of much of the burden of local taxation. Privately, Baldwin nudged a close friend, Montagu Norman, to engage the Bank of England in the task of rationalising British industry. While ready to pass permissive legislation to reorganise the mining industry and increase working hours in the hope that it would resolve the ongoing mining dispute in 1926, Baldwin was reluctant to commit the state to use compulsion. Quite apart from any ideological objection, he simply did not believe that the civil service was competent to undertake the work. The Bank of England was better placed. Norman was persuaded and established the Bankers' Industrial Development Company in 1929.

Tackling unemployment was politically essential if the serious industrial unrest, which had developed even before the war's end, was not to threaten the stability of the country and its governing system. 'The bitterness in the country was of the devil,' Baldwin recalled, and he was determined to be a healer. Hence his decision, after little more than five months in office, to seek an electoral mandate for industrial protection. Defeated, but always adroit in letting events work for him, he remained in office, resisted pressures to coalesce, and put his programme to Parliament. This course of action safeguarded his own position, forced the Liberal Party to take the responsibility for installing the Labour Party in power, and allowed the latter a chance to govern. It was a decision that conferred strength on all those within the Labour movement who believed in a parliamentary route to socialism. The decision served both national and party interest and was one of Baldwin's most significant decisions. Within nine months he was back in power.

There was no immediate cessation of industrial unrest. Knowing that the miners would receive widespread union backing if they went on strike, Baldwin conceded a temporary subsidy and a public enquiry into the problems of the mining industry in the summer of 1925. When the miners refused to accept the results of the enquiry, and the TUC called a General Strike in their support in May 1926, he was determined that it should not succeed.

Within days it was clear that the government was able to maintain essential services and would not be coerced. Baldwin's contention that the strike threatened parliamentary government was persuasive, not least with the TUC. His success dealt a mortal blow to the use of industrial action for political purposes, and when, after nine days, the General Strike was called off, Baldwin's public standing was at an all-time high. But his subsequent efforts to settle the mining dispute failed. It dragged on until November before collapsing, leaving bitter memories. The trade unions had learned their lesson, however. Baldwin used his private contacts to generate direct talks between the two sides of industry in 1927. Although the Mond/Turner talks achieved less than he had hoped, they helped create an atmosphere in which a more constructive approach to industrial relations took root. Less happily, Baldwin felt compelled to legislate not only to limit sympathetic strikes, but to make the political levy depend on 'opting in'. It was a move that left lasting bitterness, but played surprisingly little part in his election defeat in 1929.

Baldwin had a gift for explaining issues and how he proposed to resolve them in terms that could easily be grasped by his audience. He commanded audiences that on occasion ran to tens of thousands, and his speeches were reproduced at length in the national and local press. Unlike his predecessors, film and radio provided new opportunities to be heard and seen. Baldwin was skilful in adapting his message for delivery in much-shortened form straight to camera on the increasingly ubiquitous cinema newsreels, and spread further by his party's own cinema vans. He had already mastered radio, recognising immediately, as his political rivals did not, that his audience was best treated as friends sitting around their own fireside.

Nor was the content confined to politics. Baldwin was a master of the non-political address, which made use of a notable spread of cultural references. Brought together and published, they sold well and did much to buttress the resonance of his national message. However, his ability to communicate with greater audiences than those enjoyed by any previous generation of politicians would have been as nothing but for the note they unerringly struck.

The way in which he had successfully mobilised opinion against the General Strike by representing it as a threat to constitutional government and against the public interest is a striking example of how, throughout his career, he seemed to have an uncanny sense of the way public opinion was moving. An instinctive appreciation of the aspirations, appetites and interests of various social groupings enabled him to persuade enough of them that their interests were sufficiently aligned to allow him to build a successful electoral coalition. His party was depicted as a national party looking to pursue the interests of all classes and the public good, as opposed to the purely sectional interests pursued by organised labour. It proved a remarkably persuasive message.

In the five elections fought with Baldwin as leader, the party always won most of the votes cast, and only once won fewer seats than its principal opponent. Three of its victories, in 1924, 1931 and 1935, were not only large-scale, but also in each case signified that Baldwin had captured half or more of the working-class vote. Since the working class made up more than four-fifths of the electorate that was the only route to victory.

The 1935 election confirmed the party's hegemonic position, which was disrupted only by the Second World War. Not only had the Labour Party been prevented from polarising the electorate along class lines, but, even after the lurch to the left during the Second World War, Baldwin's successors could count on the continued support of at least a third of the working class. Baldwin gave his blessing also to the party's successful wooing of the women's vote, and in 1928, despite the doubts of senior colleagues, the franchise was extended to all women over the age of twenty-one.

This decision was wrongly thought to have cost Baldwin the 1929 election. In fact, it was the perception that his government had failed to solve the problem of unemployment or deliver international disarmament that put Labour in power.

It was a good election to lose, and the conduct of the trade unions throughout the economic crisis that followed did much to justify Baldwin's assertion that they would always pursue their own selfish interests.

When the Labour Cabinet split over a proposal to cut unemployment benefit in the summer of 1931, Baldwin was persuaded to come to the aid of an embattled prime minister. A temporary arrangement, made to secure a balanced budget, evolved into a durable national coalition, not least because the Labour Party's vocal opposition made the pound's departure from the Gold Standard inevitable. The subsequent General Election endorsed a National Government, but with a massive Conservative component.

Baldwin had been troubled in opposition by party splits over Empire free trade and the future government of India. The influx of younger MPs consolidated his hold on the party. In the teeth of Churchill's efforts to mobilise the party against the bill, he was able to deliver an extensive measure of self-government to India in the Government of India Act (1935). He saw it as the only way to keep India within what was fast becoming a Commonwealth rather than the Empire. Shrewdly, Baldwin emphasised the national face of the government by keeping a Labour prime minister in No. 10 and exercised his influence behind the scenes: the economic and domestic policies pursued were those of the Conservative majority. A significant number of Liberals accepted these measures, with the remainder going into opposition. The National Government was a political vehicle that commanded the support of a substantial majority of the electorate, and became the embodiment of Baldwinian Conservatism.

Baldwin's Achilles' heel is thought to be a lack of interest in foreign affairs. However, his reluctance to become involved in personal diplomacy, or to engage with the detail, should not be taken for lack of knowledge of or care for British interests. He kept in close touch with senior officials like Tyrrell and Vansittart, but for the most part saw little reason to do other than give his Foreign Secretaries solid support. His recognition that the development of air power meant that Britain could not disassociate herself from developments in Europe was evident as early as 1923, and led to his support for the Locarno Treaties. His view that Britain's frontiers were effectively on the Rhine was based as much on military considerations as on the need to reassure France. But he was conscious that the interests of the Empire lay principally in Asia; the naval strength that underpinned its defence was limited by the treaties signed at Washington (1921) and London (1930). Because of the importance of protecting imperial trade routes, Baldwin opposed the London Treaty. Concern about Japan's ambitions led him in 1925 to urge upon the Foreign Office a tripartite agreement with Japan and the United States, but he failed to convince his Foreign Secretary.

Failing that, he ensured that work on the Singapore naval base should go ahead. He knew that Japan, although limited to a smaller battle fleet than Britain and the United States, was effectively mistress in her own waters. Defence of the Indian Ocean would rest on Britain's ability to transfer her own fleet to Singapore, and a major reason for Baldwin's reluctance to risk war with Italy during the Abyssinian crisis in 1935–6 was the private estimate conveyed by the First Sea Lord that it would cost Britain four capital ships.

Japan's incursion into Manchuria in the autumn of 1931, and still more the clash at Shanghai in February 1932, had brought home Britain's vulnerability in the Far East, and Baldwin did not subscribe to Neville Chamberlain's optimism that Japan could be appeased. Rather, he shared the view of the secretariat of the Committee of Imperial Defence and the Admiralty that, if Britain became embroiled in a European war, Japan would take the opportunity to realise her ambitions in the Far East.

Of necessity, therefore, Baldwin's attention was concentrated on securing a durable European settlement. A major difficulty was

German resentment that the victorious powers had not delivered on their pledge to disarm to her level. The French would do so only if Britain would guarantee their security, but no British government would agree anything that might compromise their ability to decide whether or not to go to war. For a good many Conservatives, even Locarno was a step too far. By the time the powers assembled at Geneva to tackle the problem of disarmament in February 1932, Japan had taken over Manchuria and the growing Nazi movement had made equality in armaments Germany's goal. Conscious that Britain had disarmed to the point where she could offer only to adopt 'defensive' weapons rather than lower levels of armament, the National Government seemed reluctant to give a lead and was soon under fire for not doing so from what may have been a majority of the electorate.

In his final five years in government, Baldwin's interest in and influence upon foreign policy cannot be doubted. He read *Mein Kampf*, but remained uncertain what in practice Hitler wanted. There seemed a strong possibility that his ambitions might be confined to reunifying the German race. Long term, his ambitions lay in eastern Europe. A number of phases can be identified in the evolution of Baldwin's own views. In the first, which came to an end with the German withdrawal from the Disarmament Conference in October 1933, Baldwin ensured that the government tabled its own proposals and was the principal advocate, both in private and in public, of a scheme for the total abolition of military aviation. Even before the German walk-out, Baldwin had indicated publicly that the best way forward would be to substitute an arms limitation agreement for general disarmament. Hitler was broadly in favour, but France, failing a separate guarantee of her security from Britain, remained distrustful. Baldwin was permitted only to tell the Commons that Britain regarded the Rhine as her effective frontier. It was not enough, and in May 1934, the French vetoed the whole idea.

Throughout the winter of 1933–4 an official committee had worked on detailed plans to repair the gaps in Britain's defences, identifying Japan as the immediate threat and Germany as the long-term enemy. That the latter was rearming could no longer be overlooked. Baldwin took a major role in determining the British response. At the Treasury, Neville Chamberlain insisted that the comprehensive plan could not be afforded, but that Germany could be deterred by an expansion in the first-line strength of the RAF. Baldwin found no backing for his idea that the full plan should be financed by borrowing, and brokered a compromise, a major expansion of the RAF to deter Hitler, which he announced in July 1934, with some spending on the Fleet Air Arm and the Far East. With better intelligence to hand, the government accelerated the programme in November 1934, and when Hitler made a spurious claim to have already achieved parity the following spring, the government responded by agreeing an increased programme in May.

It was clear that a more comprehensive rearmament plan was needed, and the fourth phase began with the case made in the first ever Defence White Paper in March 1935. Mussolini threatened to invade Abyssinia that summer, providing the government with a major problem and an opportunity. Baldwin took the prime ministership in June and decided that support for League of Nations action against Italy would allow the efficacy of economic sanctions to be tested and strengthen the case for Britain to rearm. He went to the country in October, arguing that it was now necessary to repair all the gaps in Britain's defences. The Labour Party promptly charged him with starting an arms race. Confidence in Baldwin remained high and the National Government was returned with an overall majority of 247.

Although the United States had cooperated in sanctions, the French had proved reluctant partners. Vansittart, Permanent Secretary to the Foreign Office, was equally convinced of the need to keep Italy as an ally against Hitler. In the course of an informal visit to Paris in December, the Foreign Secretary was persuaded to agree that an offer to partition Abyssinia should be made to Mussolini. The plan had not been divulged to Baldwin and his Cabinet, but, not knowing why Hoare had agreed to it, they gave it their reluctant backing. They were promptly forced to reverse their decision in the face of a major parliamentary storm. Hoare resigned, and Baldwin was fortunate to ride out the crisis. More to the point, American cooperation with the League was damaged, the use of oil as a sanction further delayed, and Mussolini emerged as victor in Abyssinia and a potential ally of Hitler.

Hitler exploited the situation. In March he moved troops into the Rhineland, which the Locarno Treaties had agreed should remain demilitarised. A number of historians, making lavish use of hindsight, have agreed with Churchill that this was the right moment to stand up to Hitler. While his troops could have been dislodged, they planned to conduct a fighting retreat. Hitler would not have fallen, nor would German rearmament have been brought to an end. But the major point to note is that no one in Britain, not even Churchill himself, advocated a military response.

Baldwin and his new Foreign Secretary were disposed to see if an agreement was possible. If Hitler could be drawn into a fresh set of agreements, he might value the rapprochement with Britain sufficiently to honour them. If, on the other hand, he broke them, it would bring home to the British people the dangers they faced. Baldwin had been advised that Britain would not be ready to fight before January 1939, and he was conscious also of the danger that, with the Soviet Union as an ally, any conflict might leave Stalin in control of large parts of Germany. He nursed a hope that if there was any further fighting to be done in Europe, it would take place between Germany and the Soviet Union rather than in western Europe. In the meantime, there was a major rearmament programme to be delivered, partly financed by borrowing, and a shadow armaments industry to be created against the increased possibility of war.

It is some measure of how far the government was from that moment of decision that, for much of the remaining year of his premiership, Baldwin was locked in battle with his Chancellor about the need to equip an expeditionary force capable of engaging in a European ground war.

He was, in any case, a tired man, forced to take a prolonged holiday from business to avoid a breakdown. He came back to deal with the King's determination to wed his mistress. Once again Baldwin displayed an uncanny instinct for the reaction of Parliament and people. He prevented colleagues from taking premature action, and did his best to persuade the King to change his mind. Only when it was clear that he would not do so did Baldwin move with unerring skill to bring about his abdication. In doing so he showed himself a better judge of opinion than Churchill, who put loyalty to the King ahead of his campaign for 'arms and the covenant', and paid a price for doing so.

Baldwin's triumph lent the closing months of his premiership a golden glow. It was not unmerited. Baldwin could claim that Britain was still a bastion of liberty and democracy. He had maintained the unity of the nation and brought rearmament to a point at which Britain was likely to survive any war. Whether she could do so and retain her Empire was not a question to which he had found an answer, however, and he left his successor a foreign policy conundrum that he had been unable to resolve.

John Barnes is a former lecturer in Government at the London School of Economics and Research Fellow of Gonville and Caius College, Cambridge.

39

Ramsay MacDonald

22 January 1924 to 4 November 1924
Labour

5 June 1929 to 7 June 1935
National Labour

By Robert Waller

Full name: James Ramsay MacDonald
Born: 12 October 1866, Lossiemouth, Morayshire
Died: 9 November 1937, on the *Reina del Pacifico* ocean liner between La Rochelle and Bermuda. Buried at Spynie church-yard, Lossiemouth
Education: Drainie parish school
Married to Margaret Gladstone; 3 sons, 3 daughters
Quotation: 'Yes, tomorrow every Duchess in London will be wanting to kiss me.' (The day after the formation of the National Government in 1931)

JAMES RAMSAY MACDONALD is one of Britain's most notable prime ministers. He was the first to come from a working-class background. In 1924 he became the first ever Labour Party incumbent of 10 Downing Street, and he returned for a second term in 1929. Two years later, he led a 'national government' to the largest recorded landslide victory, and remained in office until 1935.

MacDonald played a very significant role in the transformation from clashes between Liberals and Conservatives for power in the land to the Labour versus Conservative duopoly that was maintained throughout the rest of the twentieth century. He was also a prominent figure in international affairs during the key decades of the 1920s and 1930s. Yet he is rarely celebrated, especially by the Labour Party, which has never forgiven him for what was perceived as the massive betrayal of 1931 when he formed what was in effect a Tory-dominated coalition, with a policy that included cuts in unemployment benefit during the depths of the Great Depression.

He was born in October 1866 in the small fishing port of Lossiemouth, in the county of Moray in north-eastern Scotland. His parents were never married. Ramsay MacDonald's illegitimate status was widely known. It was brought to national prominence and controversy in September 1915, when at the height of the opprobrium brought by his opposition to the First World War, the scandal-mongering populist journalist Horatio Bottomley revealed Ramsay's birth certificate in the pages of his magazine *John Bull*. Even MacDonald himself had not known to this point that his name was entered there as James MacDonald Ramsay.

For all the later condemnation by the Labour movement, Ramsay MacDonald played a major part in its political development. In the 1880s he was a member of the Socialist Union, and in the early 1890s of the Labour Electoral Association, a TUC body that effectively was the forerunner of the Labour Representation Committee of 1900, which became the Labour Party itself in 1906. However, MacDonald's real commitment for many years was to the ILP (Independent Labour Party), after it was formed by Keir Hardie in 1893. This remained significant, as the ILP might be identified as a significant home of the 'intellectual socialist' strand in Labour politics that has often clashed with the 'labourist' influence of the organised trade union movement, with which MacDonald was rarely entirely happy.

It was as an ILP candidate that he first stood for Parliament, for Southampton in 1895; and while he took a leading part as Secretary of the nascent Labour Representation Committee on its foundation in 1900, he continued to use the ILP as a power base and for his extensive writings until the late 1920s.

MacDonald entered the Commons in harness with a Liberal 'running mate' in Leicester in 1906, as part of the 'Gladstone–MacDonald Pact' that he himself had largely engineered, whereby Liberal and Labour candidates declined to run against each other, or ran together, in two-member seats.

MacDonald was a key figure in the leadership of his party right up to the outbreak of the First World War. Although there was, as yet, no formal position of overall party leader, in effect he occupied that position during his chairmanship of the Parliamentary Labour Party from 1911 to 1914. He lost the position because he consistently opposed the decision to go to war in summer 1914, and suffered much calumny, but in the chaotic politics of the early 1920s, MacDonald was best placed of all Labour leaders successfully to coordinate Labour's efforts to present itself as a potential governing party, now that the Liberals had been split by Lloyd George's coup against Asquith at the end of 1916, followed by his decision to render the split more lasting by continuing his wartime coalition after 1918. This was because MacDonald could act as a link between the socialist wing, as typified by the ILP, and the trade union paymasters who now had so much influence in the party's constitution. In the November 1922 General Election, caused by the Conservative decision to call an end to the Lloyd George coalition, MacDonald returned to the Commons. He was now fifty-six years old, and his career was about to be dramatically revitalised.

He was immediately restored to the leadership of the Labour Party that he had lost on the outbreak of war eight years earlier. When in December 1923 Baldwin called a 'surprise' election after his decision to introduce tariff reform, the Conservatives won 259 seats in the Commons, Labour 191, and the Liberals 159. It was clear that while neither Labour nor the Liberals had won the election, the Conservatives had certainly lost.

On 18 December the Liberal leader Asquith made it clear in a speech to his parliamentary party that the Liberals would not keep the Conservatives in office in the hung Parliament or keep Labour out. As Asquith put it, if a Labour government were ever to be tried, 'it could not be tried under safer conditions'. On 22 January 1924 Baldwin left office, and at midday Ramsay MacDonald went to Buckingham Palace to be sworn in as the first Labour Party prime minister.

The circumstances of MacDonald's first minority administration were well understood at the time and have been taken into account in the relatively kind judgements of historians. Even though it did not last out the year 1924, this government has not been the cause of most of the controversy and criticism that has characterised assessments of Ramsay MacDonald as a prime minister. He, and everyone else, knew that being in so severe a minority meant that no sweeping, radical changes could be enacted. Therefore, his main aim was to demonstrate that Labour could govern respectably and responsibly. Essentially, this goal was achieved, despite the fact that two scandals, the 'Campbell case' and the fake 'Zinoviev letter', were involved in the end of the administration – which, was, in any case, very likely to occur in short order whatever the reason.

MacDonald directed much of his attention to foreign affairs. It is highly significant that when forming his first Cabinet, he decided to combine the role of prime minister with that of Foreign Secretary. Not only did MacDonald as a member of the Executive have fewer restrictions on his ability to control domestic policy, but there was a golden opportunity to excel.

Since 1918, the problem of what to do with a defeated Germany had dominated diplomacy. MacDonald as prime minister (and Foreign Secretary) played a major role in improving this international flashpoint in 1924. In June of that year he convened a conference between the Great War allies to address reparations, and their consequence, the occupation of the industrial area of the Ruhr in Germany by French forces since 1923. This resulted in the London Settlement, agreed also by German delegates. It was followed by an Anglo-German commercial treaty. Next, in July and August 1924, another conference in London dealt with the enforcement of the Dawes Plan, which provided for loans for Germany to ease the repayment of the reparation burden and also led to the French withdrawal from the Ruhr.

As far as the domestic achievement of the 1924 government goes, MacDonald has received a 'worse press'. Legislative achievement was very limited, and the government ended after nine months in circumstances tainted by scandal. It is often said that the main concrete achievement was the Wheatley Housing Act, which led to over half a million council houses being built for low-paid workers – what would now be called 'social housing'. But this Act appears to be rightly named after the radical Clydesider appointed to be Minister of Health: for example, it is not even specifically mentioned in Marquand's 800-page biography of MacDonald. Much the same is true of the increased benefits for pensioners and the unemployed. Not surprisingly, given the priority the Prime Minister gave to foreign affairs, he seems to have been somewhat remote from the domestic policies of the 1924 government. He did try to initiate the building of a Channel Tunnel, but was stymied by opposition led by the armed services chiefs. Much more seriously, in the autumn of 1924 MacDonald became embroiled in high controversy – and it did not redound to his credit.

The first problem was that MacDonald had been loaned £40,000 (a large sum at the time) soon after he entered office, by Alexander Grant – who was also from Lossiemouth and had made a fortune as a biscuit manufacturer. In the next honours list, Grant was awarded a baronetcy 'for public service'. The whole business was made public by the *Daily Mail* in September 1924. Coming so soon after the scandalous large-scale sale of honours by Lloyd George, prime minister until 1922, this was not exactly 'a good look'. Worse was to follow.

The Campbell Case revolved around the August 1924 decision of the Attorney General, Sir Patrick Hastings, to advise the prosecution of John Campbell, the editor of the Communist Party newspaper *Workers' Weekly*, under the 1797 Incitement to Mutiny Act, after it had published an article calling on men in the armed services to refuse to use their guns against fellow workers, either in war or in the suppression of industrial action. A week later, the government forced the charges to be withdrawn. But the real damage to MacDonald was done as autumn replaced summer. The question was whether the Cabinet had instructed the Attorney General to withdraw the prosecution (which it was not entitled to do) and

MacDonald's own role in the decision. On 20 September, the Conservative MP Sir Kingsley Wood gave notice that he would ask parliamentary questions on these issues. In reply, MacDonald claimed he had had no notice or knowledge of the prosecution. This opened him to the very serious charge of misleading the House of Commons. At the beginning of October, both the Liberals and Conservatives supported a motion of censure against the Prime Minister. MacDonald decided that this was to be treated as a matter of 'no confidence' in his government. The time had now come for the opposition parties to combine and bring the first ever Labour administration to an end.

At first sight, the 1924 election suggests that MacDonald's first period as prime minister was a failure. Labour went down from 191 seats to 151. Baldwin's Conservatives returned to government with a landslide overall majority of over 200. Yet these figures are somewhat deceptive. In terms of raw votes, Labour actually increased compared with the previous year – up from 4.3 million to 5.3 million, and also improved from 30.7 per cent of the votes cast to 33.3 per cent: their highest ever number of votes and percentage. What is more, their main anti-Conservative rivals, the Liberals, suffered great losses, going down from 158 seats to 40, and from 30 per cent of the vote to 19 per cent.

A more subtle judgement on MacDonald's first period as prime minister in 1924 than that of ultimate failure might be that he set out to establish the Labour Party as the alternative government to the Conservatives in a predominantly two-party system for the first time – and that this goal was achieved. Although the Liberal Party never died, it has never since provided the prime minister of the United Kingdom. Although it recovered to some extent at the next General Election in 1929, it was Ramsay MacDonald himself who returned as prime minister then. As for the success or otherwise of his first administration, in particular of his own role, in retrospect his success in furthering international agreement and partially rehabilitating Germany (at this point still under the liberal democracy of the Weimar Republic) was probably the positive highlight of his prime-ministerial career.

MacDonald remained firmly in charge of the Labour party after the 1924 election defeat, and there was no serious challenge to his leadership. He was still the leader and prospective prime minister five years later, and thus able to form a second government.

In the 1929 election the Liberals did increase their share of the vote by nearly 6 per cent, but they remained firmly in third place and only advanced from forty to fifty-nine seats. MacDonald's Labour had by far their best ever result thus far: over 8 million votes, and an increase by 4 per cent to a share of 37.1 per cent; and most importantly, 287 MPs to the 260 Conservatives. This time MacDonald could form his government as the largest party in the Commons, though still not a majority. The party had resolved that this time the job of prime minister would not be combined with that of Foreign Secretary, and after he had threatened not to serve at all if he wasn't given the post, Arthur Henderson was appointed. The former railway union leader J.H. Thomas was put in charge of unemployment. At this point in the early summer of 1929, the situation in terms of the latter did not yet look too grave: the jobless total was lower than it had been a year earlier, and exports were rising. However, things were to change.

MacDonald's reluctant decision to step back from foreign affairs did not last. Right from the King's Speech of July 1929, he gave the international situation pride of place. His priority was naval disarmament, a vital issue when Britain was still the world's leading seafaring power. In particular, MacDonald was concerned about the USA's wish for naval parity. This issue took up much of his time during the first year of his second administration, and after he became the first sitting prime minister ever to visit the States, in October 1929, it resulted in a treaty in April 1930. This limited the naval power of Britain, the USA and Japan, though France and Italy were less keen on being included. It may be judged a limited success. Yet MacDonald's second government was not going to be judged on foreign policy.

After the Wall Street Crash of October 1929, a downward spiral of falling trade, output and jobs rapidly led to a worldwide crisis. American lending no longer propped up the recovery in Germany. The loss of export markets exacerbated structural problems in the British economy, especially in its older staple industries. Unemployment in the UK reached 1.5 million in January 1930, 1.9 million in June, and over 2.7 million in December 1930. MacDonald could no longer stand back and leave the government response to Thomas. In January 1930 he established the Economic Advisory Council. Though clearly ineffective in dealing with the effects of the slump, the Council was a significant innovation in government as an advisory body to the prime minister independent of the Treasury. All the same, the central judgements on MacDonald as prime minister have tended to rest on his response to the Depression in the early 1930s.

Most commentators have regarded 1931 as the year on which assessments of Ramsay MacDonald's record as prime minister and indeed his entire career may be based. This is an overly narrow view.

In February, the Chancellor of the Exchequer Philip Snowden accepted a Liberal proposal for a committee to be set up to consider the state of the economy, rather ominously recalling the Geddes Committee on National Expenditure of 1921–2, which led to the famous Axe to be taken to government spending. It was to be chaired by Sir George May, the former Secretary of the Prudential Insurance company. The May Committee report was published on 21 July 1931. Historian A.J.P. Taylor described it as 'compounded of pre-judice, ignorance and panic', while Keynes called it 'the most foolish document I ever had the misfortune to read'. May identified a government deficit of £120 million, and recommended that this needed to be eliminated by increasing taxes by £24 million and cutting government spending by £96 million – two-thirds of which should be achieved by reducing unemployment relief.

Inevitably, some members of the Cabinet felt they should side with the unions. By the late evening of 23 August, the split had come to a head. Nine out of twenty Cabinet ministers said they would resign rather than accept unemployment benefit cuts. They included Henderson, George Lansbury, and the deputy leader, Clynes. Clearly the Labour government could not continue. But what happened next came as a shock to the Labour Party and MacDonald's Cabinet. They were out, but he was still in.

On 24 August 1931 MacDonald announced that he would be forming what would now be called by some a 'Government of National Unity', a coalition. It was known as the National Government. The leaders of the Conservative and Liberal parties, Stanley Baldwin and Herbert Samuel, agreed to serve under him. In a reduced Cabinet of ten members that MacDonald appointed on his return to Downing Street, there were just three others from the Labour Party (Snowden, Thomas and Lord Sankey). They were outnumbered by four Conservatives and two Liberals. This was the first act of the 'great betrayal' identified by Labour supporters thereafter – though, as will be seen, perhaps not the most important moment.

Why did MacDonald take this dramatic step, instead of resigning himself and going into opposition or retirement? Some, like Sidney Webb, later accused him of pursuing a deliberate plan, or plot – claiming that he had long intended to drop the Labour Party and carry on himself, citing, for example, previous discussions with opposition leaders such as in November 1930. But the evidence does not support this theory, which was much influenced by hindsight. MacDonald's diary suggests that on 23 August he expected to leave office the next day. However, the intervention of King George V may well have been critical. On the morning of 24 August he implored MacDonald to stay on for the benefit of the country in the grave economic emergency. MacDonald was always strongly influenced by the conception of 'duty'. What is more, in his broadcast to the nation on 25 August, MacDonald said that the National Government would last for a short time only till the emergency was over, and there would be no continuation of a coalition at the next General Election, no 'coupons' issued as in Lloyd George's post-war election in 1918 – and thus no split in the Labour Party.

MacDonald probably did not expect that his own party would react as badly to his new government as it did. Before the end of August, the parliamentary party had met and elected Henderson as its new leader. By early September, MacDonald's own Seaham branch had voted (narrowly) to ask him to resign his seat. However, what made the split irrevocable was the decision to go back on MacDonald's pledge of 25 August and hold a General Election on 27 October 1931, which was to be fought as a coalition National Government. Just as with Lloyd George in December 1918, the effect was to divide the Prime Minister's own party to its immense damage, as the split was carried into the electoral arena. It was the effects of the 1931 election, even more than the formation of the government itself, that cast Ramsay MacDonald into the outer darkness as far as Labour was concerned, and the decision to call it needs to be examined.

There can be no doubt that MacDonald himself was reluctant to have an election, and aware of its consequences for himself. The pressure to hold one came from the Conservative Party, embracing a renewed enthusiasm for the 'protection' of tariff reform, and from another intervention from King George, who was very keen for the National Government to continue, and also told MacDonald it was his duty to carry on and that his resignation would not be accepted. MacDonald did broker an agreement that the Liberals could have a separate manifesto supporting free trade, but also agreed to lead the coalition into a General Election against the Labour Party. This was the 'unforgiveable sin'. The results of the 1931 election were to make his position even more odious.

The government won by the most crushing landslide margin in modern British electoral history – an overall majority of 497. Out of their 556 MPs, no fewer than 472 were Conservatives and just 13 National Labour like MacDonald. He himself had held Seaham with 29,000 votes to Labour's 23,000. But it was now all too clear that as prime minister he would be in thrall to the Tory Party. His former party, Labour, held on to just forty-six seats, apparently reversing all their advances since 1910, advances in which MacDonald can justifiably have been said to have played a leading part. The accusations of betrayal can easily be understood. MacDonald took little pleasure in the outcome, writing in his diary 'how tragically the Labour party has been let down . . . Conservative Head Office played a shady game . . . the size of the victory has weakened me.' Yet it now looked as if he had not so much saved the country from economic collapse as saved it from the Labour Party. The 1931 election ushered in a long period of 'national government' that was to be remembered for harsh economic policy and ultimately for weakness and appeasement in foreign affairs.

Why did MacDonald agree to lead (or be the figurehead of) the coalition in an election? Partly it was a sense of duty, that the economic problems had not been solved in a mere two months, and a response to the King's personal appeal. Partly he felt resentment against his former colleagues, whom he still thought had run away from the crisis and split his Cabinet, taking the side of the

TUC. His route back to his ancestral party had been cut off when he was expelled from Labour at the end of September 1931. Perhaps he also felt that he needed to temper the Conservative dominance; the full Cabinet he formed after the election still had only eleven Conservatives out of twenty. It has been suggested that he may have been influenced by his wish to advance the cause of India's self-government, yet his reputation would undoubtedly have been more positive if he had not continued as prime minister from 1931 to 1935.

That final period of MacDonald's prime ministership is often viewed as a period in which he was so much the prisoner of the Conservative majority in the Commons and the Cabinet that he lacked authority. To some extent that is true. In economic affairs the drive was supplied by others, principally the Chancellor of the Exchequer, Neville Chamberlain. The drive towards Protectionism throughout 1932 was clearly inspired by Conservative Party policy. Chamberlain introduced an Import Duties bill on 4 February. The Unemployment Act of 1934, which created the Unemployment Assistance Board as a new body superseding local authorities, was also very much a Chamberlain project, about which MacDonald was very unhappy, privately proclaiming it a new Poor Law. But he didn't fight Chamberlain. This government even undermined a major achievement of MacDonald's 1924 administration when it ended building under Wheatley's Housing Act in 1932.

Even on his old stamping ground of foreign affairs, MacDonald was no longer the undoubted master in his own house. The Disarmament Conference of 1932 opened at Geneva under the chairmanship of (of all people) Arthur Henderson, his principal opponent in the Labour Party split of 1931. MacDonald did introduce a disarmament plan there in March 1933, but it was largely the work of Anthony Eden and of civil servants. The conference dragged on until October 1933, but the chief United Kingdom representative was now John Simon, the Foreign Secretary. It was not MacDonald's fault that international disarmament failed so miserably at this time, with Hitler withdrawing both from the conference and the League of Nations. But the minor role he played contrasted sharply with his role in international affairs in 1924 and from 1929 to 1931.

There is one positive achievement that MacDonald can claim considerable credit for between 1931 and 1935. This was the progress made towards self-government in India. The historian Charles Loch Mowat judged this to be 'perhaps the greatest product of the partnership of Baldwin and MacDonald'. After a series of Round Table Conferences (the second of which Gandhi attended on his only visit to Britain, in late 1931), the Government of India Act was passed in 1935 against the impassioned opposition of Churchill and other 'Empire die-hards'. It provided for an all-India federation, and greater autonomy for Indian provinces – in effect a new constitution for 'the jewel in the crown'. By the time the Act received Royal Assent on 2 August, MacDonald was no longer prime minister. But he had played a major role in shepherding the process forward – Gandhi was quoted as saying that he had driven the second Round Table agreements on 'with the pitilessness worthy of a Scotsman'.

What was MacDonald's style as prime minister? In some ways he could be accused of being aloof, secretive and suspicious. He had been rendered wary long before he entered Downing Street by harsh treatment, most of all in 1914 when he had taken his principled but divisive stance against the First World War, lost his party's leadership, and been accused of treason against his country. His gradual estrangement from his earlier spiritual home in the ILP as he made the compromises he deemed necessary to govern in the 1920s was also highly painful. He never had many close friends in the higher ranks of politics. Ramsay never felt at ease with Labour colleagues like Henderson and Snowden, or Tories and Liberals from the coalition years.

On the other hand, his chairmanship of all his Cabinets was generally praised as fair and far from authoritarian. He was not a micro-manager and rarely intervened in departments except those in his areas of special interest, such as foreign affairs. In his final years as prime minister after 1931, it is a fair criticism to say that he lacked authority in all areas. However, MacDonald was clearly widely respected, for example by Baldwin, who made no attempt to supplant him as prime minister even in his evident decline through the early 1930s. King George V greatly enjoyed their regular meetings and liked him very much indeed, on several occasions, right

to the end, proving extremely keen to keep MacDonald in post
– quite an achievement considering the gap in their origins.

There can be no doubt that MacDonald ended his career as a
divisive figure. He gave up the premiership on 7 June 1935 in favour
of Baldwin, and was heavily defeated by Labour's Manny Shinwell
at Seaham in the General Election in November of the same year.
Retained in the Cabinet with the largely honorific post of Lord
President of the Council, he had a Commons seat found for him
in the Combined Scottish Universities in January 1936, but he left
the government entirely in May 1937. He died on 9 November
1937, aged seventy-one, of heart failure on a sea voyage over the
Atlantic to South America.

How should we judge MacDonald's career overall? Revolutionary
socialists will not like what he did. But it might also be pointed
out that he was the first person to become a Labour prime minister,
and he did it twice. To date, Labour has never won an election
while its far left wing has been in charge. The only Labour government with a strong socialist tinge won in the highly unusual
circumstances of 1945, after ten years without an election and
following the Great Depression of the 1930s and a total war that
overwhelmingly strengthened demands for radical change. Even so,
Attlee, Bevin, Dalton, Morrison and most of the other Labour Party
leaders then were hardly revolutionaries.

As a prime minister, MacDonald cannot be judged to be in the
first rank. His two 'Labour' governments never had an overall
majority and so their achievements inevitably remained limited. He
was far from in charge of the coalition from 1931 to 1935, with
'National Labour' representing a tiny minority of MPs. There was
no ground-breaking legislation and he was not a wartime national
leader. He split his party. Nevertheless, it should never be forgotten
how much of a breakthrough it was for someone of his background
to show that he could occupy the highest office with a degree of
competence that clearly gained the respect of the general public (in
the landslide endorsement of 1931), the other party leaders (who
were content to serve under him till 1935), and even the King, who
preferred him to any other of his prime ministers. Ramsay
MacDonald was therefore a landmark, the first from his class or
party to occupy 10 Downing Street, but also a complex rather than

stereotypical figure – and an individual, who cannot be simplified as a traitor or a hero.

Robert Waller is a British election expert, author, teacher and former opinion pollster. He is the author of eight editions of the Almanac of British Politics.

40

Neville Chamberlain

28 May 1937 to 10 May 1940
Conservative

By John Charmley

Full name: Arthur Neville Chamberlain
Born: 18 March 1869, Edgbaston, Birmingham
Died: 9 November 1940, Highfield Park, Heckfield, Reading.
Ashes interred in Westminster Abbey
Education: Rugby; Mason College (which became the
University of Birmingham)
Married to Anne de Vere Cole; 1 son, 1 daughter
Quotation: 'Peace in Our Time.'

AFTER THE MEMORIAL service for Neville Chamberlain at
Westminster Abbey in November 1940, Jock Colville congratulated Churchill on his encomium. 'Ah, but I could have said it differently,' he replied. In his memoirs he did just that. The portrait

of Chamberlain penned there is one that has resonated in history. It enshrines Lloyd George's epigram that he was 'not a bad Lord Mayor of Birmingham in a lean year'. Chamberlain emerges as a man who failed to rise to the occasion, a verdict generally accepted by historians. Yet there is something to be said for Churchill's earlier assessment, beginning with the 'physical and moral toughness of fibre', which was both the product of the environment that created him, and the quality needed to survive it.

Neville was born on 18 March 1869, the second son of Joseph Chamberlain, by his second wife, Florence Kendrick. Not only a great Lord Mayor of Birmingham in a good year, Chamberlain senior was the first truly middle-class provincial politician to become a national figure. A man of vast ambition, he nurtured his oldest son, Austen, to be his designated successor, setting him on a *cursus honorum* that included Rugby, Trinity Cambridge and a seat in the Commons at an early age; it was quite otherwise for Neville, who was expected to 'make his own way in world', and follow the family business.

Neville hated his time at Rugby, and failed to muster much enthusiasm for Mason's College in Birmingham, where he studied mathematics, engineering and metallurgy for two years before becoming a chartered accountant in 1899. Dispatched to Andros in the Bahamas to revive the family fortunes by cultivating sisal, he spent five years on what turned out to be a futile project, losing the equivalent of £1.5 million, or a third of the family fortune. Neville himself thought that the episode had exposed an inner 'hard core', which only came to the fore under pressure. It was, he wrote to his sisters, a 'character building exercise'.

Andros revealed Chamberlain's capacity for concentrated hard work, as well as an ability to rely on his own judgement; his single-minded determination to carry through the appointed task was also much in evidence. It reinforced his natural tendency to self-reliance. These characteristics helped him to build a successful business career that was translated into local politics. This culminated in his becoming Lord Mayor of Birmingham in 1915. By the time of his death the previous year, Joe had come to suspect that he had put his money on the wrong horse, and that Neville might prove to be the more successful politician.

The First World War played a decisive role in Neville's life. Impressed by Chamberlain's organisational skills at municipal level, and mindful of the need to gain support from Austen, Lloyd George asked him to become Director-General of National Service in December 1916. The experience turned into a repeat of Andros. Convinced of his own abilities, Chamberlain ignored both the complex politics of his new job, and growing evidence that despite his single-mindedness and determination, he was failing to gain traction. After eight months, he resigned. But the experience was a formative one.

Among Lloyd George's many odd beliefs, phrenology was one upon which he relied for his judgement of men. From the moment he set eyes on Chamberlain, Lloyd George decided he had made a mistake in appointing him: 'When I saw that pin-head, I said to myself he won't be any use.' For his part, convinced that he had been ill-treated by Lloyd George, Chamberlain 'resolved to prove to the world that he could be a success in public life, and not without a notion that he would get even with Lloyd George some day'. It was a feud that had serious political consequences.

Chamberlain was elected as the Liberal Unionist MP for Ladywood in central Birmingham in the 'Coupon' Election of 1918. Chamberlain pointedly refused the 'coupon' and, obtaining nearly 70 per cent of the vote, won with a majority of 6,833. The Chamberlain name counted in Birmingham.

A provincial politician entering the Commons for the first time in his fiftieth year could usually have expected to rise, if at all, to a junior ministerial position. That Chamberlain proved to be the exception to this rule owed more to circumstance, and to Lloyd George, than he ever cared to admit.

Despite his commanding majority, Lloyd George was a Liberal prime minister heavily dependent upon a Conservative majority. In the immediate aftermath of the victory, this did not matter, but as things got worse it did. While still enjoying the confidence of most of the Conservative high command, including Austen Chamberlain, by early 1922 Lloyd George's government was in trouble. An international crisis involving the near renewal of the war with Turkey in 1922 led to a meeting of Conservative MPs at which a resounding majority voted to ignore their leaders and demanded the end of the coalition. Although he took no part in the rebellion, there was no question of Chamberlain siding with his brother: 'the more I thought of it the more clear it became to me that with no fundamental difference of policy but only of personalities I could not see myself following Ll.G. and that if Austen were out of the question I would have no hesitation in remaining with the Unionists & even, if I were asked, joining the new Govt.'

In fact, given the risk of a breach with Austen, Neville did hesitate, but he made it clear that if Austen was against his joining the new government under the former leader, Bonar Law, he would resign his seat and withdraw from political life. Austen reluctantly agreed to his joining, and so it was that at the age of fifty-three, Neville entered the Cabinet for the first time as Postmaster General. He joined a Cabinet that the former Lord Chancellor, Lord Birkenhead, called one of 'second class intellects'. Nonetheless, it brought together a group of politicians who would dominate inter-war politics, albeit in circumstances no one could have predicted. It was the foundation of Neville Chamberlain's political career in the first rank; he would never again be out of high office when the Conservatives held a share of power.

The new prime minister, Andrew Bonar Law, was a kindred spirit who both liked and respected him, promoting him to Minister of Health in 1923. In the short time he held the post he was responsible for the 1923 Housing Act, which went some way to alleviating the appalling shortage of affordable houses available in the aftermath of the war. But no sooner had he done that than the Prime Minister was diagnosed with an incurable cancer and resigned. As the senior leadership of the party was still in self-imposed exile after its decision to stick with Lloyd George, the new leader, Stanley Baldwin, was not spoiled for choice in terms of selecting a new Cabinet. When his first choice for Chancellor, the Liberal MP, Reginald McKenna, declined the post, Baldwin offered it to Neville, who initially declined what he called 'the greatest compliment I have ever received in my life', before finally accepting it.

It was an unprecedented promotion. Barely five years after entering the Commons, Chamberlain was effectively the second man in the government. Despite conjecture that there was a connection between his appointment and Baldwin's decision in October to go for a General Election on the issue of tariff reform, there is no evidence that this was the case, although for obvious reasons of filial piety as well as personal conviction, Neville was an enthusiastic supporter of the idea. But although Neville held on to his seat with a reduced majority, Baldwin lost his parliamentary majority. Asquith's decision to support Labour led to the creation of the first Labour government, which, in turn, facilitated a Conservative reunion.

Neville's role in negotiating the return of his half-brother and the other coalition Tories to the fold, along with his cutting and devastating criticisms of Labour's financial policy, consolidated his position in the Conservative hierarchy. His major fear as the General Election of 1924 approached was retaining Ladywood, where a narrow majority and an intensive campaign by Labour required five recounts before Chamberlain was declared the winner by a wafer-thin majority of seventy-seven. He made it clear to Baldwin that he would prefer to go back to Health, where he had plans. The fact that the Liberal renegade, Winston Churchill, was willing to come back to the Conservative fold as Chancellor made it easier for Baldwin to grant his request.

Chamberlain came to office with a programme of twenty-five measures, involving everything from reform of the Poor Law, local government and pensions, to regulations dealing with public health; it is a measure of his ability that he pushed through twenty-one of them. His crowning achievement was the 1929 Local Government Act, which did away with the old Poor Law and reorganised local government and its financing in a way that lasted until the late 1940s. It marked him out as 'the most effective social reformer of the interwar years'. It also consolidated his reputation as an out-standing parliamentary performer, and his position as Baldwin's heir apparent. But, just as a coalition had helped lead to his speedy promotion, so another led to a delay in his inevitable rise to the top.

Anticipating that Ladywood would be too insecure, in the 1929 General Election he stood for the safer seat of Edgbaston, a wise precaution in a year when Labour won six of the twelve Birmingham seats, and when Austen held on to his seat in West Birmingham by a mere forty-three votes. The Conservatives lost the election, and Baldwin, temperamentally unsuited to the demands of opposition, struggled to retain his position. With the press lords, Beaverbrook and Northcliffe, leading a demand for 'Empire free trade', by 1930 it looked to be only a matter of time before Baldwin was ousted in favour of Chamberlain. Then the great economic crisis intervened.

The National Government that emerged in response to the crisis was largely the creation of Chamberlain. Always a believer that Labour's financial irresponsibility would lead to a calamity, when a much larger one emerged, he pursued a strategy designed to ease Labour from power and to replace it with a government committed to fiscal rectitude. Chamberlain's insistence that the Conservatives would not support the MacDonald government's request for an international loan unless there was 'retrenchment', including a 10 per cent cut in unemployment benefit, split the Labour Cabinet, leading to the creation of an emergency Government of National Unity. Though this had not been Chamberlain's primary objective, it turned into the vehicle through which the policy he wanted could be delivered; it was a sign of his power that he achieved it despite Baldwin's opposition to the very idea of a coalition.

Just as it was Chamberlain's tactics that led to the creation of what was meant to be a temporary coalition, so it was his determination to introduce tariffs that led to the resignation of its Liberal members in October, and in the ensuing General Election the coalition was returned with a massive majority. It was a mark of Chamberlain's commanding position that, despite the reluctance of the Prime Minister, MacDonald, to appoint a tariff reformer as Chancellor, he had no choice. On 4 February 1932 Neville fulfilled his father's dream with the passage of the Import Duties Bill, paying an emotional tribute to Joe in his peroration.

A display of personal feeling on the floor of the Commons was rare for Chamberlain. His usual method was the withering debunking of the opposition combined with a mastery of detail. He was the dominant figure in the National Government. While, on MacDonald's retirement in 1935, it was inevitable that Baldwin would succeed him, it was equally plain that he would not be in the job for long. On his retirement in May 1937, Chamberlain finally became prime minister.

It is hard to overstate Chamberlain's dominance of the government. Admired by his own side for his forensic skill, his command, both of his brief and of the Commons, was masterly. The young Rab Butler likened his treatment of the opposition to 'a ton of bricks falling on the unwary', while the Chief Whip, Margesson, noted the hostility that Chamberlain's 'cold intellect' engendered on the Labour benches.

Finally in a position to do as he wanted, he determined to prepare a two-year legislative schedule, which he intended would become a provisional programme for his government right up to the election that would come by 1940 at the latest. He took a similarly business-like view when it came to foreign policy.

So much ink has been spilled over Chamberlain's policy of appeasement that it is essential to be clear it always had two tracks. Contrary to popular belief, Chamberlain not only believed in rearmament, but increased government spending and refocused it around technology such as Radar and the development of the Spitfire. This was combined with a determination to end what he considered Baldwin's policy of drift. It was essential, in his view, to try, during what he called the 'danger period', to attempt to improve relations with Germany and Italy. Should this fail, the country would at least be prepared for a war that would clearly have been forced upon it.

That is not to assert that Chamberlain's self-confidence did not lead him to believe that war could be avoided, but it is to say that he took the advice of those experts who argued that while Britain might win a long war, she could only afford a short one. A policy of deterrence, as argued by Churchill, would fall at the first hurdle – who would be Britain's ally? France was committed to a defensive strategy; the USA was committed to isolation; the Soviet Union was as untrustworthy as the Nazis; and outside those powers there was no possible coalition.

Viewed through this prism, we can see that there was no practicable alternative to Chamberlain's policy. This does not absolve Chamberlain from the charge that he failed to realise that Hitler was unappeasable, although closer study reveals a growing suspicion that this might not have been the case. The image of Chamberlain waving the famous 'piece of paper' at Heston, returning from Munich to declare 'peace in our time', needs to be balanced by a recognition that the country was not ready for war in 1938. This is not to say that he was deliberately buying time until the rearmament programme was more advanced, although that was a by-product of appeasement, but it is to say that by the time war came in September 1939, the country was psychologically prepared. This was more than could be said for Chamberlain, who saw the failure of his policy as a 'bitter blow'.

An appeal to the opposition to join a reconstructed ministry failed on the back of the hostility Chamberlain aroused in Labour and Liberal circles, so the only major change in his Cabinet was the advent of Churchill as First Lord of the Admiralty.

Ironically, it was Churchill's activism that led to Chamberlain's downfall. His Norwegian campaign in April 1940, which was supposed to secure the country against the Germans, failed, and the subsequent vote of confidence in the Commons saw the nemesis of Chamberlain's career.

Shaken by the tone of the debate, Chamberlain appealed to his 'friends' to support him. Although he won with a majority of eighty-one, that was a huge falling away of support. Clear that opposition parties would not join a government led by him, Chamberlain resigned on 10 May, just as the German campaign in the West began.

But Churchill could not have formed a government without Chamberlain, so he stayed on as Lord President of the Council, standing down only in September when his health failed. Like his father, he rejected the offer of a knighthood, preferring to die as plain Mr Chamberlain.

Appeasement will ensure he never stands high in the prime-ministerial pantheon, but he deserves better from posterity than he has received.

John Charmley is a professor of modern history and Pro Vice-Chancellor at St Mary's University, Twickenham.

41

Winston Churchill

10 May 1940 to 26 July 1945
Coalition

26 October 1951 to 5 April 1955
Conservative

By Peter Caddick-Adams

Full name: Winston Leonard Spencer-Churchill
Born: 30 November 1874, Blenheim Palace
Died: 24 January 1965, 28 Hyde Park Gate, London. Buried at Bladon church, Oxfordshire
Education: Harrow
Married to Clementine Ogilvy Hozier; 1 son, 4 daughters
Quotation: 'Never in the field of human conflict was so much owed by so many to so few.' (20 August 1940)

S IR WINSTON LEONARD Spencer-Churchill, twice prime minister for a total of 8 years and 240 days, has merited far more biographies than all his predecessors and successors put together. As much a global figure as a British politician, he was one of the first international media celebrities. It is tempting to see his career through many different lenses, for his achievements during a ninety-year lifespan spanning six monarchs encompassed so much more than politics. Blessed with intelligence, wit and wisdom, he was self-educated despite – or perhaps because of – not having attended a university.

Born in the era of boots and saddles, he was the only British premier to have taken part in a cavalry charge under fire, and the first to possess an atomic weapon. Among prime ministers he was unique in being recommended for a Victoria Cross in his youth, and in old age advocating the use of weapons of mass destruction – 'I want you to think very seriously over this question of poison gas,' he ordered his Chiefs of Staff on 6 July 1944, during the stalling Normandy campaign.

Besides being known as an animal breeder, aristocrat, aviator, big-game hunter, *bon viveur*, bricklayer, broadcaster, connoisseur of tobacco and fine wines (apart from Pol Roger champagne, he enjoyed Martini made with a tumbler of Plymouth gin and ice, 'supplemented with a nod toward France'), essayist, Father of the House of Commons, futurologist, gambler, global traveller, honorary American citizen, horseman, journalist, landscape gardener, lepidopterist, monarchist, newspaper editor, Nobel Prize winner, novelist, parliamentarian, polo player, prison escapee, sailor, soldier, speechmaker, statesman, war correspondent, war hero, warlord and wit, one of his many lives was that of writer-historian. 'I have frequently been forced to eat my words. I have always found them a most nourishing diet,' Churchill once quipped at a dinner party, and on another occasion, 'history will be kind to me for I intend to write it'.

Most of his long life revolved around words and his use of them. *Hansard* recorded 29,232 contributions made by Churchill in the Commons; he penned one novel, thirty non-fiction books, and published twenty-seven volumes of speeches in his lifetime, in addition to thousands of newspaper dispatches, book chapters and magazine articles.

Historically, much understanding of his time is framed around the words he wrote about himself. 'Not only did Mr. Churchill both get his war and run it: he also got in the first account of it', was the verdict of one writer, which might be the wish of many successive public figures. Acknowledging his rhetorical powers, which set him apart from all other twentieth-century politicians, his patronymic has gravitated into the English language: 'Churchillian' resonates far beyond adherence to a set of policies, which is the narrow lot of most adjectival political surnames.

New biographers have highlighted the importance of his many secretaries, personal aides and experts; it is not generally realised that his major histories were written by teams of literary assistants and polished by Churchill, who nevertheless minutely directed each enterprise. Other in-depth studies have emphasised the role of his strong-willed wife, Clementine Hozier (1885–1977) – surprisingly little referred to in his own works – and her rock-solid, but not uncritical support for him, particularly during his Wilderness Years of the inter-war period, and her prompts for him to show humility during the wartime era of his triumph. His brother Jack (1880–1947), younger by six years, has also been airbrushed out of history – often by Winston himself – though was an engaging and honourable man who shielded his brother from the worst effects of the 1929 Wall Street Crash and lived in Downing Street during the war after being bombed out of his own home.

The behaviour of Winston's only son, Randolph (1911–68), also had a bearing on his father, who spoiled him. Churchill never referred to this, but during the 1930s Randolph's affairs with the bottle, women, and his attempts to enter Parliament caused rifts between his parents. In the war years, Randolph's domestic disagreements with his parents grew so violent that Clementine thought her husband might suffer a seizure. In 1941, Randolph's first wife, Pamela Digby, conducted an affair with Averell Harriman, Roosevelt's special envoy to Europe, then coordinating the Lend-Lease programme. Although this led to the breakdown of her marriage, her Harriman 'alliance' probably aided Britain's war effort significantly more than the younger Churchill.

The three surviving Churchill daughters (a fourth, Marigold, died aged two) also played important, supportive roles in his premiership, albeit downplayed by their father. The eldest, Diana (1909–63), served in the Women's Royal Naval Service. Sarah (1914–82) worked in photo intelligence for the Women's Royal Air Force, accompanied her father to the Teheran and Yalta conferences, and was romantically linked to the American ambassador, John Winant. Mary (1922–2014) joined the Auxiliary Territorial Service, commanded anti-aircraft batteries and travelled to Potsdam as her father's ADC. Although Winston and Clementine enjoyed fifty-seven happy years together, their four children clocked up eight marriages between them. Winston's own personality swamped those of his family. He was often away from home – 'either fighting wars or fighting elections', as Mary later observed. They accepted that he must come first – 'and second and third'. Thus, Churchill's wartime premiership was strongly underpinned by his extended family, though writers tend to be bedazzled by the man alone.

Churchill's parents influenced him in different ways. His mother Jennie Jerome (1854–1921), a noted American beauty and daughter of a wealthy New York businessman, was distant to her two sons during their childhoods in a not untypically Victorian way. The boys were partly brought up by their nanny before being sent to Harrow. Subsequently, Jennie – influential in British social and political circles – was able to shamelessly advance the cause of her eldest son. The early years of Churchill's rise to prominence certainly reflect the proactive patronage of his mother, an intelligent, witty hostess, close to Queen Alexandra and said to be romantically involved with King Edward VII.

A coda running through Winston Churchill's life was the meteoric parliamentary career of his father, Lord Randolph Churchill (1849–95). The second surviving son of the 7th Duke of Marlborough, whose appellation of 'Lord' was a courtesy title, Randolph had entered the House of Commons in 1874 and quickly became one of the leading young figures in the Conservative Party, becoming Chancellor of the Exchequer and Leader of the House of Commons twelve years later. Within months he had fallen out with his prime minister, Lord Salisbury, and resigned from the Cabinet; Randolph's political career was effectively over, though he remained an MP until 1895.

In Winston's mind was not the tragedy of his father's resignation letter of 1886, but of his death in 1895, at the very early age of forty-five. It had soon become apparent that a creeping illness was slowly robbing Randolph of his persuasive powers in a very public fashion. This was later understood to be syphilis, a contemporary diagnosis accepted – among others – by Winston Churchill all his life. Modern medical analysis suggests alternatively that a left-side brain tumour more closely corresponds to the known symptoms. The effects of this were threefold. Churchill was convinced that he, too, might die young. He therefore became 'a young man in a hurry', determined to achieve as much as possible in the brief span, he believed, allotted to him. Next, believing his father to have been possessed of a sexually transmitted disease may have persuaded him to remain chaste to 'my darling Clemmie'. He never strayed, and indeed they had a remarkably close marriage for fifty-seven years. Finally, Churchill – who lionised his father – felt that Randolph had been cut off in his prime, before he could go on to achieve greater things. Accordingly, high office and a parliamentary career were expectations for the son, who lost his father when aged just twenty.

The young Churchill left Sandhurst in 1894, joining a cavalry regiment in India, and saw action in the Swat Valley of modern Pakistan. It led to his first book, *The Story of the Malakand Field Force* (1898). This prompted a meeting with the Prime Minister, Salisbury, and attachment to Kitchener's military campaign in the Sudan. Arriving in Egypt, he joined the 21st Lancers at Cairo and took part in the Battle of Omdurman (September 1898) – the British army's last major cavalry charge with horse and lance – his subsequent book of the campaign, *The River War*, being published in November 1899.

He had meanwhile resigned from the army, narrowly failing to be elected as MP for Oldham in a June 1899 by-election. Only Churchill – then aged twenty-four – could write of his first parliamentary defeat, 'returned to London with those feelings of deflation which a bottle of champagne or even soda-water represents when it has been half emptied and left uncorked for a night'.

In 1899 he arrived in South Africa as a well-paid war correspondent to cover the Second Boer War. Armed, uniformed and passing himself off as an officer when necessary, though he had no right to any of these, within two weeks he had accompanied an armoured train that was ambushed. Churchill's leadership allowed the engine to escape, carrying the wounded to safety, but he was among twenty-three taken prisoner, the group losing thirty-eight killed and injured. His claim of civilian status as a journalist was ignored and the aspiring politician went on to spend his twenty-fifth birthday as a prisoner of war in Pretoria.

In December, armed with a biscuit and four pieces of chocolate, he vaulted over his prison wall and by jumping freight trains and walking, made his way to freedom 300 miles away, which briefly made him an international celebrity. After his escape, Churchill fought on, and was recommended for a Victoria Cross in June 1900. However, his earlier claim to civilian status while a prisoner contributed to this being denied, as well as to antipathy from the War Office towards the 'pushy young adventurer'. Later that year, two books would appear from his hand about the South African campaign; these, and the details of his dramatic bid for freedom, helped secure his first entry into Parliament as Conservative MP for Oldham in the General Election of October 1900.

Churchill soon changed parties over free trade, joining the Liberal benches, and his political career might have been over had it not been for the January 1906 General Election. Fought over Protectionism versus free trade, it split the Tory Party, and ushered in the free-trade-advocating Liberal Party, Churchill immediately beginning his ministerial career as Under-Secretary of State for the Colonies. The following year he was sworn of the Privy Council and in 1908 he was promoted to Cabinet rank as President of the Board of Trade. He found his feet campaigning in the two General Elections of 1910 and in the Commons, which won him national acclaim. His reward was, first, promotion to Home Secretary, followed by First Lord of the Admiralty in October 1911. Thus, when Britain went to war in August 1914, Churchill was not only the most experienced of Asquith's Cabinet in land and maritime matters (until the appointment of Kitchener); he was also able to closely observe his prime minister and witness how to run a country during wartime.

His major contribution to policy during the First World War was to initiate the Gallipoli campaign, a valid, but poorly executed strategy, which came at the wrong time. It drifted into helpless stalemate reminiscent of the western front and chewed up scarce manpower and resources; after eight months' fighting in January 1916, the force was withdrawn but had suffered huge casualties. Churchill resigned from the government, briefly commanded the 6th Royal Scots Fusiliers on the western front, and by 1917 was back in office as Minister of Munitions under the premiership of his old Liberal colleague, David Lloyd George.

In January 1919 Churchill moved to become Secretary of State for War, which later included Air (thus, uniquely, he presided over each of the three services), which was largely a job of downsizing budgets and personnel. By 1921 he was in the Colonial Office, but he lost his seat in the 1922 General Election; it took three by-elections over two years before he returned to the Commons. He was already drifting back towards Conservatism, winning Epping as a 'Constitutionalist', and in 1925 he was formally readmitted into the Conservative Party, observing sardonically of his own behaviour that 'Anyone can rat, but it takes a certain ingenuity to re-rat.'

In the November 1924 General Election Churchill returned to the Commons, becoming Baldwin's Chancellor, but in May 1929 he was out of office again, and would remain so for the next ten years. In 1922 a legacy enabled him to buy the run-down house and estate of Chartwell in Kent. The proceeds from his next books, including six volumes of *The World Crisis* (1923–31), *My Early Life* (1930), *Marlborough* (four volumes, 1933–8) and *Great Contemporaries* (1937) – bestsellers, all – underwrote the extensive renovations on which he embarked, supplemented by his own bricklaying and pond-building efforts, in which his many visitors were expected to help. Alterations and entertaining consumed Churchill's considerable income from writing, always slightly faster than he could generate more. The house, with its stunning views over the Kentish weald, was a refuge, good living on his own terms, grounding him in the past. At its heart is his book-lined writing room known as the study, where the wordsmith's enterprise and imagination generated the required ocean of English to keep the Churchills in the style to which Winston felt they should be accustomed.

Chartwell also functioned as the centre of an informal shadow government where Churchill's friends and counsellors shared information and devised policies to be proclaimed in Parliament or the media. During these Wilderness Years, Churchill issued warnings about German and Italian rearmament, travelling around not just the country but the world, gaining a profile that would be much needed from 1939 onwards. In December 1931, he was struck by a car in New York City, underlining less the fact that he was accident-prone (incredibly so), but that he was almost unique among British politicians in regularly crossing the Atlantic. He knew how to run government departments and had built a network of zealous admirers who were prepared to risk their positions to pass vital intelligence and information to him. The cards would not have fallen this way had he remained in office.

Thus, when the call, initially to the Admiralty, came on 3 September 1939, the day Britain declared war on Germany, almost every aspect of his life to that moment had prepared Churchill for the coming ordeal. The pleasing signal went out to the fleet: 'Winston is back.' The surname Churchill was not needed. He was the country's best-known politician, a 'brand' in modern terminology. The news indicated not only to the Royal Navy, but to the nation, that Britain was again in safer hands. Almost more important was the congratulatory message received on 11 September, from the former Assistant Secretary of the US Navy during the First World War (therefore a near-match to Churchill's First Lord of the Admiralty status). Now president, Franklin D. Roosevelt addressed his coded note to 'Naval Person' (which Churchill would amend to 'Former Naval Person' on becoming prime minister). It was an example of the informal Churchillian network at work, which no other British politician had at their disposal, or had bothered to cultivate.

Following the German seizure of Norway in April 1940, hesitant Franco-British expeditions to Narvik and Trondheim, dependent on naval assistance, failed in the face of superior German tactics and air support. Although the land–maritime operation immediately evoked harsh memories of Gallipoli, it was Chamberlain who was blamed in the electrifying parliamentary debate of 7–9 May. The Prime Minister was effectively undone by a series of spectacular anti-government speeches, though Churchill, accepting Cabinet responsibility, endeavoured to defend his boss and arch-enemy. His old friend Lloyd George gently but cleverly unpicked Churchill's defence with the observation, 'The right honourable Gentleman must not allow himself to be converted into an air-raid shelter to keep the splinters from hitting his colleagues.'

Chamberlain contemplated resignation, favouring the Foreign Secretary, Halifax, as his successor. The latter was not remotely warlike and had earlier opposed the bombing of Germany, lest the Germans retaliate. The following morning, the long-planned invasion of the Low Countries began, forcing Chamberlain's hand – by coincidence, it was the Germans who intervened to decide this most acute of British political crises. Halifax was reluctant to assume the mantle, confiding to his diary: 'Apart . . . from Churchill's qualities as compared with my own at this particular juncture, what would in fact be my position? Churchill would be running Defence . . . I should speedily become a more or less honorary Prime Minister, living in a kind of twilight just outside the things that really mattered.' No doubt also concerned by his ability to lead the House of Commons in war and rally the radical socialists of the Labour Party while, as a peer, having to sit in the House of Lords, Edward Wood, 3rd Viscount Halifax, wisely declined.

With the Labour Party stipulating that they would support a coalition government, but not under Chamberlain, it was obvious that his time had gone and – for all its traditional distrust of Churchill – the latter's time had arrived. The Finest Hour was upon the nation with no great democratic mandate but ushered in by a small multi-party coterie of Westminster politicians. Recent writers are coming around to Chamberlain, arguing that he at least bought time after Munich (September 1938) for Britain to rearm, but this ignores that he spent much of 1–3 September trying to avoid going to war. Ironically, Chamberlain's belated rearmament attempts actually left Britain more vulnerable in 1940, because they were incomplete. Identified as the leading appeaser of the pre-war period, honourable but strategically blind, Chamberlain consistently misread the international picture and clung to power until the very last second.

Churchill had been on the receiving end of Conservative venom and divisiveness throughout the 1930s, and before. He had developed the ability not to hold political grudges, was collegiate, congenial and clubbable, whether in the Commons, or over dinner at The Other Club, an informal dining society he founded in 1911, and understood that he needed as united a government as possible. He initially formed a War Cabinet of five, including Chamberlain and Halifax (a nod to their supporters, whom he had yet to win over) and the two Labour leaders, Clement Attlee and Arthur Greenwood. Having witnessed decades of weak leadership, Churchill's style was to run matters as decisively as possible, appointing himself Leader of the House of Commons and Minister of Defence. There was no such office at the time, it being devised specifically to bring him military oversight via his 'Chief Staff Officer' (a Churchillian invention), Major General Hastings 'Pug' Ismay. The latter kept his master informed of the Chiefs of Staff Committee, though Churchill often attended in person. Attlee, his deputy prime minister – another innovation – deputised throughout and wherever needed. Attlee's modest but innate intelligence was a perfect foil to Churchill's brash dominance, and they formed a very trusting duo throughout the war. Sensing he needed to offer a transparent alternative to Hitler's dictatorship, Churchill wanted Parliament to be a vital element in the day-to-day conduct of the war. It would be to the Commons that Churchill would report the highs and lows, and deliver his stirring speeches, not the media. For him to be able to concentrate on strategic decision making, he needed a tame, but not compliant, House.

Aware that Asquith had fallen from power in December 1916 as a result of domestic political intrigues, Churchill distributed power wisely, bringing in trade union leader Ernest Bevin as Minister of Labour to guarantee cooperation of the nation's workforce – a vital component he understood from his time at the Ministry of Munitions. He also deftly balanced the three Service ministries between Alexander: Admiralty (Labour); Eden: War (Conservative); and Sinclair: Air (Liberal). The latter was another of Winston's network, having served as Second-in-Command of Churchill's battalion in 1916. Dominating Parliament during the war years, Churchill was curiously vulnerable. He had no power base – as did the Chamberlains in Birmingham, MPs from the trades unions and professional classes, or some of the older political dynasties in the shires – so relied on the one weapon in his own arsenal to dominate Parliament: his familiarity with words – his oratory. The effort and polish he put into his speeches (only later issued to the BBC and print media, and rarely relayed live), underlined the respect he had for Parliament and that he never took it for granted. It also reflected Churchill's deep appreciation of British history and its institutions – Parliament was his creature, but one from which he also drew fortitude and reassurance.

On his third day in office, he addressed the Commons for the first time as its master. This was the occasion of his 'I have nothing to offer but blood, toil, tears and sweat' speech. It was a device to unify Parliament, dangerously divided only days earlier, together with a statement of the simplest of aims – victory. Here, Churchill was offering something he couldn't actually deliver. Strategically very wise, gifted with a sense of geopolitics incorporating both human and physical geography, he knew that, in 1940, his job would be to ensure Britain's survival. Victory could only be delivered later, with the assistance of Roosevelt's America. Additionally, Churchill needed both to undermine the appeasement faction still active, and to advertise to the United States, an informal and unofficial ally (despite its anti-British, pro-isolationist London Ambassador, Joseph P. Kennedy), that the country was united and focused.

The message was addressed to the British Empire, too, for Churchill was relying on the manpower, shipping and huge raw material resources the imperial partners would commit to his leadership. This was when the cartoonist David Low published a picture of a British soldier standing on a wave-drenched rock on the southern English coast shaking his fist at approaching German bombers. The caption was: 'Very well, alone.' This was a misnomer. Britain was not alone; never alone. She was but the tip of the imperial iceberg, which vastly outnumbered anything the Germans and Italians combined could bring to war – but the image helped magnify the peril Churchill understood might assault his island home. This was emphasised the very next evening, 14 May, when Churchill directed his Secretary of State for War, Anthony Eden, to broadcast a call for volunteers to join an armed citizen militia – the Local Defence Volunteers, later renamed the Home Guard.

Half a million were expected; heeding Churchill's words, three times that number joined.

The twenty-first day of Churchill's premiership, 31 May, marked the height of the Dunkirk evacuation. It is almost impossible to conceive the adversity of Churchill's position, never mind the personal stress he would have been under so soon into his administration. Operation Dynamo, the movement of shipping and personnel to and from Dunkirk, was organised and administered without warning by Bertram Ramsay, a retired admiral recalled to the colours at Dover. It again illustrated the Churchillian network in action. Ramsay's father had been the young Churchill's first CO in India. The future admiral used to spend long summers with his father, and got to know his most junior officer, Churchill. In the latter's Wilderness Years, we now know it was Ramsay who brought classified files about the paucity of naval spending for Churchill to study. The pair were old friends, trusted each other implicitly, and Churchill needed to say very little to his admiral to convey the gravity of the situation, or tell him what to do.

Four days later, on 4 June, with the bulk of the troops safely home, Churchill again addressed the Commons, as the nation expected the Germans to follow up their runaway victory in France with an immediate assault on Britain. It was still too soon to understand that events across the Channel amounted to a Franco-Belgian collapse, rather than the successful application of German military doctrine. That the Wehrmacht was unstoppable was axiomatic, but that the Nazi military machine had suffered great losses of aircraft, men and equipment, was crucially reliant on horses, not panzers, and had no amphibious capability at all was not generally understood.

The 4 June speech was when the Prime Minister unleashed the full force of his oratory on the Commons.

> We shall fight in France, we shall fight on the seas and oceans, we shall fight with growing confidence and growing strength in the air, we shall defend our island, whatever the cost may be. We shall fight on the beaches, we shall fight on the landing grounds, we shall fight in the fields and in the streets, we shall fight in the hills; we shall never surrender . . .

The effect was electric, both to seasoned MPs used to great oratory and to listeners at home, who later heard extracts read by a BBC newscaster. In the words of a Conservative MP, a noted Churchill critic, 'he was eloquent and oratorical and used magnificent English; several Labour members cried', while a Labour MP observed: 'That was worth a thousand guns and the speeches of a thousand years.' The full speech crackles with electricity, and even today has the power to move: it was a very personal extension of Churchill's unique approach to power.

On 18 June Churchill again strode into the Commons for what was to prove his third key wartime address. He might have paused to consider that the day marked the 125th anniversary of Waterloo. He was responding to the French request for an Armistice with Hitler, announced earlier. After a remarkably candid assessment of the battle just fought in France, and of Britain's losses and ability to carry on the fight, he intoned: 'What General Weygand called the battle of France is over. I expect that the battle of Britain is about to begin. Upon this battle depends the survival of Christian civilization. Upon it depends our own British life, and the long continuity of our institutions and our Empire. The whole fury and might of the enemy must very soon be turned on us.' He concluded with the call to arms: 'Let us therefore brace ourselves to our duties, and so bear ourselves, that if the British Empire and its Commonwealth last for a thousand years, men will still say, "This was their finest hour."' Here again, Churchill's messaging was directed far beyond British shores, to the Empire and the United States, to whom he had made references earlier in the speech. This was the Churchillian concept of the English-speaking peoples uniting as one against the Nazi menace.

Having predicted the Battle of Britain in his speech of 18 June, Churchill analysed it two months later, while the great aerial combat was still under way. In the Commons on 21 August he issued a rallying cry to his air warriors, to raise their morale, as well as a proclamation to the country and wider world that Britain was still in business. As *Hansard* reported,

The gratitude of every home in our island, in our Empire, and indeed throughout the world except in the abodes of the guilty

goes out to the British airmen who, undaunted by odds, unweak-
ened by their constant challenge and mortal danger, are turning
the tide of world war by their prowess and their devotion. Never
in the field of human conflict was so much owed by so many to
so few. (Prolonged cheers.)

Churchill had done his job, braced the nation for the worst possible
scenario, called everyone to arms and attracted the attention of the
wider world to Britain's plight. However, only if fortune smiled
and he survived would the United States climb off the fence and
come to join him. It was not just America's might that was needed,
but her industry. Britain needed vast quantities of war materials that
could only ultimately come from across the Atlantic. As the country's gold reserves would eventually be exhausted, loans and credits
would be needed. It would take him over a year to cement an
alliance with Roosevelt, Churchill being aware that the latter would
need to focus first on his presidential re-election campaign in
November 1940. Once secure for another term, the pair formally
met on a battleship off Newfoundland in August 1941, concluding
the first of their eleven wartime meetings together by signing a
joint policy statement of aspirations dubbed the Atlantic Charter.

Although there were moments when Churchill faced the music
alone, such as the 1940 speeches (where he presented excessively
rehearsed monologues, much altered by the army of secretaries
always in attendance and to whom he dictated throughout his
working hours), the Prime Minister's style tended towards delegation,
tempered by constant interference. Faced with irregular working
hours, weekends ceasing to exist and prime-ministerial tantrums,
his personal staff did not rebel. One spoke for many when describing
proximity to Churchill as 'the feeling of being recharged by contact
with a source of living power'. The Prime Minister forged a
successful working relationship with Brooke, his Chief of the
Imperial General Staff (CIGS), who calmed his wilder ideas and
enacted the most sane. Possessed of equally strong personalities, the
pair represented the most effective team of any nation's political–
military leadership during the Second World War. Brooke saw his
role as standing up to Churchill, recording the latter as 'genius
mixed with an astonishing lack of vision – he is quite the most

difficult man to work with that I have ever struck but I should not have missed the chance of working with him for anything on earth', whereas Churchill noted of his CIGS: 'When I thump the table and push my face towards him what does he do? Thumps the table harder and glares back at me.'

Churchill's role in the field of domestic policy was remote. This was an extreme example of his inclination to delegate, disguising the fact that social issues did not particularly excite him. As much of the wartime coalition government's effort was directed to winning the war, their legislative achievement was unimpressive compared to many administrations. The exception was the 1944 Education Act, the work of R.A. ('Rab') Butler, a noted pre-war appeaser of whom Churchill was suspicious. Yet, recognising Rab's formidable intellect, and true to his inability to bear a grudge, Churchill actually moved Butler from a junior role in the Foreign Office to his first Cabinet position as Education Secretary. His Act raised the school leaving age to fifteen, made religious instruction compulsory and introduced selection between grammar schools and state secondary moderns, at the age of eleven.

Throughout the war the political parties maintained an effective consensus on every policy. This proved the wisdom of the Churchill all-inclusive, collegiate method of government. It was best expressed by the publication in December 1942 of the Beveridge Report, enabled by a cross-party, multi-departmental initiative fostered by Greenwood. Its author was an Oxford academic and former civil servant who had worked with Churchill when the latter was at the Board of Trade. It advocated free healthcare, compulsory insurance and unemployment benefits for all. Though Labour wished to implement the report forthwith, Churchill's opposition – made partly on grounds of cost (the state coffers were already empty from prosecuting the war) – dictated that its adoption would be post-conflict. Although a logical extension of the pre-1914 Liberal reforms with which Churchill had been associated, the Prime Minister's plan would have been a means-tested, diluted form of Beveridge. A sense that the Conservatives opposed Beveridge (who became a Liberal MP in 1944), or were not as committed to it as Labour, would contribute to Churchill's surprise electoral defeat in July 1945.

By the end of the war, Churchill – in his sixties – had travelled hundreds of thousands of miles in unpressurised aircraft and across U-boat-infested oceans in pursuit of victory. Working an average of ninety hours a week, smoking heavily, he succeeded in besting three bouts of pneumonia (in February and December 1943 and September 1944) and a heart attack (while staying at the White House in December 1941), any of which would have killed a younger man. Through them all, he continued directing the country from his bed, treating his medical and clerical staff 'as intimate friends', members of his extended family. Churchill and the nation took it for granted that he would win the 1945 General Election. He wanted the wartime coalition to continue after the defeat of Germany (8 May 1945) until Japan had been vanquished, but Labour pressed for a dissolution, responding to its own grass roots.

In the end the popularity of Churchill and that of the Conservatives turned out to be two separate things. The former was undimmed, but Britain remembered the mass unemployment of the inter-war years, associating it with the predominantly Tory administrations of the period, and from 1942 Labour had won a string of by-elections. The Beveridge Report and the Butler Education Act excited a sense of wanting change, a new world. The campaign was a prolonged one, extended because of a three-week gap in which to count the ballot papers of British service personnel scattered around the globe. Initially, both sides found it difficult to break away from the warm consensus that had signified the wartime coalition, but Churchill himself destroyed it in an ill-judged speech of 4 June. This time his rhetoric worked against him when he claimed that 'some form of Gestapo, no doubt very humanely directed in the first instance' would result from a Labour victory. His former loyal foot-soldiers, Attlee, Bevin, Greenwood, Herbert Morrison (Home Secretary 1940–45) and others, were hurt and the electorate incredulous. The Labour victory, announced on 26 July in the middle of the Potsdam Conference, was as much a surprise as its majority of 145 seats. Even Churchill's 20,000 majority in Epping fell by 3,000 votes.

Winston Churchill would return to office in 1951, refusing to concede leadership of his party to Anthony Eden. Instead of leaving politics and accepting the dukedom (of Dover) offered him by King

George VI in 1945, he remained an MP but travelled widely to receive honours from the free world, write, paint and relax in sunnier climes. That Churchill was out of office actually acted in his favour, as it had done in the Wilderness Years. The literary factory at Chartwell generated books (ten volumes of non-fiction and ten books of speeches between 1948 and 1958) that kept his name in the public eye, while he was able to make speeches that as a prime minister he might have been dissuaded from delivering.

Churchill's return to office in the 25 October 1951 General Election was less a desire for the wartime leader's return (though this undoubtedly played a part) and more a recognition that Labour politicians, technically in office since May 1940, and their policies were considered stale and exhausted. The loss of several key figures, continuing austerity of the wartime kind but extending into peacetime, the prolongation of conscription, the shrinking of the Empire – both as a source of raw materials and as an overseas market – all contributed to disillusion with socialism and a desire to give the Tories another chance. Significant, too, was the fact that the Conservative Research Department (headed by Butler) had removed the blimpish image of the old party.

The newly returned prime minister was distressed that Britain and the United States had grown apart, despite the arrival of his old wartime comrade, Dwight Eisenhower, at the White House in January 1953. Churchill determined that Britain needed 'several years of quiet, steady administration', which is exactly what it got. His touch at home was light; there was no effort to unpick the innovations of the Attlee administration, and Churchill's Liberal instincts steered his second premiership towards a Disraeli-type 'One Nation' Conservatism, leaving most control of domestic affairs to his Chancellor, Butler. With Churchill chasing opportunities to host world summits, particularly after the death of Stalin in March 1953, the main obsession of Tory parliamentarians became his retirement date. The coronation of Queen Elizabeth II (June 1953) and his own eightieth birthday (November 1954), both provided opportunities, but the various illnesses of Eden, his designated heir, conspired to keep the Prime Minister in office. Churchill had suffered a hernia in June 1947, two strokes in August 1949 and June 1953 (another would follow in October 1956), but it was probably Clementine behind the scenes who more than anyone else gently persuaded her husband to quit in April 1955. Elizabeth II offered a dukedom, as her father had (this time of London), which was again declined, but he had in 1953 accepted from her the highest degree of knighthood, the Garter. Alive to his image, this did not affect the 'Winston Churchill brand' – it was merely preceded by 'Sir'.

The decline in his final decade was slow and enabled the world to shower honours on the fading knight, but he only relinquished his seat of Woodford in the October 1964 General Election. Few were surprised to learn that the former premier had suffered a severe stroke on 15 January 1965, but much of the world paused on the news of his death nine days later. Thousands filed past his coffin as it lay in state in Westminster Hall for three days (the long queue was this author's first memory) and a state funeral service was held at St Paul's Cathedral on 30 January. The sight of London crane jibs being lowered as the motor vessel *Havengore* proceeded along the River Thames towards Waterloo Station (a detail Churchill insisted on, knowing that protocol would demand de Gaulle's presence at the railway terminus named after Wellington's great victory over France) is the strongest memory of the many millions who watched, moving them to tears as Churchill's words had in 1940. He was buried in a surprisingly unostentatious grave next to his parents in Bladon, the estate village of his kinsmen, the Dukes of Marlborough.

Not only was Churchill an able administrator and effective leader, but he possessed an extraordinarily curious mind. He was what we would call today a horizon-scanner and had a knack of anticipating the course of world events. He wrote and speculated about future technology and surrounded himself with scientists and experts of every conceivable discipline.

Although the biographer Andrew Roberts reminds us that Churchill's policy was for scientists 'to be on tap, not on top', he trusted and listened to those inside and outside of government, who staffed endless committees to deal with specific problems at high speed, and had to respond to 'Action This Day' directives when the lighthouse beam of Churchill's attention fell on their activities. He understood and appreciated the human resources at his disposal. As in 1940–45, but in fact all through his life, he developed networks of people on whom he could call for advice. Churchill's tendency was to delegate, but with endless interference. He drove his civil servants and private appointees to distraction, working long hours, sparing neither himself nor those around him. If any single prime minister has found a mechanism to drag Britain through turmoil, whether domestic or global, by listening to the heart of the nation, it was Winston Churchill.

Peter Caddick-Adams is Director of the Defence & Global Security Institute, and Visiting Professor of Military History at the University of Wolverhampton.

42

Clement Attlee

26 July 1945 to 26 October 1951
Labour

By Sir Anthony Seldon

Full name: Clement Richard Attlee
Born: 3 January 1883, Putney
Died: 8 October 1967, Westminster Hospital. Buried at
Westminster Abbey
Education: Haileybury; University College, Oxford
Married to Violet Miller; 1 son, 3 daughters
Quotation: 'Democracy means government by discussion, but it
is only effective if you can stop people talking.'

CLEMENT ATTLEE WAS the most successful prime minister
domestically of all the fifty-five discussed in this volume. No
other prime minister introduced so much domestic legislation
that stood the test of time, combined with overseeing such a

ground-breaking foreign policy, nor ran a government at full pelt with such a sure touch. Specifically, no other *Labour* prime minister in history comes close to his achievement. The achievement is all the more remarkable as he faced far greater hurdles after six years of total war than many other prime ministers. The country was exhausted, its industry and housing stock in disarray, and its savings gone.

A public-school, cricket-loving romantic who liked to refer to himself after 1918 as 'Major Attlee', he oversaw the most socialist government in British history. A shy and retiring man without personal charisma and intellectual curiosity, he possessed no detailed grasp of foreign or economic policy, yet led a government that broke frontiers in both. Why did he achieve so much more than other prime ministers? Was it because of his understated qualities as a leader, or were wider factors at play?

Attlee's personal qualities lay at the heart of the success of the government. He may have been primarily the conductor as prime minister of a prodigiously talented orchestra, but he was still a brilliant conductor extracting the best from them. Born into a comfortable home in the late Victorian era, after reading History at Oxford, he became a barrister before voluntary work in London's East End prompted him to join the Independent Labour Party. Following formative experience of the First World War, he became a Labour MP and Mayor of Stepney in 1922. A minister in MacDonald's first two governments in 1924 and 1929–31, he became Deputy Labour Leader in 1932 and its leader in 1935.

Attlee radiated honesty, trust and integrity, highlighted in John Bew's seminal biography, *Citizen Clem*. Leo McKinstry, author of *Attlee and Churchill* (2019), points to Attlee's determination to be fair to all parties in his approach to the 1948 boundary changes, which McKinstry believes may have cost Labour the 1951 General Election. He remained calm and balanced, and rarely lost his touch with colleagues, though another Attlee historian and admirer, Kenneth Morgan, author of *Labour in Power, 1945–51*, believes he would have done better to have kept Aneurin Bevan in his team in early 1951. Others have criticised his lack of decisiveness during the convertibility crisis in August 1947 and the devaluation crisis of September 1949, and his timing of the 1950 and 1951 General Elections. The catastrophic collapse of the Labour majority in the first of these from 146 to 5 led to much contemporary criticism, which obscured and delayed his claim to greatness.

Of the various roles of a prime minister, Attlee was at his best as chief executive, honed in his period as Churchill's deputy from 1942. More than any other Labour leader, he had an instinctive trust in his civil servants, and was fortunate in their quality, none more so than Norman Brook, his Cabinet Secretary. Deputy to Edward Bridges, the Cabinet Secretary during the war, Brook was at the peak of his powers after 1945 and mastered every single facet of government. As his principal private secretary at No. 10, Attlee had three high-fliers in succession who could command Whitehall: Leslie Rowan, Laurence Helsby and Denis Rickett. Officials who worked for Attlee adored his passion for executing the task he set himself of delivering Labour's election manifesto, and worked tire-lessly for him, even when they found his socialist inclinations uncongenial. Mild Major Attlee was ruthless when he thought any official, or minister, was not up to the job, and was a better appointer than many prime ministers.

Attlee was in his element chairing Cabinet and its committees. No other Labour prime minister, and very few others of any other persuasion, were better dispatchers of government business. He always looked for the common ground, and to carry his colleagues with him. James Callaghan displayed similar qualities when presiding over the IMF crisis in 1976, but lacked the incisive intellect of Attlee. Forcing the pace of partition in India in 1947 was one of the rare occasions when Attlee asserted his own beliefs over those of his colleagues; another occasion was his support of Bevan over the creation of the NHS, and also driving ahead on iron and steel nationalisation in 1950–51. Other Labour leaders had qualities that Attlee lacked: Ramsay MacDonald was stronger mobilising the party. Harold Wilson was a much more persuasive communicator to the whole country. Tony Blair had more outgoing charisma and persua-sive charm. Gordon Brown had a much deeper understanding of economic policy. But none of these had the combined talents of Clement Attlee.

Prime ministers are helped immeasurably by supportive spouses and are handicapped by those who resent their role or can't cope with it. Attlee's relationship with his wife Violet ranks alongside

Robert Peel's with Julia and Margaret Thatcher's with Denis as among the strongest. Attlee preferred being prime minister to being leader of the opposition, in part because Violet could live in the (newly renovated) flat above No. 10, so he could see her several times a day. They were a close team: in General Election campaigns, she drove him around the country.

Labour's six prime ministers have been broadly in the centre of the party, a truth that admirers of Labour leaders Michael Foot and Jeremy Corbyn, who never won a General Election, ignored or overlooked. Attlee was perfectly positioned ideologically for the conditions of 1945–51, neither to the right nor the left, but with strong left-wing credentials, underlined when he defeated Herbert Morrison and Arthur Greenwood for the party leadership in 1935 (both becoming his deputies). Having credibility on the left, underlined by his support for socialist measures like the NHS, did him no harm politically in keeping the unions on side (though sat uneasily with his deep attachment to his *alma mater*, Haileybury College; he would keep a running tally of the numbers of Old Haileyburians as opposed to Old Etonians in his government).

Despite being no orator, he was surprisingly effective in the House of Commons, acquiring a reputation for being a safe pair of hands and utterly dependable. Fellow Labour MPs showed him palpable respect, bolstered by his evident superiority in debate over Winston Churchill, evident in his robust response to a censure motion in December 1945. While Parliament saw Attlee at his best on the public stage, the media saw him at his worst, where his flat voice, lacking all animation, and his absence of small talk, counted against him. Francis Williams, his press secretary in his first two years as prime minister, tried valiantly to change him, but was unable to generate any interest in him in the media, either to meeting its key figures or understanding how it worked. Although Neville Chamberlain was the first prime minister to be interviewed on television in 1938, the war held back its subsequent development, and broadcasting played little part in Attlee's premiership. This was fortunate for him: he would not have succeeded as prime minister in the television age, which dawned under Harold Macmillan.

Top ministerial quality and deep relevant experience are the second and third factors in his success. Attlee had an unusually talented and mostly loyal Cabinet throughout. The government would never have achieved as much, as quickly, were it not for them. Critical to that success was the fact that, of the six most senior ministers in the Cabinet, all but one came to office with considerable prior experience. It has become commonplace to refer to senior Cabinet ministers as 'big beasts'. These six were very big: many of their successors in key posts in the following seventy-five years have by comparison been minnows.

Prime among his team was Ernest Bevin, Foreign Secretary for all but the last few months. Bevin had organised the amalgamation of different trade unions into the Transport and General Workers Union in 1922, becoming its first general secretary. Despite him nearing retirement age at fifty-nine, Churchill appointed him Minister of Labour in the wartime coalition government (1940–45). Attlee then took the inspired decision of appointing him Foreign Secretary in July 1945 and he became the most significant figure in that government. Attlee delegated policy to Bevin, whose achievements in office were vast, not least building a close relationship with the Truman administration in the US (in direct opposition to the far left's more natural ally, the USSR) and enticing them into a permanent peacetime role in Europe in the Cold War. He helped ensure Marshall Aid, following the £3.75 billion loan from the US in 1946, poured hundreds of millions of dollars into war-damaged Europe, and constructed a series of alliances across western Europe to challenge Stalin's Soviet Union, which culminated in the formation of NATO in April 1949, his greatest single achievement. Britain took the decision in 1946 to build an atomic bomb in part because Bevin argued, 'we needed a bloody Union Jack on top of it'. When the bomb was detonated on the Monte Bello Islands off western Australia in October 1952, Britain became, after the United States and the USSR, the world's third atomic power.

Without a figure of the stature, dominant personality and vision of Bevin, Britain might not have emerged from the Second World War in such a strong position internationally. Attlee was not without strengths and interests in foreign affairs. But he lacked the larger-than-life personality of Bevin, his understanding and confidence with foreign leaders, and it is hard to see how he would have achieved nearly as much on the foreign stage without him.

Attlee knew even less about economics, and left his three Chancellors of the Exchequer to run the Treasury largely unimpeded. His first, Hugh Dalton (1945–7), was an academic who had befriended J.M. Keynes at Cambridge, where he became a socialist. A junior minister under Ramsay MacDonald from 1929 to 1931, he was appointed by Churchill to his government in May 1940, who then promoted him to President of the Board of Trade (1942–5). At the last minute, Attlee switched him from Foreign Secretary to Chancellor. Once ensconced at the Treasury, Dalton introduced heavily progressive taxation policies and nationalised the Bank of England in February 1946, introducing a Keynesian economic policy aiming for full employment. The economy moved into trouble in 1947, with a run on the pound and a fuel crisis. Dalton's response was an emergency Budget in November 1947, when he leaked tax details to a journalist at the *Star*, and was forced to resign. He returned as a minister in May 1948, but never recovered the same authority.

Attlee worked closer still with his successor, Stafford Cripps (1947–50), who he trusted completely, and who proved an abler Chancellor. The appointment showed Attlee's pragmatism as, just months before, at the time of economic jeopardy in early 1947, Cripps had led the opposition to him, placing his leadership on the line. The intervention of Bevin was decisive in seeing off the threat.

Cripps puritanical philosophy informed his austerity policies. Needing to find substantial sums for the NHS and other social reforms, he drove growth via boosting production and exports, utilising many of the direct controls still in existence from the war. Appealing to the sense of collective good, another legacy of the war, Cripps persuaded the trade unions to accept a voluntary freeze on wage increases in early 1948, which held until 1950. Marshall Aid pumping in money from 1948 gave Cripps valuable financial leg-room, though he was still forced to devalue the pound against his will in September 1949. By the summer of 1950, Cripps had become so unwell that he had to resign, and he died that October. His greatest achievement was to steer post-war Britain to an economic recovery, harnessing the mixed economy to capitalise on the strengths of the public and private sectors.

Hugh Gaitskell was Attlee's final Chancellor. A gifted economist, he had become an MP only in 1945, but had risen fast, and was appointed as a junior minister at the Treasury after the 1950 General Election. Attlee trusted him, but Gaitskell lacked the weight in Cabinet of a Dalton or Cripps. He soon ran headlong into problems with sterling, even before being caught up in the fierce debate on how the government could pay for Britain's contribution to the Korean War, which started in June 1950. His Budget in April 1951 prompted the resignation of Bevan and Wilson, in protest at its health charges to pay for rearmament. Labour's defeat in the General Election in October 1951 cut short what might have been a promising chancellorship. Gaitskell went on to succeed Attlee as Labour leader in December 1955 until his death in January 1963.

Herbert Morrison, Lord President and Leader of the House of Commons from July 1945 until March 1951, when he became Foreign Secretary, was the last of the 'Big Five' (alongside Attlee, Bevin, Cripps and Dalton) to have held senior positions in Churchill's wartime coalition. The dominant figure on the London County Council in the 1930s, Morrison had been a major figure alongside Dalton in reshaping Labour's domestic policy. Appointed Home Secretary in October 1940, he was prominent in organising Britain's civil defence during the war, and latterly became a key figure determining Labour's post-war policy, which eventually bore fruit in the manifesto, *Let Us Face the Future*. Attlee relied heavily on Morrison's organisational flair for managing the House of Commons, overseeing the passage of domestic policy through Parliament, and knocking disputatious Labour politicians into shape. Without such a capable organisational genius, Attlee would have struggled to oversee such an unprecedented volume of legislation through the House of Commons. He missed Morrison when years of overwork resulted in him withdrawing for several critical months in 1947, which coincided with the beginning of the loss of momentum of his entire government. When Morrison returned to the fray in 1948, he became a major exponent of consolidation rather than pursuing further nationalisations.

Aneurin Bevan was Attlee's final star, and the only one of the Big Six not to have had ministerial experience. As Peter Hennessy points out, only one other Cabinet minister lacked ministerial experience. A Welsh MP since 1929, he made his name as a fierce critic on the left of the party, passionate about enhancing the lives of working people. As Minister of Health, he drove the legislation to create the NHS in July 1948, in the face of strong opposition from the medical profession, with free treatment for all regardless of income. The government's greatest single achievement had deep roots in plans drawn up before 1945. Attlee worked closely alongside Bevan to secure the passage of the legislation, which saw spending on health rise from 2.1 per cent of GDP in 1945 to 3.6 per cent in 1951. Great governments introduce reforms that endure: the status of the NHS at the time of writing in 2020, during the coronavirus outbreak, is stellar. Had Attlee's government achieved nothing else, it would still have been regarded as historic because of the NHS.

None of Labour's other five prime ministers, MacDonald, Wilson, Callaghan, Blair and Brown, had so much ministerial talent at their disposal. Harold Wilson came closest with Callaghan himself, Anthony Crosland, Richard Crossman, Denis Healey and Roy Jenkins. Attlee's pool of talent went beyond his big beasts: other stellar talent besides Wilson and Gaitskell included the Lord Chancellor, Lord Jowitt; Arthur Greenwood, the Lord Privy Seal; and Ellen Wilkinson, the Education Minister who died in unexplained circumstances in early 1947.

Throughout the war years there emerged a set of clearly worked-through plans for policy, which were undoubtedly popular with the electorate. The pause on domestic policy for almost six war years, too, created a significant momentum for change. Many prime ministers arrive at No. 10, such as Anthony Eden or Theresa May, with no very clear idea about what they are going to enact in office. Yet as Paul Addison argued in his seminal *The Road to 1945*, Churchill's need to bring the Labour Party into the coalition government had shifted the centre of politics to the left, ushered in five years of meticulous planning for social and economic policy for the post-war world, and gave the Attlee government its clear theme.

Social reformer William Beveridge paved the way in his seminal 1942 report for the creation of the Welfare State from the 'cradle to the grave', with a system of social security that went far beyond the Liberals' National Insurance Act of 1911. Labour's 1946 National Insurance Act instituted a system where those in work paid a flat rate of insurance and, in consequence, the contributors as well as their spouses became eligible for pensions, unemployment, sickness and funeral benefits, while child benefits were instituted for those with no other source of income. Attlee considered it his proudest achievement. The Attlee government's education policy, too, owed much to the coalition government's Act of 1944, while its family benefit policies owed much to its Family Allowances Act of 1945. Similarly, Labour's policy of full employment owed much to the work of economist J.M. Keynes, who was to die in 1946 before the fruits began to be felt. The twentieth century is littered with the names of puffed-up public intellectuals whose ideas were never enacted. Beveridge and Keynes were two giants whose ideas most certainly were.

Prime ministers need to be secure in office. The rapid momentum of legislation and aura of confidence and unity among his government meant that Attlee was largely free of challenge, unlike Labour's other five prime ministers, whose careers were dogged by divisions, particularly in their latter stages, when disappointment and factionalism became prevalent. Serenity is the fifth factor. Attlee's only moment of peril proved to be in 1947, precipitated by the financial crisis following the bad winter of 1946–7. But the moment passed and his only other turbulent period was the divided response to the Korean War, which led to three resignations (Bevan, Wilson and John Freeman). In total, Attlee had just eight resignations in over six years, a comparatively sparse total number compared to those that have peppered the administrations of most prime ministers. Suddenly, in those final months, Attlee's government began to lose its sense of collective purpose on foreign as well as domestic policy, with his critics arguing it was overreaching itself by trying to align too much with the United States (a lesson that Wilson absorbed with his refusal after 1964 to bow to US pressure to commit British forces to the Vietnam War, to the anger of President Johnson).

No prime minister, however able, can succeed if they lack a working majority. Battles in Parliament otherwise suck up all their time and damage clarity and momentum. But Attlee had emerged as the undisputed victor in the 1945 General Election, achieving 393 seats to the Conservatives' 197, the biggest margin in Labour's history. The size was significant not just in terms of parliamentary arithmetic, but in the overwhelming boost it gave to the morale of his fellow MPs and to Attlee's personal authority, as architect of the victory. The government remained popular, losing no by-elections from 1945 to 1951 (which Bew says Attlee listed as one of his personal achievements). Even after his second General Election victory in February 1950, which saw the majority cut to five (only three Labour PMs won more elections than they lost), he had a large enough majority to push ahead with Labour's 1950 manifesto.

Strong prime ministers need to be dominant and secure, and facing a strong leader of the opposition can undermine their authority, as John Major found when Blair became Labour leader in July 1994. Attlee was fortunate to have Churchill as his leader of the opposition throughout his period as prime minister, who was far from at his best. This is the seventh factor. Initially exhausted after the war, Churchill found that being an opposition leader was not his *metier*. He took long holidays in the south of France and was preoccupied with painting and his own books (he was heavily distracted with writing his six-volume war memoirs, the first being published in 1948). McKinstry describes him as 'a useless Leader of the Opposition until at least 1949'. Much of the job of preparing the Conservative Party's domestic policy fell instead to R.A. Butler, Education Minister (1941–5) during the war. Churchill was at his happiest after 1945 on the world stage, as when he travelled to Fulton, Missouri, in March 1946 to deliver his 'iron curtain' speech about the USSR and eastern Europe. His mind was on bigger matters than domestic detail. When he returned to power in 1951, his two priorities were, revealingly, 'red meat and not getting scuppered'.

Prime ministers who battle against the grain of popular and intellectual opinion do not succeed. Harold Macmillan and John Major increasingly waded through treacle, while Stanley Baldwin in the inter-war years and Wilson in the 1960s ran with it. So too did Attlee, which takes us to the eighth factor. As Bew memorably put it: 'what happened in 1945 was that Clement Attlee and the British people arrived on the same page in history'. His government nationalised some 20 per cent of the economy, a process eased by the poor state some of the industries were in after the war and by a broad consensus that public ownership was the way forward. In 1946, it created the National Coal Board, which brought the troubled coal industry under public control; in 1947, it nationalised electricity; and in 1948, it did the same with the railways and inland water, while the new British Transport Commission took over aspects of road haulage and road passenger transport. In 1949, gas was nationalised; finally, and more controversially, so were iron and steel in 1951. Further legislation secured greater rights for workers and unions, including the repeal of the Trade Disputes Act of 1927, which had declared unlawful secondary action as well as any strike whose purpose was to coerce the government of the day. A five-day working week for miners, pay increases for police, and better conditions for fire-workers were some of the many improvements. Revealingly, the Conservatives after 1951 left many of these economic and labour changes in place.

The government's domestic achievements rolled on and on, eclipsing those of all other governments. A New Towns Act in 1946 attempted to address overcrowding in major cities and led to the growth of suburbs and new towns. A massive programme of council housing and repair work after the German bombing was initiated and over a hundred thousand new homes a year were built from 1945 to 1951, ensuring affordable housing for many. The seminal Town and Country Planning Act in 1947 instructed county councils to develop comprehensive plans for the development of their areas of responsibility, while the Housing Act in Scotland in 1949 provided generous grants for new building in the Highlands and Islands. A 1949 Act created national parks, another major innovation.

Progressive policies included a Married Women Act in 1949 to give women equal rights in property, while a Criminal Law Act in 1950 sought to safeguard prostitutes within the law. For the first time, the restrictions preventing married women working in the civil service were removed. Homosexuality, though, was not decriminalised; this, and other liberal reforms, had to wait until Wilson's government in 1966–70.

To be successful, prime ministers need the economy to be strong enough to ensure that the government is not hurled off course. It was fragile for much of Attlee's time, as suggested by the 1949 devaluation lowering the dollar exchange rate from $4.03 to $2.80. But the government always found the money to enact its policies, and Churchill never managed to undermine the credibility of

Labour's economic policies. Good relations with the Chancellor are essential for historic premierships, as H.H. Asquith found with Lloyd George (1908–15), though as David Cameron's close bond with Chancellor George Osborne (2010–16) showed, they do not guarantee it. Attlee gained greatly from the loyalty and competence of his three Chancellors.

Churchill called Attlee 'superbly lucky'. Attlee benefited from that essential ingredient of all great premierships: luck. He was fortunate that Britain emerged triumphant from the war with its international standing high, and a programme of home policy waiting to be enacted. He was lucky to peak at the right time, when Labour was strong enough to secure its first parliamentary majority, but before the era of personality leadership set in a decade later. Fortunate too to be able to draw on the ideas of Beveridge and Keynes.

Attlee went on to lose the General Election in October 1951 to the Conservatives. While Labour secured over 200,000 more votes, the Conservatives won more seats, and achieved a majority of seventeen. Attlee, aged sixty-eight, was beginning to look tired and out of touch. His momentum began to be lost from 1947 to 1948, as the party divided between consolidators like Morrison, and the Bevanites, who wanted socialist reforms to continue in intensity. The party's intellectual rigour began to be expressed by a group of Labour MPs half Attlee's age, including Healey, Crosland and Roy Jenkins. They produced a collection of essays in 1952 called *The New Fabian Essays*, which showed how much the agenda had moved on. Had Attlee won in October 1951, it is hard to conceive that his legacy would have been enhanced.

Attlee remained as Labour leader, uncomfortably, until 1955. Born in 1883, the month before William Gladstone secured agreement to outlaw bribery in elections, he died in 1967, a month before Wilson devalued the pound. One of his last appearances in public, and the first national event on television that I recall, was Churchill's funeral in January 1965, at which he was a pallbearer. 'Who is he?' I asked. 'He was a good man,' I remember my father telling me. Indeed he was.

Judgements on his premiership will always be to some extent subjective. Did his policy of high public spending, full employment and a conciliatory policy towards trade unions thwart Britain's economic progress, which didn't enjoy the same economic growth as West Germany, Japan and the United States? Did his public school attachment prevent him from seizing the golden opportunity to reform public schools? Independence was granted to India, Pakistan, Ceylon (Sri Lanka) and Burma, but did his pressure for the British to quit in 1947 lead to massive avoidable deaths and difficulties that continue to this day? Did his decision to remove British forces from Palestine, which led to the formation of the state of Israel in 1948, cause the instability in the Middle East that persists until the present day? Did his decision that Britain should have its own atomic weapon give the country ideas of grandeur that it could no longer afford? Should he have responded more positively to the first stirrings of a European economic union? Why did so little happen in Africa under him, given his passion to turn Empire into Commonwealth?

What is in no doubt is that Britain emerged stronger, more socially just and united after the Second World War than Lloyd George managed to achieve after the Great War, a historical comparison of which Attlee was always very conscious. The quiet man has been more criticised than many prime ministers, from left as well as right. But we should smell the historical documents buried in the National Archives and understand how far-seeing, wide-ranging and ethical was the government led by Attlee. Most prime ministers achieve little, and even less endures. Attlee created modern Britain. His unique qualities, coupled with the other factors discussed in this chapter, explain why he was so successful. Their collective impact explains the unprecedented success of the Attlee premiership. Such a rare combination of factors is unlikely to recur, and it is very hard to envisage another.

Sir Anthony Seldon is Vice-Chancellor of the University of Buckingham and the author and editor of more than forty books on contemporary British history.

43

Sir Anthony Eden

6 April 1955 to 9 January 1957
Conservative

By Philip Norton

Full name: Robert Anthony Eden
Born: 12 June 1897, Windlestone Hall, Co. Durham
Died: 14 January 1977, Manor House, Alvediston, Salisbury.
Buried at St Mary's church, Alvediston
Education: Eton; Christ Church, Oxford
Married to Beatrice Beckett (divorced 1950), then Clarissa
Spencer-Churchill; 3 sons
Quotation: 'A property-owning democracy.' (Conservative Party
Conference 1946)

ANTHONY EDEN TOOK after his father, Sir William Eden. His
brother Tim said of their father: 'Nature had showered upon
him with an uncontrolled hand her gifts and her curses alike, and

without control he received them all, and without control he expended them.' Anthony Eden was defined by a life of potential greatness and regular grief, both personal and political.

He was born on 12 June 1897 into a well-established North Country family, but was starved of affection by his mother. His father was prone to rages. He had an unhappy time at Eton. His fortunes changed as a result of war and university. He was both brave and bright. The youngest adjutant in the British army in the First World War, he was awarded the Military Cross for his service on the western front. He went on to gain a First in Oriental Languages at Oxford. He entered Parliament as Tory MP for Warwick and Leamington in 1923, the same year that he married. The following year he became a parliamentary private secretary (PPS) to junior minister G. Locker-Lampson and, in 1926, PPS to the Foreign Secretary Sir Austen Chamberlain. He entered government in 1931 as Parliamentary Under-Secretary at the Foreign Office.

He was a rising star. In January 1934, he was appointed Lord Privy Seal, and the following year Minister without Portfolio for League of Nations Affairs, in effect identifying more precisely what was already his principal responsibility. He was, at the age of thirty-seven, given a seat in the Cabinet. The following year, after Sir Samuel Hoare's resignation over the Hoare–Laval Pact, he was promoted to replace him as Foreign Secretary. He appeared to be having an effortless rise, but in 1938 he resigned over Chamberlain's interference in his conduct over negotiations with the Italian dictator Mussolini. In the event, the resignation proved politically fortuitous. It established his reputation as an opponent of Chamberlain's policy. Although Chamberlain brought him back as Dominions Secretary the following year, and then as Secretary of State for War, he was not a casualty of Chamberlain's fall. When Churchill took the premiership in 1940, he put Eden back as Foreign Secretary, with a seat in the War Cabinet. He was essentially second to Churchill in the party hierarchy – Churchill in 1942 advised the King that in the event of his demise, he should send for Eden – the party's expert on foreign affairs. He had a good war politically in that, though a loyal lieutenant, he was not afraid to take a different view to Churchill, not least on the position of the Poles and of General de Gaulle in France, and often was proved right in his judgement.

He complemented Churchill in that, as Jonathan Schneer observed, Churchill had an eye for the big picture, but not for details. Eden, who spent time mastering details before a meeting, could see the trees, if not always the wood.

Although 1945 saw an end to the war, it was a tragic year for Eden. His beloved eldest son Simon, a pilot, died in action. His marriage existed largely now in form only and he was thrown into opposition by the 1945 General Election. He would not have been averse to becoming the first secretary-general of the newly created United Nations, but the post eluded him. He did not relish being in opposition, having to help restore the fortunes of the Conservative Party under a frequently absent and, in terms of domestic policy, disinterested leader. He could easily have left politics, not least to build his income, but he soldiered on and was able to draw on some able young men in the Conservative Research Department to develop fresh policy and revitalise the fortunes of the party.

When the Conservatives were restored to office in 1951, he was again Foreign Secretary. He achieved success in Geneva in 1954 in brokering a compromise on Indo-China and Korea, and in London on European security. It was during this time that he remarried. Having divorced in 1950, two years later he married Clarissa Spencer-Churchill, Churchill's niece, a marriage that proved successful and enduring.

He was Churchill's heir presumptive, seen as the golden boy of British politics. Selwyn Lloyd referred to 'Eden's brilliant diplomatic skills, his intuition, charm and ability to command affectionate loyalty'. His premiership was one of the most anticipated, both in terms of inheriting the mantle of office and in delivery. His followers grew increasingly impatient with Churchill's failure to give up the reins of office. On Churchill's reluctant retirement in April 1955, Eden was called to the Palace and kissed hands as prime minister. He was fifty-seven. He capitalised on his reputation by calling a General Election the following month, in which the party achieved an increased majority.

However, although an effective lieutenant, his temperament was unsuited to holding the highest office. He had difficulty delegating, was overly sensitive and was too convinced of the rightness of his own judgement.

He also suffered from bad health, physical and mental. A gall-bladder operation in 1952 went wrong – the 'knife slipped' – requiring further operations, leaving him with irreparable damage. He was prone to acute obstructive Charcot's intermittent fever. 'When Eden became prime minister he was technically not a sick man but his health was precarious, so that at moments of stress he became unduly irritable and suspicious, and his judgement showed some signs of impairment.' He was a prime minister at a time of crisis suffering from both physical ill-health and mental stress. 'The crisis came at the end of August 1956 when Anthony Eden suffered a high fever followed by periods of lassitude and agitation.'

The Suez crisis was the event that effectively destroyed his premiership, but he was already suffering criticism of his leadership. It was not long after he entered No. 10 that dissatisfaction started to be heard. 'Even before the Suez venture there were serious rumblings against Eden, and if he had not retired through ill-health after the Suez affair, it is most likely that he would have been forced out.' He was a poor manager of others. He interfered in departments. He had no experience of domestic policy and lacked a strong grasp of economics. He was indecisive. According to Reginald Bevins, he 'ought never to have been Prime Minister. His performance prior to Suez had been feeble. He forever temporised and chopped and changed his mind.' Rhodes James writes, 'As all reports from the constituencies indicated, there was much rank-and-file discontent with the Government . . . Again, there was much talk of indecision at the top.' Suez was the culmination of poor leadership rather than an exceptional instance of it.

The Suez crisis erupted in July 1956 when Egyptian president Abdul Nasser seized the Suez Canal company from Anglo-French control. Eden saw the action through the prism of the 1930s and was determined to stand up to Nasser. 'As Eden saw it, here was a challenge to international legality as flagrant and far-reaching as Hitler's reoccupation of the Rhineland. Twenty years earlier the lessons had been ignored; now there would be no excuses' (obituary, *The Times*, 15 January 1977). After attempts to reach a negotiated settlement failed, he responded to French pressure for military action and agreed, in talks with Israel and France, for Israel to invade Egypt and then for Britain and France to intervene as honest brokers, separate the combatants and take control of the canal. A majority of the Cabinet supported his proposal for intervention, *should* Israeli forces invade. There is uncertainty as to how specific Eden was in revealing what was already planned. The Israelis duly invaded and British and French forces intervened. The action encountered strong opposition from the Labour Party and some Conservative MPs. Macmillan recorded that 'The House of Commons was in almost continuous and often tumultuous session for nearly a week.' On 1 November, the sitting of the Commons had to be suspended for half an hour because of the uproar. On 20 December, Eden denied in the House any foreknowledge of Israel's intention to attack.

The action also attracted strong opposition from the international community, not least the United States. It was not unpopular with the public, but that was insufficient to sustain the government's position. Under American pressure, with the pound under threat, the government agreed to a ceasefire.

The event caused tensions within the parliamentary party. Eden attended no fewer than six packed meetings of the 1922 Committee. Harold Macmillan also attended one and, recognising what might happen, effectively made a speech that was interpreted as a bid for the party leadership. Eden himself was required to rest on medical advice and went to Jamaica to recuperate. When he returned, he suffered pains and his doctor, Horace Evans, was insistent that he could not continue, saying he would eventually kill himself, 'but before that he would collapse, possibly in about six weeks, certainly by Easter', a view confirmed by other doctors. On 9 January, he went to Buckingham Palace to give up his seals of office. He declined the offer of an earldom.

He went to New Zealand to rest, but had to return to the UK for more operations. After that, he retired to write his memoirs, and in 1961 he finally accepted an earldom, taking the title of the Earl of Avon. He made an occasional speech in the House of Lords, but he resisted calls, including from Charles de Gaulle, to return to active political life, preferring to travel and to winter each year in Barbados. As Clarissa Eden recalled, 'In spite of two further operations, twenty years passed easily and pleasantly.' In 1976, his health started to fail, and early the next year, while in Florida, his condition deteriorated and Prime Minister James Callaghan arranged for him to be flown home. He died a few months short of his eightieth birthday.

Clarissa Eden said memorably that she felt like the Suez Canal was flowing through her drawing room. Her husband was effectively drowned by it, but even before the crisis erupted there was evidence of him being out of his depth.

Philip Norton was elevated to the peerage as Lord Norton of Louth in 1998 and is Professor of Government in the Department of Politics at the University of Hull.

44

Harold Macmillan

10 January 1957 to 18 October 1963
Conservative

By Keith Simpson

Full Name: Maurice Harold Macmillan
Born: 10 February 1894, 52 Cadogan Place, London
Died: 29 December 1986, Birch Grove House, Chelwood Gate.
Buried at St Giles parish church, Horsted Keynes, West Sussex
Education: Eton; Balliol College, Oxford
Married to Lady Dorothy Cavendish; 1 son, 3 daughters
Quotation: 'The wind of change is blowing through this continent.' (Speech to South African Parliament, 3 February 1960)

IN 1978 I met Harold MacMillan at the Royal Military Academy Sandhurst. As an academic tutor in military history I had organised an exhibition on the First World War to commemorate the Armistice of 1918. Macmillan was invited to open as a former wartime Guards officer and prime minister. I met him when he arrived in the Commandant's staff car, and after he had met every Guardsman in the Academy I slowly took him round the exhibition. He was dressed in a rather old suit, with a cardigan and brown suede shoes, and wearing the distinctive Household Division tie. Due to his war wounds he had a slow shuffle and rather a weak handshake. He was a superb play actor and pretended to be doddery and rather deaf. Later after lunch in the officers' mess he entranced all the young officers by putting on his party piece reminiscing about his experiences as a young officer in the war. I watched him playing both the gownsman and the swordsman.

I had read Anthony Sampson's book *Macmillan: A Study in Ambiguity* when it was published in 1967. Although somewhat dated and not based on the documents and memoirs now available, Sampson managed to show the many-sided facets of Macmillan's background, character and political skills. Truly he was a study in ambiguity.

At sixty-three, Macmillan was a relatively old man when he became prime minister, and although he had striven hard to gain ministerial office, he had come to the red boxes after many years as a back-bencher, and there was no certainty that he would reach the top of the greasy pole. Macmillan came from a successful publishing family, only two generations away from being Scottish crofters. The business and literary background were important to him, and as a rather shy introverted child he took to books more than people. His mother was an intelligent and articulate American, although not an heiress. She was a powerful influence on Harold until her death in 1937.

Macmillan went to Eton but was invalided home and the College had less of an emotional attachment for him than his time at Balliol between 1912 and 1914. He adored the Balliol life but never completed his degree because, as he later said, he was sent down by the Kaiser. His mother obtained a commission for him in the Grenadier Guards and he saw service in France and was wounded three times. He spent the last two years of the war undergoing a series of operations. Macmillan had shown he was physically brave and he was deeply in awe of the Guards' way of service; like many young officers of his background, he also came up against working-class soldiers, many from very poor backgrounds.

After the war he served as an ADC to the Duke of Devonshire in Canada and married the Duke's daughter, Lady Dorothy. Although the marriage produced four children, Macmillan was humiliated by Dorothy's lifelong affair with his Conservative contemporary Robert Boothby, which began in 1929 and lasted until the 1950s. She was sexually insatiable and looked for satisfaction outside marriage. But she was a very supportive MP's wife and loved his first constituency. He had married into the Devonshires but was never comfortably at home with them, although by the time he had become prime minister he played up the connection for all it was worth.

Macmillan worked for the family publishing firm in the early 1920s before he was first elected as the MP for the working-class constituency of Stockton-on-Tees in 1924, which he lost in 1929 and regained in 1931 until 1945. A marginal seat, it played to his earlier Liberal sympathies and gave colour to his belief in Keynesian economics. During the 1930s Macmillan wrote pamphlets and books and was very critical of the National Government. He tended to work across parties and to use outside experts on economic and industrial policy. His time on the back benches in the 1930s is best remembered for his book *The Middle Way*, published in 1938, which advocated a broadly centrist political philosophy both domestically and internationally.

An anti-appeaser, Macmillan resigned the government whip in 1938. To his contemporaries in Parliament he was regarded as an eccentric back-bencher.

As he was later to tell Churchill, what brought them both to their ministerial offices in 1940 was Hitler. Churchill rewarded Macmillan for his support and gave him a series of junior ministerial offices until he was made Resident Minister in the Mediterranean. This was the making of him, and for nearly three years he flourished with direct contact with Churchill and Eden and all the senior British, American and Allied commanders and advisers. Macmillan blossomed and refined his diplomatic skills and social contacts.

At the end of the war in northern Italy, Macmillan was the minister advising the senior British officer there on the difficult relations with Tito and Yugoslavia, and an agreement included the forced repatriation of up to 70,000 prisoners of war to the Soviet Union and tens of thousands of White Russians and their families who had served with Germans on anti-partisan operations in the Balkans. These deportations and Macmillan's role became a source of controversy in the 1980s.

He lost his seat in 1945, but within a few months was elected in a by-election for the safe Conservative seat of Bromley. During the first Labour government he adopted a more right-wing persona. Churchill rewarded him in his government of 1951 by appointing him housing minister with the challenge to build 300,000 new houses. Macmillan relished the challenge and achieved the target by using outside experts and uncompromising wheeling and dealing over building materials.

While Macmillan was older and had not had as comparably stellar a career in the 1930s as Eden or Rab Butler, he showed he was a ruthless achiever. When Eden became Prime Minister, Macmillan was briefly Foreign Secretary and Chancellor of the Exchequer, and in the latter role was an ardent supporter of military action against Nasser over the Suez Canal in 1957. Despite his wartime work with the Americans, and particularly with Eisenhower, who was now the president, Macmillan completely failed to grasp American opposition to the adventure. It was American pressure on the pound that forced the government to cease hostilities, with Macmillan pointing out the economic dangers to the Cabinet. Suez was not his finest hour and he was to destroy his diary entries for the period.

But Macmillan survived the debacle and, when an ill Eden resigned, used all his theatrical skills and political and military reputation to beat Rab Butler to the leadership of the party as Eden's successor. To worried Conservative MPs and party managers, Macmillan exuded confidence and style and had had two good world wars.

There is no doubt that in the aftermath of Suez, Macmillan used all his political wiliness and ruthlessness to marginalise Butler, the acting prime minister, and leading heir apparent. Butler was left to carry responsibility for the Suez debacle, and when he and Macmillan addressed a meeting of the 1922 Committee on 22 November 1956, Macmillan swept all before him. He began to discreetly lobby ministers and back-benchers, making much of his confidence and style, and generally having had a good war – unlike Butler. Undoubtedly, he was helped by Edward Heath, the Chief Whip, and the Whips Office.

Macmillan was only too well aware of the challenges for his premiership. He told the Queen that the government would be lucky to last six weeks, and drew on his acting skills to give the impression of calm confidence after the hysteria of the Eden period. On his first evening as prime minister, Macmillan dined in style, taking Heath for champagne and oysters at the Turf Club. On the door of the Private Secretaries' room at No. 10, he hung a quote from *The Gondoliers*: 'Quiet, calm deliberation disentangles every knot.'

His first aim was to restore the confidence of his parliamentary colleagues and then to rebuild relations with the Americans. Although Macmillan was to promote in government able young men of a non-traditional background like Heath, Powell and Macleod, and to bring in outside experts, nevertheless he appointed thirty-five Old Etonians, seven of them in the Cabinet. Macmillan gave the impression of someone coming to terms with what would be called the affluent society while enjoying the old lifestyle of weekends on country estates, shooting parties and mixing with the aristocracy. He continued to give the impression that he was more right wing than he actually was and practised his genuine habit of reading favourite novels at every opportunity – Austen, Dickens and Trollope. For much of his premiership he operated out of Admiralty House while No. 10 underwent substantial renovation. He preferred to use Birch Grove, his country home in Sussex, rather than Chequers.

Macmillan loved the dignified aspects of being prime minister, and unlike many others took a great interest in the appointment of senior clerics and academics. In what was regarded as an eccentric whim, he agreed to have his name put forward and was elected as Chancellor of the University of Oxford.

Initially, Macmillan succeeded in presenting himself as a One Nation Tory. The economy appeared buoyant and the Labour opposition was divided under the leadership of Gaitskell. Although he was always very nervous before the event, Macmillan performed well at the dispatch box. Relations with the press were good and he used television to good effect. The cartoonist 'Vicky' tried to mock him by showing him as 'Supermac', but it played to his advantage.

In terms of policy, Macmillan's priorities were to continue to

develop the economy, seek high or full employment, and to implement further social reforms – the influence of Stockton-on-Tees
was to haunt him for the rest of his life. In foreign policy he repaired
the rift with the USA. He was to observe that Britain's relationship
with the USA was comparable to that of Greek slaves in the Roman
Empire.

Low unemployment and improving standards of living, particularly for the working class, meant that the 1959 election saw the
Conservative majority increase from sixty to a hundred seats.

But beneath the outward signs of victory and a full-term
Parliament were increasing signs of major difficulties. The economy
was not stable and the debate over how to control inflation saw
three treasury ministers resign over their proposals for spending cuts
and an acceptance of a rise in unemployment. Macmillan survived
this and gave the impression of calm ennui.

Reaffirming his strong support for a British nuclear deterrent, he
worked hard to obtain the necessary modernisation from the
Americans. When Kennedy won the presidency in 1960, Macmillan
quickly established a close personal relationship. This was helped by
the fact that Kennedy's sister Cathleen had married William Cavendish, Marquess of Hartington, the nephew of Macmillan's wife.

Macmillan spent a considerable amount of time travelling abroad,
to the Americas and the Commonwealth. In 1960 he embarked on
what became known as his 'Wind of Change' tour of Africa. With
Iain Macleod as his Colonial Secretary, he accelerated the process
of decolonisation, believing that if the costs of holding on to a
particular territory outweighed the benefits, it should be dispensed
with. This policy was criticised by many of his back-benchers.

Relations with Europe were crucial, and Macmillan decided that
Britain should join the European Economic Community. Despite
his best efforts and those of Edward Heath, the responsible minister,
President Charles de Gaulle vetoed the application in January 1963,
believing Britain was too close to the USA. Maybe de Gaulle
remembered what appeared to be his humiliation in North Africa
when Macmillan was there.

Macmillan was facing difficulties on every front. His own back-
benchers were divided over decolonisation and the approach to the
EEC; his attempts to negotiate a Test Ban Treaty with the Soviet

Union had met with limited success; and he was trying to give the impression that Britain was still an equal partner with the USA and the Soviet Union.

By 1961 the economy was in serious difficulties with a balance-of-payments crisis and labour unrest. The government lost a series of by-elections in 1962, and Macmillan, fearing for his own position, carried out a hurried major reshuffle, sacking eight ministers including the Chancellor. He had planned to make his Cabinet changes in an orderly manner after the summer recess. But he was bounced into an early reshuffle after Butler had, with his usual indiscretion, leaked the broad details to the proprietor of the *Daily Mail*, which were then splashed over the newspapers. Known as the 'Night of the Long Knives', far from shoring up Macmillan's premiership, it gave the impression of panic and disloyalty to his colleagues – he had changed from 'Supermac' to 'Mac the Knife'.

His image as an unflappable premier in control of events was shattered by a series of spy and sex scandals, including Kim Philby, the Profumo Affair and the Vassall Affair. Macmillan's government appeared to be incompetent and awash with scandal. With Harold Wilson succeeding Gaitskell as leader of the Labour Party, Macmillan faced a formidable opponent in the Commons.

Public opinion had changed with the downturn in the economy, and Macmillan appearing unable to master new social changes. He became the butt of a new generation of satirists on television, radio and in papers and magazines, and what appeared to be a relevant persona and image had become a caricature within three years. By January 1963, Macmillan's government appeared to be in meltdown and, increasingly, he was seen as an elderly Edwardian relic. By the summer, he was pondering his future and taking soundings on whether to resign or fight the next election, although by September he appears to have decided to stay and fight. Just before the Conservative Party Conference, Macmillan was struck down with prostate problems and operated on quickly. The impression given was that the operation was serious when in fact the problem was benign. His illness gave him the opportunity for a dignified exit.

From his hospital bed Macmillan orchestrated the emergence of his successor. He wrote a memo to the Queen recommending that soundings should be taken by the whips and senior party figures, who this time would consult back-benchers and junior ministers as well as Cabinet ministers. It was high theatre played out against the background of the Party Conference, with Macmillan determined to prevent Rab Butler from succeeding him. Macmillan's preferred candidate was Alec Douglas-Home, who had been Chamberlain's PPS and a loyal supporter of appeasement, and who duly emerged as a leading contender. Macmillan later believed that he needn't have resigned and felt he had been manoeuvred out by the media and ambitious colleagues, when in fact his prostate condition and indecision had made it inevitable.

Macmillan retired from the Commons in 1964 and initially refused a peerage. To his grief, Lady Dorothy suddenly died in 1966. In retirement Macmillan took up the chairmanship of Macmillan Publishers and was active in recruiting new authors. He wrote a massive six-volume autobiography, which read like an official history. Later, his wartime diaries of his time in the Mediterranean were well received. He continued as an active Chancellor of Oxford University until his death in 1986, and was a member of many clubs, including the Carlton, Buck's, Pratt's, the Turf Club and the Beefsteak, where, as a frequent diner, he revelled in his anecdotage. He continued to take an active interest in politics, and although he was not a keen supporter of Thatcher's economic policy, he was happy to have her literally sit at his feet in awe.

In his old age Macmillan appeared to be unsympathetic to Margaret Thatcher's monetarist policies and a rejection of his One Nation ethos. In his maiden speech in the Lords he criticised Thatcher's policy of handling the miners' strike, saying, 'This terrible strike, by the best men in the world, who beat the Kaiser's and Hitler's armies and never gave in. It is pointless and we cannot afford that kind of thing.' In a speech at a dinner in November 1985 he spoke about the sale of assets commonplace among individuals or states when they encountered financial difficulties: 'First of all the Georgian silver goes. And then all the nice furniture that used to be in the salon. Then the Canalettos go.' His speech was seen as a direct attack on Thatcher's policy of privatisation, although Macmillan later said he was questioning the use of the huge sums of money as if they were income.

In 1984 Macmillan requested and received a peerage from

Thatcher and spoke a few times in the Lords, once again the old actor/manager. In his last years he was almost blind and could only shuffle along with sticks. Devastated when his son Maurice, an alcoholic, died suddenly, Macmillan lived simply at Birch Grove and died in December 1986. His last words were, 'I think I will go to sleep now.'

Keith Simpson is a military historian and served as a Member of Parliament from 1997 to 2019.

45

Sir Alec Douglas-Home

19 October 1963 to 16 October 1964
Conservative

By Andrew Holt

Full name: Alexander Frederick Douglas-Home, later Lord
Dunglass (1918–51), Earl of Home (1951–63), Lord Home of the
Hirsel from 1974
Born: 2 July 1903, 28 South Street, Mayfair, London
Died: 9 October 1995, The Hirsel Lodge, Coldstream. Buried at
Lennel kirkyard, Scottish Borders
Education: Eton; Christ Church, Oxford
Married to Elizabeth Alington; 1 son, 3 daughters
Quotation: 'As far as the 14th Earl is concerned, I suppose Mr
Wilson, when you come to think of it, is the 14th Mr Wilson.'

ALEC DOUGLAS-HOME WAS the eldest of seven children born
to Charles and Lilian Douglas-Home, the future Earl and

Countess of Home. He followed a well-trodden path from Ludgrove School to Eton and up to Christ Church. At Oxford he did not excel academically nor show interest in the Union, but he did maintain a variety of pastimes. One of these was cricket, which he played to first-class level. Motivated by a sense of duty and a desire to expand his horizons beyond those of a country gentleman, Douglas-Home decided to pursue a career in public service.

Douglas-Home's political ambitions had been encouraged by the Conservative MP and intellectual Noel Skelton. Upon his election in 1931, Douglas-Home swiftly became Skelton's parliamentary private secretary. Five years later, he took on the same role for the Chancellor of the Exchequer, Neville Chamberlain, serving him loyally until 1940. Douglas-Home learned much from his time by Chamberlain's side at the Treasury and at 10 Downing Street. He admired Chamberlain's efficient, business-like approach, but he also observed the dangers of disagreement between prime minister and senior colleagues when Anthony Eden resigned from the government in 1938. The application of these lessons was noticeable during Douglas-Home's own premiership. Shortly after parting ways with Chamberlain, Douglas-Home underwent an operation to treat spinal tuberculosis. A previously active man, Douglas-Home found himself encased in plaster and would not return to the Commons until 1944. In his intervening convalescence he read widely and developed an interest in Russia. The 1945 Labour landslide saw Douglas-Home lose his Lanark seat. Although he won it back in 1950, the death of his father and resulting elevation to the House of Lords in July 1951 posed a seemingly insurmountable obstacle to him holding the highest offices.

Douglas-Home's rise through the ministerial ranks began with the support of James Stuart, a confidant of prime minister Winston Churchill. After working under Stuart at the Scottish Office, Douglas-Home continued to enhance his reputation while serving as Eden's Commonwealth Secretary from 1955. Further promotion followed, but Harold Macmillan's decision to appoint Douglas-Home as Foreign Secretary in 1960 was controversial. The *Daily Mirror*, for example, commented that the 'ludicrous selection' would 'reduce the British Foreign Office to a laughing stock in the capitals of the world'. Douglas-Home's firmness and general sure-footedness won over many doubters. By December 1962 he was being mentioned as a possible successor to Macmillan. This speculation was informed by the increasing likelihood of constitutional change. A member of the House of Lords would not be accepted as prime minister. Labour leader Hugh Gaitskell had called Douglas-Home's appointment as Foreign Secretary 'constitutionally objectionable', and such sentiment would be magnified if a peer sought the keys to No. 10. Help in removing this obstacle came from an unlikely source: the 2nd Viscount Stansgate, Anthony Wedgwood Benn, better known as Tony Benn. Like Douglas-Home almost a decade earlier, Benn was forced to vacate his seat in the House of Commons upon inheriting his father's peerage in 1960. His energetic campaign for a change in the law led to the passage of the Peerage Act 1963, which allowed hereditary peers to disclaim their titles.

In October 1963, Macmillan was admitted to hospital and subsequently resigned. The events that led to Douglas-Home's premiership thus played out against the backdrop of the 1963 Conservative Party Conference. There were three initial leadership candidates – and Douglas-Home was not among them. The position of the Chancellor, Reginald Maudling, was already weakening, and a lacklustre conference speech saw him fall further out of contention. This left the moderate and experienced deputy prime minister, Rab Butler, and the more unpredictable and right-wing leader of the House of Lords, Viscount Hailsham (Quintin Hogg). Hailsham did little to conceal his ambition, rushing to announce his intention to renounce his peerage. Soon his supporters were wearing 'Q' (for 'Quintin') badges and Hailsham was being photographed feeding his baby daughter in what some considered to be a publicity stunt. ('Never discount the baby food,' Edward Heath later reflected.) Butler followed Maudling in failing to take the opportunity to impress at the podium, but he had already been passed over for the leadership twice and aroused feelings of mistrust within the party. His moment had passed. Douglas-Home's star, meanwhile, had been rising. He had impressed colleagues with his ministerial performance and was popular with grassroots party members. While he was seen to be on the Conservative right, he did not provoke hostility from the opposite wing of the party.

When customary 'soundings' of MPs and other senior Conservatives were taken, it was Douglas-Home who emerged as the preferred candidate. Yet his ascent remained uncertain without the backing of senior colleagues. Maudling agreed to remain as Chancellor and Butler accepted the post of Foreign Secretary. Had either refused to serve, Douglas-Home would have been unable to form a government. He remained somewhat reluctant, but his belief in duty and his feeling that he had something to offer led him to accept the call. The 14th Earl of Home became prime minister as a member of the House of Lords – the first to do so since Salisbury, and almost certainly the last – and then held office without a seat in either house. He returned to the Commons after renouncing his title and then winning a by-election on 7 November 1963. The manner of his 'emergence' as leader cast a long shadow. It was dredged up again when Iain Macleod, a former Cabinet minister turned *Spectator* editor, wrote of a 'magic circle' of Old Etonians, led by Macmillan, plotting to deny Butler the succession.

Douglas-Home knew upon coming to office that he would soon face a General Election, limiting his room for manoeuvre. His administration introduced two domestic reforms of significance. First, it restricted the right of manufacturers to set retail prices for their products through resale price maintenance (RPM). This was not a universally popular move, with small shopkeepers particularly hostile. Edward Heath, the President of the Board of Trade, guided the Resale Prices Bill through Parliament with the Prime Minister's support. Second, Douglas-Home helped establish procedures for contact between opposition leaders and civil servants ahead of a General Election. With the Conservatives in power since October 1951, the lack of government experience at the top of the Labour Party aroused some concern among senior officials. It was also known that Harold Wilson was considering major changes to the machinery of government, particularly in the economic sphere. Douglas-Home agreed to private conversations taking place between Wilson and the head of the home civil service, on the basis that the talks were discreet and that Douglas-Home himself knew nothing of them. The arrangements became known as the Douglas-Home rules and facilitated deeper contact between the opposition and civil service ahead of subsequent elections.

The new prime minister also had to contend with an unsettled international environment. Little over a month after Douglas-Home took office, US president John F. Kennedy was gunned down in Dallas. Douglas-Home struggled to establish a close personal bond with the new president, Lyndon Johnson. A dispute over the sale of Leyland buses to Castro's Cuba proved particularly troublesome and culminated in Johnson waving dollar bills at Rab Butler during an April 1964 meeting, suggesting that he would pay for the buses himself if Britain was so desperate for trade. Other issues had their origins in colonial matters. In December 1963 the British government intervened to prevent additional bloodshed between the Greek and Turkish communities in Cyprus, which had only been independent since 1960. Douglas-Home was unable to resolve the situation in Southern Rhodesia, where a white minority government sought independence while continuing to disenfranchise the majority black population, though he did manage tensions there with some skill. The impending election had a clear impact on decision making, with the government reluctant to make controversial choices such as whether to fully commit to the multilateral nuclear force (MLF), a means of giving European countries greater involvement in nuclear policy making.

Douglas-Home decided to go to the country in October 1964, by which point the Conservatives had been in power for thirteen years. The Profumo Affair had rocked the government and Maudling's 'dash for growth' had resulted in a growing balance-of-payments deficit. Reverting during the campaign to an area where he felt most at home, Douglas-Home focused on the retention of the UK's independent nuclear deterrent. The issue failed to resonate with the public however, and the Prime Minister's weaknesses were exposed. He struggled on television and suffered at the hands of hecklers. He had an especially difficult time at an event at the Bull Ring in Birmingham just a week before polling day. Despite all of this, he still led his party to within a few seats of victory. The Conservatives won 304 seats (down from 365) and Labour 317 for a majority of just four.

Douglas-Home did not immediately stand down as Conservative leader. He reformed the process for selecting his successor by putting the decision to a ballot of MPs – a system that was used to elect subsequent leaders through to William Hague in 1997. Macleod and Enoch Powell also returned to the front bench. It was nevertheless clear that Douglas-Home was not well suited to leading the opposition, and mounting disquiet with his leadership eventually resulted in his resignation in the summer of 1965. He was succeeded by Heath, who reappointed Douglas-Home to the Foreign Office in 1970.

In a ministerial career spanning almost three decades, Alec Douglas-Home was prime minister for less than a year. Sandwiched between Macmillan and Wilson, his premiership is frequently overlooked. The shortness of his stint in office makes it difficult to place him in the pantheon of prime ministers. As an administrator he was calm and measured, and he was highly effective as chair of Cabinet. He streamlined the Cabinet committee system and trusted his colleagues to do their jobs. He also avoided any major missteps of the kind that came to define Chamberlain and Eden. His achievements were limited, however. He was restricted by the forthcoming election, but the abolition of RPM was a modernising measure (albeit one driven by Heath) and he managed international affairs carefully. In comparison with Wilson, he suffered from his lack of experience of domestic matters and in economics especially. He was never able to live down a 1962 interview in which he said he did his sums with matchsticks. He was also ill suited to the media age and the rambunctiousness of the modern campaign. Yet he was widely appreciated for his straightforwardness and decency. It was these qualities, his essential assets, that helped bring him so close to victory in 1964.

Andrew Holt is a historian of twentieth-century British politics and foreign policy, and author of The Foreign Policy of the Douglas-Home Government: Britain, the United States and the End of Empire.

46

Harold Wilson

16 October 1964 to 19 June 1970;
4 March 1974 to 5 April 1976
Labour

By Rachel Reeves

Full name: James Harold Wilson
Born: 11 March 1916, Huddersfield
Died: 24 May 1995, London. Buried at St Mary's Old Church on the Isles of Scilly
Education: Royds Hall Secondary School, Huddersfield; Jesus College, Oxford
Married to Mary Baldwin; 2 sons
Quotation: 'This party is a moral crusade, or it is nothing.' (Speech to Labour Party Conference, 1 October 1962)

HAROLD WILSON IS the only leader of any political party since Gladstone to have won four General Elections. That he did so while holding together Labour's warring factions during one of the party's most intense periods of division is all the more remarkable. He kept British troops out of the Vietnam War, in the face of sustained pressure from a US president desperate for just one symbolic 'platoon of bagpipers'. And he is perhaps the prime minister who came closest of any post-war leader to settling the question of Britain's relationship to Europe. As Bernard Donoughue, who worked for Wilson, put it: where Ted Heath had 'taken the British establishment into Europe', Wilson 'would take in the British people'. And his governments helped create a country that was more liberal, more egalitarian, and more social-democratic – in which the rights of women and minorities were extended and protected by law, and educational opportunity was more equally distributed.

Yet in our collective memory, these years are less associated with the achievements of those Labour governments than with the cultural, structural and ideological tensions building within society. The 'swinging Sixties' giving way to the 'Seventies crisis', giving way in turn to Thatcher and the neoliberal revolution.

But in the 1960s and 70s, behind the pipe-smoking, HP-sauce image he cultivated, Wilson defied the political odds and, although he failed to transform an economy in decline, he shaped British society and culture in ways we still feel now. And he really was popular, at least for a while. Today, to have voted for a winning Labour leader whose name wasn't Tony Blair, you would have to be in your mid-sixties.

Wilson was born in 1916 in Huddersfield, West Yorkshire. He was a product of West Yorkshire and of Merseyside, where he moved as a teenager. His Yorkshire roots ran deep: Ben Pimlott notes that parish records trace his family line back as far as the fourteenth century to the North Riding of Yorkshire, right through to the late nineteenth century. And he was conscious to cultivate the image of the everyman.

His political career spanned from 1945 to 1976, and his background and education before entering Parliament made him in some senses an embodiment of that era. His career path was the model of post-war social mobility: from grammar school, through Oxford and an extraordinary level of academic success, followed by the civil service, working for Sir William Beveridge, and then Parliament. His northernness resonated with a sense that the North represented the beating cultural heart of a forward-looking Britain. As the historian Raphael Samuel reflected, in the popular imagination,

> the North in the 1960s . . . was definitely Mod, and on the side of radical change. It offered itself as an idiom for the degentrification of British public life. In place of an effete Establishment it promised a new vitality, sweeping the dead wood from the boardroom, and replacing hidebound administrators with ambitious young go-getters . . . As projected by the Prime Minister, a professional Yorkshireman whose accent allegedly thickened when he had a Labour Party conference to address, it was also a gauge of authenticity.

For his PPS Peter Shore, 'what Harold Wilson offered was not just an image but to some extent also the reality of a modern man . . . He knew what the modern world was all about.' He was a prime minister uniquely suited to a time of anti-establishment revolt, facing off against a third successive Old Etonian Conservative prime minister, after over a decade of Tory government. As the Labour MP Philip Whitehead observed, 'Wilson's bustling style was a deliberate contrast to the gentlemanly amateurism of . . . Alec Douglas-Home. The message of socialism was transmuted into that of modernity.'

The ambiguity around Wilson's politics – left-wing radical or technocrat, idealist or pragmatist – means that he appears a contradictory figure; some might say slippery. He was in many ways Labour's most intellectually gifted leader while also consciously anti-intellectual. Thus, for the historian Geoffrey Foote, his 'contempt for theory and public debate . . . makes it difficult to weigh Wilson's contribution to Labour's political thought. He was too responsive to party and popular moods while in opposition to have many fixed principles, while his concern with administration in government gives his record in office a sense of endurance rather than innovation.' And his place within the Labour Party was equally ambivalent. His political trajectory saw him move from a left-wing rebel, and a close supporter of Aneurin Bevan after 1945, towards a more ambiguous position as the party's leader in the 1960s. He provided one of the most famous statements of Labour's ethical character, telling the 1962 Labour Party conference that the Labour Party 'is a moral crusade, or it is nothing'. But Barbara Castle would later complain that Wilson 'always sold the left down the river'.

To understand the central role of planning to Wilson's vision and electoral appeal is to understand, equally, his greatest disappointment. Wilson took over a Labour Party that had not only spent more than a decade out of power – it had also been in majority government for just six years out of its six decades of existence. The period in power under Attlee's leadership had transformed Britain, but by 1950, the party was intellectually and politically exhausted. For the Victorian generation of politicians who led through most of the first half of the twentieth century, their work was complete. The gains of 1945–50 had delivered New Jerusalem. By the end of Attlee's time in office, most of the architects of Labour's post-war project were deep into their sixties; several were dead.

Labour was left questioning its purpose in a new society that was increasingly understood in terms of 'affluence', with Anthony Crosland's *Future of Socialism* representing the most ambitious attempt to redefine Labour's purpose for this new era. Wilson made his pitch in slightly different terms. As the historian James E. Cronin recounts, rather than arguing – as Crosland did – for Labour to adapt to a society that had already undergone a profound transformation, Wilson's argument for harnessing technology and planning in pursuit of growth 'was in a curious way a perfect reflection of a society and an economy poised on the brink of transformation but not as yet experiencing it'. This was the key to Wilson's electoral appeal. Planning thus became 'a vehicle for modernising both society and the party, a programme that gave Labour a more persuasive claim to national leadership and that linked the party's fortunes with the waxing influence of science and technology'.

His famous 1963 conference speech was a masterful articulation of exactly this worldview. It is perhaps the single greatest statement of a sentiment that Labour has captured whenever it has succeeded: the harnessing of modernity, of modern values, methods and technology in service of equality and social justice. Famously, Wilson proclaimed: 'we are redefining and we are restating our Socialism in terms of the scientific revolution. But that revolution cannot become a reality unless we are prepared to make far-reaching changes in economic and social attitudes which permeate our whole system of society.' A new Britain would 'be forged in the white heat of this revolution'.

However, despite the 'heat', when it comes to economic modernisation, Wilson's legacy is ultimately one of roads not taken. The National Plan, guided by the new Department of Economic Affairs, was supposed to spearhead the modernisation of the economy and head off Britain's relative economic decline. Blind faith that the National Plan would end a culture of complacency and conservatism within British business proved misplaced, and the DEA found itself marginalised by the Treasury. With Britain's growing balance-of-payments crisis and dire warnings from the Bank of England, a deflationary Budget in 1966 sounded the death knell for the National Plan. It was a huge disappointment and a hammer blow to Wilson's central policy programme. Many of Wilson's internal critics believed that a devaluation of the pound earlier in his premiership – in response to the appalling balance-of-payments deficit he had inherited – might have saved his economic programme. When he finally did concede to pressure to devalue in 1967, it was yet another symbolic blow to the government's already battered economic aspirations.

Meanwhile, in response to growing industrial unrest, and particularly the increasing number of unofficial 'wildcat' strikes, Barbara Castle produced the trade union reform white paper *In Place of Strife*. By the standards of today, after the waves of trade union legislation introduced by the Conservatives after 1979, its proposals appear extremely modest. But opposition by trade unions and by key figures in the Cabinet, including Jim Callaghan, meant it was fatally undermined, and its key provisions never implemented. Having come to power promising to deliver a significant 'modernisation' of the British economy, the party left office with industrial tensions mounting. When it returned to power in 1974, it was in large part based on the promise it could deliver a period of social stability after the Heath government's unhappy spell in office, characterised by industrial unrest, the 1973 oil shock, and growing tensions within British society. The means of doing this was to be the 'Social Contract': essentially a corporatist agreement between government and trade unions, in which government offered to enact certain economic and social policies, in exchange for voluntary wage restraint, to curb soaring inflation without large-scale industrial unrest. Crucially, this avoided the need for a statutory incomes policy.

In the year leading up to Wilson's resignation in 1976, this appeared to be having the desired effect as inflation decreased, despite rising unemployment. However, increasingly, after Callaghan's ascension to the premiership, the unions – and particularly their grassroots – grew frustrated. There was a strong sense that government was not delivering on its side of the bargain, as Callaghan and his Chancellor Denis Healey implemented substantial cuts to public spending. Ultimately, these tensions would boil over in the so-called Winter of Discontent, delivering a fatal blow to the Callaghan government and paving the way for historic defeat for both the party and the labour movement in the 1980s. The failure of the Wilson/Callaghan governments to deliver either the 'irreversible shift in the balance of wealth and power in favour of working people' promised in the party's two 1974 manifestos, or to resolve the growing industrial tensions that spilled over in the Winter of Discontent, paved the way for Margaret Thatcher's assault on the Welfare State and trade union movement. These governments transformed British society in ways that seemed unthinkable a matter of years before. Had the grand promise of modernisation-through-planning been realised and had Castle succeeded with her industrial relations reforms, it is not impossible to imagine that British politics, and British society as a whole, might have taken a very different course.

A more successful set of reforms were in education. In his 1963 conference speech, Wilson had called for 'a revolution in our attitude to education', to enhance equality of opportunity and to harness the talents of everyone. Social mobility was Wilson's story. He wanted to expand those opportunities to other children in Huddersfield and across the country. Wilson promised what he called 'a university of the air', in order 'to provide an opportunity for those who, for one reason or another, have not been able to take advantage of higher education'. And he was clear that this was a vision of education to provide opportunity, boost Britain's economy and enrich 'the cultural life of our country' alongside material living standards.

The Open University was, for Wilson, his proudest achievement. The minister to bring it to life was Jennie Lee, widow of the former Labour Health Secretary, Aneurin Bevan, with whom Wilson had resigned from the Cabinet in 1951 over dental charges in the NHS. As historian Philip Ziegler recounts:

> If there was one success story during his time in office which gave him unequivocal satisfaction, it was the Open University . . . Wilson had told Callaghan even before he became prime minister that this was going to be one of his priorities and that he would need money for it, and he jealously defended it when every other sacred cow was suffering in the crises of 1965 and 1966 . . . It's easy to see why it appealed to Wilson: his reverence for academic achievement and his genuinely egalitarian instincts both attracted him to a project which would extend the joys of Oxbridge . . . to a class which had hitherto been denied them.

Back in his 1963 'white heat' speech, Wilson had promised an end to the 'educational apartheid' of grammar schools and secondary moderns, as a matter of both egalitarian principle and economic necessity. The appointment in January 1965 of Anthony Crosland as Secretary of the State for the Department for Education paved the way for a revolution within schools policy. Crosland was unambiguous in his intentions. As he told his wife Susan: 'If it's the last thing I do, I'm going to destroy every fucking grammar school in England. And Wales. And Northern Ireland.' Crosland turbo-charged the drive towards comprehensive education, linking the provision of funds to local councils for new schools and buildings to concrete proposals for reorganising schools along comprehensive lines. Between 1962 and 1970 the proportion of pupils educated under the comprehensive system increased from 10 per cent to 32 per cent. By 1974, nearly two-thirds of young people were taught in comprehensive schools. It is in education that the Wilson governments came closest to achieving something consistent with his vision of a more modern, equal and dynamic society.

The changes taking place within British society during Wilson's premiership amounted to something like a 'cultural revolution'. Perhaps not what you would expect from a man who was, in some respects, instinctively conservative in his own taste, outlook and appearance. As the historian Steven Fielding reflects, this was a period in which 'the viability of what many took to be immutable identities and divisions based on class, gender and ethnicity was widely questioned'. It was a time during which 'Britain's civic culture was . . . reconfigured and placed on a more "modern" . . . basis, one notably bereft of deference. It was . . . an invigorating moment for those individuals challenging the status quo and a painful one for figures in authority.' Wilson was, to a considerable extent, both: he sought to channel a sense of the outsider rebel with a modern outlook, while at the same presenting himself as somewhat homely and conventional. He was the first prime minister to master the television, he celebrated The Beatles, and he took a modernising approach to almost every part of British economic, social and cultural life. But at the same time he was – and revelled in the image of – 'an instinctive conservative, with an unbridled admiration for the Queen and Winston Churchill, and the institutions of Oxbridge, Parliament and State . . . [an] intensely, almost parochially, patriotic Englishman . . . [and] the consciously provincial, pipe-smoking, *Coronation Street*-watching, Huddersfield Town supporting, beer-drinking everyman'.

We should be wary of reading cultural change as being all in one direction. Wilson's time in office saw the rise of Powellism and a wider backlash against the apparent challenge to the existing social order and its associated hierarchies. University expansion created a new generation of young radicals prepared to challenge every aspect of society, but this was a small minority. Despite this, Wilson's governments – thanks, in no small part, to the role of Roy Jenkins as Home Secretary – delivered a transformative wave of liberalising legislation: the decriminalisation of homosexuality and of abortion, the abolition of the death penalty, the Race Relations Act, and the liberalisation of divorce law.

If these gains are taken for granted today, for decades afterwards they were regarded by many on the right of politics as emblematic of Britain's decline. In reality, it is clear that the legacy of the Wilson government's reforms transformed the lives of millions of people and paved the way for further expansion of personal freedoms.

All of this was taking place at a time of acute uncertainty about Britain's place in the world, with increasing worries about economic decline and industrial unrest, alongside the complex geopolitics of the era of the Cold War and decolonisation. The decision to withdraw from Britain's imperial commitments east of Suez represented a logical continuation of the mindset that had prevailed since the late 1950s.

Critically, there was the question of Britain's response to America's war in Vietnam. The United States was desperate for the British government to commit troops to the conflict, in order to convey legitimacy on a disastrous war that would cost huge numbers of lives and derail Johnson's presidency. Wilson was not necessarily guided by high principle; as ever, party management played a central role in his response. The party was divided on the crisis and on the politics of the Cold War. As the historian Rhiannon Vickers observes, for the left, the Vietnam War was an anti-colonial struggle; but for many of the party's leading figures, it represented part of a struggle against communism. At the same time, the party was split over the centrality of the 'Special Relationship' to UK foreign policy, with parts of the left keen to weaken ties with the United States.

Peter Shore stressed the limited room for manoeuvre the Prime Minister was presented with: 'It is extremely hard to imagine any Labour leader resisting very strong American pressure so successfully. Enormous efforts were made by the Foreign Office, the Treasury, the Americans to get Britain wholly to identify with the war and to express this with a military presence.' Therefore, for Vickers, 'Wilson's policy of giving the United States moral support . . . while resisting the pressure to send troops did not fully satisfy either the anti-Vietnam lobby within Britain or President Johnson, but it was, perhaps, the most realistic policy option at the time.' Wilson's approach to the issue might have been shaped as much by low politics as by high ideals, but it is true that he stood his ground, and avoided embroiling Britain in a catastrophic military misjudgement. Other prime ministers have not been able to resist such pressures.

Beset by a floundering economy and a difficult relationship with the White House, Britain looked enviously upon the rapid growth and strong productivity enjoyed by the member states of the Common Market. After the failure of the National Plan, the revisionist right in the Labour Party, grouped around Roy Jenkins, increasingly saw Community membership as *the* essential solution to Britain's ills. However, the party and the wider labour movement were bitterly divided over the issue. Even in 1962, Labour's arch-revisionist leader Hugh Gaitskell had disappointed many of his closest allies by refusing to contemplate EEC entry, telling party conference that membership would entail 'the end of Britain as an independent European state . . . It means the end of a thousand years of history.'

Although not an instinctive Europhile – he preferred the Isles of Scilly to Tuscany – Wilson pursued entry to the Common Market, seeing membership as a way to re-invigorate the British economy. For his press secretary, Joe Haines, it was the experience of devaluation in 1967 – 'the biggest hurt and biggest shock of his life' – which convinced Wilson that entry was the right policy. However, Britain's application for entry in 1967 was rejected. When Heath successfully negotiated entry in 1971, Wilson struck a delicate balance, with party management once again taking precedence: while the party's official position was to oppose entry on Heath's terms, entry was secured with votes from Labour rebels led by Jenkins. When Labour returned to power in 1974, Wilson again prioritised party management, promising first a renegotiation of Britain's terms of entry and then a referendum. Wilson's careful positioning – supporting, on balance, the renegotiated 'Labour terms' of membership – played a key part in securing an overwhelming vote to remain within the Community. Wilson, in the end, is the post-war prime minister who came closest to resolving the question of Britain's relationship with Europe for longest. In hindsight, we should not underestimate that achievement.

The Wilson governments stood out for the depth of talent and experience on Labour's front benches. This included more women than ever. Figures like Jennie Lee, Alice Bacon and Judith Hart, and, most famously, Barbara Castle and Shirley Williams, joined the ministerial ranks. The former Labour MP Leah Manning believed that Wilson had 'given more chances to women to prove their ability than any other prime minister in history'.

These figures formed part of a generation of Labour politicians distinguished by their depth of talent and experience. This is obvious when we look at the names put forward in the 1976 leadership contest – Foot, Callaghan, Healey, Jenkins, Benn and Crosland. That list excludes, for instance, Castle, Williams and the recently deceased Richard Crossman. Between them, these politicians accumulated a huge wealth of experience and a long list of achievements. In fact, the profile and status of his ministers leads Wilson's own gifts to be under-appreciated. As Philip Ziegler notes, Labour's top team 'was intellectually streets ahead of anything the Tories could offer', and Wilson managed this through an approach emphasising '"creative tension", a healthy rivalry between ministers and the evolution of policy by rational argument and the eventual victory of the stronger case'.

However, these talents were never fully harnessed. Egos, factionalism and growing ideological tensions got in the way. Wilson had to be, as Joe Haines called him, 'the party manager supreme'. For Ziegler, 'given the personalities involved it was inevitable that the tension would often be destructive rather than creative'. The presence of such esteemed characters also makes it more complicated to assess Wilson's own legacy. Perhaps no other government has seen fewer of its achievements attributed directly to its prime minister. The gains for social liberalism are generally attributed to Jenkins as Home Secretary. The Open University is seen as an achievement for Jennie Lee. The large expansion of comprehensive education is credited to Crosland. Yet, as we have seen, the governments' educational agenda was a priority established by Wilson in his very first conference speech, and he ensured that the liberal reforms were political priorities – given time in Cabinet and in Parliament and money to see them through to fruition. But often, if 'Wilsonism' is seen as anything, it is reduced to the failed attempt to successfully pursue planning, or to an unprincipled and increasingly paranoid form of party management.

This would be unfair. Wilson was steering a course through rocky waters, managing widening tensions within the Labour Party while struggling to come to terms with a profound sense that Britain was entering a state of 'crisis' or even 'ungovernability'. At the exact moment Labour seemed to come closest to establishing itself as something resembling a 'natural party of government' – winning four out of five elections – there was a profound sense of pessimism about the sustainability of the party's electoral base, the ongoing viability of Keynesian social democracy, and even the durability of British democracy. In this context, the Labour Party found itself divided – on its relationship to Europe; on the future of industrial relations; on public spending; and on the appropriate response to the country's economic performance. Wilson left behind a party that was still, just about, holding together, with the economy showing gradual improvement. Soon after he left office, it all came apart. We should not judge too harshly a prime minister who kept the show on the road for the previous thirteen years. Given all that came afterwards, Wilson deserves considerable credit.

Rachel Reeves is Shadow Chancellor of the Duchy of Lancaster and has served as the Member of Parliament for Leeds West since 2010. She is the author of Women of Westminster: The MPs Who Changed Politics *and* Alice in Westminster: The Political Life of Alice Bacon.

47

Edward Heath

19 June 1970 to 4 March 1974
Conservative

By Wilf Weeks

Full name: Edward Richard George Heath
Born: 9 July 1916, 2 Holmwood Villas, Albion Road, St Peter's, Kent
Died: 17 July 2005, Salisbury. Buried at Salisbury Cathedral
Education: Chatham House Grammar School, Ramsgate; Balliol College, Oxford
Unmarried
Quotation: 'It is the unpleasant and unacceptable face of capitalism but one should not suggest that the whole of British industry consists of practices of this kind.' (House of Commons, concerning the Lonrho affair, May 1973)

UNDER A GREY summer sky that threatened rain, six men guided a rustic cart through the gates of Ted's beloved Arundells. Bearing Sir Edward Heath's coffin draped in the Union Jack, it crossed the Close to Salisbury Cathedral's Great West Door. A congregation of friends and former colleagues filled the nave, among them Lady Thatcher in deepest black. It was a far cry from the small house in the Kentish seaside town of Broadstairs where Heath was born in 1916.

His father, William, was a carpenter who went on to run a successful building company. He was a popular easy-going man and very different from his wife Ethel, who had been a lady's maid and was correct, prim and proper. She was so close to Teddy that neighbours saw him as a mother's boy, and she exerted a strong influence on her growing first son.

Teddy turned out to be a bit of loner and a swot, spending hours in his bedroom with his books. When his parents were persuaded of his musical talent, they scraped together the £42 needed to buy an upright piano on hire purchase.

When it came to Ted's brother, John, Ethel thought he should learn the violin so that he could accompany Teddy on the piano.

Bookish boys usually succeed at school and Teddy was no exception. He won praise from his headmasters and teachers, who spotted his talent and promise. He rose to become head boy at Chatham House.

Ted went up to Oxford in 1935 with his mind already set on a career in politics. It was at his college, Balliol, where he made one of his lifelong friends, Madron Seligman. He was considered genial and well liked, and gained a reputation for efficiency and organisation. In his second year he won an organ scholarship, which relieved his tight finances. His ambition was to scale the heights of The Union, and before he left Oxford, he reached his goal of becoming President.

It is impossible to write about Ted and not to mention his voice and the way he pronounced his vowels. His contrived accent combined with his distinctive heaving shoulders and laugh meant that, in time, he would cut a very recognisable figure.

Four weeks after Munich, Heath broke his loyalty with Chamberlain. During the famous Oxford by-election, he stood under the much-criticised slogan 'A vote for Hogg is a vote for Hitler'. It was a brave stand for an ambitious young man to take.

Heath's travels in Europe before the war had a profound effect on his views for the future. In 1937 he visited Germany, stopping in Dusseldorf, Frankfurt and Munich, which enlightened his understanding of the coming threat to democracy.

Much to his surprise, he received an invitation to attend a Nazi rally in Nuremberg. Sitting in a gangway seat, he almost felt Hitler brush his shoulder as he passed, and at an SS cocktail party after the rally he met Goebbels and Himmler.

One more long vacation took him and his friend, Madron Seligman, to Danzig and Warsaw. The British Embassy in Warsaw warned them to leave Poland immediately. They hurried back to England, arriving safely only two days before Britain declared war on Germany.

For Heath the war got off to a very slow start with endless training and preparations. At the end of hostilities, he was mentioned in dispatches and awarded an MBE before being demobbed in August 1946.

Shortly after the war he met Kay Raven, the local doctor's daughter. They had a lot in common and shared a great love of music. She was devoted to the Heath family and they thoroughly approved of her, but the couple's relationship floundered – he didn't want to commit, and she got tired of waiting.

By then Heath was impatient to get into Parliament and when the Bexley seat was looking for a candidate, it was just where he wanted to be. When the election came in 1950, Heath won by only 133 votes. In his maiden speech he raised his belief that Britain should go into Europe and lead it.

In the 1951 election he increased his majority and was appointed as a junior whip. This was the beginning of a nine-year stint in the Whips Office, where he rose through the ranks to become Chief Whip. However, there was no opportunity in the Whips Office to dazzle his colleagues from the dispatch box. Instead, he built a reputation as an outstanding organiser behind the scenes.

Heath demonstrated great skill during the Suez crisis, maintaining the loyalty of bewildered back-bench MPs superbly, an achievement recognised by the majority of his contemporaries. When Macmillan took over from Eden, he and Heath formed a strong partnership. Macmillan liked to talk, and Heath was a good listener. After the 1959 election, Heath entered the Cabinet for the first time.

The following year he was appointed Lord Privy Seal, with a special responsibility for Europe, and so began Heath's life mission to achieve Britain's membership of the EEC.

General de Gaulle believed that the UK wasn't European enough to make a good member and so he vetoed its membership for a second time, claiming that Britain was different from the other countries of continental Europe. Heath hated losing, and he and his colleagues were determined not to be put off the European project.

All this time Heath had been living in a flat the size of a shoebox in Petty France, St James's, until a friend recommended the palatial Albany just off Piccadilly. In April 1963 he was awarded the Charlemagne Prize for his contribution to European unity. The previous winners had been Churchill, Adenauer, Monnet and Schuman. With the proceeds, Ted bought a Steinway grand piano, which remains at Arundells, his last home in Salisbury, to this day.

As Conservatives gathered in Blackpool in the autumn of 1963, Harold Macmillan was taken ill and forced to stand down. The Conference developed into the hustings for the main candidates. The undemocratic way in which Alec Douglas-Home had been chosen was ridiculed to such an extent that it increased the prospects of Heath emerging as the victor in any future contest.

The leadership election was held within a year of the Conservative defeat at the 1964 General Election and Heath held off challenges from Reginald Maudling and Enoch Powell. His election marked a revolution in the history of the Tories, but he had inherited a demoralised, divided and unhappy party. From his early days as leader, Heath failed to get either his personality or message across. He was hopelessly wooden on television and suffered from relentless criticism, mostly from within the party.

The more he was criticised, the more defensive, tense and withdrawn Heath became. But the loyal team around him kept the show on the road.

Heath never enjoyed the wholehearted enthusiasm of his own back-benchers and at the next conference Conservative MPs could be heard asking whether they had made a terrible mistake.

The 1966 election was as crushing as the polls predicted and Labour piled up a majority of ninety-six. Although Heath took defeat well, the whingers made the most of their disappointment and of the daunting prospect of how long a haul it would be to the next election. By now many Tory MPs believed that their leader despised much of his own party.

It was also in 1969 that Ted bought his first boat, and in no time he was commissioning his next one, *Morning Cloud*, to be built on the Medway. He kept the same name for all four subsequent boats. In 1969 he put together a crack crew and persuaded them to enter the 640-mile Sydney Hobart Yacht Race. *Morning Cloud* won. It was a tremendous achievement, which captured the headlines, and was perfect timing for good publicity with an election not far away.

Ted Heath had few friends, but the ones he had were very important to him. Among them were several strong women who were not afraid to stand up to him. Sara Morrison was just such a friend. She was one of the few people who could tell Ted when he was behaving atrociously. She was his best, strongest and most candid friend, who understood his odd sense of humour and would always answer him back. They talked constantly on the telephone and, like all his other friends and colleagues, she experienced the line going dead when he had finished the call. There was never a 'goodbye'.

There was a strong element of sheer stubbornness in Heath's character. The more he was criticised, the less ground he would give to his critics. His confidence that he would win in the end was sustained by an immediate circle of loyal supporters who admired his courage, integrity and humour, among them Jim Prior, Douglas Hurd and Willie Whitelaw. He inspired great loyalty in those who worked closely with him, a loyalty that was repaid though never in a demonstrative way. But even to those closest to him he remained a puzzle and an enigma.

The Cabinet and senior Tory officials gathered in January 1970 at Selsdon Park Hotel in south London. The resulting policy platform was portrayed as a lurch to the right and it turned the spotlight on Tory policies. After a pretty awful time in opposition, at last it was a good week for Heath, and for the first time since 1966 Conservative politicians were convinced that they could win.

The problem with Selsdon Park was that Heath allowed himself to be identified with ideas and attitudes that were not really his own. By doing this he encouraged expectations among the right that he was bound to disappoint. Fatally, he ended up falling between two stools, committing the mistake of permitting himself to be thought to have more radical intentions than in fact he had. Heath's failure of government stemmed from this confusion.

As the June 1970 election approached, the polls showed Heath losing. Those around him admired his confidence when everything seemed to be slipping away. When Heath won, the result of the election was the greatest upset in British politics since the Attlee victory of 1945. *The Times* claimed that Mr Heath was going to Downing Street full of 'authority to govern and command' and in Heath's words, 'To govern is to serve.'

But in no time the optimism of the new administration was shattered by the heart attack and death of the Chancellor, Iain Macleod. It is impossible to over-estimate the impact this had on the prime minister and his colleagues. It could be argued that it rates as one of the greatest political tragedies of the twentieth century. It was certainly a bitter personal blow to Heath, who since 1965 had learned to place great trust in the wisdom and judgement of Macleod. We shall never know, but the Heath/Macleod Downing Street partnership could well have been one of the great political double acts of the century. MacLeod was simply irreplaceable.

Tony Barber was Macleod's successor, but he lacked the critical strength and independence of thought that would have played such an important part in Macleod's influence on Heath.

One of the most successful Whitehall innovations introduced at the time was the so-called Think Tank, led by Victor Rothschild. The introductory meeting, like so many with Ted, was full of long pauses, which he didn't appear to mind, but it always made the other person or people involved in the conversation feel distinctly uncomfortable.

President de Gaulle had resigned in April 1969, reopening the chance to reverse the French veto on EEC membership. The new president, Pompidou, would turn out to be the key to success. He and Ted warmed to each other from the beginning and built a very successful relationship. Indeed, Douglas Hurd suggested that winning the President round was probably the single greatest feat of Heath's premiership. When it came to the vote in Parliament, those in favour had a majority of 112. Heath naturally wanted to celebrate and appeared at the requisite round of parties. He then went back to No. 10, where he played Bach's First Prelude and Fugue on his clavichord, surrounded by a few of his closest friends.

A traumatic year for the Heath government was to come in 1972. Suddenly there were problems across the board: unemployment hit a new level, the miners went on strike and there was a new wave of bombings in Northern Ireland. Power cuts meant that Cabinet meetings were held in the dark and babies were born by candlelight. The miners' strike of 1972 led directly to the second strike of February 1974. Attempts to bring the communities together in Ireland were shattered when, on Bloody Sunday, thirteen demonstrators were shot dead by paratroopers in Londonderry. It was to Heath's credit that he grasped the nettle and introduced direct rule.

After endless discussions with the trade unions and the CBI, the government had to admit defeat and abruptly carried out a U-turn on statutory pay policy. As the problems piled up, Heath responded to each crisis with drastic measures, announcing the three-day week and a wider range of power restraints. This was the background to calling the 'Who Governs Britain' election of 1974, set for 28 February – one in which the Conservatives emerged with 297 seats, 4 fewer than Labour. Despite garnering 6 million votes, the Liberals only managed to win 14 seats. Many of Heath's colleagues thought that if they had gone to the polls three weeks earlier, they would have won. They believed that having declared a state of emergency, they needed to act more urgently. An attempt to negotiate a coalition with the Liberals failed and Heath was forced to resign.

That year, 1974, was proving to be a dreadful one for Heath, and there was more to come. On 3 September, *Morning Cloud 3* sank in a gale in the English Channel. Tragically, two members of her crew were drowned, including Ted's godson, George Chadd.

Heath had fought four elections and lost three. He would have been wise not to offer himself for re-election, as many of his friends agreed, but this was Ted at his stubborn worst. Supported again by Toby Aldington, he put his name forward. When nominations closed on 30 January 1975 there were three runners: Heath, Thatcher and

Hugh Fraser. Thatcher won on the second ballot and the day after-wards received a frosty reception when she made a courtesy call on Heath at Wilton Street.

Heath was then offered a platform to lead the 'in' campaign in the European Referendum. His main argument for staying in the Community was, as always, that Britain would be left behind by history if it chose to come out. This was Heath at his campaigning best.

However, Ted felt deeply hurt that neither he nor his government were ever referred to by the new administration. It was as if he was being airbrushed out of history. Although this of course helps to explain his extreme sulkiness, it remains impossible to excuse the graceless way in which he behaved. Despite an occasional, knowing twinkle in his eye, he made his own life infinitely more difficult and became an easy target for his critics.

In 1977, Robert McNamara of the World Bank was appointing members to the independent Brandt Commission, and Heath was an obvious choice. He liked his fellow Commissioners and enjoyed the status of the group. The report at the end of the enquiry made quite a splash and the North–South dialogue became an important part of Ted's message in his programme for survival in relation to global challenges.

Heath found it particularly difficult to get around to writing his memoirs. So, when a couple of publisher friends suggested he should write books on different aspects of his life, he took up the challenge more enthusiastically. In what seemed a very short time, he produced illustrated books on sailing, travel and music, and a slim volume on Christmas carols. The inevitable signing sessions that accompanied their publication all over Britain were a huge success. A grinning Heath could be seen surrounded by piles of books to sign and chatting to his audience. He was never happier.

These were uncomfortable times in the political world, but Heath remained loyal to the Conservative Party. He was never tempted to join the SDP and every year after he lost the leadership he attended the annual party conference. He would stay in the best hotel in the area and invite journalists to a series of dinners throughout the week.

Life continued to disappoint and delight. In his bid to succeed his old friend Macmillan as Chancellor of Oxford University, he was beaten by Roy Jenkins. But in time he inherited the title of Father of the House as the longest-serving MP and he was very proud to be made a Knight of the Garter by the Queen. Like Winston Churchill, he decided to remain in the Commons for the rest of his political life.

Heath's search for a home was finally resolved in 1985 when Robert Key, the MP for Salisbury, and his PPS, suggested Arundells, a beautiful eighteenth-century house in the Close. Ted was smitten and immediately abandoned his dream to live by the sea. It was the first house he had owned, and he was, justifiably, very proud of it.

Every year Ted celebrated his birthday in the garden, inviting his friends to join him. At what was to be the last party in 2005, he was barely able to leave his bedroom to join his guests. However, he eventually appeared being wheeled around by his carer Stuart Craven.

A week later he died.

Wilf Weeks served as private secretary to Edward Heath and is a public affairs consultant.

48

James Callaghan

5 April 1976 to 4 May 1979
Labour

By Lewis Baston

Full name: Leonard James Callaghan
Born: 27 March 1912, 38 Funtington Road, Portsmouth
Died: 26 March 2005, Ringmer, East Sussex. Ashes scattered at Peter Pan statue, Great Ormond Street Hospital
Education: Portsmouth Northern Secondary School
Married to Audrey Elizabeth Moulton; 1 son, 2 daughters
Quotation: 'We used to think that you could just spend your way out of a recession and increase employment by cutting taxes and boosting government spending. I tell you in all candour that that option no longer exists and that insofar as it ever did exist, it worked by injecting inflation into the economy.' (Conference speech, 28 September 1976)

CALLAGHAN (HE WAS 'Len' rather than 'Jim' for the first decades of his life) was born among the dense terraces of Portsmouth. His naval officer father, of an Irish Catholic and Jewish background, changed his name from Garoghan to Callaghan when he joined the navy in the 1890s. His mother was from Devon. She imbued him with many West Country Nonconformist habits of thought and speech – in radicalism and puritanism, and in a knowledge of hymns and the Bible that stayed with him all his life even though he abjured religion in the 1930s. His father died when Jim was aged only nine, making him one of many political leaders with paternal loss in his background.

Looking back, he was deeply disappointed in his secondary school education; although he was bright enough to have gone to university, the family simply could not afford it. He took the civil service exam and joined as an Inland Revenue clerk in 1929. He moved to Maidstone to work and was increasingly active in the clerks' trade union, elected national assistant secretary of the Inland Revenue Staff Federation (IRSF) in 1936, and serving under general secretary Douglas Houghton. He joined the Labour Party in 1931, then the Fabian Society, and read a wide range of socialist authors of whom his biographer, Kenneth Morgan, records Harold Laski as being the biggest influence.

The labour movement gave him the education that he felt he had been denied as a boy. His values were formed by this interaction of West Country radicalism, trade unionism, Fabianism and his own experiences. He was never drawn to communism. He described himself in the 1990s as 'original Labour', not 'New' or 'Old', and he was right.

Callaghan was the last prime minister whose political identity was forged by wartime service. He applied to the Royal Navy in 1940 and was finally allowed to join up in 1942, serving until 1945 in a fleet based in the Indian Ocean. He was encouraged by IRSF colleagues to seek a parliamentary nomination and was selected for Cardiff South, although he had no previous connection with the city. The dockland constituency was a patchwork of communities, including the pre-Windrush black and multi-ethnic working-class area of Tiger Bay. Callaghan gained it in 1945 and represented it, through several boundary changes and a lot of urban redevelopment, until 1987.

He was a hard-working but unexceptional junior minister in the later years of the Attlee government, a party loyalist rather than a combatant in the Bevanite/Gaitskellite conflict, but came to prominence during opposition in the 1950s. He was appointed Shadow Colonial Secretary in 1957 and developed good relations with the leaders of the independence movements, based on his belief in racial equality, democracy, independence, and economic and cultural partnership through the Commonwealth. He became Shadow Chancellor in 1961 and stood for the party leadership in 1963 after the death of Gaitskell. He polled forty-one votes in the ballot, coming third behind the more divisive figures of Harold Wilson and George Brown ('everybody's second choice and nobody's first,' he groused).

Callaghan did not have a happy time as Chancellor between 1964 and 1967. He had to fight a turf war with George Brown's Department of Economic Affairs over economic policy, and had been hobbled by the early decision not to devalue the pound. This meant being imprisoned within the 'stop–go' fluctuations of policy even while the government tried to lift growth in the National Plan. His tax reforms had a rough passage through Parliament. Eventually, he had to devalue in 1967 and was transferred across to the Home Office. His time there is known mainly for his overt opposition to Wilson's proposed *In Place of Strife* reforms of industrial relations, and his decision to send the British army into Northern Ireland in August 1969.

During Labour's troubled period in opposition between 1970 and 1974, Callaghan became Shadow Foreign Secretary – reflecting the party's turn towards Euroscepticism, he made a strikingly crude nationalist speech in 1971, but when Labour returned to power, Callaghan as Foreign Secretary helped renegotiate EEC membership and win the 1975 referendum for staying in.

His high-level ministerial career gave Callaghan the distinction of having served in all three 'Great Offices of State' before he became prime minister, the only premier to be quite so experienced on taking office. He came to No. 10 late in life, aged sixty-four, four years older than the man he replaced.

Callaghan succeeded to the office of prime minister after Harold Wilson announced his resignation on 16 March 1976 and triggered a leadership contest. Callaghan, the incumbent Foreign Secretary, entered the contest as the heir apparent and had been given a few days' head start by Wilson. Five other members of the Cabinet stood – Tony Benn and Michael Foot to the left of Callaghan, Roy Jenkins clearly to the right, and Tony Crosland and Denis Healey whose position is harder to classify. The election took place over three rounds of balloting among Labour MPs, and on 5 April 1976 Callaghan won the final ballot by the relatively close margin of 176–137 over Foot. He took office later that afternoon.

In a relatively short premiership, Callaghan encountered two major crises. The first was the IMF crisis that dominated the second half of 1976; the second was the wave of strikes in early 1979 that was dubbed the 'winter of discontent'. His handling of the first was masterful, but the second was mismanaged and born of his own miscalculations.

Callaghan inherited a precarious political position. Labour had won an overall majority of three seats in October 1974, and this disappeared on the very day that Callaghan became prime minister. Callaghan's prime ministership was therefore dominated by the tense parliamentary situation, worsened by the divisions within the Labour Party. Rather as the Eurosceptics operated as a party within the Conservative Party for the thirty years after 1990, the Labour left in the form of the Tribune Group virtually had its own parliamentary whip and had the support of most of the constituency parties.

With this limited stock of political capital, Callaghan had to address a menacing economic situation; the pound was sinking on the international markets, the budget was heavily in deficit and an inaccurate analysis that suggested that the state accounted for 60 per cent of GDP had been published by the Treasury. Spending cuts failed to satisfy the markets, while antagonising the Labour Party membership and the trade unions, who had pledged to hold down pay increases in the 'Social Contract' on the understanding that the government would deliver improved social conditions. The economic crisis, combining inflation and rising unemployment, was hard to understand and confounded conventional economic analysis. Callaghan and Chancellor Healey turned to some unfamiliar instruments, such as control of the money supply, and Callaghan told a hostile Labour conference in 1976 that the option of fiscal stimulus was not available – his words were written by his economist son-in-law Peter Jay.

After a long series of Cabinet debates and some heated international diplomacy, agreement was reached with the IMF in December 1976. This meant harsh cuts in public spending – investment in public services never really recovered. But sterling bottomed out, and by the late 1970s, with rising North Sea Oil production and increased confidence, the pound risked becoming dangerously high. The IMF loan was repaid early. The economy grew steadily, even strongly, throughout the Callaghan years – there have only been two years since 1978 when GDP growth has been stronger.

Callaghan sacrificed a lot of political capital to solve what was essentially a confidence problem, but it was hard to see a realistic alternative at the time. His Cabinet management was sufficiently skilled that no members resigned from that very ideologically broad, able and potentially truculent Cabinet, four of whose members had stood against Callaghan in the leadership election. He was adept at letting ministers have their say, playing left and right off against each other, waiting and occasionally bullying people to a conclusion. There was no inner Cabinet in Callaghan's time. For good or ill, it was as close as we have got to the ideal model of Cabinet government.

The two central relationships throughout Callaghan's government were with Denis Healey as Chancellor and Michael Foot as Leader of the House of Commons, neither of them Callaghan intimates in the past. Healey was doing the dirty work of keeping the economy on track, Foot was the loyal negotiator with the left and the smaller parties in Parliament who kept the government in business. From March 1977 onwards, the other relationship was with David Steel, the Liberal leader, whose parliamentary support in the Lib–Lab Pact gave the government eighteen months of relative stability during which Callaghan was a successful prime minister.

Jim Callaghan's working-class conservative personal and political temperament met the mood of the time, following two self-conscious reformers in Wilson and Heath. His personal style was calm and courteous, with but the occasional flash of irritability. His metaphors and references drew on a reassuring – self-taught – shared English literary culture; he taunted the Tories for bringing back

MPs 'from Far Cathay' for a tight parliamentary vote. It would have sounded wrong from anyone else. He was a good-humoured uncle about contemporary fashions, posing balanced on a skateboard in the year of the craze (1978), but his own culture was older. When he teased the TUC with the idea that he might not call an autumn election in 1978, he sang, 'There was I, waiting at the church . . .' and credited the song to Marie Lloyd. Callaghan knew well that it had actually been sung by Vesta Victoria, but he was shrewd enough to realise that most of his public would not get the reference.

'Jim is a populist,' Cabinet minister Bill Rodgers told journalist Hugo Young in 1977. 'He is conscious of this, welcomes the description.' Callaghan was comfortable among trade unionists, business people, Labour stalwarts: 'what he cannot abide is the long-haired intellectual and all his works'. While not an instinctive progressive, Callaghan was on the liberal side in the key votes on social reforms of the 1960s and was the Home Secretary who abolished theatre censorship and took the death penalty off the statute book. His conservative instincts led him to start a 'Great Debate' on education with his speech at Ruskin College in 1977, focusing on standards rather than structures and teaching methods, which had dominated the progressive argument for two decades. His attitudes to crime were similarly governed by his identification with the interests of the respectable, aspirational working class, and his respect − sometimes ill-founded given that the police and other forces of the state did not behave well in the 1970s − for the forces of law and order. He was a communitarian rather than an individualist, less a New Labour prototype than what Blue Labour tried and failed to become.

Callaghan's populism stopped short of the point where that implies a distrust of experts. He valued a neutral, professional civil service. Always sensitive about the limits of his knowledge and when he needed to expand them, he recruited experts to help him − from the Nuffield College group, who helped him prepare for the Treasury in the 1960s, to his capable Policy Unit in No. 10. His closest political supporters were often unimaginative Labour and trade union tribalists, but his policy makers were experts.

The decision not to have the election in autumn 1978 was Callaghan's fatal error. It was a wrong decision, but not a stupid one; without the benefit of hindsight, the arguments on each side were finely balanced. But Callaghan suffered from his own version of the hubris that descends on prime ministers in time. The likely outcome in 1978 would have been a hung parliament and the need to keep the Liberals and various nationalists and Unionists sweet, and he was tired of hung parliaments.

On top of this, Callaghan tried to renew the government's incomes policy for another year, asking for no more than 5 per cent pay rises. But first the skilled workers of Ford revolted (and Parliament voted against sanctions against Ford for settling the pay claim at 17 per cent), then lorry drivers, then public sector workers in the winter of discontent. The NHS and basic services were severely disrupted in January and February 1979, and the disputes were conducted with a meanness of spirit that profoundly distressed Callaghan as a union man. The government lost its way until it and the Trades Union Council (TUC) signed a concordat on the auspicious date of 14 February. It promised working towards reducing inflation to 5 per cent by 1982, and raised the possibility of no-strike agreements in some services, but it never had the chance to bed down because the Parliament was running out of time and the Callaghan government was losing its will to live.

The government's position became much worse after the devolution referendums of 1 March. Wales voted solidly against, and Scotland's 52–48 Yes vote was insufficient under the Scotland Act. It might have been possible to cobble something together to keep the SNP on side, or buy a few more votes from Northern Ireland, but Callaghan was tired and fatalistic. The government lost a vote of no confidence by 311 votes to 310 on 28 March 1979 and a General Election followed.

Callaghan was Labour's greatest asset in the campaign; his personal popularity had taken a hit during the winter of discontent, but he was still preferred as prime minister over Margaret Thatcher by double-digit margins. Labour recovered support during the election campaign, but started too far behind and lost the momentum at the end. Callaghan himself was listless and ambivalent. Some of his aides wanted him to fight a tough negative 'broken bottle' campaign, but he did not want to shed his statesmanlike image in order to, at best, deprive Thatcher of an overall majority. Part of him felt that he had let the nation down. It was in this mood that he made his famous comment about a 'sea change'. But an offhand remark burnished into a lapidary quotation is not an infallible guide to the politics of an era, and the result would have been very different in October 1978, and probably, given that every month's distance from the winter of discontent helped Labour, if the Labour whips had pulled out the stops and gone on until October 1979.

The election result of May 1979 was decisive. The Conservatives won with a clear majority. Labour had done particularly badly among skilled working-class voters in the south who had lost out from incomes policy and were attracted by Thatcher policies such as council house sales (a policy that had been considered by Wilson's Policy Unit but dropped under Callaghan). It was sad and ironic that Callaghan's premiership came to an end because he had alienated the people from whom he had come, because he could not manage relations with the trade unions he loved, and because he had tried to build a consensus that collapsed into bitter class conflict.

Callaghan's year as leader of the opposition was inglorious. He had hoped to give the party breathing space to reunite, but its divisions had become even worse by the time he announced his resignation in October 1980. He served a final term between 1983 and 1987 as Father of the House, after 1984 being the last MP in the House who had served continuously from the Attlee landslide to the middle Parliament of the Thatcher ascendancy.

When historians and politicians try to draw up league tables of prime ministers, Callaghan tends to be ranked in the middle of the table, perhaps slightly further than halfway down the list. The historical reputations of tail-enders like Callaghan, Brown, Douglas-Home and Major tend to be dominated by the problems that led to electoral defeat, rather than the crises successfully handled or the policies developed. Tail-enders, by virtue of their experience in office and the wiliness that gets them into position as designated successor, have particular merit in keeping governments together in difficult times and steering past dangerous rocks. But they are accused of being stale *fin-de-régime* leaders. However, they all had visions of broader horizons, different from their predecessors and successors. Callaghan's 1979 manifesto envisaged North Sea Oil revenues fuelling industrial modernisation and public sector investment, and a tripartite collaboration between government, business and unions to set the framework. It was a promise of Scandinavian social democracy. The question was whether British institutions could deliver such an outcome. Callaghan, the small-c conservative man of 1945, thought they could, but thanks to his risk taking in 1978 and his fatalism in 1979, he never got the chance to test the proposition. It was a road not taken, not a dead end.

As a chief executive, Callaghan was clearly a 'good' prime minister – his management of Cabinet, the mutual trust he enjoyed with Healey, Foot and Steel, and his consistently high ratings with public opinion are testament to that. He was well regarded by his international contemporaries, and instrumental in establishing what is now the regular series of G7 summits; he was as successful as anyone has been at keeping the three circles of British foreign policy (Europe, Commonwealth, transatlantic) in harmony. If one assesses Callaghan on his worst moments, he was a poor prime minister (although he did not have the opportunity to make amends). But taking his time in office in the round, he was a dependable, competent, honest and realistic captain of the ship of state. He had an unusually choppy passage to navigate, and did it with skill. Callaghan was not a great prime minister. But he was a good one.

Lewis Baston is a writer on elections, politics and history.

49

Margaret Thatcher

4 May 1979 to 28 November 1990
Conservative

By Julia Langdon

Full name: Margaret Hilda Thatcher, née Roberts, later
Baroness Thatcher of Kesteven
Born: 13 October 1925, 1 North Parade, Grantham
Died: 8 April 2013, The Ritz Hotel, London. Buried at the
Royal Hospital, Chelsea
Education: Kesteven and Grantham Girls' School; Somerville
College, Oxford
Married to Denis Thatcher; 1 son, 1 daughter
Quotation: 'You turn if you want to. The lady's not for turn-
ing . . .'

THERE WAS A certain symmetry to the rise and fall of Margaret
Thatcher as prime minister. It was a surprise that she got the

job in the first place and it was startling how she lost it. She became the first woman prime minister quite unexpectedly, and in the course of the ensuing eleven years won two more General Elections, both by a landslide. During this time she had established herself as one of the most successful, influential and best-known politicians on the face of the earth, and then, having never lost a vote – either in the House of Commons or at a General Election – she was precipitously dispatched from office totally against her will and to the complete astonishment of much of the British electorate and the other leaders of the watching world. She ended her extraordinary political life in the same manner as she began it: as a woman alone.

She was a woman who had stood alone, among men, to become leader of the Conservative Party. Against expectation, she had then won her first election to become prime minister and thereafter she governed with a single-minded determination which enhanced her individual authority with every passing year. She fought to establish an enterprise economy in the United Kingdom, to limit the expansionism of Europe, to control inflation and trades unions, to improve East–West relations in the post-Cold War world, and to bring about an end to White colonial rule in Rhodesia, apartheid in South Africa and a terrorist war in Northern Ireland. She sent the Royal Navy to the South Atlantic to fight a war against Argentina on behalf of the British territory of the Falkland Islands.

Thatcher did not only display courage in taking on established interests. She survived a number of attempts to assassinate her, by guerrillas who tried to shoot her plane out of the sky over Malawi ('Fortunately they missed', she wrote with airy dismissiveness in her memoirs) and, most notably, by the IRA in Brighton, who failed to kill her but (to her great distress) succeeded over the years in murdering a number of her colleagues. Her list of achievements is remarkable, not least because she embarked upon so many challenges against the better judgement of her ministers, her officials and often in the teeth of public opinion. And what distinguishes her primarily in these successes of her term as prime minister is not, actually, that she secured these results as the first woman in the job, but because her motivation in almost all circumstances was that she refused to accept defeatism.

She did not do any of this, of course, without making a great number of enemies. She was widely disliked in many quarters because of her personality and her policies. She was regarded with a degree of patronising snobbery by some intellectual elites, exemplified by her being refused – by a vote of two to one – the award of an honorary doctorate by Oxford University, thus becoming the first Oxford-educated prime minister in the last century to be so humiliated. The social disquiet during her years in office provoked a number of serious riots across major cities of the country, which were ascribed to her political divisiveness. The adoration shown her by the Conservative Party's rank and file was more than matched by a visceral hatred she inspired among others, particularly those whose industrial heritage had been sacrificed in the name of what became known as 'Thatcherism'. When she died, there was reportedly some singing and dancing at impromptu street parties. In what had once been the country's coalfields, until the effective closure of the industry following a bitterly fought year-long miners' strike between 1984 and 1985, her name would still induce bitter antipathy for many years to come.

It was a price she had recognised, long before, that it was necessary to pay. 'If you just set out to be liked,' she said once, 'you would be prepared to compromise on anything, wouldn't you, at any time? And you would achieve nothing!'

And it was a lesson she had learned early in her political career in her first Cabinet job as Education Secretary in Edward Heath's government. She abolished the provision of free school milk in secondary schools, an expensive hangover of the paternalistic policies that had accompanied post-war food rationing, and she was immediately vilified as the 'Milk Snatcher' for having done so. It was a soubriquet that stuck and was still remembered forty years later when she died. Only when the official records were released years afterwards did it emerge that Mrs Thatcher herself had actually opposed the change in policy and that it had been imposed upon her department by an insistent Treasury.

But it was this refusal to accept defeatism, this belief that anything was possible if you tried hard enough, that got her into politics in the first place. It got her into Parliament at her third attempt as a mother of young children at the age of just thirty-three, and at a time when most would-be women Conservative candidates were being asked questions like 'Does your husband know where you are this evening?' if they were so bold as to attend a political selection conference. When she arrived at Westminster in 1959, she was one of only eight Conservative women among the 19 women elected to a House of Commons of 630 members.

Twenty years later it was the same indomitability in the face of what to others might have seemed an insuperable obstacle that got her to Number 10 Downing Street, waving in her matronly bright-blue costume from the nation's most distinguished doorstep and promising to try to fulfil the trust and confidence that the electorate had placed in her and the things in which she believed. That first doorstep delivery is remembered more for her evocation of St Francis – harmony, truth, faith and hope all having subsequently proved somewhat in short supply at times in the years that were to follow – but it was the last phrase that mattered. At that point in 1979, the British people hadn't really got a clue what it was that she did believe in, but they were about to find out. 'We have work to do,' she said briskly, evoking the name of Airey Neave, her first colleague to have been murdered by the IRA, at the outset of the election that had just brought her to office, and she disappeared through the door for eleven years of putting her ideas into practice.

The difficulties that Mrs Thatcher had surmounted to reach that historic point were mostly about tradition within the Conservative Party. She got selected and elected as an MP, which was difficult enough for anyone, and then proved herself sufficiently competent to be promoted within the ranks. Harold Macmillan was in government when she first got in, and there was, of course, always going to be room for a capable tax lawyer with the forensic brain of an industrial chemist in a department like the Ministry of Pensions and Insurance. Alec Douglas-Home kept her on and she was a minister there for three years until Labour swept into power in pursuit of the white heat of the technological revolution. Thereafter, she had a range of shadow appointments – Housing, the Treasury, Fuel and Power, Transport, Education, and, when she stood for the leadership, at Environment. Not all of these were regarded then as areas of concern to women, and they all served to provide her with a useful breadth of experience. Heath resisted appointing her to the shadow Cabinet initially, but her claim to membership could not be denied after 1967.

What was all the more surprising therefore about her eventual arrival in Downing Street was the fact that she had herself appeared defeatist about the prospects for a woman reaching that address. When she became a Cabinet minister in 1970, a reporter from the local paper in her Finchley constituency whipped round to ask about the extent of her future ambitions, only to be told: 'There will not be a woman prime minister in my lifetime – the male population is too prejudiced.' She said much the same three years later, this time on BBC television in *Val Meets the VIPs*. Mrs Thatcher was the only politician to be questioned by Valerie Singleton and a collection of schoolchildren in eighteen editions of the programme. Three years at the top of the Tory Party had not changed her mind, yet within two more years she was herself leader of the party. By then Heath had lost two elections, been told by the electorate that it wasn't him they wanted running Britain – and then shown by the party that they didn't want him either. Shaken by the size of the revolt against him (as one day she would be, too), he had resigned.

Mrs Thatcher may not have changed her views about whether she could reach the top, but neither had she changed her philosophy about how to make possible that which seemed to be impossible. There were four components to this strategy, which she pursued throughout her life: she decided on an objective; she decided how to achieve it; she prepared to defend her intent; and she embarked on the attack. She got on with it. At least half the population knew what she meant when she said: 'In politics if you want anything said, ask a man; if you want anything done, ask a woman.'

The Conservative Party was nevertheless surprised to find that it had elected a woman leader, and as uncertain as the rest of the political world about how the voters would respond when asked. One of the Labour Party leaflets issued on the eve of polling day in 1979 put it baldly: 'The day after you forgot to vote, Mrs Thatcher became prime minister!' It may have reflected what seemed like the improbability of such an outcome; it did not reflect the views of the electorate on the public sector strikes that characterised what came to be known as the 'winter of discontent', as James Callaghan's tottering minority government finally collapsed over devolution.

When she got into office, Mrs Thatcher already knew that the British public wanted a resolute leadership. She proposed to give it to them. She always admired intellectuals with a political ideology that concurred with her own, men like Friedrich Hayek whose *Road to Serfdom* she had read when she was at Somerville. It wasn't on her syllabus. She had been studying X-ray crystallography, but she had known even as a schoolgirl, before she won a place at Oxford to read Chemistry, that really she would have preferred to be a lawyer. It wasn't exactly that it was a mistake; she was immensely proud of her training as a chemist and, indeed, would often say that of all the firsts she notched up, the one that pleased her most was being the first prime minister with a Science degree. She read Hayek because she was involved in the Conservative Association when she wasn't in the laboratory or the library. And the former head girl who didn't do things by halves wasn't going to be a back-room girl; she was president of OUCA.

So now, when she got her hands on the reins of power, bolstered by her friends at the free-market think-tank, the Institute of Economic Affairs, she embarked on a government programme of deregulation and market competition. The answer to what had been termed the British disease was not socialism, she asserted. On one occasion she banged down a copy of Hayek's *The Constitution of Liberty* at a meeting and declared: 'This, gentlemen, is what we believe!' When the Russians dubbed her 'the Iron Lady' (in 1976, even before she was elected) it was meant to be an insult. 'Zheleznaya Dama' actually translates as 'Iron Maiden' and was intended as a reference to a medieval instrument of torture, but in any case Mrs Thatcher seized upon the phrase with delight. She put on a red chiffon evening dress and marched off to Kensington Town Hall to address a party audience. All leaders need a bit of steel in their backbone, she told them, and they loved it. It wasn't long before an 'Iron Lady' (tonic water and angostura bitters) was a drink in Annie's famous bar in the House of Commons.

The first two years were very difficult but very crucial. There was an economic recession. Mrs Thatcher's radical departure from the post-war consensus was not proving popular with the public. An opinion poll in December 1980 ascribed her a popularity rating of 23 per cent, which was lower than any previous prime minister. She had a number of dissenters in her Cabinet and many more in the government. It did not affect her resolve. She wasn't having any of it. 'Wet, wet, wet!' she scrawled over a ministerial paper submitted to her for approval. When Sir Geoffrey Howe delivered his 1981 Budget on her behalf, it was against the backcloth of 3 million unemployed. Most professional economists took a critical view of the emerging polices of Thatcherism. The Prime Minister herself was said to be good at finance, but not very good at economics. A letter was circulated and signed by 364 of the country's economists to make the point. While Edward Heath, who had already embarked on the longest sulk in contemporary history, glowered with pleasure from the back benches at her evident discomfort, the shadow of Selsdon Man was also lurking. Heath had begun his government in 1970 with a commitment to free-market policies, previously agreed at a meeting in Selsdon in Surrey; it had been ditched very swiftly.

All politicians need both luck and good timing if they are to survive, let alone succeed, and Mrs Thatcher was to benefit from both. She was lucky that the Labour Party was engaged in a fratricidal civil war. She also proved the fortunate victor of the Falklands War. The Argentinian invasion of the Falklands in 1982, caused ironically enough by British spending cuts that reduced naval patrols in the South Atlantic and thus encouraged Argentina's General Galtieri to attempt to recapture the Malvinas for his own domestic political reasons, was shockingly unexpected. As was the consequent British declaration of war and the dispatch of a naval task force. Mrs Thatcher showed both resolve and steel. At early meetings of the War Cabinet, she would bang the table until the empty water glasses rang with the reverberation of her anger. What she didn't know, and wasn't told until one of the admirals present plucked up the courage to speak, was that there is a long-standing naval superstition that when a glass rings on a table, a sailor dies at sea.

But she won the war ('Rejoice! Rejoice!' she exultantly exclaimed over the recapture of South Georgia) and the consequence was that she won the election that followed with a stonking majority. She had also already arrived at a view of the way ahead. As a newspaper journalist, I had worked at Westminster since 1971. I had covered the 1979 election. I heard the bomb explode that killed Airey Neave at the outset and I was at Finchley Town Hall and then at Conservative Central Office when she won. In the 1983 election I was on the Thatcher battle bus, and it was in that charabanc, parked in the unlikely surroundings of Newbury racecourse, that she told the world what she was going to do next. We licked our pencils and wrote down what she said, and then went and told the rest of the world to look out. Her message was that she planned to export the perceived success of her policies which, she correctly anticipated, would be reflected in the result of the election.

There was a great deal of travelling and not much tourism in the years that followed, and I went everywhere that she went for much of it. In the course of her years in office, she attended thirty-two European summits, twelve Group of Seven (G7) summits of the leading economic nations, seven Commonwealth Heads of Government Meetings (CHOGM) – 'This place Choggum,' said one of my colleagues, arriving in the Bahamas, 'is it the capital?' – and three NATO summits. She took tea in an army trench with three African presidents. She was mistaken for the Queen all over Africa. I was mistaken for her in the Soviet ministry of foreign affairs. I had become detached from the press corps, the greeting party was expecting Mrs Thatcher to emerge from a lift, and the doors opened to reveal me instead. On the way back from her hugely successful first visit to the Soviet Union, when she proved that she could do business with Mr Gorbachev – not least by keeping the audience waiting at the Bolshoi for about half an hour over the allotted interval because the two of them were talking politics – I asked her if she also liked him. I had to ask the same question three times. 'Yes, I liked him,' she eventually conceded.

We once went round the world backwards in six days. We flew to Beijing to give them back Hong Kong and then we went to Hong Kong where she had to defend this decision. Mrs Thatcher famously only needed four hours sleep a night on weekdays (she would catch up sometimes at Chequers at the weekend) and on one day of this trip she stretched us all. We left Hong Kong after breakfast, landed on the island of Guam in the Pacific Ocean at teatime, before taking off for Hawaii which we reached in time to watch the sun rise over the day we had just travelled through. We arrived in Washington DC in time for dinner, drove up to Camp David to breakfast with President Reagan, and flew home overnight to arrive on Christmas Eve.

Someone had told Mrs Thatcher when we went to Egypt that, really, she ought to show some interest in the cultural glories of the countries she visited, so we got to see the temple at Karnak and she instructed the pilot of her RAF VC10 to take the plane down to a height at which she could catch a glimpse of Abu Simbel at Aswan. She made a similar gesture on the next overseas visit, this time in Australia, when the aircraft circled Uluru, then still known as Ayers Rock. It wasn't that she wasn't interested in the culture – it was that she had so much else to do that was so much more vital. She had the same approach to holidays. She was worried about 'vegetating' – a very Thatcherish word – about not having enough to occupy her. She used to stay in Switzerland on holiday with friends and was said to have looked out of the window one morning and announced that, having climbed the only visible mountain, there was clearly nothing else to do. In the early years of marriage when obliged to take an interest in gardening, she grew dahlias the size of dinner plates, but leisure activities didn't interest her. In his masterful authorised biography, Charles Moore observes that she regarded holidays as occasionally necessary, but unpleasant, rather like going to the dentist.

She set herself superhuman tasks, yet she retained a human comprehension of other people's everyday concerns. Her thoughtfulness to her staff was legendary. When we went to Australia, by way of the Middle East and Singapore, I had looked at the itinerary and made a mental note that, as there was no more than one night anywhere for about ten days, there would be no opportunity to do laundry until Bangkok. On the first leg of the journey, I asked Mrs Thatcher what she thought of the schedule that lay ahead. 'We can't do any laundry until Bangkok!' she said. Travelling with her on a long flight when I was visibly pregnant, she offered me the use of the bed in her cabin; to my eternal regret, I declined.

When she first became a figure of public attention, she was

derided as something of a suburban housewife, but nothing could have been further from the reality of her early married life. She married Denis Thatcher in 1951, the year she fought Dartford for the second time, and when their twins were born in 1953, she was already en route to qualifying as a barrister. Since leaving Oxford, she had been working for J. Lyons as a chemist, working on the emulsification of ice cream, before also studying for the Bar. Her husband was wealthy and could pay her bills for law school. When she was called to the Bar, the candidates being ranked in alphabetical order, Margaret Thatcher was called between Dick Taverne and Jeremy Thorpe, both of whom she would later meet again at Westminster. Denis Thatcher was also quite happy for her simultaneously to pursue a political career to try to get there: he shared her views, although, of course, in a rather more relaxed fashion, and had himself turned down the opportunity to stand for selection as the Tory candidate in Dartford. It was how they had met. Interestingly, Mrs Thatcher was rejected for a job with ICI during this period. The reason given, after she had been interviewed, was that the candidate was unsuitable because she was headstrong, obstinate and dangerously self-opinionated.

In her early years as an MP, she did conform to the necessary image of the busy, well-organised mother. She claimed in an interview during that time that she would dash in from work and put the supper in the oven before she even took her hat off; a curious picture of what life was like as a Tory woman MP in the 1960s. But according to her daughter, Carol, Mrs Thatcher 'would have hated being a housewife' and she herself once admitted that, on the few occasions when she was not working, she felt 'no more than a drudge'. The reality was that she had a nanny for the children when they were small and they were later sent away to school. Mrs Thatcher was hurt by the cutting remark of a newspaper columnist that by having twins who were born by Caesarean section she had even managed efficiently to minimise the inconvenience of childbirth, yet she was nevertheless somewhat defensive about her role as a mother. She would tell other women MPs that it was the quality of the time that a mother spent with her children that was important, but she clearly suspected that Mark might have been less of a tearaway as a young man and

Carol might have achieved more success, had their mother put more time into parenting.

Her own childhood in Grantham had been so vastly different, raised as she had been in Methodist austerity, the younger of the two daughters of Alfred and Beatrice Roberts, born at home, above the corner grocery shop in an atmosphere dominated by work and religion. The family didn't have much in terms of material possessions, but they had enough. When Margaret won a scholarship and got to the grammar school, she could afford to pursue her interests and do the things that girls did in the straitened days of the 1930s. She swam and walked and played hockey and the piano, but she aspired to a better lifestyle and recognised that education was the route. 'People from my sort of background need grammar schools to compete with children from privileged homes, like Shirley Williams and Anthony Wedgwood Benn,' she told the Conservative conference with real feeling in 1977. It was her father who had the greatest influence on her; it was listening to him speaking in public, as a lay preacher and as an Alderman, that provoked her interest in public affairs and, even then, in public speaking. Margaret Thatcher loved poetry. At school she won prizes for reciting Kipling and Tennyson and de la Mare in what were known in those days as 'declamation competitions'.

She also learned to love clothes and always cared what she looked like. Worried about her weight all her life, she frequently spoke of the need to lose half a stone. Quite simply, Mrs Thatcher liked looking good, and in maturity as prime minister, she looked better all the time, particularly after she began to take advice and got rid of the pussy-cat bows at the neck of her blouses. Instead, she wore more frequently the double row of pearls that Denis gave her when the twins were born; she listed them among her favourite things. The grooming and the elocution lessons – first started in childhood to remove the slight trace of Lincolnshire in her accent and because she had trouble with her 'Rs' – now enhanced her elegance and her oratory. The lessons of the Grantham grocery store were always with her. 'Open all hours – and dressed for it,' was how her press secretary Bernard Ingham described her approach when he talked years later about what he jokingly termed 'Life with the Lioness'. She was also, he claimed, 'the fastest woman in the West' when it came to changing her clothes; she would be tapping her fingers or her heels with impatience in the hall while waiting for the mere men around her to get ready on time. One of her Cabinet ministers, the famously fastidious Norman St John-Stevas, once asked to be excused early from a meeting because he had to change for a formal evening dress event. 'But Norman,' she protested. 'I am going too . . .'

Mrs Thatcher was feminine, but not a feminist. She made no bones about that. She was a meritocrat and saw no need to promote other women because they were women. In the course of her entire period as prime minister, the only woman to be appointed to the Cabinet was Lady Young, who was briefly the leader of the House of Lords. When Mrs Thatcher was a back-bencher and in her first parliamentary years, she was perhaps more unexpectedly liberal on some social issues than her background might have dictated. She supported the first successful private member's legislation to legalise abortion and to decriminalise homosexuality; she voted to ban hare coursing. As a new MP she won the back-bench lottery to introduce a private member's bill, and her maiden speech was to introduce her own bill to oblige local authorities to hold their council meetings in public. In those early years, however, she also voted to retain capital punishment and against relaxing divorce laws. She would say later that she felt the permissive society of the 1960s had been taken too far.

Throughout her life, she enjoyed being a woman among men, increasingly using her handbag as a metaphor for her authority. When talking about the practice of politics, quite late in her career, in 1987, her statement to an interviewer, 'perhaps, you know, women are better at it than men', wasn't a question and it was not meant to be a generalisation. It was herself she was talking about. She had begun to believe in her own invincibility. 'Get the policy right and everything else follows,' she would say, and she thought she had cracked it. Inflation had been at nearly 22 per cent in the spring of 1980, but it was down to 2.4 per cent by the summer of 1986. The proportion of people owning shareholdings increased by 25 per cent as a result of her policies and more than a million people bought their council houses. She had made the case for 'getting her money back' from Europe and was continuing to resist its federal impulses. She had defeated the National Union of Mineworkers, 'the enemy within'; overall trade union membership had begun a fall from which it would not recover. She won the 1987 General Election with ease.

And then she entered what was characterised as the 'Gloriana' period of her premiership. She talked more and listened less. She embarked upon a reform of local authority financing, through what was called a poll tax, and didn't hear the arguments that were made against it. She was now a fierce and dominating character and she exhibited her strength as much against her colleagues in Cabinet as she had once shown to the enemy without, those who did not share her views. Before her last election, she had already lost one member of her Cabinet, Michael Heseltine, who presented a real threat to her from the back benches, but this did not inhibit her determination. Denis Thatcher had always thought that the 'old girl' should call it a day after ten years, before they cut her off at the stocking tops, but she didn't listen to him any more than to anyone else. She had a show-down with her Chancellor, Nigel Lawson, over future policy towards European finance and about her retention of an independent financial adviser, and he resigned, too. She made John Major his successor. She had always had a weakness for charmers among her ministers, but her judgement was sometimes faulty about their capabilities or, as in Major's case, about their commitment to her cause. When she first put him in the Cabinet, I asked him if he was really a Thatcherite, what she used to call 'people like us'. He was very direct: 'I believe in tight control of the money supply. She has never asked me about social issues.' The next – and last – to go was Geoffrey Howe. He had been her faithful supporter from the first, but by now she had exploited his goodwill to the point of exhaustion. It was to be his resignation speech that triggered the leadership election that brought her down. At the height of her authority she had once boasted that she would 'go on and on'; even now, she valiantly asserted that she would fight on, she would fight to win. But after 11 years and 209 days in office, the longest-serving prime minister continuously in office since Lord Liverpool, she had lost. It was predictable, when they came for her at the end, that she would refuse initially to accept that she was defeated. But then, as she said, a woman alone once more: 'It's a funny old world.'

She was lonely in her long retirement. A foundation to promote her ideas was set up in her name. In her old age, she fought her declining mental powers in the company of a few faithful friends and died in the Ritz Hotel, aged eighty-seven.

Julia Langdon is a political journalist and biographer.

50

John Major

28 November 1990 to 1 May 1997
Conservative

By Julian Glover

Full name: John Major, later Sir John Major
Born: 29 March 1943, Surrey County Hospital, St Helier, Surrey
Education: Rutlish Grammar School, Wimbledon
Married to Norma Johnson; 1 son, 1 daughter
Quotation: 'The harsh truth is that if the policy isn't hurting, it isn't working.' (27 October 1989)

B Y ANY STANDARDS other than those set by much of his own party, John Major's premiership was a real and lasting success. He left office with inflation lower, employment higher and economic growth stronger than it was when he entered it. He led the country through a major war in the Gulf and at the end of it persuaded the US to adopt a plan that brought peace to Kurdistan.

He made progress in ending the conflict in Northern Ireland, even though he came close to being killed in an IRA attack. He played a confident role in building a new relationship with Russia and a reunified Germany at the end of the Cold War, welcoming new eastern states into what become the European Union. He stood firm in backing a degree of democracy in Hong Kong as its return to China approached.

He scrapped the poll tax. He introduced the National Lottery and with it unleashed British sporting success and cultural renewal. He was part of the first response to climate change at the 1992 Rio Earth Summit. He negotiated the Maastricht Treaty, securing British opt-outs from the single currency and the Social Chapter on employment rights. He oversaw the privatisation of the rail system, which, though flawed, was followed by growing investment and a doubling of passenger numbers.

He understood that to survive, public services had to treat the people who used them as customers with rights, not lucky supplicants. In the NHS, models such as GP fundholding and patient choice set a model for reform that continues to be followed. In higher education, he sought to break down old class divides such as between polytechnics and universities, and increase participation.

He ran Downing Street with a small and effective team, among them Jonathan Hill, Sarah Hogg and George Bridges, and led a Cabinet that contained several heavyweights who might have hoped to become prime minister themselves, including Ken Clarke, Michael Heseltine and Chris Patten. Intellectually, he gave his party an identity that went beyond the tremendous shadow created by his then unhappy and interfering predecessor, Margaret Thatcher.

Most of all, in April 1992 he won a fourth General Election victory for the Conservative Party, something that many had written off as impossible. He won the biggest single vote for a political party in British history and did it against a talented Labour opposition after taking charge of the campaign himself and facing up to voters directly, as no prime minister has been able to since, on a soapbox.

So why did he also go down to a thumping defeat in the 1997 election and depart, if not as a joke figure, then at least as someone widely seen at the time as not up to the job? And what is it that

449

in the years since then has caused many of his old critics to reassess him, so that by the time of his Brexit interventions in 2019 he was seen by many — although again not by some in his old party — as a wise and admirable elder statesman?

The roots of the answer lie in the circumstances of his birth. Class identity is never far from the surface in British — or at least English — politics and it counts as much on the right as on the left.

John Major was born in St Helier, Surrey, on 29 March 1943. It was in the middle of the war. Glass from a widow broken in a German rocket attack was found soon after on the baby's cot. His childhood was fractured in other ways, too. His mother Gwen, whom he adored, had married a former music hall artist, Tom Major-Ball. Born in 1879, shaped by the attitudes of the late Victorian and Edwardian age, he was already an old man during Major's childhood (and his antique phrases shaped the curious figures of speech Major himself became noted for using).

He was a colourful chancer who had roamed the United States and South America in his youth, and fathered at least five children with four different women over many years.

Neither father nor son ever settled into the stratigraphy of English class identity. The future prime minister did not grow up in the hard but identifiable poverty of a coal-mining family. Nor did he know the gentility of a suburban childhood or Etonian ease. He was tricky to place, which left him short of solid allies when he needed them. Even his accent, soft, modulated south London, seemed rootless.

His father ran a garden ornaments business (much mocked as gnome making) but in 1955, short on funds, he moved to the bottom flat of a shared house in Brixton, which later came to define his son. 'What does the Conservative Party offer a working-class kid from Brixton?' asked an ad in the 1992 campaign. 'They made him prime minister.'

An election broadcast from the same contest showed Major peering through the windows of his Jaguar (not wearing a seatbelt) at his old home: 'It's still there,' he cried. Some laughed, but the emotion was real and Major cringed at using it.

Brixton made him into a rebel. A lonely education at a dreadful grammar school miles from home was ended by the teenage Major, who told his headmaster he was leaving (he never shared the Tory nostalgia for grammars). He had a handful of O-Levels (and in later life could not remember exactly which and did not want to know).

He filled his time and taught himself through reading and cricket – Major has remained literate and cultured as well as more committed to sport than most prime ministers since.

A succession of false starts in office jobs followed. More significantly, he joined the Young Conservatives at a time when the party was building success ahead of what turned out to be its London highpoint in the 1968 local elections.

He met and moved in with a local activist, Jean Kierans, twelve years older, who lived nearby. 'Dark-haired, attractive and fun', as he recalled in his autobiography, she helped open his eyes to the possibilities of politics. In 1966 he joined Standard Bank, tempted by the pay and excitement of a post in Nigeria. A car crash there nearly killed him and left him with injuries that ended any serious attempts to play cricket and caused pain that affected him more than anyone knew as prime minister.

In 1970, only ten days after he met her, he became engaged to a teacher, Norma Johnson. Despite a later-publicised affair with a fellow MP, Edwina Currie, in the 1980s, their relationship underpinned his later success and continued to do so after he left office. Her clarity, wisdom and straightforward way of thinking has mattered immensely to him. When married to a prime minister, she loved the man but was not in awe of the job.

Major rose quickly. He stood as a candidate in the unwinnable seat of St Pancras North in both 1974 elections and in 1976 was selected for the very safe seat of Huntingdon.

Tall and physically impressive, Major always cut a more striking figure in the flesh than when photographed. He dressed unmemorably and wore heavy-rimmed glasses until switching to a less intrusive design after leaving office, but he could always command a room.

He was lucky, too, that he entered the House of Commons in 1979, as the party was tipping towards new men like him, self-made, pro-market, post-war. It was assumed by most fellow Tories then, as now, that someone from a modest background could only have joined the party because they had hard-right views. Thatcher herself probably never stopped to listen to the actual opinions of a man she was soon promoting fast as a whip and junior minister.

A whips' dinner in which he famously and outspokenly clashed with her over winter welfare payments ought to have given her a clue that he was not 'one of us' as she assumed. So might his membership of the largely wet, posh Blue Chips dining club, formed after the 1979 election and comprising new young and ambitious MPs – men (only men) who went on to form the bedrock of his government in the 1990s.

Major rode his success: he joined the Cabinet in 1987 as Chief Secretary, a job, as a former banker, he loved. In July 1989, as the Thatcher government began to implode, he succeeded Sir Geoffrey Howe as Foreign Secretary – 'for August' he later joked, pointing out it was a short but golden age with no wars and no disasters. He disliked the scarcely hidden sneer for his inexperience on the part of some Foreign Office grandees, but did not have time to prove them wrong. In October 1989 he replaced Nigel Lawson as Chancellor.

Unknown two years before, he was now one of the most famous politicians in the land if still a mystery to most voters. He remembered the shock when, watching the satirical show *Spitting Image*, he first saw himself portrayed as a grey man eating peas – which he didn't even like in real life.

By now he was rising almost as fast as Thatcher was falling. His only Budget, in early 1990, introduced tax-free savings accounts – Tessas – but the issues that mattered were Europe and the poll tax. Major backed membership of the Exchange Rate Mechanism, as did Lawson, who resigned over No. 10 interference. Major threatened resignation himself on the issue at least once in a call from Northern Ireland to an intransigent prime minister.

In October 1990 he got his way on the ERM. Tory Eurosceptics, many of whom later turned on him, might have done well to note that the man they mostly soon backed to be prime minister did not share their views on Europe and never pretended to. He, in return, might have done more to point it out to them before it was too late.

Major did not cause Thatcher's downfall a month later, but he benefited more than anyone from it. Heseltine, the obvious successor, was not forgiven by many of her supporters for triggering the contest, in which Major voted for her in the first round. Conveniently, but genuinely, he was recovering at home from a wisdom tooth operation as rumours swirled at Westminster. Under pressure to sign her nomination papers for a second round when she did not win on the first ballot, he played for time, aware, along with the rest of the Cabinet, that she was finished. Later, she felt he had been disloyal. At the time, she picked him as her successor.

In the short contest that followed, Major was the most obviously Thatcherite candidate by dint both of his background and his supporters. Norman Lamont, whom he made his first Chancellor, ended up leading his campaign, but much of the work was done by Blue Chip members such as Tristan Garel-Jones, his close friend, who were not on the right of the party. With little time for policy discussion, the seeds of rapid disillusionment were sown.

On 27 November 1990, Major gained 184 votes, two short of a winning total but well ahead of his two rivals, who withdrew. The next morning he became prime minister, less than three years after joining the Cabinet.

His stated ambition outside Downing Street – 'I want to see us build a country that is at ease with itself' – seemed a welcome break with the tensions and divisions of the late Thatcher years. But his inheritance was troubled: a currency under pressure, an economy in difficulty, a nation split by the poll tax and a looming war to drive Iraq out of Kuwait, which it had invaded in August. On top of that, an election was expected within a year.

Major made some early mistakes, such as replacing a Cabinet led by the first female prime minister with one that contained no women. Lamont was also a mistake as Chancellor, given the pressures caused by the ERM and the fact that the pair were never close.

At his first Prime Minister's Questions, Major used the phrase 'Oh, Yes!' repeatedly – eventually leading to the sort of gentle mockery that needled him more than it should have done. Having grown up reading the *Daily Express* on long journeys to school, he was a newspaper addict and could never rise above the hurt caused by the criticism that came with his new profile. It was an insecurity that cost him. Unable to build an easy relationship with the media, he was in the end damaged badly.

The first eighteen months were a triumph, however. No. 10 and the Treasury took charge of defusing the poll tax with a simple solution that has endured.

Major, along with his Foreign Secretary Douglas Hurd, rapidly built a close relationship with President George H.W. Bush – later a firm and lasting friend. He also worked in a coalition of thirty-five nations, the largest military alliance since the Second World War, which launched an assault on Iraq on 16 January 1991. The first war to be televised live, it went better than most feared. Iraq did not use chemical weapons and its forces collapsed under the might of the allied attack. Kuwait was recaptured and British captives in Iraq, including airmen who had been shot down, were returned.

Major – whose televised address on the night the war began ended with a gentle 'God Bless' – was seen as a successful unifying force. His one big strategic intervention came at the end when he persuaded President Bush to back a no-fly zone in northern and southern Iraq and create so-called Kurdish safe havens. It saved many lives and created a degree of stability that lasted until the errors of the second Gulf War launched after he left office.

The second foreign adventure of 1991 was the Maastricht European summit, which ended in December and was signed the following year. Major was widely held to have played an effective role, and initially many Eurosceptics in his party were satisfied at the outcome. Had he decided to ratify it in the Commons rapidly, with a large majority, before an election, he and his party might have been spared much later grief.

As it was, he waited until 11 March 1992 before calling an election. Most polls in the campaign put Labour ahead. Turnout, at 77 per cent, was high. Labour struggled initially in the so-called War of Jennifer's Ear, over a film on the NHS. But its downfall lay in overconfidence, setting out a shadow budget that allowed Patten, the Party Chairman, to hammer home a message about 'Labour's Double Whammy' on tax.

Major's biggest contribution was to rip up his party's initial over-designed campaign and portray himself as a man of the people, happiest debating out in the streets. Enough of that was true to leave Labour's Neil Kinnock exposed when he appeared to accept victory at a rally in Sheffield before polling day.

In the end, the Conservatives won 41.9 per cent of the vote against Labour's 34.4 per cent – a trouncing that did not turn into seats. A majority of just twenty-one, which fell to nothing by the end of the Parliament, spelled trouble ahead.

After a calm summer, all hell was unleashed on Black Wednesday, 16 September 1992, when sterling fell out of the ERM. Major's premiership never recovered, nor did his reputation in the party. He felt that Lamont could have handled things better and Germany could have offered support – as it did to keep France in the ERM. The seeds of Britain's later departure from the EU can be traced to that day.

Trapped in Admiralty House, while No. 10 was being rebuilt after an IRA attack, Major could do little to manage events, and the public sensed it. Britain, and he, looked weak. Unemployment passed three million in early 1993.

Under Ken Clarke, who became Chancellor soon after, Black Wednesday was followed by eventual economic recovery. Major's two great economic achievements were to break the inflationary cycle – which had endured through the Thatcher years – and restore public finances, which were destroyed not just by recession but by the poll tax, which virtually wiped out local government revenue.

In 1997 a New Labour government would be elected on a promise to back Conservative spending plans. But Major got no credit for economic reconstruction and little for his other policy efforts, which included a central role linking Europe, the US and Japan in the creation of the World Trade Organisation in 1995 – the same body that twenty-five years later allowed Brexiteers to claim there was an alternative to EU membership. There has been no successful world trade round since.

Major's efforts to bring peace to Northern Ireland also relied on bold negotiation. In December 1993 he agreed to the Downing Street declaration, which asserted that the United Kingdom had no 'selfish strategic or economic' interest in Northern Ireland. In 1994 a tentative ceasefire began, which ended with the bombing of Canary Wharf in 1997. Blair resumed the peace process on taking office and got much of the credit, but would have got nowhere without the foundations laid under Major.

On the other great issue affecting the Union, Scotland, Major had no equivalent strategic response. The rise of Scottish nationalism was not countered by the tactical stunt of bringing the Stone of Scone from London to Edinburgh in 1996.

By early 1993 Major was under siege. The Liberal Democrats were winning by-elections and Lamont accused the Prime Minister of 'being in office but not in power'. The charge that he was weak hung over him for the rest of his time in No. 10, although he persisted with a domestic policy agenda that was more effective than many saw at the time, including the National Lottery, which launched in 1994.

But in the Commons all attention was on the ratification of the Maastricht Treaty. On 22 July the government was defeated in a vote on the Social Chapter. The next day, this was reversed in a vote deemed an issue of confidence – Major had a resignation speech ready in case he lost. Any momentum he gained was thrown away two days later when, at the end of an interview, he was caught calling some in his Cabinet 'the bastards'.

For the rest of his time in office, he seemed to be at war with parts of his party. In October 1993 a party conference claim to go 'back to basics' – by which Major meant standards in things such as education – backfired when it was seen as an attack on personal morality. The media enjoyed exposing Tory ministers, unaware of Major's own affair with Currie. He came to dread the call from No. 10 each Saturday night telling him what was in the Sunday papers.

In July 1994 Blair's arrival as Labour leader seemed to point to inevitable defeat when the election came. Tory rebellions did too. That same year, the government was defeated in a vote on VAT on fuel, and eight MPs lost the whip for another rebellion on Europe.

On 22 June 1995 Major took the extraordinary step of resigning the leadership and putting himself up for re-election. It spooked some of his senior critics, such as Michael Portillo, who did not stand. John Redwood, who did challenge, lost badly, but over a hundred MPs failed to support Major and he came close to the limit he had set himself privately and below which he would have quit.

The following year was miserable. The disease BSE caused widespread fear about the safety of beef. The Cash for Questions affair seemed to blend financial sleaze into existing alarm about morality among Tory MPs, all adding to the sense that the Major government had run out of road. There was little any leader could have done about this, especially not one who had lost the support of so much of his own party.

The 1997 General Election, which Major announced on 17 March, was never likely to be won. 'Whether you agree with me or disagree with me; like me or loathe me, don't bind my hands,' he pleaded with his own party midway through.

The result was one he was prepared for: a Labour landslide. 'When the curtain falls, it's time to get off the stage – and that's what I propose to do,' he said, heading off to watch the cricket. Apart from an autobiography, published to good reviews in 1999, Major mostly held firm to his promise. He spoke occasionally in the Commons before standing down in 2001.

Mostly not hated, but disparaged, Major slowly recovered his reputation. He did not support the 2003 attack on Iraq, and was proved right. Nor did he welcome the Eurosceptic direction taken by his successors in opposition. When the party returned to power in 2010 in coalition, he was enthusiastic, although he was not close to David Cameron.

Only when the Brexit referendum led to Britain's departure from the EU did he begin to speak out, despairing of the prospect of no-deal. Old adversaries in the Lib Dems and Labour saw him in a new positive light. Old Tory enemies had their dislikes reaffirmed.

A steady but sceptical pro-European all his life, Major was always puzzled by the passion the issue caused in others. It made him prime minister by helping destroy Thatcher. But it brought him down in turn, just as it did successive Tory leaders.

He became wiser the longer he served, but with that wisdom came a knowledge of what could go wrong. He was at his best not worrying but getting on with what his instincts told him was right – speaking on a soapbox, leading in the Gulf War, trading deals in the negotiating room at Maastricht.

His six and a half years as prime minister seemed tumultuous and were not always happy ones for him. He might have been a better leader of a government of national unity than a single party full of guilt about Thatcher's destruction. But he left the country in better shape than he found it, he departed with good grace, and he took great pleasure from life in the years that followed. Not many former PMs can claim all that.

Julian Glover is Comment Editor at the London Evening Standard *and a former political adviser.*

51

Tony Blair

1 May 1997 to 27 June 2007
Labour

By Andrew Adonis

Full name: Anthony Charles Lynton Blair
Born: 6 May 1953, Edinburgh
Education: Fettes School; St John's College, Oxford
Married to Cherie Booth; 3 sons, 1 daughter
Quotation: 'A day like today is not a day for soundbites, really.
But I feel the hand of history upon our shoulders. I really do.'
(On the Good Friday agreement, April 1998)

POSSIBLY THE MOST gifted natural politician to have become
prime minister apart from David Lloyd George, and with fewer
personal flaws, Tony Blair held the supreme office continuously for
ten years and fifty-seven days, a tenure exceeded only by Margaret
Thatcher in the democratic era. His impact on the British state is

matched or exceeded since the Second World War only by Thatcher and Clement Attlee.

Blair was an electoral genius. He won all three elections he fought as Labour leader, two by landslide majorities (1997 and 2001). His third victory, in 2005, was the first time the Conservatives had lost three elections in a row since the introduction of the democratic franchise in 1918. The common view at the time, that 'any' Labour leader would have won the 1997 election and might have carried off the other two as well, looks less plausible in the light not only of the party's poor previous electoral history but also of the four elections since 2005, all won decisively by the Conservatives over Labour despite unspectacular leaders and unfavourable economic and political conditions in the 2010s.

Blair's greatest governmental achievements were lasting peace and power-sharing in Northern Ireland, devolution to Scotland and Wales, the refinancing and transformation of the National Health Service and England's public education system, and the introduction of a national minimum wage. These fortified the progressive reformist and constitutional tradition of Liberal and Labour governments since Earl Grey's Great Reform Act of 1832. However, like most Liberal and Labour governments since Palmerston, Blair also became embroiled in bitter disputes with left-wing and liberal supporters over the use of military force abroad as he wrestled with Britain's security and global role. His decision to participate in President George W. Bush's invasion of Iraq in 2003 created deep and lasting controversy on a par with Gladstone's conquest of Egypt in 1882, Asquith's entry into the First World War in 1914, and Attlee and Bevin's military resistance to Jewish immigration and the creation of the state of Israel after 1945.

Anthony Charles Lynton Blair was born into a comfortable professional family on 6 May 1953. His father, a youthful communist, became an establishment barrister, law lecturer at Durham University and aspirant Conservative MP. He set his younger son on a similar path, sending him to a prestigious private prep school in Durham followed by Fettes College, an Edinburgh public school. From there Tony progressed fairly effortlessly to St John's College, Oxford, to study law, like his father and elder brother, who also became a barrister. His early years were privileged but not untroubled: his father suffered a stroke when Tony was ten, putting an end to his parliamentary ambitions, and his mother died of cancer when he was twenty-one.

The young Blair's preoccupation at Oxford was pop music, not politics, in which he evinced little interest until he reached the Bar. A serious side developed at Oxford from engagement with Christian socialism at the behest of a charismatic Australian graduate theologian, Peter Thomson, who introduced Blair to the communitarian philosopher John Macmurray, shaping his social-democratic convictions. His later speeches, especially on international affairs, contain frequent biblical phrases and overtones.

Following the family tradition to the Bar, Blair fortuitously got a pupillage in the chambers of Derry (Alexander) Irvine, a dominant and domineering barrister well connected with the Labour leadership as a friend of fellow Scots lawyer and ex-Cabinet minister John Smith. A fellow 'pupil' barrister, with whom he was soon going out, was Cherie Booth, a politically driven Liverpudlian who went on to become a successful human rights specialist and later QC and Recorder (part-time judge).

Derry Irvine's chambers gave the young Blair the triple whammy of a job, a wife and a political career. Cherie Booth was initially the more politically ambitious of the two, but after fighting the 1983 election in a safe Tory seat she concentrated on her legal career and the couple's two boys and a girl (a third son followed much later, in 2000, when they were in Downing Street). Irvine remained a powerful influence and ally, and was later to drive the radical constitutional reform legislation of his ex-pupil's government as Lord Chancellor, including a Human Rights Act and freedom of information. Lord Irvine of Lairg, as he became, also had an eye for the fine things of life, which left its mark on both his pupils.

Blair quickly built an employment and commercial law practice, including trade union work, and he joined the Labour Party as the Callaghan government limped to defeat in 1979. In 1981 he was sufficiently rooted, connected and left wing not to defect to Roy Jenkins' SDP, as so many aspirant politicians with backgrounds like his did. Instead, in 1982 he fought a by-election for Labour in unwinnable Beaconsfield, impressing party leader Michael Foot. His personable and energetic performance helped him gain the last-minute nomination a year later for the then safe Labour seat of Sedgefield, an ex-mining constituency in County Durham. Winning the selection contest by a single vote after the 1983 election had been called, at the age of thirty he became one of a handful of new Labour MPs in a year when Labour was decimated nationally. Gordon Brown was among the other newcomers. By such fine margins are political careers forged, even the foremost.

Blair was content to go along with the left orthodoxies of the day: he stood on a platform of leaving the EEC in 1983, and in these years was also a member of the Campaign for Nuclear Disarmament. Left conformity was partly why he was able to rise so smoothly through Labour ranks in the 1980s and ultimately accede to the party leadership just eleven years after election to Parliament – the same interval between first election and party leadership as for John Major, his sparring partner for his first three years as leader, although Blair became prime minister three years younger than Major (aged forty-four).

Tony Blair was a rare, exotic creature on the Labour benches in Neil Kinnock's party after 1983: youthful, charming, articulate, informal, with matinée-idol looks, a young family, sensible judgement – and English. He was quickly promoted into deputy leader Roy Hattersley's shadow Treasury team, and was widely tipped for the top from the outset because he was so well attuned to 'Middle England'. At a time when Labour needed to advance massively in suburban England to stand any chance of power, being quintessentially modern English middle class was a huge asset in a shadow cabinet top heavy with Scottish and Welsh MPs, including all four party leaders between 1976 and 1994 (Callaghan, Foot, Kinnock and Smith).

Elected to the shadow cabinet in 1988, Blair worked closely with Peter Mandelson, Herbert Morrison's grandson, who became Kinnock's media manager and increasingly his 'modernisation' strategy director too. A decisive break came a year later when Blair was appointed shadow employment spokesman. This pitched him into the most sensitive area of Labour policy – relations with the trade unions – in the aftermath of the Thatcher trade union reforms and the industrial militancy of the early and mid-1980s. Over three years up to the 1992 election, Blair accomplished a delicate political balancing act of vigorously opposing Thatcher's trade union reforms while not committing to reversing them, all the while projecting a strong positive public narrative of industrial partnership and renewal.

He repeated the performance, on a bigger canvas, as Shadow Home Secretary under John Smith, who became leader after Kinnock's defeat by John Major in 1992. His mantra, 'tough on crime, tough on the causes of crime' resonated and was thought to be politically brilliant, while his ethical 'broken society' response to a moral panic sparked by the murder of a Liverpool toddler, James Bulger, by two ten-year-old boys in 1993, struck a national chord.

John Smith's sudden death on 12 May 1994 was the moment of Blair's rise to power. Opinion polling showed him far ahead in public preferences for the succession and it was soon clear that party members, as well as Labour MPs, backed him *en masse* as the candidate most likely to win power for Labour after fifteen years in the wilderness. At this stage he had few enemies and his nickname was 'Bambi'. Gordon Brown, Shadow Chancellor under John Smith, regarded himself as far more heavyweight, but he saw the writing on the wall and the political siblings did an uneasy deal – the 'Granita pact', after an Islington restaurant near Blair's home – whereby Brown said he would not stand for the leadership in return for an assurance of the chancellorship and an indication that Blair would not go 'on and on' in the event of a Labour government. What this actually meant was much disputed in future years, and Blair would have stood and won in any event. However, by choice it made him beholden to Brown, who in the second and third Blair terms claimed he was 'owed' the succession.

Blair's relationship with Brown was the crux of his leadership, like Attlee's with Ernest Bevin and Asquith's with Lloyd George. It was to be one of his greatest assets, because of Brown's force and command at the Treasury and beyond, but it also caused endemic frustration, especially when the political siblings started arguing over domestic policy and Blair's departure after 2001.

Blair was separated oceanically from other British politicians and elite leaders for nearly a decade between 1994 and the Iraq war of 2003. Elected Labour leader in 1994 by a landslide, a year later in 1995, by another landslide, he carried a symbolically and strategically significant Labour conference vote to change the highly charged

Clause 4 of the party's constitution from a commitment to public ownership to a social-democratic statement of communitarianism. From now on, the party's name changed from 'Labour' to 'New Labour', and it was treated as if it was indeed a new party of the centre and centre left, unlike anything that had gone before. Major and the Tories hadn't a clue how to counteract the Blair phenomenon, and few ad campaigns have bombed as badly as their 'demon eyes' posters against him in the 1997 campaign. 'Weak, weak, weak', and 'I lead my party, he follows his', Blair's refrains on Major, pierced Major to the political core, while his two slogans summing up his mission – 'education, education, and education' and the still endlessly recycled 'tough on crime, tough on the causes of crime' – gave him compelling urgency and freshness behind the cause of 'New Labour for a New Britain'. Major was reduced to the quip that on education he had the same three priorities but not necessarily in the same order.

Blair proceeded to win the 1997 election with the greatest landslide in seats gained by any party since the Second World War (416 Labour, 165 Conservative), then repeated the coup in 2001 (413 Labour, 166 Conservative). In his first term, Blair also won four transformational referendums rewriting key parts of the British constitution: to implement power-sharing and a devolved assembly in Northern Ireland, building decisively on Major's brave rapprochement begun in 1993 and bringing an end to the civil war in the province that had been ongoing since the late 1960s; and to create a devolved parliament for Scotland, a devolved assembly for Wales, and a mayor of London, an office with the largest direct democratic mandate in Europe besides the president of France.

Blair outlasted four Conservative leaders. The three after Major (William Hague, Iain Duncan Smith and Michael Howard) never became prime minister, the only Tory leaders of whom that was true since 1922. His reach extended even to the monarchy, the aristocracy and the military. The death in a Paris car crash of the recently divorced and highly popular Diana, Princess of Wales, on 31 August 1997 left the monarchy reeling. Lauding Diana as the 'people's princess' in a pitch-perfect tribute on the Sunday morning of the crash, outside his parish church, Blair orchestrated the dramatic national and royal mourning.

In the first Blair term, the hereditary aristocracy was mostly removed from the House of Lords and its inbuilt Tory majority was ended, a reform no previous Liberal or Labour government had been able to accomplish. The Lords became a largely nominated chamber and did not trouble Blair thereafter. The armed services were equally deferential and readily subscribed to his escalating military commitments, notably interventions in Kosovo (1999), Sierra Leone (2000) and Afghanistan (2001), which paved the way for the Iraq war in 2003. All three interventions were to a greater or lesser extent in explicit pursuit of a new and bold 'doctrine of liberal interventionism' set out in a seminal Blair speech in Chicago on 22 April 1999, which asserted a substantial international military role for Britain, beyond keeping Russia out of western Europe, for the first time since the end of Empire.

Blair forged a wary but working relationship with media mogul Rupert Murdoch, whose lowbrow *Sun* and highbrow *Times* newspapers, hitherto fiercely hostile to Labour, were fairly supportive throughout his leadership. Murdoch supported Blair partly because he was a winner. His editors were also cultivated intensively by Blair's ebullient communications director Alastair Campbell, the most prominent No. 10 media spokesman in history, who was widely regarded as deputy prime minister until his departure in the wake of Iraq in 2003.

It was the received wisdom of the time that Blair maintained a cautious approach to tax-and-spend policy and relations with the European Union to appease the right-wing media, Murdoch in particular. This is to underplay Blair's charismatic skill at playing both sides of electorally sensitive issues − 'you shouldn't be in this game unless you can ride two horses at the same time,' he used to say − and his skill in securing a progressive policy when he wanted to while appearing to appease the right. Equally, he sometimes located policy to the right by design, particularly on law and order, while carefully neutralising the left. He had these qualities in common with Bill Clinton, President of the United States from 1993 to 2001, who was a 'third way' model for Blair and became a friend and collaborator for the first four years of his premiership.

With a strongly growing economy, Blair and Brown were able to increase spending on public services substantially in their combined thirteen years of office, especially on health and education, by the expedient mostly of pegging taxes rather than increasing them, in an environment where a Thatcherite Tory government would have cut them. This enabled a trebling of spending on the NHS and a doubling of state spending on education, substantially renovating these key public services without appreciable direct tax increases. Spending also doubled on overseas aid, a cause of both Blair and Brown.

Alongside extra investment Blair championed radical reform of the public services. The key elements were ambitious published performance targets and data, rapid workforce expansion and upskilling, the promotion of patient choice within the NHS, independently managed 'foundation trusts' within the NHS, and the creation of new state schools with independent sponsors, called 'academies', to replace failing comprehensive schools and drive up school standards in deprived areas. These changes involved a 'reform' battle with trade unions and opponents on the left, including some ministers within his own government and increasingly with Gordon Brown, who after 2001 exploited the unpopularity of public service reform on the left to tweak and weaken Blair. In a celebrated speech (7 July 1999), Blair talked of 'scars on my back' from public service reform, but partly from this perception of struggle he generated wide public and media support for this 'invest and reform', 'something for something', 'investment not cuts' strategy, and it made a highly effective rallying cry and dividing line with the Conservatives in the 2001 and 2005 elections.

Blair's most controversial state reform in England was the introduction of student tuition fees of £3,000 a year for university education in 2004, justified as the *quid pro quo* for a substantial increase in student numbers. This provoked a massive Labour backbench rebellion, encouraged by Brown, and the legislation only passed the House of Commons by a majority of five on 27 January 2004. But the reform endured and was generally seen as progressive. Fee levels were trebled by the incoming Conservative/Lib Dem coalition in 2010, using the Blair legislation.

Blair's policy on Europe was highly consequential and highly ambiguous. Like Major before him, who had agreed the framework for European monetary union with Helmut Kohl in the Maastricht

Treaty of 1991, including a British right to opt in, he was anxious to keep British membership of the new Euro currency in play should Germany and the other core members decide to proceed, as happened in 1999. But in the event, Blair did not take Britain into the Euro, and it was only with difficulty that he managed even to maintain UK support for the Brussels institutional reforms necessitated by EU enlargement, culminating in the Lisbon Treaty signed shortly after his resignation by his successor. Brown symbolically and deliberately arrived at midnight in Brussels to do so with no media coverage, and with no other European leaders present.

Ironically, there was near universal political and media support in Britain for the enlargement of the EU to include the former communist states of central and eastern Europe after 2004, after a treaty negotiation begun under Major after the collapse of the Berlin Wall in 1989, although this gave rise to the substantial immigration that was to turn British Euroscepticism into a mainstream political movement at the behest of Nigel Farage's United Kingdom Independence Party, culminating in Brexit. Ironically also, Blair had attacked Major before 1997 for being weak and irresolute on Europe, although his policy of rhetorically projecting Britain at 'the heart of Europe' without it being so was the same as Major's and he took no political risks as great as had his predecessor at Maastricht. On the contrary, his decision to go to war with Bush in Iraq in 2003 vitiated the geopolitical unity with France and Germany, for which Blair was to pay a high personal price, undermining his ambition to become President of the European Council, a key new EU post created by the Lisbon Treaty, after his time at Downing Street.

Blair anguished about whether Britain should join the Euro. There was disagreement between Blair and Brown about how to express Britain's refusal to sign up, but not about the decision itself. However, at the time Blair was far keener to join than his retrospective account in his 2010 memoirs suggests. Between 1997 and 2007 no issue preoccupied his inner team in Downing Street so much and for so long as the Euro. At a No. 10 Policy Unit Awayday at Chequers in July 2001, after one of his frequent riffs on wanting to 'do' the Euro, I recall asking him over lunch what his game plan was to get there, with the following sequel:

He promptly disappeared into sun-drenched rose garden, scribbled notes, and came back to give us pep talk at the start of the afternoon session. 'If we can we should do the Euro in this Parliament. I am absolutely clear how I see this. There are two sides to the British character: the cautious and the adventurous side. The cautious side has dominated us for the last 40 years and done untold damage. John Major and David Owen epitomise it perfectly. It is the cautious side which wants us to wait another four to six years, to wait and see how it all goes, but I tell you if we do that – and I can already see all the forces of caution uniting, on our side also – we will repeat the mistakes of the past . . . We should do it in this term. There is no point being Prime Minister unless you take risks to do the right thing. If we don't go in, we will be a supplicant in five or six years' time.'

But it was not to be. After years of to-ing and fro-ing between Blair and Brown, a formal government statement by Brown on 9 June 2003, shortly after the Iraq invasion, ruled out British membership of the Euro for the foreseeable future. Even after this 2003 announcement, Blair still thought it might be possible to re-open Brown's negative Treasury assessment of the 'economic case' for membership and hold a referendum in 2004. But this option silently disappeared in late 2003 without being explicitly abandoned.

Blair had come to power in 1997 on a manifesto that was deliberately negative on the Euro: 'There are formidable obstacles in the way of Britain being in the first wave of membership if EMU takes place on 1st January 1999', it stated. Anxious not to lose media or provincial English support during the election, which he thought would be far closer than transpired, he reinforced even this negative stance during the election campaign, with Campbell placing an article in Murdoch's *Sun* a few days before the poll under the headline: 'WHY I LOVE THE POUND'. But Blair's ardent desire – riding two horses at the same time – was nonetheless to find a way to take Britain into the Euro, and he said this frequently and with great earnestness to Roy Jenkins, Britain's only president of the European Commission, who launched European monetary union in 1977, and who had become his friend and mentor by the mid-1990s. In the event, for all his natural charisma, Blair lacked the skill and maybe the imagination to transfer from one political horse to the other at the moment of greatest urgency, in the manner of the greatest modern master of constructive democratic ambiguity, Franklin Delano Roosevelt. The same was perhaps true of his dealings with George W. Bush on Iraq.

The decision not to join the Euro, and the decision to invade Iraq, were the two determining international acts of the Blair government. From the outset, Iraq set him against France and Germany. This is reflected in Blair's memoirs, where he bluntly and undiplomatically attacked Chirac of France and Schröder of Germany, with whom he previously had a good relationship, for being 'brilliant at ringing statements of intent, which then evaporated into thin air when the consequences of seeing them through became apparent . . . In truth, without the US, forget it; nothing would happen. That was the full extent of Europe's impotence.' Chirac replied in kind in his memoirs (2011):

> Having tried, on coming to office, to free himself from the control of Washington, Blair had not been long in bowing down to it. What saddened and angered me, to be frank, was that he did not make greater use of the former experience that his country had of the Middle East and of Iraq in particular. By immediately rallying to the American side, Blair unfortunately deprived himself of any real ability to influence the analysis made by the American government of a regional situation that it knew less well than Britain.

The watershed moment for the Blair premiership was the Islamic terrorist attack on the twin towers in New York on 9 November 2001, shortly after George W. Bush had replaced Clinton in the White House, which was also a target for the 9/11 terrorists. The events of that day led to the invasion of Afghanistan, where the terrorists were based, a relatively uncontroversial international decision taken with United Nations support, although one that became increasingly problematic, as the pacifying not only of terrorist-related activity, but also of hostile and provoked indigenous communities, proved far harder than anticipated, and indeed was never accomplished. Nonetheless, before this was clear, George W. Bush decided to move on from Afghanistan to invade Iraq, also in the name of quelling Islamic terrorism orchestrated by the Al Qaeda organisation of Osama bin Laden.

Bush's motivation in Iraq was always transparently to remove the Iraqi dictator Saddam Hussein, left in place by his presidential father George H.W. Bush after the Kuwait war of 1990–1, to the filial disapproval of his son and, more particularly, the younger Bush's ultra-hawkish vice-president Dick Cheney and Defense Secretary Donald Rumsfeld, both pugilistic veterans of Richard Nixon's administration of the 1970s. For all his crimes against his own people, Saddam was not an international Islamic terrorist, so from the outset his removal proved a difficult and controversial mission for Blair to share. He was, however, determined to do so, partly to stick close to the United States for security considerations, partly from a belief that Saddam was an urgent and imminent security threat – on this the case in international law for removing him by invasion crucially depended – and partly in pursuit of his doctrine of liberal inter-ventionism.

The frenetic diplomatic and political activity in the months leading up to the Iraqi invasion of 19 March 2003 was fraught, as bitter in its domestic political argumentation as the events surrounding the Munich conference in 1938, with similar language deployed on both sides. But Blair was confident that the invasion would be a success, fortifying British prestige as well as security. It was not to be.

The intervention started well, with the passage of a parliamentary vote in favour on 18 March 2003 by an overwhelming 412 to 149, as most Labour MPs stayed loyal and the Conservatives swung behind Blair. Public opinion was also majority supportive at this stage. The initial invasion removed Saddam with less Iraqi military opposition, and fewer British and American casualties, than expected. But the security and executive situation in Iraq rapidly disintegrated. US and British troops became bogged down in a desperate guerrilla war with insurgent forces militarily supported by neighbouring Iran and its continuing anti-American revolutionary government. Well-publicised atrocities took place on both sides, including by American and British troops. The failure to find 'weapons of mass destruction' steadily sapped Blair's moral authority, particularly after the suicide of British weapons inspector Dr David Kelly on 17 July 2003, who was hounded after speaking to a journalist about his long-standing doubts as to the existence of WMDs. All this reignited domestic opposition, manifested before the war in a march in central London of more than a million anti-war protesters. Over the course of 2003, the left defined itself against the Iraq invasion with a bitterness and intensity not seen since Eden's Suez invasion of 1956. Successive judicial and public inquiries into governmental decision making in the run-up to the war dominated Blair's last years in office and subsequently.

In Iraq, Blair wanted his Falklands but got his Suez. It was 'never glad confident morning again', although he did a political Houdini in surviving with substantial political authority for four more years in office. He not only contained growing internal and international opprobrium but also won the May 2005 election, gaining a new lease of political life until September 2006 when Brown, deploying lieutenants to threaten a leadership challenge, forced him to set his departure for 27 June 2007. This period saw the successful British bid for the 2012 Olympic games, pipping Paris for the honour on 5 July 2005 after a highly personal duel between Blair and Chirac.

One of Blair's greatest stated regrets is that he was not able to take Britain into the Euro, and it is hard to believe that he does not wish that George W. Bush and Iraq had not come upon him. So the big counterfactual of his premiership is: what if he had expended the huge political capital he amassed in 1997 on the Euro instead of Iraq? Having been there with him, it is possible to imagine this; the margins were fine on both. Britain and maybe the world would be fundamentally different had he done so. Ultimately, Blair poses in especially stark relief the profound remark of Pierre Mendès-France, who got France out of Vietnam: 'To govern is to choose.'

Andrew Adonis is a writer and former Labour Cabinet minister. He was elevated to the peerage as Lord Adonis of Camden Town in 2005.

52

Gordon Brown

27 June 2007 to 11 May 2010
Labour

By Stewart Wood

Full name: James Gordon Brown
Born: 20 February 1951, Giffnock, Renfrewshire
Education: Kirkcaldy High School; University of Edinburgh
Married to Sarah Macaulay; 2 sons, 1 daughter
Quotation: 'Under this Government, Britain will not return to the boom and bust of the past.' (9 November 1999)

GORDON BROWN BECAME prime minister on 27 June 2007 after a decade as Chancellor to Tony Blair, his fellow architect of the New Labour political project. Brown arrived in No. 10 having been elected unopposed by his party. Few men can have entered the highest British political office equipped with comparable levels of political skill, stamina, intellectual ability, dedication to public service and ambition as Brown. But his tenure would prove to be a short and rocky road, full of friction with his own party, errors of judgement and sheer bad luck. Brown's premiership plunged the political depths of the MPs' expenses crisis. But it also delivered one of the most astonishing displays of peacetime political leadership in response to an economic crash that threatened to engulf not just the UK but the world economy.

Brown is a son of the Manse: his father, John, was a Church of Scotland minister in Kirkcaldy in Fife. From his father he inherited much: his evangelical zeal, though directed at politics rather than heaven; an affection for Israel, where his father travelled extensively representing his Church; and an austere but sincere dedication to public service. Like his father, Brown had no interest in material gain. His passions remain simple: family, history, football and politics.

As a young man he became enamoured of the transformative idealism of the Kennedys (RFK more than JFK) and the Camelot court around it. But in his inexhaustible energy, tactical cunning and capacity for ruthless politics when necessary, he was perhaps as much inspired by JFK's successor Lyndon Johnson, of whom he was also a keen student.

In 1967 Brown lost the sight in one eye after a rugby match at school: only a young eye-surgeon's experimental procedure prevented him from losing sight in both eyes. He became a crusading Rector of Edinburgh University aged just twenty-one. After stints in lecturing and television journalism, Brown entered Parliament as MP for Dunfermline East in 1983. Like his soon-to-be best political friend Tony Blair, his politics were profoundly shaped by the struggle of Neil Kinnock to revive Labour after its near-terminal episode of the early 1980s. In 1985, just before listening with Blair to Neil Kinnock's famous repudiation of Militant at the Bournemouth Conference, Brown recalled being advised by an usher where the nearest exits were, 'in case everything kicked off'.

Brown was the senior partner in the Blair–Brown partnership. Both were driven by a passion to return Labour to electability: reconciling the party to a market economy and a sceptical England to Labour. Though they agreed on much (more than Brown would admit) their politics were subtly different.

Brown was a child of the Edinburgh Enlightenment. Like fellow Kirkcaldy resident Adam Smith, he saw the potential of free markets to bring prosperity and challenge established interests, when combined with responsible behaviour. But he was also a Scottish Social Democrat: optimistic about the use of the state to deliver prosperity and social justice; egalitarian, but not anti-capitalist. And like the founding fathers of his beloved United States, he was enamoured with the Madisonian tradition of constitutionalism, building and redesigning political institutions to improve people's lives. On international affairs, Brown was also no Blairite: he was a hard-headed pro-European without affection for the activities of the EU, and an Americanophile who did not want UK policy dictated by Washington.

Brown's brilliance was widely recognised, and to many he seemed the obvious successor to John Smith as leader of the Labour Party. Yet when Smith's death in 1994 forced a leadership election, Brown and Blair agreed (allegedly at the Granita restaurant in Islington) that Blair would be the reformers' candidate. A sense of grievance would remain with Brown for the rest of his political career, re-inforced a decade later by Prime Minister Blair promising to step down before seeking re-election, only to change his mind in mid-2004.

Brown spent three years as Shadow Chancellor relentlessly re-establishing Labour's credentials as a responsible custodian of public finances. Once in power, a series of radical reforms – including making the Bank of England independent, and transformative invest-ment in public services – made him a hugely successful Chancellor, presiding over strong growth while increasing spending. Though private and public tensions continued with Blair (over university tuition fees, the war in Iraq and Brown's decision to stay out of the Euro), it was a period of seemingly unchallengeable ascendancy for Labour.

Once he became prime minister, it may have felt to Brown as though the long shadow of Blair's tenure could be brushed aside. But the tension between being a repudiator and an inheritor of Blair's New Labour project was to be a hallmark of Brown's premier-ship. Brown wanted his own distinct policy agenda, yet, without an electoral mandate, and having been CEO to Blair's Chairman for ten years of Labour government, he found it difficult to create one, despite a litany of initiatives and vision documents. He was not helped by a Blairite establishment inside Labour that portrayed any opposition to Blair's public services policies as anti-reform; and a press dominated by Rupert Murdoch (whom Brown continued to court until the spectacular rupture of 2009) that saw any departure from Blair's policies as a return to Labour's unelectable past.

Brown defied his critics in his first two months in power with skilful political management in response to a series of national crises (terrorist attacks in Glasgow and London on day two of his premiership, a foot-and-mouth epidemic, and extensive nationwide flooding). A series of domestic policy initiatives also earned attention and praise. Some of them turned a page on Blair (abolishing plans for super-casinos, reintroducing university scholarships for poorer students), while others spoke to new agendas, in particular a draft blueprint for constitutional reform.

By August, opinion polls showed enthusiastic public support for Brown and Labour. Despite Blairite fears that Brown would be a leaden-footed, stolid PM, his assiduous, strong and relentless style of crisis management had proven a popular antidote to what the public saw as the 'spin' culture of the Blair years. A Labour billboard with the phrase 'Not flash, just Gordon' seemed to capture his strengths well.

Privately, Brown reminded his team these poll ratings were honeymoon froth. But he was sufficiently encouraged by them to allow open talk of an early autumn election, and began privately exploring options. The summer months saw a disastrous combination of open speculation encouraged by Brown's advisers, with continued internal indecision about when and whether to call an election.

By October, this indecision had led to public humiliation. A Conservative conference policy announcement on reducing inheritance tax finally propelled Brown into abandoning any ambitions for an autumn election. The final rejection of the idea in a hastily arranged BBC interview smacked of full-scale retreat and tactical defeat. It was an episode that inflicted lasting damage to public perceptions of Brown's judgement and authority, and to the unity of the previously tight Brown advisory team, who now launched into mutual recriminations.

In the months ahead, the self-inflicted wound of Brown's 'election that never was' was compounded by a sequence of mistakes and misfortune. In October, a Child Benefit database with confidential details of over 25 million claimants was lost by a government department. A month later, illegal loan donations to the Labour Party (of which Brown knew nothing) raised the spectre of sleaze, generating damaging internal rows between the PM, his deputy leader Harriet Harman and his own party staff. That same month, senior army representatives attacked Brown in public for starving them of resources needed to fight the war in Afghanistan – the first in a sequence of barbed exchanges between the UK military and a No. 10 that was keen to move on from the military engagements of the Blair era.

The year 2007 ended with an own goal. Instead of joining his fellow twenty-six heads of government in Lisbon for the ceremonial signing of the controversial EU treaty, Brown decided to stay at home to answer parliamentary committee questions, and sent his Foreign Secretary David Miliband in his place. Rather than succeed in symbolic distancing from a treaty whose origins had brought such grief to his predecessor, Brown's elaborate avoidance instead signified indecision and posturing at the expense of gravitas and leadership.

The early months of 2008 hinted that a recovery from the lows of late 2007 was possible. In health, education and immigration, Brown began to set out a coherent agenda for reform, building on New Labour reforms but extending them with new emphases on teacher quality, raising minimum standards of service and a comprehensive Children's Plan. Meanwhile, visits to China, India and, in particular, his speech at the JFK Memorial Library in Boston showed his significant authority on issues of international governance and reform of the global economy.

Yet again, however, momentum was derailed. In Brown's last Budget as Chancellor he had decided to axe the lower 10p rate of income tax, with effect from April 2008. Now, as the date loomed, the Parliamentary Labour Party launched into open revolt for fear of its effect on the lowest earners, and forced Brown to find money to compensate them. Of far greater importance was the prelude to the global economic crisis that would dominate Brown's premiership, when the Northern Rock bank faced liquidation in February. After heated arguments with the Treasury, Brown authorised the emergency nationalisation of Northern Rock – a move that, while hugely against his New Labour instincts, also served as an important intellectual liberation for the more significant decisions he would have to take later in the year.

These economic woes, combined with PLP anger and the recurrent return of stories of dysfunctionality inside No. 10, led to a protracted political crisis. May saw Labour's worst local election results in forty years, Boris Johnson elected as the first Tory Mayor of London, and the first Conservative by-election gain in thirty years (Crewe and Nantwich). A further PLP rebellion over the attempt to extend the length of time terrorist suspects could be detained without charge to forty-two days further strained relations with Brown's own party. In addition, relations with David Miliband and Brown's friend and Chancellor, Alistair Darling, were severely tested by an article outlining an alternative vision for governing by the former, and an interview predicting economic doom by the latter.

Alistair Darling's pessimism would be proved right. What no one could predict, however, was that Brown's response to the unprecedented economic crisis that began to unfold would be the greatest political achievement of his career.

On 15 September 2008, Lehman Brothers filed for bankruptcy. Like many banks across the Western world, it had become overexposed to subprime mortgages in the US housing market, leaving it hugely vulnerable to the downturn in property prices. At the time of Lehman's collapse, Brown's future as PM was being openly questioned in the wake of a flurry of ministerial resignations and threatening briefings from Blairite MPs. Within hours, the domestic political crisis was shaken off as he turned to confront the economic crisis facing Britain and the world.

Whatever the various errors and low points of Brown's time in power, Britain was fortunate indeed to have the right man at the helm in September 2008. He had the skills, experience, stamina and vision to understand what needed to be done. For a few short months he proved adept at handling febrile markets, intellectually uncertain world leaders, a panicking financial elite and a frightened British public.

His interventions came in four waves. First, in September 2008, immediate action was needed to bail out HBOS, Lloyds and Bradford & Bingley. Second, in two scary weeks in early October, Brown launched a £500 billion plan to recapitalise UK banks (coordinated with parallel unprecedented intervention by the Bank of England) and immediately set out to persuade George Bush and European leaders to abandon their own responses – bailing out toxic assets in Washington, guaranteeing bank deposits in Berlin – in favour of a global version of his recapitalisation plan. On 12 October he was invited to and effectively ran the Eurogroup meeting in Paris specially convened by French President Sarkozy. He emerged having won the argument, despite the UK not being a Euro member state. By early January 2009, a third initiative was needed for another domestic banking bailout, though one whose political impact was somewhat derailed by a national scandal over leading bankers continuing to collect their bonuses despite the economic carnage they had helped cause.

The fourth wave was the highpoint of Brown's premiership. In early April, Brown hosted a meeting of leaders from the G20 economies in London, at which he announced a market-reassuring collective stimulus totalling over $1 trillion. It was a triumph of global shuttle diplomacy, as Brown flew around the world in preparation to secure national contributions. It also marked the highpoint of global economic cooperation in the post-Cold War era. Brown was a leader who gave personal chemistry short shrift as a political ingredient. For him, interests, not personalities, drove politics. Yet here was a deal of global importance that was secured by Brown combining his personal authority, relentless work ethic and insistence on securing the personal commitments of world leaders.

For a brief moment, Brown looked as though he might be able to perform a political Houdini act and resurrect his electoral chances. Once again, however, the slings and arrows of misfortune and mistakes combined to make the remainder of the year the most difficult time in his No. 10 life. Immediately after the G20 triumph, Brown's controversial chief press adviser Damian McBride resigned after emails were leaked showing his attempts to spread false stories about Tory opponents. The Budget later that month began the tax-raising measures essential to pay for the enormous public support to save the banks – and immediately opened up a predictable but profitable anti-tax line of attack for Tory leader David Cameron.

But the domestic crisis that derailed Brown more than any other was a parliamentary crisis. In early 2009 it became apparent that the entire ledger of detailed expense claims of every MP had been leaked to the press, in advance of their planned publication in summary form later in the year. Public outrage was swift and widespread – at the pettiness of claims as much as at their scale. MPs of all parties protested that they had followed existing parliamentary rules, but in the court of public opinion their cause was hopeless. Brown, unusually for him, listened to his MPs' complaints too closely. While Cameron forced his MPs to repay, Brown took refuge in a review of the system, a series of proposals for alternative expense calculation systems, and eventually the idea of an independent regulator. Brown spent weeks playing catch-up with both the public and the leader of the opposition, and his public standing suffered considerably.

The result was a summer of threatened coups and senior ministerial resignations from inside his own Cabinet. The August night that Work and Pensions Minister James Purnell resigned – angry at what he saw as Brown's refusal to embrace the need for spending cuts – Brown's team assembled in 10 Downing Street, fearing that David Miliband would follow in Purnell's footsteps and trigger a leadership challenge. Miliband stayed silent, and talk of full-scale mutiny subsided, reappearing briefly in January 2010 for one last anaemic effort to depose Brown.

The remainder of the year was dominated by international issues. Brown's sense of obligation in supporting Tony Blair's ill-fated bid to become the first President of the European Council led to the UK being allocated a portfolio for the new Commission that Brown did not want (EU High Representative, a position that went to Cathy Ashton, and not, to his lasting annoyance, Peter Mandelson).

When Brown became PM, British troops were still engaged in both Iraq and Afghanistan. Quietly but effectively, Brown managed the full disengagement of UK forces from Iraq. Over Afghanistan, however, he wrestled uncomfortably with a UK defence establishment and military leadership, and after 2009 with the newly elected President Obama, who wanted the UK to match the USA's increase in troop commitments to secure the peace. He also faced increasing criticism from the right-wing press, culminating in November 2009 with the *Sun*'s wildly unfair accusation that in a handwritten note to a mother of a UK solider killed in Afghanistan he had misspelled the soldier's name. The Murdoch press had switched political horses, and Brown bore the brutal brunt of their opposition.

The run-up to the 2010 election held one more triumph for Brown. Over three days of emergency all-party talks at Hillsborough Castle outside Belfast, Brown secured the foundations for the elusive phase 2 of the Good Friday Agreement's devolution settlement, transferring police and justice powers to Northern Ireland. Blair is rightly credited for the landmark 1998 achievement that ended The Troubles, but Brown's contribution in completing the deal, and knowing when and how financial support would enable agreement to happen, is considerably under-appreciated. As is the courage he showed in calling for the Chilcot Inquiry into the 2003 Iraq War, a move much of his party and Cabinet resented. It was the right thing to do to enable a country scarred by the war to begin to move on, even though it undoubtedly rebounded to Labour's elec-toral disadvantage in the May election.

The 2010 election campaign will be remembered for two moments: the first TV debate, when Lib Dem leader Nick Clegg became a box-office hit with the electorate; and the day that Gordon Brown met Gillian Duffy, a disaffected Labour voter in Rochdale, who complained to him on camera about immigrants 'flocking in' from eastern Europe, only for Brown to forget to remove his microphone in the car driving away and be heard calling her 'a bigoted woman' in chatting to his aide. It was a moment that for many crowned a lacklustre Labour campaign, and seemed to herald a resounding defeat for Labour. But when 10 p.m. on Thursday 6 May came around, the election exit polls surprised everyone by projecting a Tory lead in a hung parliament rather than an outright majority.

Brown had a slender lifeline. He returned to Downing Street, and over the next five days plotted an unlikely rainbow governing coalition of Labour, Liberal Democrats and other minority parties. The result always made such a deal look impossible. Brown's logic, though, was not to create a viable government, but to scramble together a vote of confidence that would give his new government a few weeks or months in power: enough time for the Tories to depose yet another leader who had not won a majority, and prepare for a second election. Quickly, however, it became clear – from public statements and from the intensity of discussions between their teams – that a coalition government between David Cameron's Conservatives and Nick Clegg's Liberal Democrats would be forged.

On Tuesday 10 June 2010, a day after announcing his readiness to resign as Labour leader if it would make a progressive coalition possible, Brown accepted his fate. He left Downing Street for the last time at 5.45 p.m. in the last throes of daylight, so that Cameron would arrive in the first throes of darkness thirty minutes later. With him was Sarah and, on camera for the first time, his two boys John and Fraser.

Brown was always demanding, often irascible. His work ethic was astonishing. Aides would wake at 6 a.m. to find lengthy emails written to them at 3.30 a.m., and joke with each other about whether they were sent before Brown went to sleep or after he woke up. His inability to articulate a 'Brownite' domestic agenda once in power was both tragic for his own ambition and damaging for Labour's electoral fortunes. But, on occasions – responding to domestic crises, on international affairs, and in response to the 2008 Financial Crash – Brown showed that he could be a statesman like few others. And how many prime ministers leave office knowing that when their country faced a crisis of previously unimaginable proportions, it was fortunate indeed to have had exactly the right person at the helm when they were needed most?

Stewart Wood is a political academic and former adviser to Gordon Brown. He was elevated to the peerage as Lord Wood of Anfield in 2011.

53

David Cameron

11 May 2010 to 13 July 2016
Coalition, then Conservative

By Adam Boulton

Full name: David William Donald Cameron
Born: 9 October 1966, Marylebone, London
Education: Eton; Brasenose College, Oxford
Married to Samantha Sheffield; 2 sons, 2 daughters
Quotation: 'Conservatives believe in the ties that bind us.
Society is stronger when we make vows to each other and we
support each other. I don't support gay marriage in spite of
being a conservative. I support gay marriage because I am a
conservative.'

D AVID CAMERON SAID he wanted to be prime minister because
he thought he would 'be good at it'. He fulfilled the role for
six years with self-confidence, charm and mild authority. But it

ended with a dire legacy of failure. Cameron's great mistake was to call a referendum on leaving the European Union too casually; only to lose.

At home, Cameron presided unflinchingly over unbroken financial austerity. Public services were cut and squeezed while public employees had their pay capped. Abroad, especially around the Middle East, human misery thrived unabated, with Great Britain more uncertain than ever what it could do to alleviate these scourges.

The future of the Union remains an open question. Cameron failed to build on the 55 per cent to 45 per cent rejection of Scottish independence in 2014. Northern Ireland, Scotland and Wales are restless while no sense of unity prevails among the people of England.

Yet the chief beneficiary of this mess appears to have been Cameron's own party, which emerged in power at four General Elections, two under Cameron in 2010 and 2015, and subsequently under the leadership of Theresa May and Boris Johnson.

David Cameron's ascent to No. 10 felt like an irresistible rise, driven by the English ruling class's belief in its entitlement to power should it choose to reach for it. Cameron was the nineteenth prime minister to be educated at Eton.

On his mother's side, the Mount family have returned a series of Tory MPs since the early nineteenth century. The warmest conversation I ever had with Cameron was after an interview in his West Oxfordshire constituency. We had something in common, having grown up as boarding schoolboys, home for the holidays in the Thames Valley. Cameron talked about previous Mount MPs, including an ancestor whose campaign literature solely focused on the promise of cheap food. 'That's the way to do it,' he joked.

Cameron's father, Ian, was a successful stockbroker, whose name came up in the Panama Papers leak about offshore tax havens. David idolised his father, not least for the way he made nothing of a serious disability in his legs. Cameron's mother was a local JP.

David followed the conventional pattern of private education for one of his social position and time. First, Heatherdown, an exclusive boarding prep school from age seven, also attended by young 'senior' members of royal families.

Next, David became the latest in a long line of his family to attend Eton. His elder brother Alexander was already there, as was

Boris Johnson. Unlike those two, Cameron was not a schoolboy star. He was not elected by his peers to the prefects' society, 'Pop', and he narrowly escaped expulsion for involvement with cannabis.

In his final year at school, Cameron began the academic surge that took him to Oxford University and, eventually, a first-class degree in PPE (Philosophy, Politics and Economics). When I asked a contemporary at Brasenose College what else the future prime minister had got up to, he replied, 'He hung out with the other Etonians.' His tutor, Professor Vernon Bogdanor, described him as 'one of the ablest students' he's taught, 'with moderate and sensible' Conservative views.

The best-known image from Cameron's Oxford years is a group photograph of the Bullingdon Club, which his allies tried to suppress. It depicts young men, including Cameron and Boris Johnson, posing in silk-upholstered tailcoats on the steps of a grand college building.

By the time he was twenty-two years old, in 1988, Cameron had a job in the Conservative Research Department. Rumours persist that discreet expressions of interest from Buckingham Palace helped ease the young man's passage.

He soon became an aide to Prime Minister John Major and his hapless Chancellor of the Exchequer, Norman Lamont. Dealing with the media on his masters' behalves, he was airily self-confident to the point of conceit.

In the news footage of Black Wednesday, 16 September 1992, a glum-looking Cameron can be seen in the background in the Treasury courtyard, literally carrying the Chancellor's bags, as Lamont tries to explain sterling's enforced exit from the European Exchange Rate mechanism and subsequent dramatic increases in interest rates.

Cameron forged some key contacts for the future during this painful time for the Conservatives. His next boss, Michael Howard, became one of his greatest fans. Other CCHQ staff, including George Osborne, Kate Fall and Steve Hilton, would go on to be key aides in his Downing Street years, most of them well connected and posh. Kate, now Baroness Fall, denies that this was the formation of a 'chumocracy'.

Cameron left Westminster in 1994 to work as a public relations man for Carlton Communications, a media company created by

Michael Green, a prominent supporter of and donor to the Conservative Party. Those seven years were the only time Cameron was outside professional politics in his adult life until his resignation as prime minister, aged forty-nine.

During this period, Cameron married. If anything, his wife Samantha Sheffield, initially a friend of his sister, came from a smarter background as the daughter of a hereditary baronet and landowner. But she can take much of the credit for rounding out her 'posh boy' husband and making him more approachable.

Samantha is much less conventional and more down to earth than David, perhaps because her family life as a child was less sheltered. She studied art in Bristol and famously has a small tattoo of a dolphin on her ankle.

Their first child, Ivan, was born in 2002. He was severely disabled from birth with epilepsy and cerebral palsy. His parents cared for him devotedly and David Cameron repeatedly praised the NHS and welfare services for the care they gave his son. Ivan died in 2009. The Camerons have three other children. Nancy born in 2004, Elwen in 2006 and Florence in 2010, just months after the family moved into No. 10.

Cameron continued to be politically active in the Conservative Party while away from Westminster. He blooded himself as a candidate, standing, and losing, in Stafford, as Tony Blair swept to power in Labour's landslide election victory in 1997. After that, the race was on to find a winnable seat.

Cameron toured the circuit of selection meetings by Conservative associations and was turned down by some of them. The constituency of Witney proved a perfect fit. Cameron had grown up in the area and was reliably sound, unlike his immediate predecessor Shaun Woodward, who inherited the seat from Tory grandee Douglas Hurd only to defect to New Labour.

David Cameron was duly returned as MP in 2001. A good night for him but a second landslide burial for the Conservatives by Tony Blair. The election was a watershed for the party. Ted Heath and John Major stood down as MPs, while George Osborne and Boris Johnson entered Parliament.

But the folly of Iain Duncan Smith's leadership led to a third hammering by Labour in 2005. Michael Howard took on the mantle of the caretaker Conservative leader and fixed on Cameron and Osborne as his preferred successors. The younger Osborne was Howard's first choice, but instead Osborne threw his weight behind Cameron, who had no similar reservations about running for the leadership. (For once, this partnership and friendship would survive their time as prime minister and Chancellor.)

Cameron began the race as the outside candidate, but quickly eclipsed David Davis, the unenergetic former Europe Minister. He promised to modernise the party and acted out the part of a tie-less and informal new CEO. 'Call me Dave' became a catch-phrase. Instead of delivering stodgy speeches from a lectern, he prowled the stage seemingly speaking without notes or prompting.

Cameron was elected leader and continued in show-and-tell mode. He replaced the Tory Party's logo with a green oak tree and visited the Arctic Circle to underline a renewed commitment to act on climate change. 'Hug a husky' was followed by 'Hug a hoodie' when Cameron posed on a run-down council estate for what was essentially a repetition of Blair and Brown's 'tough on crime, tough on the causes of crime' government by slogan.

In 2007, Gordon Brown at last forced Tony Blair to hand him the premiership, only to miss the chance to call an early General Election. The UK was instead caught in the unfolding financial crisis that saw the collapse of such UK institutions as Northern Rock and RBS.

By the time the election had to be held in 2010, Labour was bitterly divided, not only over economic policy but also over the New Labour government's record and legacy, especially the Iraq invasion.

By contrast, a vanguard of 'Cameroons' coalesced around the new Tory leader. Named after the fashionable area of London where many of them lived, the 'Notting Hill Set' included Michael Gove, Nicholas Boles and Ed Vaizey, and the so-called 'A-list' of Cameron's preferred candidates, who stood in 2010 with mixed success.

But there were also deepening divisions on the right. Nigel Farage's UKIP was emerging as an electoral force demanding a referendum on UK membership of the EU. Cameron dismissed UKIP members as 'fruitcakes, loonies and closet racists', but tacked in their direction. He had already attempted to secure election as party leader by taking the Conservatives out of the EPP, the main centre-right grouping in the EU – a significant step that greatly antagonised Angela Merkel. In his condescending way, Cameron reckoned he knew how to win over the German Chancellor: give her a box set of *Midsomer Murders*.

The Conservatives were the largest party after the 2010 General Election, but they were short of an overall majority. Five days of frantic negotiations followed, during which both Brown and Cameron tried to form a government with support from the Liberal Democrats. The maths was against Labour, but Cameron still made the boldest move of his career: 'a big, open and comprehensive offer' to the Lib Dems to be full partners in a coalition government lasting five years.

It was an offer the Lib Dems, who had been out of power for eighty years, could scarcely refuse. Cameron made it lightly, seeming only to care about getting into power rather than who he shared it with. William Hague, a wilier negotiator with a long-term perspective, commented to his wife Ffion, 'I think I've just killed the Lib Dems.' But it was all smiles in the summer sun as the new prime minister and deputy prime minister Nick Clegg held their news conference in the Downing Street Rose Garden.

Cameron honoured the agreement to the letter. The top of government was conducted by 'the quad', consisting of himself, Clegg, Chancellor Osborne and his Lib Dem deputy Danny Alexander. As promised, the Fixed-term Parliaments Act was put into law. A referendum took place on electoral reform, though Cameron did all he could to ensure it was defeated. As a gesture of solidarity to the coalition, senior Lib Dems broke their election promise not to raise university tuition fees.

Environmentalism was a key policy that bonded the two parties. Cameron had campaigned with the slogan 'vote blue, go green'. But he infuriated his coalition partners in 2013 when he ordered, 'get rid of all the green crap' from electricity bills. When the 2015 General Election came around, Cameron enthusiastically fronted the Lib Dem 'decapitation strategy' devised by Lynton Crosby. The twenty-seven seats the Tories captured from the Lib Dems were enough to make Cameron prime minister in command of a slim Conservative majority.

Prime Minister Cameron shouldered the burdens of office with ease. He rose at five to go through his red boxes in the kitchen of the flat above Number 11 Downing Street previously occupied by the Blair family. The Camerons followed the Blairs in having another child during the premiership.

He was determinedly not a 24/7 prime minister. The word 'chillax' entered the national lexicon after Cameron spoke of his love of down time with a bottle and a box set to watch. He admitted, however, that leaving his young daughter Nancy behind at the pub after an extended Sunday lunch probably took chillaxing too far.

Cameron was seldom caught out on policy detail and took steps to avoid potential embarrassment. He did not hold monthly, or even regular news conferences, and cut down on the number of interviews prime ministers had previously done with serious news journalists.

When on camera, he could be surprisingly careless. In short TV interviews with me, he variously revealed the date by which UK troops would be withdrawn from Afghanistan; insisted that Britain was 'the junior partner' of the United States, even in 1940 when the US had not yet entered the Second World War; and professed himself 'humbled' by India's state of advancement compared to the UK.

Perhaps the two finest moments of his premiership were presidential rather than prime ministerial. In Parliament he delivered a pitch-perfect apology for Bloody Sunday, the massacre of Catholic civilians in Derry that took place when Cameron was barely a schoolboy.

The London Olympics of 2012 are also looked back on as a golden moment of national pride and inclusivity. Cameron trumpeted how 'the greatest show on earth' was an opportunity 'to show the world the best of Britain, a country that's got an incredibly rich past but also a very exciting future'.

Soft power thrived at the Olympics. Cameron's use of hard power around the world was less impressive. Under President Barack Obama, the US 'took a back seat', providing only air support when Britain and France intervened militarily to try to restore calm in Libya. But according to Obama, Cameron took his eye off the ball, resulting in the 'shit show' of civil war in Libya that persisted into the next decade.

Meanwhile, Western euphoria over the so-called Arab Spring again proved ill-founded in Syria. In 2013, President Obama's red line was crossed when the Assad regime was caught using chemical weapons in direct violation of international law. Cameron hastily reconvened Parliament at the end of the summer recess for a vote to authorise a punitive strike. But his preparations were slapdash and the Commons voted against the Prime Minister's recommendation in what was a stunning blow to the UK's international credibility.

The situations in Libya and Syria were the main drivers of the mass migration of refugees into Europe in 2015 and 2016 that would feed into the debate during the UK's EU referendum.

This Prime Minister's record of domestic policy achievement is slim, hemmed in as he was by his insistence on austerity to put the national finances back in order after the credit crunch. Cameron imposed a cap on public sector pay increases and bore down hard on welfare claimants. His belief was: 'We spend billions of pounds on welfare, yet millions are trapped on welfare. It's not worth their while going into work.' But measures such as the clampdown on incapacity benefit, the so-called bedroom tax, and the introduction of Universal Credit often seemed to be targeting the less well-off while the more affluent felt little pain.

'The Big Society' will be remembered more as a slogan than as something that actually made a difference. As a Thatcherite Tory, Cameron was instinctively sceptical of state spending and intervention, declaring, 'real change is not what government can do on its own. Real change is when everyone pulls together.' But he failed to devise effective ways for civil society and the private sector to fill the breach.

David Cameron says his single proudest achievement as prime minister was the introduction of same-sex marriage. This was an extension of the civil partnerships introduced by Tony Blair, or 'the Master' as George Osborne called him. Going one better, Cameron even claimed himself to be 'the heir to Blair'.

Copies are seldom as successful as the original. Tony Blair manipulated referendums and the promise of referendums to his political advantage; Cameron fell foul of them.

The referendum on Scottish Independence in September 2014

was a less narrow squeak than Downing Street had feared when a poll showed that 'Yes' supporters were ahead a few weeks out from the vote. Though he denied it in advance, victory for 'Yes' would have finished Cameron's premiership two years before it actually ended. But incongruously, for all the promises to Scotland made, in Downing Street the morning after, Cameron failed to mobilise a counter-offensive against the SNP. His most notable action was to be overheard indiscreetly describing how the Queen 'purred down the phone' when he told her the referendum result. For Cameron, Scotland remained a place to shoot stags.

Cameron habitually described himself as 'a Eurosceptic Conservative'. He followed up the Conservatives' withdrawal from the EPP with the unprecedented use of the UK veto at a European Council in 2011. This was a characteristically nonchalant and ineffective manoeuvre that left the UK with less leverage in the EU.

Cameron shared none of his partner George Osborne's reservations about the risks inherent in a referendum on Britain's continuing membership of the European Union, blithely confident that he would win it. He injected the possibility of a referendum into his conversation long before he committed to hold one in his speech of 23 January 2013 at Bloomberg's London headquarters.

For Cameron the promise of an in/out vote was a tool of party management to keep the Tory right flank in step. UKIP's stunning victory in the 2014 European Parliament Elections only strengthened his resolve. In retirement, he continued to insist that he would have held a referendum even if the coalition had extended beyond June 2015.

Since he advocated Remain, David Cameron must have thought that continued membership was beneficial to the UK. But he did not frame the Remain campaign as a celebration of Britain in the EU. He began his campaign by seeking a renegotiation of the terms. This strategy had been a convenient fig leaf for Harold Wilson a couple of years after joining the EEC, but it made no sense after forty years of membership. The package of minor concessions Cameron obtained pleased no one and left him telling the British people to vote to remain in an institution he disliked and that had rebuffed him, in contrast to Leave's easier proposition to just get out and 'Take Back Control'.

Like Harold Wilson ahead of the 1975 referendum, Cameron dissolved collective Cabinet responsibility and let his ministers take sides. His personal appeals to Michael Gove failed, and the Prime Minister was surprised when his old pal, the ambitious Boris Johnson, also opted for Leave.

Unlike Wilson, Cameron did not step back. He appointed himself head of the campaign for Remain, but refused to debate his position on TV. By his own admission, he held Remain back from going full throttle and vetoed attacks on Tory ministers on the other side.

The Prime Minister's warm personal relationship with the American president led Barack Obama to reply, when asked at a news conference during a visit to London, that the UK would be 'at the back of the queue' seeking an independent trade deal with the US. This outside intervention was judged to be counterproductive for the Remain cause.

On 23 September 2016, Leave won by 52 per cent to 48 per cent. Cameron had stated that he would not resign if defeated, but he immediately announced he was quitting. The mirthless ditty he was overheard humming as he headed back through the front door of No. 10 Downing Street was a fitting theme tune for his careless years as prime minister – years that left his country weaker, poorer and bitterly divided.

Adam Boulton is editor at large of Sky News *and the presenter of* All Out Politics.

54

Theresa May

13 July 2016 to 24 July 2019
Conservative

By Rachel Sylvester

Full name: Theresa Mary May, née Brazier
Born: 1 October 1956, Eastbourne
Education: Wheatley Park School, Holton, Oxfordshire; St
Hugh's College, Oxford
Married to Philip May; no children
Quotation: 'Brexit means Brexit.'

THERESA MAY HAD one job when she became prime minister
in the summer of 2016: to deliver on the result of the Brexit
referendum and take the United Kingdom out of the European
Union. She did not do so. Instead, she left the country more divided
and her party torn to pieces by the effort of reconciling its differences over Europe. At the end of her premiership, politics was more

toxic, the Union weaker and Britain more marginalised in the world than when she arrived in Downing Street. The reputation of key institutions, including the courts, the civil service and the House of Commons, had been undermined by the constitutional crisis she presided over. Instead of healing the wounds created by the referendum, she inflamed the tensions by denouncing liberal Remainers as 'citizens of nowhere' and failing to condemn headlines about the judges being the 'enemies of the people'. The social revolution that she heralded on her first day in No. 10 when she promised to end the 'burning injustices' in modern Britain never materialised.

On these terms it is hard to see May's time in office as anything other than a failure. During her 1,106 days as prime minister, she suffered thirty-five ministerial resignations (outside of reshuffles) and multiple Commons humiliations, including the biggest government defeat in parliamentary history. Although she was undoubtedly given a difficult task, it was she who made it impossible through a series of political misjudgements and character flaws. None of those who worked with her question her integrity, stamina or dedication, but she lacked fundamental leadership skills. Chris Wilkins, who was her director of strategy between 2016 and 2017, says:

> If you look back at her time, on any of the metrics you would set for her job, she didn't succeed. She never delivered Brexit, and her domestic ambitions also remained unfulfilled. The question is: could anyone have done it? I'm more sympathetic to her on that front. There are people who would have been more adept but I don't think it was entirely down to her failings.

I had a small role in May's elevation to the top job. In July 2016, I interviewed Andrea Leadsom for *The Times*. The Tory leadership contest had descended into chaos. Boris Johnson had been knifed in the back by Michael Gove, who had then also been eliminated. Leadsom, who was then an energy minister, was the only candidate left apart from May. She told me that she believed motherhood gave her an advantage because 'being a mum means you have a real stake in the future of our country'. It was a crass line to use at any time, but it seemed particularly cruel because, only a few days before, her rival had spoken about her sadness that she could not have children. Leadsom pulled out and May became leader by default with extraordinarily little scrutiny of her character or policy platform. 'There was always a sense that she was a slightly accidental prime minister,' Wilkins says. 'She hadn't been tested in a leadership campaign and because it happened so quickly she then made mistakes.'

On moving into No. 10, May immediately set out to distinguish herself from her predecessor. She signalled an end to the 'chumocracy' favoured by Cameron by throwing out the comfortable sofa in the Downing Street 'den' and replacing it with a table and hard-backed chairs. The table was supposed to be a symbol of a new seriousness in government, but as time went on, those around her began to see it as a barrier that made it harder for her to build alliances. May always made a virtue of her lack of 'club-ability', which she contrasted with the easy bonhomie of the public schoolboys in the Tory Party. An only child, she was naturally shy and rarely visited the Commons bars or tea rooms. Instead of socialising, she preferred to eat alone with Philip, a devoted husband and also at times her most trusted political adviser. One former newspaper editor who sat next to her at a dinner found it so difficult to make conversation that he asked to move after the first course.

There was also a slight chippiness. The vicar's daughter, who had gone to a grammar school, hated the culture of privilege that she associated with Cameron and his circle. Soon after she became prime minister, she told her aides that they should not expect peerages or knighthoods in her retirement honours list – 'she said it was an honour to work in No. 10 and if we were lucky we might get a Jaffa Cake,' one recalls. Although May was in many ways a traditional shire Tory, she always thought of herself as an outsider. Instead of 'chillaxing' at Chequers, she worked late into the night on her red boxes. She had a ferocious work ethic and was admired by her civil servants for her grasp of policy detail.

There was something admirably high-minded about her approach, but she also alienated people while failing to make friends. George Osborne, dismissed as Chancellor with a humiliating lecture about how he should get to know the party better, went on to edit the

Evening Standard and became one of her greatest critics, once describing her as 'a dead woman walking'. Wilkins says:

> If I'm honest it went wrong on day one. The decisions that were made about the way the Cabinet was put together, and the way people who left the Cabinet were dealt with, was all problematic. If she wanted to be the domestic reforming prime minister she shouldn't have made Philip Hammond [a cautious economically dry Conservative] her chancellor. She spent too long trying to balance the Cabinet between Leavers and Remainers rather than having the right people in her team.

May had survived for six years as Home Secretary, one of the most politically treacherous jobs in government, by being controlling, careful and uncollegiate. But the strengths that had helped her at the Home Office turned into weaknesses in No. 10. Ken Clarke, the former chancellor, once described her as a 'bloody difficult woman' and she wore it as a badge of honour, even drinking her tea from a mug printed with those words, but a prime minister needs to be flexible and charming as well as stubborn.

The two fiercely loyal chiefs of staff, Nick Timothy and Fiona Hill, who had protected her in her previous job, became a liability as they tried to act as a filter between the Prime Minister and the rest of Whitehall. The Cabinet became increasingly frustrated about May's refusal to delegate and her inability to make decisions. Amber Rudd, who succeeded her at the Home Office, and also later served as Work and Pensions Secretary, says: 'The characteristic that defined her really was as an extension of being Home Secretary. It's a very cautious job, you don't take risks, but as prime minister you have to win people round and persuade them and lead. There was very little leadership.' Meetings were excruciating, with long periods of silence. 'In Cabinet she would ask everyone for their opinion but there was no resolution,' Rudd recalls. Chris Wilkins says that for all the disloyalty that was shown to May during her time as prime minister, she ultimately had only herself to blame. 'You never left a meeting knowing what she thought. That is a dysfunctional way to work. There were many many problems but ultimately they all came from the top and the lack of decisiveness.'

At a time when the government had to resolve the most difficult political dilemma for a generation, that was a disaster. On taking office, May had issued the meaningless platitude that 'Brexit means Brexit', then boxed herself into a series of positions, at times apparently oblivious to the full consequences of what she was saying. On 29 March 2017, she invoked Article 50, which gave two years for the UK to agree the terms of its departure from the EU, even though she had no clear idea about what she wanted to achieve in the negotiations with Brussels. She ruled out membership of the customs union and the single market without any Cabinet debate about the trade-offs that would be involved. In an attempt to keep the factions of her party together, she infuriated both sides. 'I think that she was in a difficult position because she was undecided about where she stood on Brexit except that she knew we had to do it,' says Rudd, who had campaigned for Remain in the referendum.

With a parliamentary majority of just seventeen, May also realised that she would struggle to get any plan on such a divisive issue through the Commons. The Tories were riding high in the opinion polls and she was enjoying a political honeymoon, and so, less than a year after taking office, she called a snap General Election that was held on 8 June 2017. Her aim was to get a mandate for her version of Brexit. In fact, she lost her majority and her authority was destroyed both at Westminster and in Brussels. The flaws that had been apparent to Cabinet ministers during the early months of her premiership were on display to the country during a campaign that put the Tory leader centre-stage. She was uncomfortable in the public eye, and awkward in interviews, even sending Rudd in her place to a televised leaders' debate. Having promised to be 'strong and stable', May was left looking 'weak and wobbly' after she abandoned a flagship policy on social care that had been branded the 'dementia tax'. Wilkins recalls:

Halfway through the campaign there was a meeting in Conservative campaign headquarters when she said: 'I absolutely hate this campaign. It's not the campaign I wanted. I'm being told where to stand, what to say even what to wear and I'm not allowed to be me.' And I thought – 'Well change it then.' But she didn't. She just didn't have the confidence. Again, the problem was indecision.

May returned to No. 10 as leader of the largest party but running a minority government. She was dependent on a 'confidence and supply' agreement with the Northern Irish Democratic Unionist Party while also being at the mercy of the Brexiteer Tories in the European Research Group. Her two chiefs of staff were sacrificed, but it was not enough to salvage the Prime Minister's own reputation. From that moment on, power seeped away from her. Between the 2017 election and her eventual departure just over two years later, there were twenty-eight government defeats in the Commons, the second highest number since 1945. At the European elections in May 2019, the Conservatives suffered their worst result in a national election since the 1830s when they came fifth, with just 9 per cent of the vote. Yet May failed to understand the weakness of her own position and instead of trying to build consensus across party lines after the General Election, she continued to try and govern as if she had a huge majority. By the time she did eventually open up talks with Labour – towards the very end of her premiership – it was too little too late and positions had become entrenched on all sides.

There were moments that played to her strengths – including the Novichok attack by Russian agents in Salisbury, which she responded to quickly and confidently. But her reaction to the Grenfell Tower tragedy in 2017 exposed a lack of emotional intelligence when she failed to meet survivors in the immediate aftermath of the fire. Her Home Office years began to catch up with her – most notably during the Windrush scandal, when British citizens were wrongly arrested and deported for failing to have the right paperwork, a result of her 'hostile environment' policy towards immigration.

On Europe, the issue that dominated her premiership, the Cabinet rapidly descended into open warfare. When David Davis, the Brexit Secretary, and Boris Johnson, then Foreign Secretary, resigned in 2018 because they could not sign up to May's proposals for taking the UK out of the EU – the so-called 'Chequers deal' – it was clear that the Eurosceptics in the Tory Party were never going to be happy. 'I think she was given an impossible situation to deliver this in the face of a party that was becoming the Brexit party and they wanted their Brexit leader,' says Rudd. 'I suspect there was also an element of sexism. The European Research Group is very male.' But the pro-Europeans were also dissatisfied. Conservative MPs, who had voted Remain, were instrumental in inflicting a series of defeats on the government, and the pro-Europeans in the Cabinet became increasingly outspoken in their attempts to block a 'no deal' Brexit. Any sense of discipline or collective responsibility evaporated, with ministers even sometimes texting journalists with live updates of confidential discussions. 'Cabinet became more and more polarised,' according to Rudd. 'There was epic leaking as everyone was positioning themselves for the fight on Brexit and the leadership which was coming.'

May kept her job for two years after the 2017 election only because the multiple plotters could not agree on who should replace her. She survived a no confidence vote by Tory MPs, and a no confidence vote in the House of Commons, triggered by the opposition, but when it became clear that she would never be able to get her Brexit deal through Parliament her position was unsustainable and on 24 May 2019 she announced her resignation. By then she was, one aide said, 'like a wounded beast being chased'. According to Rudd: 'the reason she went is because nobody trusted her any more. It wasn't that she lied but she just didn't deliver for anyone. She implied to everyone that they would get what they wanted.'

Unlike most of her predecessors, May stayed as a back-bench MP after resigning as prime minister. 'I don't think she has much of a hinterland,' says one former minister. 'I'm slightly amazed she stood as a member of parliament again. I think at the core of her that's what she is – she is a good Christian English woman, who is very strong on duty and her community.' She is happiest in her Maidenhead constituency, attending drinks parties and charity coffee mornings or shopping in the local Waitrose.

The mystery for many of the people who worked with her is why she wanted to be leader, a role for which she seemed so conspicuously unsuited. A member of her Cabinet argues that most prime ministers have 65 per cent of what is needed for the job, and hire people around them who can do the rest, but May only had 55 per cent and never built a team that would compensate for her shortcomings. 'There are all these stories about her wanting to do it when she was younger but she didn't seem to enjoy it,' Rudd says. 'You look at David Cameron, Boris Johnson, Gordon Brown, Tony Blair or John Major, they had a swagger about being prime minister. There was a pride about it. With Theresa May it was all just terribly difficult, which of course it was.'

Those who know her best say 'duty' was the main driving force behind May's premiership, but that was not enough for a leader at a uniquely difficult moment in the nation's history.

Rachel Sylvester is a political journalist and columnist for The Times.

55

Boris Johnson

24 July 2019—
Conservative

By Iain Dale

Full name: Alexander Boris de Pfeffel Johnson
Born: 19 June 1964, New York City
Education: Eton College; Balliol College, Oxford
Married to 1. Allegra Mostyn-Owen; 2. Marina Wheeler; 3.
Carrie Symonds; 2 sons, 3 daughters
Quotation: 'I have as much chance of becoming Prime Minister as
of being decapitated by a frisbee or of finding Elvis.' (21 July 2003)

IT WASN'T SUPPOSED to be like this, at least not quite. Boris
Johnson is a man whose belief in his own destiny has been
unshakeable. From professing at the age of five to wanting to be
'World King', he overcame many self-imposed hurdles to eventually
become prime minister half a century later.

He set himself up as the nation's Brexit saviour, the only politician in the land who could lead it through the troubled waters of Brexit into the sunlit uplands of an independent Britain basking in the afterglow of sovereign, free-trading nationhood.

And then Coronavirus descended on the United Kingdom, not just casting a deep shadow over the whole of society and the economy, but very nearly consuming the Prime Minister himself.

Born on the Upper East Side of Manhattan in 1964, Boris Johnson experienced a nomadic childhood. In his first nine years he was carted across the Atlantic several times, living in New York, Oxford, Crouch End, Maida Vale, Somerset, Washington DC, Connecticut, Primrose Hill and Brussels. He was sent to Ashdown House School in East Sussex before gaining a scholarship to Eton, where he abandoned his first name and took on the role of Boris. It was here that he befriended David Cameron. His school reports give early mention to idleness, complacency and lateness – three words that would dog his adult life. Despite this, he excelled at Eton, winning prizes in Classics and English. Before going up to Oxford, Johnson spent a gap year teaching English in Australia.

He was a popular and successful undergraduate, becoming Secretary of the Oxford Union and, at the second attempt, President. Much to his disappointment, but perhaps not surprise, he failed to be awarded a First.

Johnson spent a week as a management consultant with LEK Consulting after leaving university, but then joined *The Times* newspaper journalist training scheme in late 1987. This came to grief when he was fired for inventing a quote. *Telegraph* editor Max Hastings, later to become an über-critic of Johnson, came to his rescue, and within two years made him Brussels correspondent. It was here that he could lay claim to be the man who started to stoke the nascent flames of Euroscepticism in Britain. The then British EU Commissioner Chris Patten later claimed that Johnson was one of the 'first exponents of fake journalism'.

Upon his return to London he carved out a niche as a controversial columnist in both the *Telegraph* and *The Spectator*. In 1999 he became editor of the latter, having promised proprietor Conrad Black he had abandoned any parliamentary ambitions following his unsuccessful attempt to secure the unwinnable seat of Clwyd South in 1997. A few months later he was selected to replace Michael Heseltine in the safe seat of Henley.

Johnson's parliamentary career took some time to take off. He was more noted for appearances on TV comedy shows like *Have I Got News for You* than any speech he made in Parliament. But the public seemed to like him. He continued to edit *The Spectator*, but riding two horses was proving more and more difficult to justify. An editorial he published (but not written by him) accusing Liverpool of having a 'victim mentality' led to the Conservative leader ordering Johnson to go to Liverpool to apologise in person. A month later, Howard sacked him for lying to him over an affair with the journalist Petronella Wyatt. In 2005 he was sacked as *Spectator* editor by its new chief executive Andrew Neil, and he backed David Cameron in the Conservative leadership contest. Cameron rewarded him by appointing him Shadow Universities Minister.

It was in 2008 that Boris Johnson achieved political stardom. He had to be persuaded, but he sought the Conservative nomination for London Mayor after the favourite, his friend Nick Boles, pulled out of the race following a cancer diagnosis. Not for the last time, Labour totally underestimated his electoral appeal and he beat the incumbent, Ken Livingstone. Much to most people's surprise, he repeated the feat four years later. Possibly learning from President George W. Bush, from the outset Johnson appointed a team of deputy mayors and advisers designed to compensate for his own weaknesses. His eight years as mayor can be seen as moderately successful, even if some people would acknowledge the 'Boris Bike' scheme as his only notable success. They ignore the glory of the 2012 Olympic Games, which Johnson himself looks back on as his greatest achievement, and in many ways rightly so. They showed off the kind of Britain Boris Johnson now wishes to be prime minister of – open, liberal, maverick and making waves.

Despite still being Mayor, Boris Johnson returned to the House of Commons at the 2015 General Election as MP for Uxbridge and South Ruislip, but it was to be the Brexit referendum where he was to next hit the headlines. Despite coming under huge pressure from Prime Minister David Cameron and most of his family and friends, in February 2016 he declared his support for the Leave campaign, thus becoming its de facto leader. Some pundits say this was the key moment in the whole Brexit saga.

His electoral popularity gave the Leave campaign the momentum it needed, and it never looked back. Johnson himself was less than confident of winning, but calculated that whatever the result, he would gain politically. It didn't quite turn out that way.

The morning following Leave's victory David Cameron resigned, triggering a leadership contest. Johnson wasn't ready for it. His old flaws all came to the fore. His mistreatment of fellow leadership candidate Andrea Leadsom led to his running mate Michael Gove deserting him and standing himself, leaving it to someone else to inform Johnson of his decision. Boris was distraught. His campaign launch turned into a wake, and off he went to lick his wounds, but only for fourteen days.

On 13 July 2016 the new prime minister, Theresa May, astonished the whole of Westminster and appointed him Foreign Secretary. His two years in the job were not happy ones. His counterparts across the world divided into those who loathed him and those who adored him. Repeated gaffes led to a bunker mentality forming in the Foreign Office, where he seemed marginalised by Downing Street with the Brexit Secretary, David Davis, ensuring he played little role in the Brexit negotiations.

His cack-handed handling of the response to the imprisonment in Iran of the British-Iranian dual citizen Nazanin Zaghari-Ratcliffe and his reported blurting out of the phrase 'fuck business' after the CBI expressed concerns about a 'hard' Brexit did little to enhance his reputation. However, his handling of the diplomatic response to the poisoning of the Skripals in Salisbury in March 2018 drew widespread praise, after he persuaded more than thirty countries to expel Russian diplomats.

Inevitably, it all ended in tears. Following a Cabinet agreement in July 2018 at a summit in Chequers to decide the way forward on Brexit, David Davis beat him to resigning from the government by twenty-four hours. Johnson's resignation went off with a whimper and he proceeded to spend the next ten months in the political wilderness. But in May 2019 Theresa May finally departed and Johnson had a second chance of a tilt at the prize. Having been written off as a no-hoper only months previously (not least by me), he triumphed in a play-off with his successor as Foreign Secretary, Jeremy Hunt.

On 24 July 2019, Boris Johnson achieved the office he must have begun to think he would never rise to. And it was there that the fun started. He fashioned a Cabinet very much in his own image, expunging virtually all trace of political opponents or Hunt supporters. He declared that his job as prime minister was to 'Get Brexit Done' – three words that would dominate the political lexicon for the next six months.

Given that Johnson enjoyed no parliamentary majority and a substantial part of his party was determined to thwart his Brexit policy, it was a minor miracle that he ever managed to do a deal with the European Union. He and his chief adviser Dominic Cummings tried every trick in the book, including unlawfully proroguing Parliament, but they were outmanoeuvred at every turn by a combination of the Speaker of the House of Commons and a parliamentary ragtag of Remain-supporting MPs from across the House.

The 31 October deadline loomed and, with no prospect of getting a deal through, Johnson rolled the dice and called a General Election for 12 December. He stormed to victory with an eighty-seat majority and with that the whole political atmosphere changed. He immediately started the process of taking the necessary Brexit legislation through Parliament, and the UK formally left the EU on 31 January 2020. Johnson's poll ratings continued to bloom, and as the negotiations started with the EU to secure a free-trade deal by the end of 2020, he appeared master of all he surveyed.

And then the Coronavirus hit.

In the initial stages of the crisis, his government seemed unsure about which strategy to adopt to mitigate the spread of Covid-19. Johnson insisted he was following scientific advice, but appeared uncharacteristically devoid of certainty in front of TV cameras.

At the height of the crisis he started displaying symptoms himself, and self-isolated, followed quickly by his Health Secretary and Chief Medical Officer. He struggled on, working from the Downing Street flat, but his state of health worsened and he was hospitalised at exactly the same time as HM The Queen was addressing the nation. Two days later he was moved to an Intensive Care Unit and reportedly came within an inch of losing his life. Four days later he was released from hospital and spent the next few weeks recuperating at Chequers.

The next few months proved very difficult for the government and Boris Johnson in particular. Its messaging was mixed and various Covid-19 initiatives appeared to be ill thought out and incompetently administered. Repeated promises and pledges were broken and by the end of August infection rates were on the rise again, leading to Boris Johnson addressing the nation and imposing renewed restrictions on day to day activities. He did this amid rumours that he himself was suffering from so-called 'Long Covid' and was not back to functioning at full tilt. There was even speculation that the state of his health could even lead to an early departure from office.

Meanwhile, negotiations with the EU over a free trade deal were getting nowhere fast. In early September Johnson let it be known that he was willing to breach the EU Withdrawal Agreement (and consequently breach international treaty law) to protect the integrity of the four nations of the United Kingdom. The controversial Internal Market Bill came before Parliament, provoking fury among all sides of the House of Commons with even the former Prime Minister Theresa May vowing to oppose it.

Boris Johnson is portrayed by his opponents as a right-wing Tory extremist. In reality, he is a mixture of a social liberal and old-fashioned Tory paternalist. His election victory gave the Conservatives the majority they hadn't enjoyed since Margaret Thatcher won a landslide in 1987. He won so well, largely because he managed to appeal to die-hard Labour voters in seats the Tories hadn't dreamed of winning for decades – in some cases, ever – across the Midlands and the North. Many of them said they were 'voting for Boris', rather than voting Conservative.

Westminster commentators and his political opponents have consistently underestimated Boris Johnson's appeal outside the M25. His longevity as prime minister will largely depend on whether he can retain that support at the next General Election.

It is of course too early to form a judgement on whether Boris Johnson will go down in history as a great prime minister or a poor one. He's the most intellectually capable prime minister Britain has seen, despite often appearing to be a clown. Somehow, he inspires loyalty and devotion – first it was *Telegraph* readers, then *Spectator* readers, then London, and now he seems to have acquired that same loyalty from large parts of the electorate. He has confounded many of his critics, and gripped both the Conservative Party and the country.

Whatever the verdict of history, it will be how he leads the country out of the Coronavirus crisis that will have more impact on his legacy than the free-trade deal he does with the EU. Despite his personal failings and bad behaviour – which are factored in by the country – he will be seen as a prime minister who changed the political weather.

Iain Dale is a political commentator and radio presenter with LBC. He is editor of this book.

Acknowledgements

This book has been an absolute pleasure to edit, even if the main challenge has been to keep it to a reasonable size and word length. I hope I have got the balance right, and I am grateful to each of the contributors for their forbearance.

I would like to thank my agent, Martin Redfern, at Northbank Talent Management, and everyone at Hodder who have done so much to bring this book to you. Rupert Lancaster is one of the country's leading commissioning editors and it is an absolute honour to be published by him. He has been a patient listener and a wise counsel during the whole process, coping especially well with my post-midnight emails. Thanks also to Cameron Myers and Karen Geary at Hodder, to Nick Fawcett, who copyedited the final manuscript, and to the proofreader, Simon Fox.

My thanks also to each and every contributor. Without exception, they have all been a pleasure to deal with, and none of them sent me into a blind panic over failure to meet delivery deadlines. Many were very helpful in suggesting other contributors and all were a source of wise advice throughout the commissioning and editing process.

Earlier this year I published a book called *Why Can't We All Just Get Along?*, which sought to discuss the issue of the decline in public discourse. In the acknowledgements for that book, I thanked everyone who has played a role in encouraging me throughout my broadcasting and writing career. I won't repeat that long list here, apart from mentioning three names, without whose inspiration I am not sure I would have taken such an active interest in history and politics.

My two O- and A-Level history teachers at Saffron Walden County High School were superb at both teaching and inspiring. Bob Crossan and Nigel Wills each taught at the school for more than twenty years.

507

At university I had the honour of being taught by Richard Evans about German history. UEA's loss was the University of Cambridge's gain, and his knighthood in 2012 cemented his reputation as one of Britain's premier-league historians. We met up for lunch a couple of years ago and it was as if the intervening thirty-five years hadn't happened.

This book is also available as an audiobook, read by me, and there is a podcast series to accompany it called 'The Prime Ministers'. Download it wherever you get your podcasts from.

I hope you have enjoyed the book. I take full responsibility for any mistakes, but if you spot any, please let me know (I'm easy to find) so that they can be corrected for any reprint or new edition. If you have enjoyed it, do tell people, because the best way of marketing any book is by word of mouth. Yours.

Iain Dale
Tunbridge Wells, September 2020

Index